THE MIDLAND PEASANT

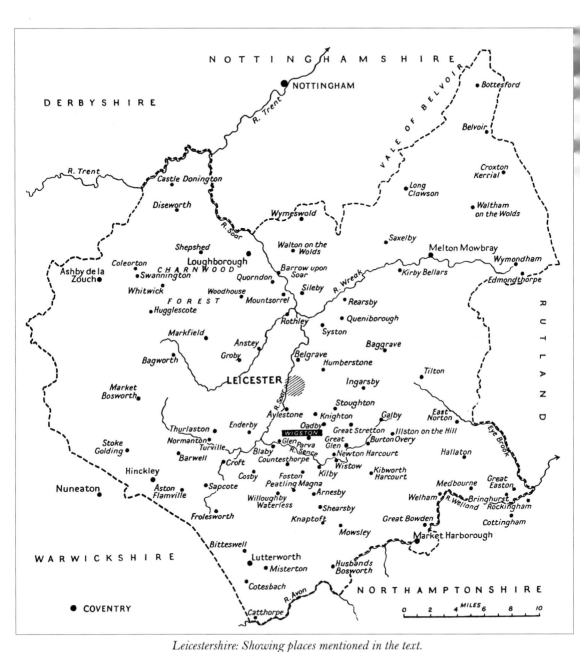

Leicestershire: Showing places mentioned in the text.

THE
MIDLAND PEASANT

THE ECONOMIC AND SOCIAL HISTORY
OF A LEICESTERSHIRE VILLAGE

W.G. Hoskins

PHILLIMORE

First Edition 1957
Reissued 1965
Macmillan and Company Limited

This paperback edition, 2008

Published by
PHILLIMORE AND CO. LTD.
Chichester, West Sussex, PO20 2DD
www.phillimore.co..uk
www.thehistorypress.co.uk

ISBN 978-1-86077-525-3

Printed and bound in Great Britain

To
R. H. Tawney
this book is offered as a
grateful tribute

CONTENTS

LIST OF MAPS, PLANS AND PLATES   IX
ABBREVIATIONS   IX
ACKNOWLEDGEMENTS   X
FOREWORD by Professor David Hey   XI

CHAPTER

   I. ORIGINS AND EARLY HISTORY

      Beginnings   1
      The Danish Conquest   6
      Early Growth   10
      The Two Churches   15

  II. THE MEDIEVAL MANOR, 1066-1509

      The Manor down to 1207   18
      The Winchester Manor, 1207-1509   23
      The Duchy Manor, 1207-1509   24

 III. THE FREE TENANTS, 1086-1509

      The Larger Free Tenants   31
      The Free Peasantry   34
      The Balle Family and its Lands   49
      Conclusions   52

 IV. THE MEDIEVAL VILLAGE AND ITS FIELDS

      Medieval Leicestershire   56
      Medieval Wigston   61
      The Village Fields   62
      The Medieval Crops   68
      Peasant Families   70
      The Church and the Rectory   80
      The Fifteenth Century   83

  V. THE MANORS AND THE LAND, 1500-1606

      The Village and its Fields   89
      The Break-up of the Turvile Manor   95
      The Break-up of the Oxford Manor   102
      Peasant Buying and Selling of Land   115
      Wigston Leaseholders   125
      The Rectory Farm and Tithes   130

VI. THE PEASANT FARMER IN THE TUDOR PERIOD

The Distribution of Wealth   141
The Peasant Farm   147
Open-Field Husbandry   152
Craftsmen and Tradesmen   166
Cottage Economy   171
Subsistence Farming   175
Church and School   179

VII. THE PEASANT SOCIETY, 1600-1766

The Village in 1625   185
The Peasant Economy   190
The Village in 1670   194
Parish Government and Officers   205
Summary and Conclusions   211

VIII. WIGSTON ON THE EVE OF THE REVOLUTION

Owners and Occupiers   216
The Framework-Knitting Industry   227
The Relief of Poverty   229
The Farmer and his Fields   231

IX. THE ENCLOSURE, 1764-66

The Enclosure Act   247
The Enclosure Award   250
The Costs of Enclosure   259

X. THE END OF A PEASANT SOCIETY

Farming after the Enclosure   261
The End of the Peasant Economy   267
The Last Phase, 1870-1900   276

AN EXCURSUS ON PEASANT HOUSES AND INTERIORS,
1400-1800
Plan and Evolution, 1400-1642   283
Peasant Interiors, 1500-1642   295
Plan and Structural Changes, 1650-1800   299
Peasant Interiors, 1675-1725   307

Appendix: SUMMARY OF THE WIGSTON ENCLOSURE
AWARD, 1766   311

INDEX   315

MAPS

The Site of Wigston Magna 4
Medieval Wigston: the Village 91
Medieval Wigston: the Parish and the Fields 94
The Beginnings of South Wigston (1885) 280
Leicestershire: showing places mentioned in the text ..... *Frontispiece*

PLANS

Two Sixteenth-century Farmhouse Types at Wigston 149
A Yeoman Farmhouse of the Early Seventeenth
   Century (1636) 187
A Yeoman Farmhouse of the Late Seventeenth
   Century (1691) 213
A Peasant-Gentleman's House (1752) 243

PLATES

Wigston Magna: Parish Church and Rectory Farm ..... *after page 125*
The Old Mere .... ”
Canal Settlement at Kilby Bridge .... ”
Framework-Knitters' Workshop at Wigston .... ”

ABBREVIATIONS USED IN THE FOOTNOTES

B.M.	British Museum
Ec.H.R.	*Economic History Review*
E.H.R.	*English Historical Review*
Farnham	*Leicestershire Medieval Village Notes* (6 vols. privately published)
Farnham MSS.	Unpublished Medieval Village Notes in Leicester Record Office
H.M.C.	Historical Manuscripts Commission
J.H.C.	*Journals of the House of Commons*
L.C.R.O.	Leicestershire County Record Office
L.R.O.	Leicester (City) Record Office
Nichols	*History of Leicestershire (Guthlaxton hundred)*
P.R.O.	Public Record Office
T.L.A.S.	*Transactions of the Leicestershire Archaeological Society*
V.C.H	*Victoria County History of Leicestershire*
W.H.R.	*Wyggeston Hospital Records*, ed. A. Hamilton Thompson

ACKNOWLEDGEMENTS

It is a pleasure to thank the Rev. Canon G.H. West, vicar of Wigston Magna, for his past kindness in giving me full access to all the parish records in his charge. I owe much also to two former students of mine at Leicester: to Miss D.C. Valentine for transcribing many wills and inventories, and to Mr. V.R. Webster for visiting and making plans of several Wigston houses when I was unable to do so personally. To the archivists of the Leicester City Council (formerly Mrs. A.M. Woodcock) and the Leicestershire County Council (Dr. L.A. Parker) I am grateful for years of patience with my demands on their time. To my old friend Sir Cyril Fox, my thanks for reading the excursus on peasant houses and for his valuable comments thereon; and to Professor R.H. Tawney, the friend and teacher of so many of us, my warm gratitude for reading the whole of my typescript at an early stage and for advice on many matters contained in it, not least the title of the book itself.

FOREWORD

The Midland Peasant was published in 1957, two years after *The Making of the English Landscape*, William Hoskins's most famous book. The great success of the landscape book had made Macmillan more receptive to the idea of publishing a detailed local study of a Leicestershire village, for which there had not previously seemed to be a market. *The Midland Peasant* is usually thought of as a successor to *The Making of the English Landscape*, but in fact Hoskins had been working on this study of Wigston Magna since the 1930's and had largely finished it during the Second World War, when he was a civil servant in London. This new book was his major scholarly work and, despite the huge and deserved fame of his general book on the English landscape, many of us regard it as his greatest contribution to the study of English Local History.

During his first period at the University College of Leicester, as a young lecturer in Economics, Hoskins and his wife, Jane, lived at Wigston Magna, four miles to the south of the county town. His knowledge of the topography of the parish and its records grew at a time when he was becoming deeply interested in the agrarian history of the whole of his adopted county – so very different from that of his native Devon – and when he was presenting the fruits of his research to his extramural classes at Vaughan College, Leicester. During the four or five years that he was forced to spend in London during the war, he no longer had access to local records, except those held as part of the national collections at the Public Record Office, and so he was forced to think about the wider context of his research and to fit his findings into general historical patterns. He was inspired by the historical studies of F.M. Stenton, Mildred Campbell, G.C. Homans and R.H. Tawney, by Lewis Mumford's concept of a 'cultural humus' of layers of the past, and by the condemnations of the effects of parliamentary enclosure in the poems of John Clare and in George Bourne's *Change in the Village*. When contemplating Wigston Magna, the idea of a lost peasant culture and its final collapse upon the enclosure of the open fields and commons in the 1760's emerged as the central theme. His original title for the projected book was 'The History of Wigston Magna: A Study in Peasant Civilisation'.

Hoskins's notebooks (preserved at the Centre for English Local History at Leicester University) include one devoted to Wigston, headed 'The Economic and Social History of a Midland Village', which he started in 1943 or 1944. His jottings reveal that his wider reading and contemplation eventually showed him how to shape the book that he had in mind. Professor Charles Phythian-Adams has identified the key passage in this notebook, which is headed *The Old Pattern*:

> I have the theme now: the old pattern of life slowly built up – describe at length – then the disintegration of the pattern, shattered beyond recognition. The old peasant tradition where men and women were 'at home' in the world, rooted in a place that had meaning and significance for them, among their own people, embedded in an ancient mode of living and conduct. They 'took care of a few fundamental things', not nobly or beautifully perhaps, but they took care of them nevertheless. Attached to a place, and to a family and neighbours, the strongest cement a society can have. And gradually we see the attachments being loosened, the cement crumbling, and the walls of that old society falling into ruin – the visible signs in the ruined church of St. Wistan, the silent water-mill, the tumble-down cottages in the village … The lost pattern of living, the lost pattern of integrated life that everyone once knew, of a time when we were all 'at home' in the world among our kindred and in our native places, conforming to the pattern of life handed down from the immemorial past, having our roots deep down in the 'cultural humus' deposited by generations of ancestors before us in the same place, the same house, the same village, or the same small town.[1]

The new title, *The Midland Peasant*, which was suggested by R.H. Tawney, to whom the book was dedicated, was more appealing to the publishers than the original one, for it emphasised the wider historical patterns behind this detailed local study. In his Introduction, Hoskins wrote:

> This book is intended to be primarily a study of the Midland peasant-farmer and of the open-field system in which he worked all his life, as

revealed in the records of one village in the heart of England. It is a
contribution to English economic and social history, and not a history
of the village as such. With this in mind I have rejected a considerable
amount of material that would ordinarily have gone into a local history
here as generally understood and which would doubtless have interested
the people of Wigston and its neighbourhood.

The Midland Peasant then was 'a study of a peasant culture, of the
way it was built up (as far as we can discover it), of the way it worked,
and of the way in which it was finally dissolved'. Despite his caveat in the
Introduction, however, the book remained essentially a detailed study of
one rural community that has shown local historians a way of studying
a single parish by taking into account its topography, population trends,
family histories, vernacular buildings, the farming and craft economy,
and the wider concerns of the inhabitants.

Hoskins began by emphasising that 'the village of Wigston Magna
stands very near the centre of England' and that it was 'a completely
nucleated village, profoundly characteristic of the Midlands'. Its open
fields lay all around, with the commons stretching beyond. He claimed
that Wigston's geographical position was responsible for two main themes
from the earliest times to the closing years of the eighteenth century:
it lay at the heart of open-field England, and it lay within the Danelaw.
Wigston was a large parish for the Midlands, stretching to almost 3,000
acres, twice the average size for Leicestershire. By the time of Domesday
Book, it was the most populous parish in the county, a leading position
that it retained throughout the following centuries. Hoskins was one of
the pioneers of the study of population history and in the same year as
the publication of *The Midland Peasant* his essay on 'The Population of
an English Village, 1086-1801' traced Wigston's demographic history
in more detail in the *Transactions of the Leicestershire Archaeological and
Historical Society*. Hoskins's early interest in topography is also evident from
his recording of the parish bounds and his observations on local soils as
the basis of the farming economy. A deep knowledge of the landscape of
Wigston and its neighbouring villages is evident throughout the book.

Manorial records for Wigston are almost entirely lacking but an
exceptional number of over 200 charters from the late twelfth to the early

sixteenth centuries provided Hoskins with rich information about peasant holdings. In the Domesday survey about 40 per cent of Wigston's land was owned by free tenants. Wigston was one of several 'double vills' of free and unfree peasants in the Midlands. In line with the orthodox view at the time, Hoskins argued that intensive Scandinavianisation during the last quarter of the ninth century, when Danish farming families settled in the territories that had been conquered by their army, had produced a considerable class of free peasant proprietors. Wigston's two, relatively small manorial estates were owned by absentee lords and hardly any land was held by monastic institutions. The village was, therefore, very different in character from neighbouring settlements such as Foston, which were dominated by their lords and which shrank, sometimes to the point of desertion, in later centuries. The supposed descent of the free peasants recorded in Domesday Book from the Danes and the unfree tenants from the Anglo-Saxons, as Hoskins surmised, is now doubted; this division seems to go back even further in time, and Hoskins himself pointed out that some of Wigston's medieval charters were granted to freeholders with Old English personal names. But whatever the origins of this group of freeholders, he was right to emphasise their prime importance in the community throughout the succeeding centuries down to the enclosure award of 1766.

William Hoskins's interest in and detailed knowledge of long-resident peasant families was one of his many strengths. (His own descent from a long line of Devon yeomen gave him much personal satisfaction.) Another of his early essays in the *Transactions of the Leicestershire Archaeological and Historical Society* was on 'Leicestershire Yeoman Families and Their Pedigrees' (1946). In *The Midland Peasant* he traces the history of individual families, such as the Randulls, Herricks, Codwins and Balles to typify 'a vigorous thriving free peasantry' in the thirteenth century and beyond. The charters revealed the continued buying and selling of land, mostly in very small parcels, between one peasant family and another, and 'somewhat larger transactions between the lord and a peasant family', in the years when the population was rising between the Norman Conquest and the Black Death. Hoskins was one of the first historians to provide detailed evidence for the 'great reshuffle' of the population at parish level after this disaster. During the fifteenth century the population of

Wigston Magna changed considerably, then afterwards it settled down again, a phenomenon that is now widely recognised throughout the country. But 'a solid core of middling peasant freeholders lasted right through this century of change and movement' and 'a peasant aristocracy, or a class of capitalist peasants who owned substantially larger farms and capital resources' emerged across the Midlands.

At the heart of his book is a study of the minute workings of 'The Peasant Economy'. Wigston 'produced all its own food, clothing, light, power, and building materials, and nearly all its own heat, out of the most commonplace natural resources'. Rather defensively, Hoskins noted that much of what he wrote here

> may seem obvious, a great deal about trifles; but these trifles, down to the pebbles under the clay or the beehives in the garden and the feathers on the goose's breast, were the very foundation of that old peasant economy which thought all the time in terms of goods and services and not of money. And unless one has a proper understanding of this peasant or thrift economy, of the foundations on which it was built up, the way they thought about it and the way it worked in practice, one cannot begin to understand the economic and social history of a good deal of rural England between the sixteenth and nineteenth centuries.

This is the essential message in all of William Hoskins's writings. To some historians it now seems an idealised view of the English peasantry and a romantic attachment to an imagined better world before the supposed rootlessness and hectic pace of modem life, but at the time this emphasis on the lives of ordinary countrymen and women as revealed in both the visual evidence and new sets of documentary records (notably probate inventories) was an inspiration to a whole generation of scholars, showing them what could be done. Soon, several studies of other rural communities in different parts of England were attempted along these pioneering lines, using *The Midland Peasant* as their model in methodology and as a yardstick for comparisons.

Although he emphasised the underlying continuity of life in Wigston Magna, Hoskins was well aware of change. He showed that the population of Wigston doubled from 70 householders in 1525 to 140 or so by 1625 and that the inevitable consequence was the growth of a poor cottager or labourer class. He was one of the first to study hearth tax returns to reveal the existence of 'a social pyramid' of householders. In 1670 Wigston was a large village of 161 households, including 47 that were exempted from payment of the hearth tax on the grounds of poverty. Of these, 120 households were taxed on one hearth, 25 on two, nine on three, two on four, and five on five. No rich family dominated their neighbours. The majority of the inhabitants were still the middling fanners of old, but the number of landless cottagers was growing. Hoskins also used the returns in a pioneering way in his study of peasant housing and to emphasise the longevity of many of Wigston's families. The 161 householders had 82 different family names. Thirty-six of these names (44 per cent) had been present in Wigston for at least 100 years and 15 or 16 (20 per cent) had been there for over two centuries. The most remarkable of these longestablished families were the Boulters, who had lived in Wigston for 100 years or so and who now formed eight different households. The Freers were equally prolific at a slower pace, with eight branches after 200 years of residence. The Smiths, Vanns and Wards each had six branches, the Johnsons five, the Langtons, Holmeses, Noones and Abbotts four, and several other families had three. In addition, kinship links through frequent intermarriage and numerous personal friendships had cemented the bonds that provided the inhabitants of the village with a real sense of belonging. Hoskins was one of the first social historians to point out the importance of long-resident, 'core families' such as these in preserving the traditions and culture of a local community.

The peasant system long remained vigorous with large numbers of middling farmers with 10-30 acres of land or more who managed to hang on to their holdings over the generations. But by the eve of parliamentary enclosure in 1764-66 the population had grown so much that only three families in every ten occupied any land; the majority of the villages were now framework knitters or other wage earners. This change was happening in many parts of Leicestershire, where framework knitting was introduced about 1640. The industrialisation of Wigston from the late seventeenth century onwards began long before parliamentary enclosure.

Enclosure was nevertheless 'one of the most momentous events in the long history of the village. It transformed the physical landscape of the parish of Wigston within a few years, altered its farming almost beyond recognition, and changed the entire culture and habits of the peasant community'. In his chapter on 'The End of a Peasant Society' Hoskins wrote about the conversion of the arable lands to permanent pasture and the transformation of Wigston into an industrial village with a large population and a calamitous rise in the poor rates: 'The peasant economy had been finally extinguished by the enclosure award, though it took a long time to die; the crucial blow had been the extinction of the common rights of the peasantry.' Yet the enclosure Act had not been pushed through Parliament by grasping lords, but by the leading group of freeholders.

The final phase in the life of the village covered the last three decades of the nineteenth century. The village of 1870 still retained much of its rural character, for the framework knitting industry was largely a domestic one, but the rise of the population appeared unstoppable. In 1894 Wigston became an Urban District Council and the old ecclesiastical parish was split into two, when nearly 1,200 acres on the cast side (away from the industrialised section) broke away as the separate civil parish of East Wigston, attached to a neighbouring Rural District. The ancient parish of Wigston Magna was no more: 'The peasant village had been swamped and then submerged completely, and the tide of industrialism rolled over it unchecked … a whole culture, a qualitative civilisation, had perished to bring about this quantitative triumph.'

Hoskins had once intended to use his information on the buildings of Wigston in a separate book on *Peasant Houses and Interiors, 1400-1800*, but settled instead on a shorter final chapter entitled 'An Excursus on Peasant Houses and Interiors, 1400-1800'. Long after publication, he regretted that he had reluctantly agreed to Macmillan's decision that a similar chapter, bringing together the histories of the peasant families of Wigston, should be omitted.

The importance of *The Midland Peasant* as an outstanding work that did so much to help establish English Local History as a respectable academic study was well expressed by William Hoskins's former colleague, Dr. Joan Thirsk, when she wrote his obituary:

This sensitive study of peasant society is regarded by some as as Hoskins's finest original work of scholarship. It expressed better than anything else the importance he attached to ordinary people of no particular eminence in forming the foundations of a stable society. In it he explored the changing social structure of a whole community over a long period, from the fifth to the end of the nineteenth century. It appeared at a time when the social and economic development of single villages in different regions of the country was attracting young scholars to similar studies, but its chronological range and its impassioned sympathy with some of the simplest basic assumptions of peasant life put it ahead of all the rest.[2]

Fifty years on, *The Middle Peasant* remains an outstanding study, well worthy of a new edition.

David Hey

David Hey, a former postgraduate student of William Hoskins, is Emeritus Professor of Local and Family History, the University of Sheffield, and the President of the British Association for Local History.

---

[1] Charles Phythian-Adams, 'Hoskins's England: A Local Historian of Genius and the Realisation of his Theme', *Transactions of the Leicestershire Archaeological and Historical Society*, LXVI (1992), 143-59.

[2] Joan Thirsk, 'William George Hoskins, 1908-1992', *Proceedings of the British Academy*, 87 (1995), 33954.

INTRODUCTION

The village of Wigston Magna stands very near the centre of England, four miles to the south of the town of Leicester. It was, before its ancient plan was destroyed by the modern builder, a completely nucleated village, profoundly characteristic of the Midlands. Its farmhouses, cottages, and shops gathered together along the village streets; the little crofts lay behind the farm houses or to one side of them, and the farmyards opened directly off the street. The village stood in the centre of the parish with nearly three thousand acres of open fields all around it, the spire of the parish church visible from almost every corner of its territory. Until 1766, when the parliamentary enclosure award revolutionised the local landscape, not a house stood away from the village. It was as unlike the scattered settlement of the Norfolk parish of Forncett, studied by Miss Davenport some fifty years ago, as it was the hamlet country of south-western England, and its economic and social history was correspondingly different.

The position of Wigston Magna in the centre of the Midlands is responsible for the two main threads which run through its entire history from the earliest times up to the closing years of the eighteenth century. It lay in the heart of the open-field area and its whole life, social and political as well as economic, was coloured by that major fact. And it lay in the Danelaw, not in the heart of it, it is true, but in the middle of a county which was as intensively Scandinavianised as any part of England, with the exception of Lincolnshire and East Anglia. The dual nature of Wigston in pre-Conquest days is revealed in its name: it is *Viking's tun*, a Scandinavian personal name compounded with the commonest place-name element in Old English.

This intensive Scandinavianisation in the last quarter of the ninth century produced at Wigston a considerable class of free peasant proprietors, who persisted down to the enclosure of the village fields and for some time afterwards. During that time, a period of nine hundred years, these free peasant landowners were subjected to important changes: their personnel largely altered as the centuries passed (though a small solid core of the original families persisted) but their estates remained and passed mostly to other peasant families like themselves; and there was, too, the inevitable concentration of property in fewer hands as time went on, some families rising in the social scale, others selling out and disappearing into the town or working on in their ancestral village as small tenant-farmers. or even labourers. Later still they are to be found working in the Victorian factories of the village.

In spite of these changes, the broad pattern of Wigston's social and economic history between the ninth century and the eighteenth is abundantly clear: it is a village with a large and persistent class of free peasant landowners without any resident lord of the manor at any time; and it is a village which maintained unimpaired its traditional open-field husbandry when so many other villages in Leicestershire, and in the Midlands generally, were being enclosed and depopulated for sheep and cattle pastures in the fifteenth, sixteenth, and seventeenth centuries.

These two distinctive threads, which run all through the recorded history of the village, are themselves connected. In those Midland villages where no free peasantry appear in Domesday, or where for some reason they disappear at an early date, the enclosing squire or monastic house encountered no opposition when they turned over all the village lands to pasture. Or, if there were a small handful of freeholders, the landlord had a reasonable chance of buying them out or of securing their agreement to enclosure in some other way. Such agreements between the lord of the manor and the free tenants (and occasionally the leaseholders) became increasingly frequent from the middle of the sixteenth century onwards in the Midlands. But in villages like Wigston, with nearly a hundred freeholders to cope with, no such action was possible. No squire could ever buy out such a multitude or secure their unanimous agreement to proposals for revolutionary change. Such villages remained open until the machinery of parliamentary enclosure overrode the multitude of small peasant proprietors in the interests of the wealthier minority.

Besides these two fundamental characteristics of Wigston's economic history, there are others which we ought to touch upon briefly in order to bring out the salient points of the story before plunging into the detailed evidence in the following chapters. It seems likely, for example, that Wigston was relatively overpopulated at an early date: it was already the largest village in Leicestershire if in 1086 and remained so in all probability until the late fourteenth century, when a decline set in which lasted for over a hundred years. Then came a remarkable increase of population in late Elizabethan times, and by 1600 the population had recovered to the level of 1377. It continued to rise throughout the seventeenth century, though at a slower pace after about 1630, until over-population – so far as one may employ such a relative term historically – set in again, and brought about an early industrial development, making use of the landless and surplus labour of the village. This development is apparent in the last quarter of the seventeenth century, and during the following century the village became increasingly industrialised and its agricultural life correspondingly less important.

It may well be that one can attribute the over-population of the village, which is suggested as early as the end of the eleventh century, to the dual nature of its settlement: a heavy Scandinavian settlement in the late ninth century superimposed bodily on an Old English village which had existed, as we know from archaeological evidence, since the first years of the sixth century. Elsewhere in Leicestershire, and indeed in the East Midlands as a whole, there is considerable evidence to suggest that the Scandinavian settlers occupied in the main new lands hitherto unoccupied by the English, or only thinly settled by them; but at Wigston, and probably at other villages in the neighbourhood of the military centre of Leicester (one of the Five Boroughs), there is reason to suspect a deliberate superimposition of one colony upon an older one, perhaps for military reasons. However this may be, medieval Wigston shows marked signs of over-population which has its origin in pre-Conquest times and colours the course of its economic development down to the eighteenth century, when the ancient agrarian economy began to be transformed into the full-blooded industrial economy of the present day. One might almost have called the economic history of Wigston a study in overpopulation, but the materials are lacking to make such a study completely convincing, and it would, in any event, be a gross simplification of a thousand years of history.

The fact that the village never had a resident lord (though down to the end of the sixteenth century there were two absentee lords) but had, on the contrary, a large and solid class of peasant proprietors, meant also that it appears as an active self-governing community during the whole period for which we have the relevant records. Even the copyholders at Wigston, so far as they were distinct in personnel from the freeholders, were in a far stronger position *vis-à-vis* the lord than in the great majority of English villages, certainly outside the East Midlands. They appear in the sixteenth century as copyholders of inheritance, subject only to a small fine on entry to their tenements and a small rent thereafter; and both fines and rents were certain and not alterable at the will of the lord. The economic position of the villagers, both freeholders and copyholders, was therefore strong and their political and social life correspondingly vigorous; and this peasant democracy lasted until the enclosure of the open fields killed it at the roots. For one of the roots was the open-field system which, so long as it lasted, called for continuous co-operation by all the cultivators of the soil. It called for a real self-government, of which the annual general meeting of the village to consider the by-laws of the fields was one sign and the election of field-reeves, pinder, 'eveners' and other officers was another. And the other root of this peasant democracy was the existence of a body of independent peasant proprietors, ranging from substantial yeomen down to cottagers with a strip or two of arable and proportionate rights over the common pasture.

Another respect in which Wigston differed from many other English villages, and from several in its own neighbourhood, was in the almost total absence of monastic property among its 2944 acres. Only one virgate out of ninety-six found its way into the hands of a religious house. Hence the dissolution of the religious houses in 1536-9 was not followed at Wigston, as it was in so many other English villages, by large-scale transferences of land to wealthy laymen with all the economic and social consequences that usually ensued. Life went on in Tudor and Stuart Wigston with a monumental stability. Such changes as there were, notably the breaking-up and selling off of the two manors, in 1586 and 1606 respectively, strengthened rather than weakened the ancient peasant economy of the village.

Although the materials for the social and economic history of Wigston

are considerable in bulk, both locally and in the national archives, and
enable us to tell a fairly full story, there are some important deficiencies
which make it less informative than one would like, particularly in the
medieval period. It is necessary to say something at this point of the
merits and defects of our sources, even allowing for the fact that the
historian can rarely find all the materials that he would like, especially
in the field of local history where time and chance have played greater
havoc with the records than with most.

Manorial records are almost entirely lacking for Wigston. There are
no reeves' accounts or custumals such as Professor Gras used so fruitfully
for the economic and social history of Crawley in Hampshire, nor any
of those detailed account-rolls which Miss Davenport drew upon for
the early history of Forncett in Norfolk. The Hundred Rolls of 1279,
which are so rich a source for so much of the Midlands, fail us where
Wigston is concerned. Nor do any court rolls survive, save for two short
fifteenth-century rolls and a few isolated and uninformative rolls for the
sixteenth century. There is no manorial extent or survey, not even a map
until the days of the six-inch Ordnance Survey, for the enclosure map
of 1766 has vanished and cannot be traced.

The by-laws of the village fields, to which there are tantalising
references from time to time, have likewise perished. To go yet farther
back, some of the poll tax returns for Leicestershire villages in 1377
and 1381 give us a good picture of the economy of a fourteenth-century
village with its variety of trades and crafts all based upon the land;
but for Wigston only a portion of the 1377 assessment survives, and
this does not give the occupations of the taxpayers. Nevertheless, this
fragment is sufficient to form the basis for an accurate estimate of the
total population of the village at that date, and is therefore important
for the understanding of its economic history.

On the credit side, so far as the surviving records are concerned, the
existence of an exceptional number of medieval peasant charters (more
than two hundred of them), running in date from the late twelfth century
to the early sixteenth, compensates to a large degree for the absence of
much purely manorial material. We know very little about the customary
tenants of the medieval Wigston manors and almost nothing of the
manorial organisation; but from these charters we are able to discover a

great deal about the free peasantry of the village, who were the largest and most important social class in the community.

From the time of Henry VIII onwards, the record material is fairly voluminous. It does not tell us all we would like to know of the economy of the village and of its social life generally, but it is enough to form a detailed picture of the working of a typical open-field township in the Midlands. There are law-suits in the courts of Chancery and the Exchequer, in the Court of Requests and in the Court of Star Chamber; and there are local suits in the archdeacon's court at Leicester. All of these suits throw light upon the economy of the village in the sixteenth and seventeenth centuries. From the hundreds of Wigston wills and inventories now in the County Record Office at Leicester we can build up a picture, such as no other class of records could provide, of the economic life and the intimate social history of the village between the early sixteenth century and the middle of the eighteenth. Such records as these are particularly valuable since legal records of one sort and another, upon which the historian is so often obliged to rely for his material, give us by their very nature a somewhat false and pathological picture of the past.

There are, too, great numbers of conveyances, leases, mortgages, marriage settlements and other legal documents, with which we can carry on the story of the medieval charters, and all the usual parish records (registers, churchwardens' accounts, overseers' accounts, constables' accounts), together with a short series of less usual records such as the accounts of the field reeves (1752-64) and of the eveners (1750-64). One need not mention at this point the mass of other records which are common to all historical enquiries such as this, most of which are in the Public Record Office. All I have drawn attention to here is the general nature of the available material, its principal deficiencies on the one hand and its principal merits on the other, in so far as these are bound to influence the scope and treatment of this history.

This book is intended to be primarily a study of the Midland peasant-farmer and of the open-field system in which he worked all his life, as revealed in the records of one village in the heart of England. It is a contribution to English economic and social history, and not a history of the village as such. With this in mind I have rejected a considerable amount of material that would ordinarily have gone into a local history as generally understood and which would doubtless have interested the people of Wigston and its neighbourhood. In this book I trace in detail the working out of the economic and social forces in one Midland village, set in the middle of its three thousand acres of land, to see if any light can be thrown on the precise manner in which general changes come about; and particularly I have tried to trace the break-up of the ancient economy of the open fields. This is a study of a peasant culture, of the 'way in which it was built up (so far as we can discover it), of the way it worked, and of the way in which it finally dissolved. It is a study of a rural society based upon an open-field economy, and though it cannot be called typical in all its aspects, for every community is a unique organism in some way, with its own peculiar flavour and individuality, it may perhaps be regarded as a portrait of the kind of society which existed over a considerable part of central England for the best part of a thousand years.

A few years ago I spent the greater part of a fine April afternoon at the bottom of a newly-dug grave in the modern cemetery at Wigston. This cemetery was opened in 1882, half a mile south of the village, and was by chance laid out almost exactly over a large burial-ground of the heathen Anglo-Saxon period, the cemetery of the sixth-century village. The finding of a few broken pieces of pottery at the bottom of this grave led me to it immediately, to discover in the almost pure sand (a fact of archaeological significance in itself in a clay country like the Midlands) a Roman ditch of unknown purpose, dating from the later years of the first century.

On emerging from the grave into the bright sunshine once more, I saw all around the visible evidence of the continuity of life in this community whose history I was trying to unravel. Beneath my feet ran the Roman ditch, and within a few yards lay the remains of the old gravel-pit where in 1795 Wigston labourers, digging gravel for the new turnpike road close by, turned up a collection of objects of sixth-century date and so brought to light one of the largest Anglian cemeteries in Leicestershire. A few hundred yards away to the north lay the village on its gravel ridge above the colder clays. The sun shone upon the handsome limestone tower and spire of the parish church, built when the village was larger and more prosperous than it was to be for many a generation afterwards; it flooded over the pastures that had replaced the open arable fields in the year 1766, and fell alike on the whitewashed Georgian farmhouses on the edge of the village and the bright red brick of the Victorian villas and the hosiery factories – for today the village lives almost wholly by industry and hardly knows its own fields.

Beneath the modern field-pattern, laid out nearly two hundred years ago, I saw the rolling succession of ridge and furrow that spoke of arable cultivation for a thousand years before that. Dividing these ridges at intervals one could see the balks and headlands where the medieval peasant drove his cart into his strips or turned his plough, curving his strip as he approached the headland, so that the enclosure commissioners' hedge (the hedge of today) was obliged to follow the same ancient line dictated by the ox-drawn plough; and in one place a broader bank of grass showed where the medieval footpath to Kilby, the next village to the south, clearly ran – *Kylebygate* in an early fourteenth-century charter – until broken by the modern cemetery wall.

Over the cemetery fence, on their allotments, the men of Wigston were turning over the earth for another year – good loam from the sandy mixture near by and not the usual backbreaking clay – and behind me, for it was a Saturday afternoon, a funeral was going on, another Wigston man gone to the cemetery on the hill where his pagan forefathers had been buried fourteen hundred years before. All this, the long history of this village set in the green Midland landscape, was visible without moving more than a few yards: Roman, Old English, Scandinavian (some of the names on the headstones told of Danish ancestry), medieval and modern, it was all there. Coming back to the village one talks to a man whose surname appears on the Wigston poll tax assessment of 1377, the descendant of *John Mold and wife*. Over a decaying shop the name of Vann shows that a descendant of Thomas Vanne, a Wigston farmer in Henry VII's time, lives on, rather precariously perhaps in these difficult times. Pawleys were peasant proprietors in the village in the 1440's and a Pawley still does building jobs in the village. Dands were here in Henry VIII's reign, and their name is still called on the school register. Several other names go back to Elizabethan and Stuart days. *Ross's Lane* commemorates a yeoman family who farmed here from the early-sixteenth century to the early nineteenth, and until the other day a Ross kept a baker's shop in the village. The Boulters first appear in the village in Elizabethan days, and they still survive.

As one walks up Bullhead Street, the only street to retain much of its village character, one passes farmhouses whose history can be traced continuously back to the thirteenth century, in one instance perhaps to the very birth of the house on a toft enclosed out of the demesne in the time of Henry III, when Nicholas de Campania, lord of the smaller manor, granted to Ralph Balle and Hysenda his wife, for their homage and service, 'a plot of land in the town of Wykingstone, lying in Hecroft … to enclose, build, and inhabit.'

Out in the upland fields, solitary windmill-mounds, all traces of their mills long since gone, speak of the ancient cornlands of open-field husbandry. Farther out towards the frontiers of the parish the 'black spring' bubbles up out of the earth exactly as it did in the thirteenth century when the rough pasture on either side of it was named *Blacwelsick*; and nearer the village the 'horse spring' – *Horswelle* in a charter of 1348 – can still be found. Below the parish church, where Newgate ('new' in the reign of Edward I) enters the fields, the faint traces of a moated homestead site can be seen, probably where the Wykyngeston family lived in the thirteenth and fourteenth centuries; and well out on the south-western side of the parish the water-mill still stands on the river Sence, silent now, the descendant of the mill recorded in a twelfth-century charter.

In spite, however, of the apparent continuity of life in this village, which is reflected in a multitude of ways wherever one walks in the streets or fields, there has in fact been an almost complete break with the past. Such families as survive from the fourteenth, fifteenth, and sixteenth centuries have done so in spite of the revolutionary changes which destroyed the old village and the kind of peasant society it once represented; and such ancient street-names and field-names as survive are only the meagre remnants of a once-rich galaxy of their kind. And the other evidences of the past we have seen on our walks reveal by their very nature the dissolution of the former way of life: the decrepit water-mill, the untenanted windmill-mounds, the one-time arable ridges now under pasture, the hosiery factories and the older framework-knitters' cottages, the shopkeeping and factory-hand descendants of the yeoman-farmers of Elizabethan days – they are all symptoms of the economic and social changes that crept over the older village and slowly dissolved its life beyond present recognition; so much so that the old peasant society of Wigston and its former mode of life, its culture (for such it was) can only be reconstructed with the greatest of difficulty. The reconstruction of this former society is the principal theme of the book that follows.

I

ORIGINS AND EARLY HISTORY

Beginnings

More than fourteen hundred years ago, in the last years of the fifth century, Anglian invaders who had landed on the desolate shores of the Wash, with the wildfowl crying above them at this disturbance of their ancient solitude, pushed slowly up the Welland valley, past the sites already occupied by early kinsmen at Spalding, Deeping, and Stamford, until the low wooded hills of Leicestershire, the edge of the forested Midland clay country, came into view to the north and west. Here they founded another little group of villages – Rockingham and Cottingham on the southern (Northamptonshire) side of the valley, and Bringhurst and Medbourne on the northern or Leicestershire side. The Welland at this point is an inconspicuous stream in a broad valley, and it may be that this group of settlements represented the limit of navigation for boats. At any rate the main course of early colonisation seems to have diverged from the valley here, to run northwestwards over the low watershed into the Soar basin, where the Roman town of Leicester lay, and perhaps northwards also into the upland country of east Leicestershire where numerous Anglian cemeteries of the pagan period (about A.D. 450-650) have been found.

Where the watershed began to dip gently down to the marshy basin of the Soar, Peotla's people settled in a small territory – 'the land of the *Petlingas*' – covering some three thousand acres and represented today by the parishes of Peatling Magna and Peatling Parva, some eight to ten miles south of Leicester. From Peatling small groups made their way along old beaten tracks through the woods, northwards towards what had been the Roman town of *Ratae Coritanorum*, now perhaps surviving, if at all, with a flickering, sub-human life three generations after the departure of the Romans. At intervals they pitched camp just off these old paths close to running water. We find another group of early settlements along or near the little river Sence, originally called *Glen* from its clean water that was suitable for drinking.

The remains of these early English colonists – bones and broken pots, brooches and beads, horse-trappings and weapons – have been found in gravel-pits at Glen Parva (half a mile north of the village of Blaby), at Wigston (again about half a mile outside the present village), and at Brock's Hill, half a mile to the south of the village of Oadby. The rich burials at Glen Parva may be dated as early as the year 500; those at Wigston belong to the middle and later years of the sixth century; and those at Brock's Hill are of unknown date, since none of the finds has been preserved. It seems likely that the Glen Parva cemetery was associated with the present village of Blaby and that of Brock's Hill with Oadby; just as the Wigston cemetery can only be the burial-place for the early settlement of Wigston. In each instance the cemetery is between half a mile and a thousand yards away from the present village.

Thus the continuous history of Wigston as a village begins in the first half of the sixth century (allowing for a slight interval before the first burials took place).[1] Even at that early date it was flanked by two other settlements, one about two miles to the west, and the other rather nearer on the north-east. The three villages formed a line on the southern side of the town of Leicester, about four miles in front of it, and it is safe to say that all were well-established communities by the second half of the sixth century. Yet two of them (Oadby and Blaby) have pure Scandinavian names, and the third (Wigston) has a Scandinavian personal name as its first element. This raises a question which is not only of interest to the archaeologist but may well concern the economic historian also, and we shall try to answer it in due course.

The burial-place of the first settlers at Wigston was discovered accidentally in the year 1795 by workmen digging for gravel for the purpose of repairing the new turnpike road near by, the usual way in which archaeological discoveries of this period have been made. Throsby describes the circumstances of the discovery in a letter to Nichols, the Leicestershire historian.[2] The site is wrongly identified

---

[1] The discovery in the present cemetery on Welford Road of a short stretch of Roman ditch containing native pottery of the late first century, in April 1946, though interesting archaeologically, does not form part of the continuous history of the village and has no apparent bearing on its economic history.

[2] Nichols, iv, 377.

on the present twenty-five-inch Ordnance Survey map of the parish as being in the middle of the village, in what is now the Memorial Park, anciently the Gaol Close. But this site does not tally at all with the description given by Throsby, and the discoveries in recent years of brooches of sixth-century date in digging modern graves in the Welford Road cemetery make it clear that the pagan cemetery also lay in this area. Topographically this site corresponds in all respects with Throsby's description, and the visible traces of an old gravel-pit beside the southern fence of field no. 303 (O.S. map, 1930 edn.) enable us to fix the exact site of the discoveries of 1795. The more recent finds have come from the south-western quarter of the modern cemetery between two and three hundred yards south of this old gravel-pit, so that the pagan burial-ground was very large. This may indicate an extended occupation over the greater part of the heathen period (as at Saxby in north-east Leicestershire), though so far only the second half of the sixth century is represented by finds.

The sixth-century cemetery lay in a long narrow island of sands and gravels, capping the high ground to the south of the village, about half a mile to the south-east of the parish church of All Saints, which probably represents the nucleus of the original settlement. The original village itself lay on a large island of glacial sands and gravels. All over Leicestershire, and particularly to the east of the Soar, these patches of drier and warmer soils, easier to clear and cultivate than the surrounding clays, formed islands of varying size in a rolling sea of inhospitable, forested clays, and on the larger islands the old English settlers built their first villages.

Wigston Magna, as it was called in later centuries, stood very near the centre of England, in the heart of Leicestershire, on a ridge of high ground between two small tributaries of the Soar, and just four miles to the south of the ancient town of Leicester. As we shall become familiar in the course of this book with the topography of this Midland village, its fields and its soils, its slopes and streams, it is necessary to say something here of the details of the site and what led to its first settlement in the early days of the English Conquest.

The east-west ridge on which the village stands is formed in the main by an extensive cap of glacial sands and gravels overlying the boulder clay and rising to between fifty and eighty feet above the surrounding valleys (see map). To the north of the ridge, in the direction of Leicester, the ground falls sharply down to the Knighton Brook about a mile away; and southwards it falls more gently to the banks of the little river Sence, about the same distance from the village. Along both these streams lay the meadows of the medieval village.

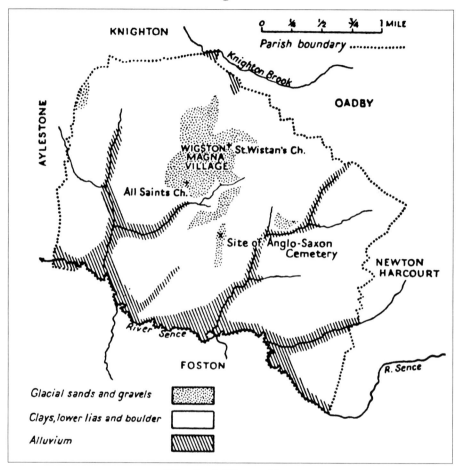

The site of Wigston Magna.

Westwards the ground falls away again towards other meadows (now under a network of railway-lines), known as *Hillymedowe*, in the fourteenth century; but to the east and south-east the clays rise in long, rolling slopes towards the Old Mere, an ancient boundary where the parish reaches its greatest elevation (386 feet above the sea), commanding wide views over the Leicestershire countryside out of all proportion to this modest height.

The centre of the original village, which has now lost much of its ancient shape by reason of its industrial growth during the nineteenth century, lay almost exactly three hundred feet above the sea, and about sixty feet or so above the meadows to the north, south, and west. Thus, although the scale would be a miniature in many parts of England, the site is a commanding one for the Midlands: both from the north and the south the two medieval spires of Wigston are visible for some miles, so that from Henry VIII's time onwards it was known as 'Wigston with Two Steeples'.

Not only did the sands and gravels give rise to a ridge of high ground commanding the southern approaches to the town of Leicester, but they provided also about two hundred acres of dry, well-drained, and lightish soil for the village-site itself, ranging from a pure sand (useful for building material) to a fertile easily-worked loam. Where the sand and gravel cap met the clay, on the fringes of the village, numerous springs welled out, each of which had a distinctive name in the medieval village; and in the village itself shallow wells tapped the drinking-water on the clay bed thirty to fifty feet below. Most of the farmsteads had wells in their yards. A hundred yards to the south of the parish church, where the fields even now begin abruptly, a small stream (nameless today) provided a larger supply of water for cattle and other purposes. The village 'wash-pit' lay here in later times, as we learn from the seventeenth- century Constables' Accounts, and had probably been here since time immemorial.

Thus the site met all the primary requirements for early occupation: an abundant supply of water for human beings and animals, a dry site for building surrounded by a considerable tract of loamy soils before the heavier unmixed clays were reached, and a position commanding both the hollow in which Leicester lay four miles to the north and the approaches from the south. The road beside which the original village grew up was an important medieval traffic-route, the principal of the two main roads between Northampton and Leicester from the thirteenth century onwards; and it may well be that it existed as a pre-Roman ridgeway. For there was no deliberate road-making after the Norman Conquest: like the Anglo-Saxons the Normans made use of tracks and ways that were ancient even to them. If such a trackway existed then, when the first English settlers were pushing northwards towards Leicester from the Welland valley, their earliest corridor into this part of the Midlands, the planting of a village-site at Wigston was obvious, for it was here that the old road surmounted the last ridge of high ground before dropping down to the Soar valley in which Leicester lay. Whether or not the town of Leicester was entirely deserted and lifeless after the Romans went, it is certain that it had been reoccupied by Anglian settlers soon after 500. This being so, an early settlement on the site of Wigston was an obvious choice.

The parish and manor of Wigston, as it was afterwards demarcated (probably in the tenth century), was large for Leicestershire. It covered almost three thousand acres or roughly twice the average for this county. It seems probable that this area represents the original territory settled or staked out in the sixth century, just as the three thousand acres of Peatling represented the original territory of the *Petlingas*. But at Wigston, unlike the great majority of ancient village-sites, there was no later fission into daughter-settlements with churches and fields of their own. Apart from the sand and gravel patches we have already spoken about, and the alluvial borders of the little streams, where the meadows later lay, the greater part by far of this territory consisted of boulder-clays, fertile and rewarding enough in later centuries when they had long been well cultivated. But many centuries went by before they were wholly cleared and broken up. The long process of clearing the natural landscape and of bringing it into cultivation, begun in the first years of the sixth century, was not finally accomplished, so far as we can tell, until the end of the thirteenth. Between seven and eight hundred years were needed to reach the frontiers of the parish at all points with the plough and the spade.

❧ THE DANISH CONQUEST ☙

For some three hundred and fifty years after its foundation the life of the village subsisted, mostly occupied with the felling of the acres of encircling forest and the clearing of the land for cultivation. Twelve generations came and went in this anonymous back-breaking toil of which we know nothing. Then in the ninth century there came to the village from time to time rumours of the Northmen who appeared in summer and ravaged the eastern coasts; but these were vague reports of far-away events and nothing happened in the Midland countryside. In the autumn of 865, however, 'the whole fabric of English society was threatened by a great army, which landed in East Anglia, prepared to spend many consecutive years in the deliberate exploitation of all the opportunities for profit which England offered';[1] and two years later this army took up its winter quarters at Nottingham. More years of fighting followed, culminating in a short and decisive war in Mercia. The king of the Mercians abandoned his kingdom in 874 and three years later the Danes appropriated half of Mercia for division among the members of their army, leaving the other half to the English. The exact lines of the division are not known, but Leicestershire certainly fell entirely within the Danish province. For centuries afterwards its economic and social history was strongly influenced by this momentous event, and its social structure deeply coloured by it. This Danish settlement set up a large number of villages of free peasant landowners who persisted, to a varying degree in different places, down to the time of the parliamentary enclosure of their open fields. Wigston was one of these villages, and its history is typical in its broad outlines, though not in its details, of hundreds of others in the Midland plain from the Humber southwards to the Chilterns.[2]

Exactly what form the Danish settlement took at Wigston we do not know. We know, however, that the village had already been in existence between three and four hundred years when the Danes came in 877 and that as a result of the Scandinavian Conquest its name was changed from an Old English name (now lost) to *Viking's tun* after some Scandinavian leader who occupied it with his men and their families. We do not know whether the original English village had been wholly destroyed in the fighting which must have occurred before the Mercian kingdom was surrendered in 874, and refounded by the Danes a little later, or whether they found a large English village more or less intact. Nor do we know whether they dispossessed the native landholders

[1] Stenton, *Anglo-Saxon England*, 243.

[2] How far south we can trace the effects of the Scandinavian settlement on the subsequent economic and social history of the Midlands is still a matter of doubt. Danish place-names peter out rapidly south of the Welland, but Stenton observes that 'even in the eleventh century the free peasants of the southern midlands were numerous enough to distinguish the social structure of this region from that of the shires towards the west' (*op. cit.*, 252).

and turned them into 'their harrowers and plowers' as the Anglo-Saxon Chronicle records happened to the Northumbrians the year before, when their lands had been seized and divided similarly. We can, however, trace the existence of English landholders at Wigston in the twelfth century, as we shall see, and there is therefore some reason to suppose that the native English were not entirely dispossessed at the Danish settlement.

To some extent, Domesday Book throws a little light on these problems, though even here the evidence is not without ambiguity. In the first place, Wigston appears as the largest village in a thickly settled county, with a recorded population of eighty-six. It was more than a quarter the size of Leicester, which had a recorded total of 318 houses, and more than twice as populous as Melton, which was to become the second town in the county.

The high population of both Wigston and Oadby (with fifty-six tenants), taken together with the numbers of sokemen in both places, suggests the deliberate superimposition of a Scandinavian settlement on an existing English village, possibly for military reasons. Many of the villages between the *burh* of Leicester and the frontier of the Danelaw along Watling Street, only fifteen miles away, show a remarkable concentration of sokemen as though considerations of military defence may have been in mind. Cosby, Frowlesworth and Willoughby Waterless, all within a few miles of Wigston to the south and south-west, consisted entirely of sokemen in 1086; and other villages in the neighbourhood, such as Blaby with 28 sokemen, four villeins and four bordars, were nearly as strongly Scandinavianised. On the other hand, Arnesby and Shearsby, only four or five miles to the south of Wigston, have pure Scandinavian names but their Domesday population shows a very low proportion of sokemen. In the former village, the two Domesday manors have a total recorded population of twenty-five, of whom only two (described as 'men') may be regarded as free, seventeen were villein families, five were bordars, and one was servile. At Shearsby, a mile away, only three of the recorded population of twelve were free. Other villages in the same district, such as Kilby and Knaptoft, also have Scandinavian names but relatively few free peasantry.

The wording of the Wigston entry in Domesday Book suggests the existence of two distinct communities in the village even at that late date. Apart from the demesne land on which were two serfs and a bondwoman, there is a hint that the village was divided between 'thirty-two villeins with a priest and twelve bordars' who had five ploughs between them, and 'thirty-one sokemen, with one clerk and two knights and four Frenchmen' who had eight ploughs. There is the possibility, too, though it is only a faint echo of the past in thirteenth- and fourteenth-century charters, that the north-eastern side of the village may have been Danish in origin. The Wyggeston Hospital charters, the main source of our information about the free peasantry of Wigston from the twelfth century to the sixteenth, relate, it is true, only to houses and farms centred on that side of the village; but they are rich in Scandinavian family names. Many, if not the majority, of the peasant families on this side of the village seem to have been free landholders in the thirteenth century and subsequently. It will be noticed also that there was in 1086 a marked economic difference between the two communities, if such they were, the one having five ploughs to forty-five households, and the other eight ploughs among thirty-eight households. The latter were relatively nearly twice as well-off as the former, judged by this test.

It may be observed that there are in the Leicestershire Domesday half a dozen clear examples of 'double vills', of which Wigston is one. In all these cases the wording of the Domesday entry suggests two distinct communities, and in most cases the 'free' community is twice as well-off as the 'unfree'. Thus at Croxton Kerrial, in the extreme north-east of the county, 22 villeins and 2 bordars shared 2½ ploughs, while 30 sokemen shared 8 ploughs. In the former community there were nearly ten households to every plough, in the latter fewer than four. At Shepshed, 42 villeins and bordars shared 15 ploughs (about three households to every plough) while in the other community there were only 1½ households to every plough.

At Barwell, on the western side of the county, the discrepancy was even more remarkable. After reciting that 14 villeins, 3 bordars, and a priest shared only 2 ploughs (i.e. 8½ families to every plough), the scribe goes on to say 'in this vill there are eight sokemen having 5 ploughs', or about 1½ households to every plough. At Husbands Bosworth, in the extreme south of the county, 12 villeins and bordars shared two ploughs, while 20 sokemen and 5 bordars had 6 ploughs. Assuming, as we may, that in the latter community the sokemen possessed all the ploughs and the bordars none, we again find – as at Wigston – one community, twice as well-off as the other. Only at Waltham-on-the-Wolds, not far from Croxton Kerrial, do we find two communities not markedly different in wealth. Here 24 sokemen, a villein, and a bordar shared only 6 ploughs – about four households to every plough – while a knight and 7 bordars had 1½ ploughs. But this entry is difficult to interpret in any case. In general, the 'double vills' reveal not only two distinct communities, but also two communities with very unequal economic standards as judged by the number of ploughs available to them.

Where there was still land to spare it seems likely that the Danish host settled down on new sites away from the English villages. Such examples occur at many places in Leicestershire and may easily be detected on the Domesday map. Wigston lay in thickly settled country, with villages equally old on either side of it. There was no room for another settlement between them; yet the site of Wigston was militarily important and could not be ignored. Hence, if this theory be correct, the Danish community settled in the existing English village, segregating themselves in a distinct quarter of the village but imposing their agriculture on the fields as they found them, since there was no room to develop their own field-system. They moved in, dispossessed many if not all of the English landowners, and cultivated their lands as they lay. From the thirteenth century, when the village records begin effectively, until 1766 when the open fields disappeared by Parliamentary Act, Wigston had only a simple three-field system and it was never at any time more complicated than this.

❧ EARLY GROWTH ❧

The growth and evolution of the village and of its fields during the pre-Conquest period is a matter of almost complete obscurity. As for so many English villages, the first recorded reference to its existence occurs in Domesday Book; but the Domesday village was already as far separated in time from the original settlement as we are from the village of Edward III's day. Much had happened in that great stretch of time of which we have not a single record, but only such faint hints as the Ordnance map, and the present topography of the village, can be made to yield.

The course taken by the boundaries of a medieval parish will often tell us something significant about the early settlement of a small piece of country, particularly about the evolution of a group of parishes or townships out of an original large estate. One can detect this, for example, in the country which adjoins Wigston on the south-east, in which it is possible to reconstitute from a number of medieval parishes on the map a large and compact estate that may well have been the Mercian royal estate of Glen from which Beorhtwulf issued a charter in 849. But the parish boundaries of Wigston tell us almost nothing of its earlier, unrecorded history. There are hints here and there that when the boundary of the township was drawn, probably in the tenth century and certainly not later than the eleventh, the arable fields had already reached the frontier in some places. The irregularity of the boundary, making frequent short right-angled turns can only arise from the existence of strip cultivation at that date. This is especially noticeable on either side of the ancient road from Wigston to Wistow, south-eastwards out of the village, and on either side of the equally ancient road to Oadby, on the north-east. One would expect the frontiers of cultivation in the eleventh century to be most advanced along known trackways to neighbouring villages of similar antiquity, and to be least advanced in the forest away from the roads; and the frontiers of Wigston bear this out.

In some places, the parish boundaries run direct along straight lines of hedge for hundreds of yards, reflecting an artificial frontier drawn through country as yet uncultivated. The change in the nature of the Oadby Wigston boundary from a zig-zag line to a long straight hedge at *Blackwell Sike* strongly suggests that this *sike* or long narrow belt of rough pasture on either side of a small stream represents the limit of expansion of the Wigston fields at the time the parish boundary was drawn (see map, page 94). Clearance and cultivation must have stopped at that marginal land for some considerable time; but to the south of the Wistow road (which existed in pre-Conquest times) the woodman's axe had hacked much farther to the south-east and had reached the frontier of the township at an early date. Thus the examination of the course of the parish boundaries throws a little light on the nature of pre-Conquest expansion of the arable into the forest. We get a glimpse here and there of the limits of cultivation in the tenth or early eleventh century from the record of the Ordnance map.

Wigston, though of such antiquity as a settlement, produced no offshoots. It never became the mother-church of a group of townships around it, like Wistow or Tilton or Bringhurst, to cite a few examples at random in Leicestershire, or like Blaby, just to the west, which had given birth to the daughter-settlement of Countesthorpe by the eleventh century. The absence of such offshoots means that the original area of the Wigston territory (so far as we know it) has not been reduced by 'the fission of vills', as Round called it. Wigston remained a large parish as Leicestershire parishes go, covering according to later measurement 2944 acres, or about twice the average for the county. Leicestershire parishes, like those of Northamptonshire or East Anglia, are usually small, indicating thereby the comparative prosperity all density of population of these regions in the tenth to the twelfth centuries when most of these boundaries were being drawn.

The parish boundaries told us a little of the pre-Conquest history of the settlement and its fields. What light, if any, can the village plan throw on the course of its development in those dark centuries?

Although the later plan of the village assumed the shape of ring-fence enclosing an open space, it is likely that its origin may have been very different. The parish church of All Saints lies on the southern edge of the large sand-and-gravel island on which the village is built. It is probable that the original village grew along the southern edge of this island, parallel with the small stream that flows to the south and along a small track running into the prehistoric road now represented by the Welford Road. Thus the first village may well have been a simple 'street-village' running roughly east to west. From this original centre, the settlement grew down the slope (now Moat Street) towards the hollow known as 'Little Dale' in medieval times, where the village green formerly lay.

Running northwards from Little Dale is the present Bullhead street, known as *Spowtewell Street* or alternatively as *Moseho* in the fifteenth century (page 91). From the thirteenth century onwards this street formed part of the main Northampton-Leicester road where it ran through the village. At the northern end of this street is St. Wolstan's church, originally St. Wistan's, the second of Wigston's two medieval churches. It is on this side of the village, along both sides of Bullhead Street, that I have suggested the Danish colony of the ninth century may have established itself, forming a separate community so far as their houses were concerned though sharing the village fields. We know that this street was built up as far north as St. Wistan's church by the end of the thirteenth century, for a Wyggeston Hospital charter (undated, but *c.* 1286-1300) speaks of 'a messuage which lies next the churchyard of St. Wistan'. The village had expanded no farther than this even by the middle of the nineteenth century.

Of the other two streets, which form the remaining sides of the rectangle, we know little. We have no medieval charters relating to property adjoining them but it is significant perhaps that neither is referred to as a 'street' until the enclosure award of 1766. One suspects that they originated as built-up streets not earlier than the seventeenth century, and quite possibly not until the eighteenth. If this is so, the ring-fence plan of the village appears to be an accidental and a late development.

Although the upshot of this discussion of the village-plan is inconclusive, it may serve some purpose as illustrating how difficult the science of village morphology is likely to prove. Even maps of the pre-industrial period, before modern changes have begun, may be misleading as a clue to the original plan of a settlement. We shall have to reconstruct the growth of villages from their original centres with the aid of medieval charters more than anything else, coupled with an eye for the geology and topography of the site. The map can help only in the later stages.

There is some evidence for believing that the fields of the village of Wigston were expanding fastest towards the north, the north-east and the south-east down to the twelfth century, rather than towards the west and the south. There is the evidence of the parish boundaries which we have already considered, which suggested the most rapid growth of the fields along the north-eastern road to Oadby and along the south-eastern road towards Wistow. Secondly, there is the fact that Wigston had no watermill in 1086, although it was the largest and most populous village in the county and although it had a considerable stream along its southern and south-western boundary. After more than five hundred years of existence, and nearly three hundred since the water-mill had been introduced into England, the village of Wigston had not begun to use the waters of the Sence, only a mile away. This can only mean that the expansion of the fields, which by 1086 covered nearly three-quarters of the available land of the parish, had been away from the Sence or it would surely have been harnessed to a mill by that date. Scores of smaller places in Leicestershire had their own water mills, but Wigston did not build one until about the middle of the twelfth century.

Again, Domesday Book confirms that the village fields had reached the frontier of the township on the north-eastern side by the eleventh century. We are told that the countess Judith held 7½ virgates of land in *Oldebi* and *Wichingestone*, a small estate of about 240 acres where the townships of Oadby and Wigston met. This land lay, in all likelihood, mainly along the zig-zag boundary line between Oadby and Wigston, from just north of the present road joining the two villages and extending south-eastwards to the edge of *Blackwell Sike* which, as we have already seen, marked the frontier of cultivation in the eleventh century. Thus the evidence of Domesday Book helps to confirm the evidence of the Ordnance map.

On the far western side of the parish of Wigston there is a good deal of low-lying alluvial land that must have been marshy and drained under natural conditions, and there would have been a tendency to avoid this at first. There are slight traces in the parish boundary that the arable may have reached the frontier at one point on this side (round Cowpasture Farm on the modern six-inch map) but it is pretty certain that the north-western and south-western corners of the township had not been reached by the time of Domesday. The fact, however, that a water-mill was built at the south-western corner by about the middle of the twelfth century suggests that the arable had reached the frontier at that point, as a result of renewed effort in the two generations immediately following the Conquest. On the north-west, the medieval name of *Shakresdale* (1342),[1] with the meaning of 'the robbers' valley', may indicate the remoteness and late clearance on that side, perhaps the last corner to be brought under cultivation.

Northwards, too, the ground falls away rapidly to flat alluvial land, partly meadow and partly marsh in early medieval times.[1] The northern

---

[1] Represented by Shackerdale Farm today.

boundary of the parish follows a straight line of hedge on either side of the main road to Leicester for some considerable distance, indicating that the arable did not reach this frontier in all probability until post-Domesday times.

Let us sum up our reading of the map and of such small hints as other documents can give us. Such evidence as there is suggests that the village fields were expanding outwards from the village most rapidly towards the north-east and the south-east in the pre-Conquest period, and that the frontiers of the territory had been reached along a line of several hundred yards on these sides by the late-eleventh century. It is possible also that the western frontier had been touched at one point. But to the north and the south the limits of the cleared and cultivated area still fell far short of the frontiers of the township, though how far short we do not know. An examination of the modern field-boundaries would probably have thrown some light on this question, were it not for the fact that these have been much altered on the southern and western sides of the parish by the making of the railway and the canal, and on the northern by recent building developments, all of which have obliterated even the hedge-lines laid down by the enclosure award.

∽ THE TWO CHURCHES ∾

Wigston is unusual today in possessing two churches, that of All Saints on the southern side of the village and that of St. Wistan (now wrongly called St. Wolstan) on the northern side. All Saints is the mother-church but we have no clue as to its antiquity as a site beyond the fact that it almost certainly existed at the time of Domesday. The priest who served the thirty-two villeins and twelve bordars unquestionably officiated in the church of All Saints. But the clerk who served the sokemen, knights, and Frenchmen in the other community in 1086 is less easy to place. There is no documentary reference to St. Wistan's church before the late thirteenth century; yet the existence of a clerk serving what appears to be a distinct community strongly suggests that such a church (or more strictly a chapel) existed at that date. Wistan

---

[1] *le Kerresheued* occurs in charters of 1306-8 in Mucklow Field meaning 'the headland by the marsh'. This was somewhere near the southern end of the present race-course.

is a purely local saint, a Mercian prince who was in all probability murdered at Wistow, three miles away, in the year 849.[1] His body was taken to Repton for burial and would have passed through Wigston and perhaps rested here for a night. A small church might well have been erected on such a site in the late ninth, or more probably the tenth century. In medieval times there was a jewelled image of the saint in the church at Wigston to which an annual pilgrimage was made. It seems likely in view of the Domesday reference to a clerk that this second church at Wigston existed in pre-Conquest times and served a distinct community.

[1] T.L.A.S., xxix, 30-41. 'The Murder of St. Wistan.'

II

The Medieval Manor, 1066–1509

The manorial history of Wigston is somewhat complicated and is made more so by the confused and often inaccurate account of it given in Nichols' *History of Leicestershire*. Down to the partition of 1207 the story is simple enough; after that date it is one of increasing complexity, above all in the lesser of the two manors, but the detailed changes are fortunately of little importance for the economic and social history of the village. The lot of the villager, free or unfree, remained much the same whether the lordship passed from one great family to another: the change was merely of one absentee lord for another, and village life continued to flow along its accustomed channels from generation to generation without much concern for the vicissitudes and interminable lawsuits of the great. Not until the second half of the sixteenth century did the changes in the lordship of the Wigston manors affect the life of the village at all profoundly.

Throughout medieval times the absentee lords ruled their tenants through bailiffs on the spot. There was freedom from the immediate eye of the lord. Moreover, a great part of the land – perhaps nearly a half – was owned by native peasant landowners, men 'of free condition' as the later records say. This economic freedom has influenced the history of Wigston profoundly through many centuries and given it a stamp of its own. For a thousand years, as far as we can tell, it was never subservient to one man or family but was a place where many men were free and roughly equal, socially if not economically. No squire dominated Wigston at any time as the Turpins did Knaptoft or the Faunts did Foston (the next parish to the south), or the Pultneys did Misterton, to cite only three out of a score or more of similar examples in Leicestershire where the whole course of village history was changed in a generation or two as a result of this dominance. There were far more villages in Leicestershire, and probably in the east Midlands as a whole, which were like Wigston in being free of a dominating lord, villages of peasant proprietors, than there were villages like Foston, Knaptoft and Misterton where the squire ruled on the spot.

❧ THE MANOR DOWN TO 1207 ❧

At the time of the Norman Conquest the manor of Wigston belonged to Ralph, earl of Hereford and nephew of the king, a man of Norman descent who had been entrusted with the protection of Herefordshire and endowed with considerable estates in Leicestershire as well as elsewhere. The gift of Wigston by the king suggests that it had been a royal manor before that time, though of this there is no specific evidence.

The large and rich manors of Wigston and Stoughton[1] had been granted by the Confessor to Earl Ralph, who had also been given Lutterworth, Misterton and Catthorpe in the extreme south of the county, Great Easton on the south-eastern border, and a small estate at Welham in the Welland meadows between Medbourne and Market Harborough. The large manor of Great Easton was, however, granted by Ralph to Peterborough Abbey before the Conquest and remained in the abbey's possession until the Dissolution in 1539: it later belonged to the Dean and Chapter of Peterborough, to whom the abbey property was transferred in 1541.

At the Conquest, or immediately afterwards, Ralph's manors of Wigston and Stoughton were given by the king to Hugh de Grentemaisnil; the Lutterworth estate, together with Misterton and Catthorpe, passed to Maino the Breton; Great Easton remained with Peterborough Abbey; and Welham was given to Robert de Buci. In this manner Earl Ralph's considerable estate in Leicestershire was broken up and parcelled out among various great landowners, though the larger part passed into the hands of Hugh de Grentemaisnil.

The latter, a Norman magnate who had accompanied the Conqueror to England, had been richly rewarded with lands in five counties. In Leicestershire he was by far the greatest landowner, having, in addition to Wigston, no fewer than thirty-six other manors in his

---

[1] Stenton identified the Domesday *Stoctone* with Stockerston in the south-east of the county (*V.C.H.*, i, 314) but there is no doubt from its subsequent history that it is to be identified as Stoughton, including Bushby and Thurnbly.

own hands, while in fifty-four other places in the county tenants held lands under him.

The vast estates of Hugh passed, about the year 1101, to Robert, count of Meulan (or Mellent), who became the first earl of Leicester. For the next hundred years, down to the year 1204, the manor of Wigston remained in the hands of the earls of Leicester, through four generations, until the death of the last earl without issue. During this period the manorial history of Wigston is uncomplicated and almost nothing is recorded of it. There were, however, two events during the rule of the earls of Leicester which affected the later history of the village and it is necessary to say something of them. The first was the grant of the church of Wigston (i.e. the rectory with all its revenues) by the first earl to Lenton Priory in Nottinghamshire; and the second event was the grant, some time during the twelfth century, of a considerable part of the manor to a local magnate, one of the Croft family, so called from the village not far away to the south-west. This property came to be regarded as a manor in itself and we can trace its subsequent history down to its dissolution in 1586 when it was broken up and sold off to the tenants and others.

Nichols says, of the first transaction, that Robert, earl of Meulan and earl of Leicester, gave the church of Wigston, together with the tithes of all his demesne there, to the Cluniac priory of Lenton early in the reign of Henry I, and that this gift was confirmed by his son Robert Bossu about the year 1140.[1] An entry in the Charter Rolls enables us to date the gift as having been made between 1109 and the earl's death in 1118. Another entry confirms the original gift of the first earl and reveals that his son, while confirming his father's gift of the church and the tithes of the demesne, added to it three virgates of land with three tofts and crofts.[2]

Professor Hamilton Thompson has stated most succinctly what the gift of a parish church meant in these circumstances. The monastery became the permanent patron, with the right to fill the living with someone of its own choice, and it could also, if it wished, enter upon and appropriate the rectorial or great tithe, i.e. the tithes arising from

[1] Nichols, iv, 373.

[2] *Cal. Charter Rolls*, iii, 317-8; v, 149. In plain English the gift was of three farms, each of one yardland or roughly 32 acres, and in later centuries known as the Rectory Farm.

the corn and hay of the parish. In most instances it chose so to do and thus became the rector of the church, appointing a vicar to perform the actual spiritual duties of the parish. On the other hand, 'monasteries with large possessions often were content to receive annual pensions out of the fruits of parish churches to which they could present influential clerks in orders and so avail themselves of their help in business affairs.'[1] This is what happened at Wigston. The priory appointed rectors and was content for several centuries to receive an annual pension of one hundred shillings out of the rectorial revenues, which were worth the handsome sum of fifty-six marks per annum.[2] Not until 1506 did it enter upon and appropriate the rectorial tithe, so becoming rector of the parish, and ordaining a vicarage for the cure of souls at Wigston. The significance of all this for the village of Wigston was that the parish rarely if ever saw its rector, who fulfilled his spiritual duties through a number of chaplains whom he paid. Wigston was one of the richest livings in the county and the rector much too important a man to spend any time in the place whence so much of his income came. In the early fifteenth century, at least, he was farming out the rectory to local men and drawing a rent from them over a term of years. Thus the village had an absentee parson for many centuries as well as an absentee lord, and not until the early sixteenth century did it acquire a resident vicar. Perhaps the spiritual loss was not great: for all we know their chaplains, often men of local peasant families, performed their duties as well as any well-fed prelate would have done, possibly better. But a further and more remote effect of the alienation of this opulent rectorial tithe into monastic (and later into lay) hands worked itself out as late as 1766 when the Duke of St. Albans, to whom the great tithes had eventually come by a devious route, was able to appropriate in the enclosure award nearly one-seventh of the land of the parish in lieu of the great tithe, so becoming the largest single landowner in the parish.

The other event of the twelfth century to which we have referred is a matter of more conjecture. Even in the thirteenth century the origin of

---

[1] T.LA.S., xxii, 4.

[2] The *Taxatio* of Pope Nicholas in 1291 sets down the church of Wigston as worth 48½ marks per annum after meeting the annual pension of 100 shillings to the prior. The gross value of the rectory was therefore 56 marks or £37 6s. 8d.

the second and smaller manor in Wigston was the subject of conflicting stories in lawsuits. This manor descended to the Champayne or Campania family and in 1274 a dispute broke out over the wardship of Robert, son and heir of Nicholas de Campania, who was then under age. Ralph Basset of Sapcote, a member of the powerful family who had given so many sheriffs to Leicestershire since the early years of the twelfth century, was summoned to the Easter assizes at Market Harborough to answer Edmund, the king's brother, who had obtained the honor of Leicester (of which the Champayne manor was part) in 1265. Edmund claimed the custody of the heir because Nicholas de Champayne had held the manor of him by knight service. To this Ralph Basset answered that the custody belonged to him because Nicholas had held the manor of Thurlaston of him by knight service and had been enfeoffed in this manor before that of Wigston. He recited the descent of both manors from Robert de Croft, giving details which need not detain us here since the jury rejected this account and found, in their turn, that the first earl of Leicester had enfeoffed Hugh de Champayne, the ancestor of Nicholas, in all his lands in Wigston before any other lands. Thus the verdict was that the Champaynes held their manor of Wigston by knight service of Edmund, the king's brother, who recovered the custody of the ward. And since the latter had married without the permission of his guardian he was ordered to satisfy Edmund with a fine of £341 8s. 9d. or two years' rental of all his lands, the usual penalty for this offence.[1]

Ralph Basset appears to have ignored this judgement. Two years later he was again summoned to the court of King's Bench in London to answer Edmund. Apparently the decision of the jury in 1274 that Robert, first earl of Leicester, had enfeoffed Hugh de Champayne in his Wigston lands before any other was afterwards shown to be false though it had won the suit for Edmund at the time. At any rate, Edmund's claim was advanced on different grounds in the second suit, in which both parties were agreed that Robert de Croft had originally been seised of the Wigston lands under the earl of Leicester and that he had left two daughters and co-heirs, one of whom married a Champayne, so bringing the Wigston property to that family. The jury decided once more in favour of Edmund and at Michaelmas

---

[1] Farnham, V, 286.

1276 the sheriff was ordered to take £341 8s. 9d. from the goods and chattels of Ralph Basset in his bailiwick because the wardship of the heir, and consequently his marriage, belonged to Edmund.[1]

Other scattered references provide independent support for the second version of the origin of the smaller Wigston manor. Hugh de Grentemaisnil had held the manors of Thurlaston and Croft in 1086 besides that of Wigston, and all three manors had passed to the earls of Leicester in the twelfth century as part of their Grentemaisnil inheritance. At some time in the twelfth century, probably before 1170-80, the Crofts, under-tenants of the earls in the village of that name, were granted in addition substantial estates in Thurlaston and Wigston by one of the earls. Thus there came to be formed the group of estates in these three manors which went together as a whole for centuries afterwards, until Sir William Turvile separated them again by leaving the manor of Thurlaston to his eldest son and the manor of Wigston to his second son.[2]

Robert de Croft died leaving two daughters and co-heirs, one of whom, Alice, married Hugh de Champayne before the end of the twelfth century. The Champaynes thus became possessed of the Croft estates in Thurlaston and Wigston. This second manor at Wigston had probably come into existence before the 1170's when Robert de Croft witnessed a Wigston charter.[3] There is good reason to believe also that this grant may have represented the original demesne of the Domesday manor, which was assessed at one-third of a hide out of a total of one and one-third hides for the manor as a whole, i.e. at one-quarter of the whole. For we know that in the sixteenth century the lands of John Turvile, to whom the Champayne manor eventually descended, amounted to 23 virgates out of a total of 92¾ in the whole parish, again a quarter of the whole. Moreover, these lands were not geldable, as we are told in an early seventeenth-century record, strong, presumptive evidence that they had originally been the Domesday demesne.[4]

---

[1] Farnham, v, 287-8.   [2] See page 98, below.

[3] *W.H.R.* no. 867. No date, but assigned by Hamilton Thompson to 1170-80.

[4] Inq. post mortem on John Turvile's lands, 1506. Assessments of land are not always reliable in such inquisitions, but there is independent evidence on this point in some Court Proceedings in the Archdeacon's court at Leicester in 1633-4 in which it was stated that the Leicester or Duchy fee contained 22 yardlands (as one deponent thought), the remainder of the township being in the Winchester fee. Sir William Faunt in 1634, in the same suit, said that he was lord or owner of one part of the village 'commonly called the Gildable' and that a 'good part of the town stands in the fee of the Duchy of Lancaster' which we deduce was not geldable.

Robert, fourth earl of Leicester, died without issue in the early autumn of 1204. His estates were partitioned between his two sisters, Amicia, who subsequently married Simon de Montfort, father of the better-known Simon, earl of Leicester, and Margaret, the wife of Saer de Quincy, who was created earl of Winchester in 1207. The division of this great inheritance was delayed by other circumstances, but the partition had been finally accomplished by the early months of 1207.[1] The principal manor of Wigston was assigned to Margaret, and was thenceforward known as the Winchester fee, and the overlordship of the smaller Champayne manor went to Amicia and was known as the Leicester fee.

✎ THE WINCHESTER MANOR, 1207-1509 ✎

Saer de Quincy died in 1209 and was succeeded by his son Roger, who died without male issue on 25 April 1264. The earldom of Winchester lapsed to the Crown and Roger's lands were divided between his three daughters and co-heirs.[2] This further partition was of no practical significance for Wigston, however, for some years earlier the Winchester manor in Wigston had been granted to Hugh de Vere, fourth earl of Oxford, on his marriage with Hawise, daughter of Margaret, countess of Winchester, who had inherited it in 1207. This marriage took place shortly before 1240 and by it the earls of Oxford acquired the principal manor of Wigston, amounting to three-quarters of the whole parish. The inquisition post mortem on the lands of Roger de Quincy shows under Wigston: '£40 land held by the countess of Oxford in free marriage of the gift of Roger de Quincy her brother.' The earls of Oxford continued to hold the manor for the next three hundred years, free of all service. Thus, although the overlords might change (as at the further partition of 1264) there was no change in the mesne tenants of the manor through all these years. For all practical purposes the earls of Oxford were lords of the manor from about 1239 to 1526, when they failed in the male line.

[1] Fox, 'The Honor and Earldom of Leicester', *E.H.R.*, liv, 391-3.
[2] Ibid., 391, n. 5.

It is they who draw the revenue from the lordship and it is they with whom the tenants always deal.

Only once was the long tenure of the earls of Oxford at Wigston seriously interrupted and that was between 1474 and 1485. John de Vere, thirteenth earl of Oxford, was attainted and all his honours forfeited in 1474 for his support of Henry VI; and in January 1476 we find his manor of Wigston granted to Sir Walter Devereux, Lord Ferrers, to hold by the accustomed rents and services and all issues from 14th April 1471.[1] It was not long before the Veres resumed their ancient patrimony. The earl fought at Bosworth Field with Henry Tudor and in the same year all his honours were restored. At the close of our period (1509) we find the thirteenth earl of Oxford securely in place once more as the lord of the principal manor, which passed to his nephew in 1513.

↣ THE DUCHY MANOR, 1207-1509 ↢

The history of the smaller manor, that held of the honour of Leicester and subsequently of the Duchy of Lancaster, is more complicated than that of the principal manor. In 1207, when the division of the earl of Leicester's lands was made between his sisters, the Champaynes were already in possession as mesne tenants and they remained undisturbed. The Champaynes held their estates in Wigston, Thurlaston, Croft and elsewhere for six generations, the male line dying out with Sir William de Champayne who died on or about Christmas Day, 1355. During their tenure of the manor, changes took place in the overlordship, again without affecting the mesne tenants. The earldom and honour of Leicester descended to Simon de Montfort who was killed at Evesham in 1265, whereupon his estates were forfeit to the Crown. Later in the same year, the honour of Leicester and all the lands belonging to it, were granted to Edmund, the second surviving son of Henry III and brother of Edward I. It is as 'the king's brother' that he is referred to in the suits of 1274 and 1276 already discussed.

The honour of Leicester descended with the earls of Leicester, who were also earls and later dukes of Lancaster, coming eventually to John

---

[1] *Cal. Patent Rolls, 1476-7, 565.*

of Gaunt and thence to his son Henry, who became Henry IV. Henry
settled the Lancastrian lands upon himself and his heirs as an appanage
to the Crown, under a distinct and independent administration, which
became known as the Duchy of Lancaster. Thus the Leicester fee became
known as the Duchy fee and it is under this description that we hear of
the smaller manor in Wigston in later centuries.

Meanwhile, the actual tenants of the manor remained, as they had always
been since some time in the twelfth century, local families – Leicestershire
squires for the most part. The Champaynes were, as we have said, lords for
six successive generations. In the third generation their right was disputed
by the Skeffingtons, another Leicestershire family of some note, and was
the subject of prolonged litigation. The origin of the trouble was the
second marriage of Joan, widow of Nicholas de Champayne, who had died
shortly before 1274, leaving Robert, his son and heir, under age. By 1277
Joan had married Robert de Skeffington and trouble began almost at once
over the Champayne lands, dragging on for almost twenty years.

In a suit dated Hilary 1279, Robert de Skeffington sued Robert de
Champayne and Nicholas his brother 'in a plea wherefore they by night
entered the house of Robert de Sceffington at Thurlaston, broke open
a chest of his, and took and carried away his charters and other of his
goods there found to his damage of £100'. The court made an order
to distrain the defendants and produce them in court at Easter. We do
not learn the sequel of this burglary, evidently chiefly concerned with
getting hold of the 'deeds and evidences' of the lands in dispute, but in
July 1281 'the assize came to recognise whether Robert de Campania and
Henry le Leper unjustly disseised Robert de Skeftyngton and Joan his
wife of their free tenement in Thurlaston and Croft, namely, a third part
of a water-mill in Thurlaston and a rent of twenty pence to be taken
from the water-mill of Croft at the hands of the miller at the time, as
dower of Joan, of the gift of a certain Nicholas de Campania, formerly
her husband.'[1] The court decided that Robert and Joan were in mercy
for a false claim.

Two more law-suits followed, relating to the Wigston portion of the
estate. In 1291 Robert de Skeffington and Joan his wife were summoned to
answer Peter the Chaplain of Wigston 'in a plea that they render him the

[1] Farnham, v, 288.

custody of the land and heir of Laurence, son of Roger, son of Thomas de Wykyngeston, which belongs to Peter, because Laurence held his land of Peter by knight service.[1]

Finally, in 1296, some twenty years after Joan's troublesome second marriage, Robert de Skeffington brought Robert de Champayne to court once more, accusing him of unjustly keeping possession of the manor of Wigston, which is described as consisting of 16 messuages, 16¼ virgates of land, a windmill, an oven, 13s. 3¼d. rent and rents of a pound of cummin and two capons. Robert de Champayne recovered his seisin and Robert de Skeffington once more was 'in mercy for a false claim'.[2]

The suit is only interesting to the economic historian as giving some indication of the extent and degree of organisation of the smaller manor at the end of the thirteenth century. It reveals a manor already equipped with its own oven and windmill (and indeed with its own church also, as we discover from other records at this time), a smaller version of the larger manor from which it had evolved, except that it could have no water-mill for there was no stream large enough for this purpose within its bounds. In all its jurisdiction covered 22 or 23 virgates of land, as we have already discovered from other evidence, of which an unknown amount had already been granted out or sold freely to villagers who paid small sums of money, or a pound of cummin or a couple of capons, as chief rents to the lord. We shall learn more of this process of granting or selling of freeholds to peasants in the village in the following chapter.

When William de Champayne died at the end of 1355, he left an only daughter and heir, Margaret, who married Sir John Sulney and took the Champayne lands with her. At this point, and for the next two or three generations, the descent of the Wigston property becomes a matter of great complexity which is, fortunately, of little significance for the economic history of the village. The manor came eventually to Baldwin Bugge who died in 1435, and then passed from him to his sister and heir, Margaret, who had married as her first husband Richard Turvile of Normanton Turvile. When she died in 1474, seised of the five manors of Thurlaston, Stoke, Normanton, Croft and Wigston (all in Leicestershire), her large estate passed to John Turvile, her grandson by her first marriage. So the Duchy manor of Wigston came to the Turviles,

[1] Farnham, v, 289.   [2] Ibid. 289.

an ancient family of squires settled a few miles away from Wigston since the twelfth century. John Turvile died in 1506 and his manors came to his eldest son, William, later Sir William Turvile, who held the family estates until his death in 1549.

Thus, in 1509 when our survey of the manorial history of Wigston comes to an end for the time being, the larger manor was held by John de Vere, thirteenth earl of Oxford; and the smaller manor was held by Sir William Turvile, one of the largest landowners in Leicestershire, lord of seven manors, principally in the country to the south and south-west of Leicester. Both were absentee landlords, but whereas the earls of Oxford probably never came near their Wigston property (as it was their only land in Leicestershire), the Turviles, living not many miles away at Normanton Turvile, may have been known to the villagers at least as occasional visitors.

III

THE FREE TENANTS, 1086–1509

Beneath the lords of the two manors were a large number of tenants who held their land freely, most of them peasants but a few of more considerable rank. In general it is not until the thirteenth century that the records begin to yield information about these freeholders and their lands, and even then they rarely tell us enough. The absence of manorial extents or surveys makes impossible anything but an incomplete account of this important social class during the medieval period.

In Leicestershire Domesday enumerates nearly 2000 sokemen, about one-third of the recorded population of the county. Many of them were, in all probability, direct descendants of the Danish settlers of the ninth century, though a number were of English descent from men who had retained possession of their small estates through both the Danish and the Norman Conquests. At Wigston for example, we see distinct traces of English landholders in the late twelfth and early thirteenth centuries.

Even in Leicestershire, however, there were Domesday villages where the lord owned all, or the greater part, of the land, and where the peasant families were merely occupiers of land they could not call their own. So it was at Knaptoft, six miles south of Wigston, in the upland country of south Leicestershire, where in 1086 there were only two peasant proprietors (sokemen) out of some eighteen or twenty families in the village, and nine acres out of ten, as we discover from later records, belonged to the lord. As a result of this fundamental difference between Knaptoft and Wigston as far back as the eleventh century, the subsequent history of the two villages was entirely different. There were a number of other Domesday villages in Leicestershire like Knaptoft, and in the main it was these which were swept away under the sheep and cattle pastures between 1450 and 1550.

Villages like Wigston, however, with a high proportion of free peasantry, are typical of a much larger number of East Midland villages which succeeded in retaining their traditional husbandry of small mixed farms, based on the open fields, until the age of parliamentary enclosure in the second half of the eighteenth century; and it is important therefore to trace the history of this class of free peasantry in as much detail as the records will allow.

How much of the land at Wigston in 1086 was held freely and how much was not? Of the sixteen ploughlands on the manor of Hugh de Grentemaisnil, four were in the lord's demesne and the remaining twelve were 'village land', occupied by a population of 32 villein households, 31 sokemen households, 6 persons of superior rank (knights and Frenchmen), and 12 bordars or cottagers. The amount of land occupied by the cottagers would not have been large: perhaps fifty acres at the outside, if we allow about four or five acres to each. Of the remaining households, the free outnumbered the unfree by 37 to 32. In view of this we can be reasonably certain that at least a half of the village land (outside the demesne) was held freely in 1086.

Even if we assume that the free tenants held on an average no more than the villeins we find that the 37 free men owned about 6½ ploughlands of the total of 16½ (including the small de Buci estate) or about thirty-eight per cent. This is a conservative figure, since it is likely that the knights and the Frenchmen held somewhat larger tenements than the average. We shall be somewhere near the truth if we say that in 1086 about forty per cent of all the land in Wigston was held by free tenants of all kinds.

Though the sokemen, who roughly equalled the villeins in number at Wigston, were a superior class tenurially, being free of nearly all the burdensome restrictions under which the latter laboured, they were not necessarily superior economically. The land they occupied they could call their own, but it was rarely more land than was occupied by a villein. There is plenty of evidence from all over Leicestershire that the 'normal' tenement of both free tenants and villeins was a virgate in the twelfth and thirteenth centuries,[1] though by the time of the inquest of 1279 this uniformity had been greatly modified in some places by subdivision on the one hand and the accumulation of several tenements by one family on the other.

---

[1] Examples abound in Farnham and in Nichols. Cf. also Stenton, *Danelaw Charters* (Introduction, xxii), though Stenton also notes that 'departures from this average were frequent and considerable'.

At Wigston, with its densely peopled streets in 1086, there must have
been considerable variations from this uniform pattern even by that date.
The village had more people in 1086 than it had at the beginning of
Elizabeth's reign. The pressure of population must already have been
acute, with a consequent early subdivision of tenements. It may be that
some of the Domesday cottagers held small free tenements cut out of
original virgate-holdings as a result of the natural increase of population.
That whatever uniform pattern of land-holding there may once have been
had been greatly modified by 1086 is clear enough from the fact that 81
households (ignoring for the moment the priest and the clerk, the serfs and
bondwoman) shared between them the fifty virgates of the village land.
Clearly, the 'normal' tenement of one virgate, though it still survived in
the thirteenth century and later records of the village, was beginning to
break down into smaller tenements as early as the eleventh. Only on this
assumption can we fit some eighty households into fifty virgates at that date.
Later, the leasing of the demesne or the granting of parts of it outright,
by sale or otherwise, to village families, coupled with the expansion of the
cultivated area to the boundaries of the village territory, may have eased
the pressure to some extent. Whether it did more than keep pace with the
increase of population between the late eleventh century and the early
fourteenth is something that remains to be considered.

It seems reasonably certain that in 1086 about forty per cent of
the Wigston land was held by free tenants, and that they constituted
about forty-five per cent of the enumerated population of the village.
Numerically, as well as otherwise, they were the most important class of
the tenantry. But our information as to particular tenements and families
does not begin effectively until about the middle of the thirteenth century
(with a few hints that take us back into the late twelfth century at times).
From about 1250 onwards, the Wyggeston Hospital charters provide a
good sample of families and tenements in one part of the village, and
these, coupled with a number of final concords and other records in
the national archives, are our main source of information for the next
270 years, up to the endowment of the Hospital in 1521. These records
between them bring out abundantly:

(1) the frequent grants of land by and to the larger tenants, who

subsequently re-grant land in smaller parcels to lesser men, usually free peasants of the village;

(2) the continual buying and selling of land, mostly in very small parcels, between one peasant family and another;

(3) the continual use of money by peasant families, which presupposes the sale of crops for cash on a not inconsiderable scale; and

(4) the slow accumulation of property by a few energetic, acquisitive or fortunate families in the village, and the emergence of what we may call a 'peasant aristocracy' by the fifteenth century.

❧ THE LARGER FREE TENANTS ❧

Among the largest of the under-tenants of the manor at the end of the thirteenth century was Sir Simon Friday, knight. An inquisition taken in 1296 shows that he held nine yardlands of the honour of Winchester, held of the heirs of the earl by serjeanty,[1] but we have no information about the antiquity of this grant nor much as to its subsequent disposal among the smaller men in the village. One Ralph Fryday witnessed the earliest Wigston charter (*c.* 1170-80) and his descendants in the village witness other charters throughout the thirteenth and fourteenth centuries. Another Ralph Fryday was living in Wigston in the first half of the fifteenth century and Richard Fryday his brother appears as a substantial landholder at the same time.[2] Besides possessing a capital messuage and three virgates of land together with a croft, he drew 22s. 2d. yearly in chief rents from a dozen properties in the village. Some of these chief rents are substantial sums as chief rents go (4s. 6d., 3s., 3s. 4d.) and must have come from tenements of some size. There can be little doubt that they represent chief rents reserved to the lord from the grant of virgates and half-virgates of land in former times to the Cooks (or Cocks), the Pollyngs, the Smiths, the Herricks and the Huttes, all of whom are known to have been free tenants, and who are named in 1443. Indeed, these chief rents may represent the regranting or sale of six virgates,

---

[1] Nichols, op. cit. 373.
[2] W.H.R., *passim*, between 1419 and 1455.

the difference between the original Fryday holding of nine virgates in 1296 and the three virgates they retained in 1443.[1]

A fine of 1344 tells us that these tenements had been granted away by that date, for it records a transaction 'between John Fryday of Wigston and Emma his wife, plaintiffs, and Thomas Lewyn of Wigston, defendant', relating to a messuage, three virgates and five acres of land, and 22s. 2d. rent in Wigston. At first sight it would appear that this fine records the purchase of the property by the Frydays from Lewyn but it represents in fact the final stage of a rather tortuous method of ensuring the succession to the Fryday property.[2] We shall return to this method of disposing of land in a later page, but for our immediate purpose it is sufficient to say that the large original grant to the Fryday family in Wigston seems to have been redistributed in smaller parcels to various peasant families by the early years of the fourteenth century.

The same inquisition of 1296 says that William de Winterborne held lands by serjeanty of the honour of Winchester in Wigston. This appears from inquisitions taken between 1371 and 1457 to have been only a small estate of 2½ virgates (about eighty acres) which in 1444-57, and probably earlier, was held by Thomas Hutte by the service of a moiety of a knight's fee. The Huttes were a peasant family of some antiquity in the village, who held other property also.[3] The Winterborne estate may have been one of considerable antiquity, for in a late twelfth-century grant we read of property held by Reynald Wynturborn 'of the Englishmen' in Wigston.[4] It is possible that the Huttes acquired the Winterborne lands by marriage, as we are told that William Hutte (fl. 1250-1300) married Amice, daughter of Reynald Wynter.

In the 1270's Jordan le Flemyng had acquired a substantial estate in Wigston. We find him disposing of eight messuages and six virgates of land in two grants in 1274-5. At Michaelmas 1274 he granted to

---

[1] *W.H.R.*, no. 1023, dated 22 June 1443.

[2] Farnharn MSS., Wigston. Final concords or fines are amongst the most deceptive and misleading of all the records we have to deal with.

[3] William Utte or Hutte appears frequently in records of *c.* 1290-1300 both as a witness to charters and occasionally as a grantee (see *W.H.R.*, nos. 900 to 940, passim). No. 940, dated March 6, 1319-20, tells us that he held a messuage and a virgate of land in his lifetime, which was conveyed to Roger Huth by this grant. In the fifteenth century they held lands of the Frydays also.

[4] *W.H.R.*, no. 867.

Joan, widow of Martin de Bayl, four messuages and four virgates of land in Wigston for the term of her life and after her death to John, son of the said Martin, and his heirs for ever. A fine in the following year (Easter, 1275) records that Philip le Fraunceys and Joan his wife, acquired from Jordan le Fleming four messuages and two virgates of land in Wigston.[1] Some of the property which came to the Bayls was leased to local families but at least one small parcel of half a virgate was sold off to Robert Balle in or about the year 1295.[2] We find two half virgates being released to John de Bail in 1292 by Simon de Wykingeston and William Hutte, to whom they had previously been leased for life, and a quit claim by Reynald Pikeman of Wigston to John de Bail of a messuage in Wigston which had been leased to him for the term of his life,[3] but of the subsequent disposal of these lands and the rest of the Bail inheritance in Wigston we find no trace.

Another family of gentle descent who acquired land in Wigston were the Harcourts, who held considerable estates in Leicestershire, notably at Newton Harcourt (adjoining Wigston to the south-east) and Kibworth Harcourt, a few miles away, and elsewhere in England. Before his death in 1118 Robert, first earl of Leicester, had given four virgates in his manor of Wigston to the hospital of Brackley in Northamptonshire, the gift being confirmed by Robert his son.[4] In 1236 the prior of Brackley exchanged these four virgates for certain lands and a barn near Brackley which had been part of the inheritance of Orabel de Quincy, wife of Richard de Harcourt. Richard and Orabel had been tenants of the priory lands in Wigston, as appears from the fine recording the transaction, and by this exchange became the owners of the four virgates, with the usual appurtenances in the meadows and common pastures. For a time the part of the village where the tenements lay, to which these lands pertained, was known as Wigston Harcourt. The Harcourts, a younger branch of the more illustrious family, lived in Wigston from the early thirteenth to the mid-fifteenth centuries, but they appear to have regranted their four

[1] Farnham MSS., loc. cit.
[2] W.H.R., nos. 899, 900, 919. At first this half-virgate, 'which Robert Spire sometime held', was leased to Balle and his wife at a rent of 10s. yearly during their lives and in survivorship (no. 899), but no. 900 (n.d.) records the outright sale of the property for a sum of money not specified.
[3] W.H.R., nos. 916–9.
[4] Nichols, 373.

virgates of land to the Wykyngestons, who held them in 1301 of John de Harcourt, lord of Bosworth, by the service of one barbed arrow.[1]

The small Domesday estate of Robert de Buci – two virgates on the Wigston side of the boundary and five on the Oadby side – seems to have come into the hands of the free peasants also before the end of the thirteenth century. We can trace its descent through various medieval Midland families (Basset, de Bases, Dyve) but in actual fact the property (which also included four virgates in Evington, the next village beyond Oadby) was held in the last resort by peasant freeholders. Some time in the fifteenth century the original Buci estate came into the hands of the Brooksbys of Oadby, and in the following century (through one or two intermediaries) to the Waldrams or Waldrons of the same place. A rental of John Waldron's lands in 1580 shows that the Wigston portion of his estate was then let to two freeholders of Wigston, John Cartwright and one Coultman, at an annual rent of 3s. each.[2] They must have held a yardland each.

✐   THE FREE PEASANTRY   ✐

So far we have been mainly concerned with the larger free tenants, holding directly under the chief lords. These, as we have seen, regranted the greater part of their estates in Wigston to smaller men – peasant families most of them – though some, with smaller estates, like the Bails, lived on them and kept them mostly in hand for their own farming.

We must turn now to the native peasantry of the village, whose names occur repeatedly in the period 1200-1500 among the Wyggeston Hospital charters, often as grantors and grantees of small pieces of land, ranging from single selions up to a virgate or more, and more frequently as witnesses to such grants. We may presume the freedom of any man who attests a charter. This is certainly true at Wigston where many of the witnesses to thirteenth-century charters themselves grant or receive grants of land or are otherwise known to have been free tenants. Further,

[1] Nichols, 378-9.
[2] B.M. Add. MS. 6702, fo. 110. The Wigston men probably held a lease for lives, paying a substantial fine on entry and a nominal reserved rent per annum thereafter for the term of the lease.

says Stenton, there is a 'general probability that the native witness of the twelfth century represents, in the second or third generation, a sokeman of the age of Domesday'.[1] This, too, is suggested by the earliest Wigston charters (though these fall into a rather later period, *c.* 1200-*c.* 1260), in which Scandinavian personal names are still to be found. In a grant which may be dated as not later than 1202, we find Rannulf the clerk receiving 'the virgate which Ketel held' and 'the half virgate which Turbertus held';[2] and a grant of *c.* 1250 is witnessed by Henry Eyrig and Adam Toki, among others, both of whom derive their surnames from Danish personal names. 'Fridai', which appears from the late twelfth century onwards, may be a Scandinavian name also. In charters of the second half of the thirteenth century we find the names of Robert Gamel (*c.* 1270), Roger Swan (1273) and John Wyking (1273), descended ultimately from Gamel, Swein, and Viking.[3]

The early charters also make it clear that native Englishmen survived as landowners in the village. Not only do we read of land 'held of the Englishmen' in Wigston in the twelfth century, but there are such Old English personal names as Godric, Godwin, Edwin, Alwyne, all of whom must have been alive in the late twelfth century as their sons witness charters or appear as landholders in the early thirteenth. In a late thirteenth-century grant we read also of 'those 2½ virgates which William Hengleis sometime held'.

It is clear that the free peasantry of Wigston, as we find them in the thirteenth century, were descended from both native English and Scandinavian landholders, but the evidence is too late and too meagre to draw any conclusions from this as to the respective numbers and importance of the two peoples.

The most important of the native Wigston families who held land freely probably descended from one of the two knights or four Frenchmen mentioned in the Domesday record as possessing land here. This was the Wykyngeston family, who took their name as early

---

[1] *Danelaw Charters*, ciii.

[2] *W.H.R.*, no. 868 (n.d.). Turbertus is rendered as Thurbern in no. 871.

[3] *W.H.R.*, nos. 867-89, passim. On the formation of Leicestershire surnames in the thirteenth century from Scandinavian and Old English personal names, see my '*Leicestershire Yeoman Families and their Pedigrees*', in *T.L.A.S.*, xxiii.

as the twelfth century from their native place, and who lived here as
considerable free tenants until the middle of the fourteenth century,
when they disappear suddenly from the records. The earliest Wigston
charter (*c.* 1170-80) is a grant whereby Robert, third earl of Leicester
and lord of the manor of Wigston, gives to Sir Symon Wykingeston
of Wykyngestona, knight, 'for his love', two chief messuages and a
virgate of land, together with the mill and an acre of land.[1] The rank
and surname of Sir Symon may indicate that he was not of peasant
stock but sprang from one of the Domesday tenants of superior rank.
However this may be, his descendants are distinguishable from other
peasant families in the thirteenth- and fourteenth- century village only
by their larger holdings of land.

As early as the reign of John we find Simon de Wikeston involved in
a suit concerning six virgates of land in Wigston.[2] A later Symon, who
flourished in the last decades of the thirteenth century and the early
years of the fourteenth, appears to have been the bailiff of Wigston,[3]
probably acting in that capacity for the earls of Oxford. There are
many grants of parcels of land to and by the family from *c.* 1170 to the
early fourteenth century among the Wyggeston Hospital charters. By
Edward I's time they had acquired a considerable property not only in
Wigston but in the villages of Burton Overy and Ullesthorpe elsewhere
in Leicestershire. An inquisition *ad quod damnum*, taken at Leicester early
in the year 1301 and arising from Simon's desire to found a chantry
in his parish church, shows that he had endowed the church for this
purpose with three houses and 2½ virgates of land in Wigston, together
with 40s. worth of rents arising from two virgates of land in Burton
Overy. The jurors found that he still retained land and rents in Wigston
and Ullesthorpe to the value of £6 per annum, which was sufficient
to enable him to carry out his obligations to the king. A document of
1334 indicates more precisely the extent of the Wigston property as
'a messuage, 8¼ virgates and 3 roods of land, and a windmill, with
meadows, grazings, pastures and all other lands and tenements, rents

---

[1] *W.H.R.* no. 867. This is the first mention of the water-mill at Wigston, which had apparently existed
a generation earlier. Its appearance may be dated as *c.* 1150.

[2] Assize roll, 613 (temp. John). Farnham MSS., under Wigston.

[3] *W.H.R.*, no. 939 (dated 1320) refers back to 'Simon le Baylif' who is clearly identifiable with Simon
de Wykingeston.

and services, in Wigston'.[1] Before the gift of 1301, therefore, assuming that they had acquired no further land between that date and 1334, the Wykyngestons had already accumulated an estate of some 10¾ virgates and were by far the largest resident landowners in the village.

The name of Wykyngeston disappears suddenly from the Wigston charters after 1343, in which year William de Wykyngeston, son of Simon, witnessed a grant. It seems certain that they migrated to the town of Leicester, to which other members of the family had gone in earlier centuries. We know that William had a son Simon, to whom his lands were released in 1334, and it is probably significant that we find among the freemen enrolled at Leicester in the year 1344-5 the name of Simon de Wykyngston, 'ernemongere'.[2] In Leicester they rose to an eminent position in the town in the course of the next hundred years or so, becoming merchants of the staple and supplying mayors and members of parliament for the town on many occasions between 1448 and 1520.

Whether or not they sold some of their ancestral lands in Wigston on their migration into the town we do not know, but they certainly retained part of their property for two or three generations afterwards. A grant in 1432 by Richard Randolf of Wigston, representative of another ancient family of free tenants, speaks of 'a messuage and two virgates of land, lying within the commodities of Burton Nouerey, and of a messuage and half a virgate of land lying within the commodities of Wykyngeston, which lately descended to the said grantor by hereditary right, after the death of Henry Wygston his cousin, and lately were called Wygstonland'.[3]

Among the smaller peasant families we find some nineteen whose names recur in the thirteenth-century records: Randolf, Herrick, Smith, Coke, Godwin, Balle, Freman, Gamel, Toki, Mabile, Simon,

---

[1] John Swan of Wigston, chaplain, released the property, to Simon, grandson of the Simon of 1301. William, father of the younger Simon and son of the elder, had devised it to Simon his son and John Swan jointly, for the life of William. Again, the transaction is really the termination of an arrangement to settle the succession of the estate in the Wykyngeston family.

[2] *Register of the Freemen of Leicester*, 1196-1770, ed. Hartopp (1927), 39. The name of Roger de Wykingston, 'barkere', appears in the same year.

[3] *W.H.R.*, no. 1012. This small property in Wigston is referred to again in no. 1065 (dated 1515) as 'a messuage and a half yardland of Richard Randell's, lying within the precinct of Wynchestre fee called Chaunters lond'.

Polling, Swan, Betrich, Hutte, Aldwin, Pauey, Clark and Amory. Other free tenants whose names appear at Wigston during the fourteenth century and mostly before 1350, are Walton, Cage, Clay, Faukes, Penne, Mathew, Lawe, Love, Bryges, Haukyn, Peris, Bacoun, Abbot, Noreys, Jewet, Astell, Palmer, Sweyn, Robyn and Attewelle. Altogether we have about forty free tenants named in surviving records, most of whom go on for generations and some for centuries. There is no sign whatever at Wigston of the depression of the free peasantry 'on the morrow of the conquest' such as we find elsewhere.

The Randolf family originate, so far as the Wigston records are concerned, with 'Rannulf the clerk of Wikingeston' to whom Hugh de Champayne, lord of the smaller of the two manors, sold two virgates of land in Wigston about the year 1200 or shortly before.[1] The grant is interesting, furthermore, because we are told of these two virgates that one was that which Ketel had held; a half-virgate together with a toft had been held by Turbertus; and a half-virgate by William, son of Godric, also with a toft. Rannulf was to hold this property of Hugh freely, for a chief rent of four shillings per annum in lieu of all service, and was specifically allowed to 'give the said two virgates to whomsoever he will, and that he to whom he will give them may hold them, he and his heirs, of the said Hugh and his heirs freely and quietly, in fee and heritage, by the said service'. For this land Rannulf paid four marks in silver.

Rannulf had two sons, John and Helias, to whom he granted one virgate of land each from the above purchase. John received the virgate which had been Ketel's, paying therefor a chief rent of five shillings per annum in three equal instalments of twenty pence at the Purification of Blessed Mary, at Pentecost, and at Michaelmas.[2] Helias was apparently granted the other virgate by his father, though no record to this effect survives among the Wyggeston Hospital charters. By two subsequent grants it appears that he sold his share to his brother John for six marks in silver, reserving to himself and his heirs a chief rent of five shillings per annum in lieu of all service, save foreign service.[3] By a subsequent

---

[1] *W.H.R.*, no. 868. The grant is undated, but was certainly made before 1202 as Hugh de Champayne was dead in that year.   [2] *W.H.R.*, no. 869. Undated, but *c.* 1202–21.

[3] *W.H.R.*, nos. 870, 871. The documents are not entirely clear as to the nature of the transaction but it appears that John paid Helias (who dwelt at Newton Harcourt, an adjacent parish) three marks in silver for each of the two half-virgates which had been Helias's share.

grant the chief rent due from Helias's virgate in Wigston was reduced to three shillings in silver, which Adam, grandson of John, later extinguished by paying to Robert, son of Helias, forty shillings in silver.

This chief rent of three shillings in silver per annum was apparently only temporarily extinguished, for it reappears in later years and serves to identify the property with that sold to Rannulf the clerk so long before. In January 1309, Adam Randolf granted one of his houses in Wigston to Joan, his daughter, together with 'two selions abutting on the said messuage and (extending) as far as Faucous Sty',[1] for which she was to render yearly three shillings, in three equal instalments at Michaelmas, the Purification, and Pentecost.

Several generations of Randulls (as the name had now become) continued to dwell in this house and to occupy the two half-virgates of land that went with it and that had been the lands of Turbertus and William son of Godric in the twelfth century. By a grant dated 1 May 1424, John Randull of Wigston made over to Margaret his mother (who had married John Waleys as her second husband), as part of her dower, 'a messuage and a virgate of land, with meadow, etc., in the town and fields of Wykynston, and also three shillings yearly rent payable out of the premises, the which messuage is situate between the tenement of William Coke and that of William a Penne, with one head abutting upon the king's way called Spowtewell Stret, and with the other head extending opposite towards the cast, and was called of late Helys Randyll lond, or John of Wykynston lond.'[2]

With the death of this John Randull, the family disappeared from Wigston. Richard Randull, his son, had migrated to Leicester where we find him described as 'Richard Randolff, otherwise called Richard Randull, of Leycestre, grocer' from 1436 onwards.[3] In 1462 we find him leasing part of his property in Wigston – 'a messuage in Wygeston and 3 quarters of land with meadow and pasture in the fields of the same town' – to William Clerke and Markett his wife for the term of twenty years from Michaelmas 1463 at an annual rent of fifteen shillings,

[1] *W.H.R.*, no. 930.
[2] *W.H.R.*, no. 1007.
[3] cf. *W.H.R.*, nos. 600, 616, 1020.

payable at the three most usual times of the year. William and Markett paid 6s. 8d. in hand in earnest of the bargain, and Richard Randull undertook to make the house habitable before they entered. It was further provided that the tenants 'shall maintain all repairs, with hedging and ditching, during the said term, and shall leave the premises in repair at the end thereof, by view of six persons of this present covenant'.[1]

Two years later, on 20 December 1464, Richard Randull leased the remainder of his Wigston property to William and Markett Clerke for a term of 12 years from Michaelmas 1465 at an annual rent of forty shillings, payable at the three usual times of the year, together with the chief rent of four shillings per annum payable to 'the lady Markett Effreyngam at the said terms for the services done beforetime'.[2] The property is described as 'his capital messuage with a croft on the east side thereof called the tenmentt, and a croft called Malkeyn Randull croft, and a croft called Swettynges croft, and a toft called Reddeleiz tofth, in Wygiston, and three yardlands and a quarter land, and seven acres of land, with meadow, pastures and leazes, in the fields of the same town, with all the commodities of old time to the said messuage pertaining or belonging, with all manner of " sherdeynges" within the said messuages; for the ingression whereof the said William and Markett have paid in hand twenty shillings of good and lawful money'. Richard Randull agreed to make the house habitable before the entry of the tenants and the tenants agreed on their part to 'uphold all manner of repairs except laying of slate and great timbers, and shall leave the premises sufficiently repaired at the end of the said term'.[3]

---

[1] W.H.R., no. 1040, dated 10 November 1462. This farm can be identified as having belonged formerly to the Swetyng family who appear in the Wyggeston Hospital Records from the late thirteenth century (cf. nos. 895, 898) up to 1417 (ibid. no. 992). Richard Randull had taken it over some time before 1462.

[2] *W.H.R.*, no. 1045. Margaret Everingham was lord of the duchy manor, or Leicester fee, at Wigston. She married three times, her first husband being Richard Turvile and her third Sir Thomas Everingham. This part of the Randull property was therefore in the smaller of the two Wigston manors, that which went eventually to the duchy of Lancaster, and the chief rent of 4s. per annum identifies it with the two virgates bought by Rannulf the clerk from Hugh de Campania *c.* 1200 upon which a chief rent of 4s. per annum was reserved to the lord.

[3] Of the 3¼ yardlands in this transaction, two are the ancient inheritance of the Randulls (as we have seen by the chief rent that was payable). In all probability one other yardland had formerly been Redley's farm, and the odd ¼ yardland had perhaps been taken out of the Swetyng Farm and attached to another for convenience of working. The remaining 7 acres had presumably come by casual purchases or may be the remains of a disintegrated tenement.

In these two leases, Richard Randull disposed of two houses in the village, both of which had been held by his ancestors of old, and of four yardlands or virgates of arable, meadow, and pasture, together with an odd seven acres – in all about 135 acres of land, which represented the property of a free tenant accumulated in the course of several generations. All this property passed eventually to Elizabeth, daughter of Richard Randull, who married Richard Kent of Kirby Muxloe, and thence to her son Thomas Kent who sold the whole to William Wigston the younger of Leicester, merchant of the staple of Calais, in 1514 for the sum of £37.[1] The latter in turn endowed his hospital with the property.

Besides the four yardlands described above, and the messuages, tofts, and crofts belonging to them, the indenture of bargain and sale in 1514 between William Wigston and Thomas Kent also included 19½d. of chief rents yearly from three holdings in the village. These are the tenement of William Symon which paid 1s. 6d., the tenement of William Frem one penny, and the tenement lately of William Gower one farthing. They probably represent parcels of land sold by the Randulls in the past upon which they had reserved these chief rents. It is further recorded that apart from the four yardlands lying within the Duchy fee at Wigston, Richard Randull had possessed a messuage and half a yardland 'lying within the precinct of Wynchestre fee called Chaunters lond'. This is the property which has already been referred to as that which came to 'Richard Randolff of Wykyngeston, gentleman' by the death of his cousin Henry Wygston, sometime before 1432.[2]

In the Randolff or Randull family we have a good picture of a substantial family of free tenants who in the course of some 250 years (c. 1200-c. 1450) accumulated, partly by purchase, and partly by inheritance, about 150 acres of land in the village fields, two or three substantial farmhouses, and a number of chief rents, so that by the fifteenth century they had become, like other free tenants we shall encounter, 'gentlemen'. Nevertheless, Richard Randolff, gentleman, of

[1] W.H.R., no 1061.
[2] W.H.R., nos. 1012, 1065.

Wigston did not disdain to be come Richard Randolff, grocer, of Leicester, making the transition from the land to commerce that was made by others from his native village also.

Other families whose names occur in every generation in these early Wigston records are the Herricks (far ancestors of the poet), the Smiths, and the Cooks, though we have few details of their lands as, unlike the Wykyngeston and Randolff property, they did not become part of the Wigston Hospital endowment. The Herricks appear in the middle decades of the thirteenth century with Henry Eyrig or Eyrek as a witness to several grants of land.[1] There can be no doubt that the family were numbered among the free peasantry of the village, for they witness many charters in common with other families of the same class: the same family names occur again and again as witnesses in every century. Every grant or charter was witnessed by an aristocracy of peasant families in Wigston, if one may employ such a term for a class which nevertheless had not cut itself off in any way from the common life of the village but always formed an integral part of it.

It seems likely that the Herricks could trace their ancestry back to one Erik, one of the original Danish settlers, perhaps, of the last quarter of the ninth century in the same village; and they may well have occupied the same piece of land since that distant date knowing what we do of the immense continuity of village ownership in Wigston in medieval times. They above all emerge into recorded village history from the mists of pre-Conquest days, from the Danish army of the ninth century and the sokemen of the eleventh, and we find them flourishing vigorously in the village when Henry VIII came to the throne. We shall indeed find them in every subsequent century, too, down to the twentieth, having lived more than a thousand years in one village.

Like the other families of the same class, the Herricks made the familiar migration into trade and commerce. John Herrick appears in the Leicester borough records in the 1470's[2] and from that time onwards the family played an important and influential part in the affairs of the town. Nicholas Herrick, goldsmith, became mayor in 1552, and John Herrick in 1557; and in 1588 Robert Herrick represented the borough

---

[1] e.g. *W.H.R.*, nos. 873, 875, 886–91, etc.

[2] The earliest mention of the name at Leicester is in 1471 (*W.H.R.* no. 649).

in Parliament. The *White Hart* in Leicester, just outside the East Gate, belonged to the Herricks from 1570 onwards, in which year it had been conveyed to John Herrick for the term of 1,000 years for the annual rent of a rose flower.[1]

Besides the John Herrick who migrated to Leicester, probably shortly before 1470 as Richard Randull had done some thirty years before him, there was another John Herrick who migrated to London about the same time, where he became a citizen and carried on the trade of skinner until his death in 1494. In his will[2] he left 100 shillings or 10 marks to the building of an almshouse in the churchyard at St. Wistan far away in his native Wigston, the little church which lay at the north-eastern end of the village in the Duchy fee, and which was the family church of the Herricks, as their wills disclose in the sixteenth century.

Like the Herricks, the Smiths appear as witnesses in the earliest records and afterwards in almost every generation up to the end of the period we are now discussing, and far beyond. They take their name from the occupation of a distant ancestor, an occupation which was pursued by father and son for at least four generations, and probably many more, in conjunction with a small property held freely. John the smith (*Faber*) of Wykingeston is named as a juror in an Assize roll of 1247. 'John the smith' witnessed a grant made between 1260 and 1274, the other witnesses all being prominent people in the village – clerks, chaplains, etc. There is no doubt that the smith ranked with these as a personage. Then, after John's death, we find 'Henry son of John the smith' witnessing a grant dated 20 December 1269; elsewhere he is called 'Henry the smith'. For forty years between 1269 and 1309 he was called in to witness transfers of property in the village, and then he too died and his place was taken by 'Robert the smith', who witnessed several grants between 1318 and 1321.

'William le Smyth' witnessed a grant in 1342, and is so referred to in another grant in 1376, suggesting that he carried on the occupation of his forefathers into the fourth generation at least, but after this date we have no further reference to the trade. There are, however, many references in the records indicating that the Smiths were possessed of lands of their

[1] Billson, *Medieval Leicester*, 30.
[2] An abstract of his will is given in *T.L.A.S.*, vi, 127.

own in Wigston, though nowhere are we told their extent. In 1395, for example, 'William Smyth the elder' granted to his daughter Alice Smyth a messuage standing next to another belonging to him, together with 3¼ acres of land.[1] Nearly twenty-four years later, on 12 February 1418-9, John Smyth, brother of Alice, granted the same property to Beatrice his wife: 'a messuage with a horse mill in Wykyngeston, lying between the messuage which is in the tenure of Henry Jewet and that of the said John Smyth; and three acres and a rood of arable land, lying in the fields of Wykyngeston, which Alice Smyth the sister of the said John, sometime had of the gift and feoffment of William Smyth their father … to the said Beatrice for the term of her life, with reversion after her decease to the said John and his heirs'.[2] Evidently this small property, a cottage and three and a quarter acres of land in the fields going with it, was treated by the Smiths as providing, when necessary, for unmarried daughters during their lifetime or alternatively as dower for a widow; and there seems to have been other property besides which went with the larger house.

The Godwins, too, were of great antiquity, going back to an English peasant landowner of the twelfth century. 'Robert son of Godwin' witnessed the charter, some time between 1202 and 1221, by which Rannulf the clerk granted a virgate of land to his son John. In later documents he is called Robert Godwine, another illustration of the origin of a family name. Godwin was alive in the second half of the twelfth century and later records suggest that his tenement consisted of a virgate of land in the Champayne manor and a farmstead on the east side of what is now Bullhead Street. Two documents (one dated 20 December 1269, and the other undated but about the same time)[3] show Ralph, the son of Robert Godwin, buying two small pieces of property and are worth quoting more fully than usual as illustrating the nature and size of typical transfers of property between village families at this early date.[4] The first relates to the sale of a toft by Richard Coc (one of the family referred to above) and his wife to Ralph Godwin for the sum of sixteen shillings in silver.

---

[1] *W.H.R.*, nos. 880-979, passim.

[2] *W.H.R.*, no. 1000.

[3] *W.H.R.*, nos. 883, 884.

[4] Another typical 'peasant' transaction is illustrated in doc. no. 921 by which William Cook (le Keu) granted a rood of arable to Robert Balle and Alice his wife, for a sum of money not specified.

Grant by Hawise, daughter of Hugh Coc, to Ralph son of Robert Godwine, for his homage and service and for 16s. of silver paid in hand, of a toft in the town of Wikingeston, with the ditch appertaining thereto, lying next the toft of Robert Godwine, which abuts upon the toft of Robert Gamel, with free entry and exit to the said toft; that toft to wit, which Richard the spouse of the said Hawise, and she formerly sold to the said Ralph. To hold of the chief lords and of the said Hawise and her heirs freely rendering therefor yearly at Christmas a penny for all service save foreign service… . And for the more surety of this gift and grant, the said Hawise has made affidavit and has sworn upon the Gospels that never in her life, whatsoever may befall concerning the said Richard her spouse, will she move a plea against the said Ralph, his heirs or assigns, by occasion of the said toft, subjecting herself to the jurisdiction of the archdeacon of Leycester or his official, to compel her by sentence of excommunication to keep the said grant, renouncing all cavilling and all suits of writs from the court of Rome or the King's court.[1]

On 20 December 1269 Alice, daughter of Serlo of Wikingiston and widow of Richard son of Symon of Wikingiston, granted to Ralph Godwine for fourteen shillings in silver a rood of land in the west field of Wigston 'upon Gonewarehil' between the land of Henry son of Symon and the land of William Juwet, to hold for a chief rent of a halfpenny a year payable at Pentecost. On the following day, Henry son of Alice, renounced all his right and claim in the piece of land.[2]

The earliest dated reference to the Godwin farm is in 1330 when John, son of John Godwyne of Wigston, granted to Adam, his brother, a messuage and a virgate of land with meadow and pasture and all other appurtenances in Wigston which had formerly belonged to John's father. Included in the grant were 'seven selions of land abutting upon the said messuage' and the remainder of 51 roods of land held of John by Richard Godwyne which should revert to John upon Richard's death (no. 945). The seven selions of land abutting on the messuage, which like the other farmsteads was in Bullhead Street, are interesting as showing the origin of the typical croft or homestead close behind the toft or farmhouse and buildings. In a survey of c. 1844 these appear as a long narrow strip of land immediately behind the

---

[1] *W.H.R.*, no. 883.   [2] *W.H.R.*, nos. 884, 885.

house, with a total area of 3 roods 25 perches. Each selion was therefore about half a rood. The reference to 5½ roods in the occupation of Richard Godwyne is also noteworthy: he is almost certainly a younger son of John Godwin the elder, who, in default of inheriting any of his father's farm, is granted a small holding out of the ancestral farm with reversion at his death to the eldest son and his heirs.

Although there is no earlier dated reference to this farm as such, we find John Godwin the elder witnessing charters in 1292 and 1295, and some undated charters which are probably somewhat earlier than this in time (nos. 894, 898, 900, 901, 915, 919, and others) which carry the history of the property back to the 1280's at least. Indeed 'Robert son of Godwin' witnesses a Wigston charter between 1202 and 1221 (no. 869). This takes us back to an English landholder of the twelfth century, from whom the main line of descent can be traced from the charters, generation by generation, down to the disposal of their property by Joan Godwyne in 1351.

Though there can be no certainty that the farm of one virgate held by John Godwin c. 1280-90 represents the twelfth-century holding of Godwin, it is probable that this is so for a grant (no. 883) made about the middle of the thirteenth century shows that Robert, son of Godwin, had a farmstead abutting on to the same street as the later Godwin farmstead. Moreover, this mid-thirteenth-century farmstead (a toft with a ditch) came into the hands of the Wigston Hospital. The deed is endorsed in a sixteenth-century hand '1 toft & fossat', which strongly suggests that it is identical with the later farmstead. On the whole it is reasonable to assume that the Godwin farm of one virgate can be traced back to an English landholder of the latter part of the twelfth century whose farmstead lay on the east side of Bullhead Street.

The exact site of this farmstead is shown on the survey of Wigston Hospital property (c. 1844) as a few yards south of Spa Lane and on the east side of Bullhead Street, but the site has since then lost its identity. The house which was standing in 1844 has been pulled down and the croft behind it has been cut up unrecognisably for the purpose of late Victorian building.

The early descent of the farm, assuming its identity with that of Godwin who was certainly a free peasant, is as follows:

Godwin fl. second half of the 12th century
Robert son of Godwin *c.* 1200-*c.* 1250
Ralph Godwin *c.* 1250-*c.* 1290
John Godwin *c.* 1290-early fourteenth cent.
John Godwin early fourteenth cent. to 1330
Adam Godwin 1330-1343
Joan Godwin sold the farm in 1351 to Roger Bridde.

Adam Godwin was killed by Alice Walton in 1343, and we hear no more of Richard his brother, who perhaps died in the plague-year shortly afterwards. At all events we find Joan Godewyne, whose relationship to the others is not stated, selling the family farm to Roger Bridde on 9 January 1350-1 (no. 956). She may have been the daughter and heir of Adam Godwin and Alice his wife, both of them dead by this date. The property is described as a messuage and virgate of land, with meadows, pasture and all other appurtenances, and there is mention of a further gift of 4½ roods of land in the fields and 7 selions of land abutting on the said messuage. Richard Godwin must have been dead, and a rood of his land is missing from the grant of 1350-1.

Robert Faucous or Faukes acquired the Godwin farm from Roger Bridde very shortly afterwards, though there is no surviving record of the purchase. We find him witnessing a grant in this part of the village on 25 December 1352 which suggests that he was already in possession of the farm. A John Faucous, probably his father, appears in the subsidy list of 1327 at Wigston, assessed to pay six shillings, one of the highest assessments in the village. He was almost certainly a free tenant at this date as he pays as much as, and more than, other known free tenants in the village. His property was probably elsewhere in the village before 1352, since the Faukes do not appear as witnesses to Wyggeston Hospital charters before that date. These charters are concerned solely with property in and off Bullhead Street (with the appurtenant farms out in the fields) and are witnessed by free peasants on that side of the village. The appearance of Robert Faukes's name in 1352 suggests therefore that he had recently become a free tenant of the Godwin farm.

The Faukes held the farm for only two generations. In 1367 John Faukes, son and heir of Robert, was holding the farm (nos. 967-8) and in 1397 he leased a dovecote and a bridge over a fish-pond within his messuage to Richard Love of Wigston for a term of twelve years, at an annual rent of 3s. 2d. Richard had paid six years' rent in advance (19s.) and agreed to pay the second instalment at the beginning of the second term of six years (no. 981).

It is possible that John Faukes was falling increasingly into financial difficulties, which culminated in his giving up the farm by about 1416, and this lease of part of his property with six years' rent in advance may be the first symptom of his distress. A plea roll for 1393 reveals him being sued by Thomas Walshe, chivaler, in a plea of 40s. In the following year he is sued by John de Bellomonte in a plea of rescuing cattle in the former's fee at Wigston 'which John Wodbrugh, servant of John de Bellomonte, wished to impound for customs and services due from John Faucous'. (Farnham MSS. under Wigston, from Plea Rolls.) Then in 1416 he was sued with his daughter Amice by William Freman of Leicester, in a plea of 40s. The Wyggeston Hospital documents also suggest growing financial trouble; it may well be that the deepening agricultural depression of these years was the primary cause of all this. This must have been the story of many a small peasant farmer in these decades, less able to weather the storm than some of his fellows, who eventually emerge with a number of other men's farms in their possession.

At any rate it appears from a record of 1412 that John Faukes was obliged to mortgage his farm to Richard Penne of Wigston (no. 989), for we find him taking a lease of his own farm from the latter for a term of three years at a yearly rent of 13s. 4d., but 'if the said John, his heirs or assigns, or one of them, pay or cause to be paid to the said Richard, his heirs or assigns, 8 marks 9s. silver within the said term of three years, then a charter with seisin, made therefor to the said Richard, his heirs and assigns, shall be re-delivered to the said John Faukus, with all the muniments that the said Richard has in his custody. And if it happen, which God forbid, that the said John make default in the said payment of 8 marks and 9s., then the said Richard shall have and enjoy the premises with all their appurtenances and all the muniments aforesaid, to hold to him, his heirs and assigns, for ever according to the tenor and force of the said charter with seisin, made to the said Richard.'

In 1414 John Faukes the younger bound himself in the sum of

twenty marks to Richard Love and John Brown of Wigston, with the condition that he would indemnify the grantees against the sheriff of Leicester or his deputies. In the following year, however, we find John Faukes (presumably the elder) recovering his property at the end of the term of three years for which it was mortgaged (no. 992) but only for a short time. From no. 993 it seems that in December 1416 he finally parted with his ancestral farm to Henry Coc and John Morley both of Wigston. Between 1416 and 1424 the farm passed through a succession of hands (nos. 993-1006, passim) but by 1421 we see the hand of Richard Penne once again, and in 1424 he receives the final grant and confirmation of the property (no. 1006). Two months later, on 30 May 1424, Richard Penne granted to John Faukes and Joan his wife a yearly rent of nine shillings 'payable out of all those lands and tenements in Wykyngeston, which were sometime of Robert Faukes, the father of the said John, and were late of the said John, in Wikyngeston'. John Faukes must have been an old man by this time (it was almost fifty years since he had entered into his inheritance, perhaps a little more) and this payment may have been a sort of pension out of his own farm, made as an act of grace by the new owner.

Richard Penne's two farms descended to his son John Penne, as we have seen, by 1440, and in 1453 he sold both to John Love. The subsequent history of the Faukes farm has already been traced in the previous notes.

When the Wyggeston Hospital acquired the property they leased the farm as 'a messuage one yardland and dovecote' to Richard Heryck at a yearly rent of 18s. 8d. It was then subject to a chief rent of 1½d. a year to the Turviles as lords of the manor.

∾ THE BALLE FAMILY AND ITS LANDS ∾

We may choose, as the last of our examples of the numerous free tenants of Wigston, the Balle family, who figure in a great number of Wigston deeds. They first appear in a series of undated deeds, probably of the third quarter of the thirteenth century.[1] In the first transaction Ralph Balle paid Alexander, son of Thomas of Wykinston, thirty shillings in silver for four selions of land. In the second, he gave 48 shillings for five selions 'and the quarter of meadow which

[1] W.H.R., nos. 876-80. No. 880 may certainly be dated as c. 1260-72.

pertains to a virgate of land'. These five selions include the four referred to in the first purchase.

The third transaction was the purchase for sixty shillings of five selions of land (the same five already mentioned) and of the meadow pertaining to half a virgate of land which Alexander, the grantor, sometime held. Another deed referring to six selions (five as before and one other) and the same meadow records the payment of six marks in silver. This was the last of four transactions with Alexander of Wykyngeston, but some time between 1260 and 1272 Ralph Balle bought from Nicholas of Champayne, the lord of the smaller manor, for the sum of twenty-four shillings, 'a plot of land ... lying in Hecroft, next the land of Henry son of Symon on the south, containing in itself length and breadth with the land of William Cocus (Cook): to enclose, build, and inhabit, with free entry and exit ... ' and to hold at a chief rent of three shillings per annum for all services except foreign service.

A house was built on this toft and was granted by Ralph Balle, together with one strip of arable and a third part of the above meadow, to Alice his daughter, the other five selions and two-thirds of the meadow referred to above having been granted to two other daughters: Amice had received two selions from her father and Joan three. Some time later (all these deeds are undated) Amice sold her portion back to her brother Robert for twenty shillings in silver. Ralph Balle had died before the end of the winter of 1272-3 and his lands were inherited by his son Robert who in addition made several purchases. First, there was a single selion bought from Robert de Champayne, 'rendering yearly therefor a rose at the Nativity of St. John Baptist'. Then another tenant died and we find him renting from the overlord – John, son of Martin of Bayl, of Whetstone – half a virgate of land at an annual rent of ten shillings in silver. Shortly afterwards, however, he bought this land, together with the meadow pertaining to it, for a sum of money not specified.[1]

Next came an acre of arable in the east field bought for 26s. 8d. from Matthew of Wykingston, clerk, and a single selion bought from the son and daughter of Richard Symunt for seven shillings in silver. For an unspecified sum Robert Balle also bought from one of the minor overlords (William of Whetstone) 1½ roods of arable in one place and 'two butts of arable' in another part of the same field; and two selions were acquired from Simon of Wykingeston for an unspecified consideration. Early in 1298 he purchased a rood of arable land from William le Keu (Cook) for an unspecified price, the last recorded purchase.

Robert Balle died in the early years of the fourteenth century and was succeeded by Richard his son, who continued his father's activities by acquiring first three roods of arable land from the widow of William of Whetstone, then a rood and a selion from Richard Randolf.[1]

In December 1357, nearing the end of his life, Richard Balle made arrangements for the disposal of his property by enfeoffing therein William Dicoun, then a chaplain at Wigston.[2] The property is described as a messuage, half a virgate of arable land, half a virgate of pasture and a virgate of arable land, half a virgate of pasture and a virgate of meadow 'with all other the appurtenances', together with the two selions acquired from Richard Randolf.[3] William Dicoun granted and confirmed the property to Richard Balle, Isabel his wife, and John their son, to have and to hold to Richard, Isabel and John, and the heirs of John's body begotten, under the chief lords of the fee. Elaborate provisions followed as to remainders: if John's heirs failed then Richard, another son, and his heirs should inherit the property: in default of heirs to Richard, the remainder passed to Alice and Amice, daughters of Richard Balle the elder, and their heirs: and in default of heirs to Alice and Amice, the property was to go to 'William of Penne', another son of Richard Balle the elder, for the term of his life, with reversion after his death to the heirs and assigns of Richard Balle the elder.

This transaction has been set out in some detail in order to illustrate the complexity of the arrangements that could be made by a medieval peasant for the disposal of his modest property. Richard Balle died

---

[1] *W.H.R.*, nos. 901, 902, 903, 932, 941-2.

[2] *W.H.R.*, no. 959. The process here described, whereby Richard Balle granted the property to the chaplain, who then re-granted it on certain terms and conditions as to remainders &c., was a tortuous way of ensuring the succession to a peasant tenement.

[3] The half virgate of pasture and the virgate of meadow must be interpreted as the amount of common pasture and of meadow appurtenant to a half-virgate and a virgate of arable respectively, not as a half-virgate and a virgate in themselves, since common pasture and meadow were not reckoned in this way.

shortly afterwards, certainly before 1364 when we find 'William Penne of Wykyngeston' releasing all right and claim in the property.[1] Some of the Balle property, however, eventually came to William Penne for in 1393 we find him occupying the house which in 1309 had been that of Alice, widow of Robert Balle.[2] and in 1424. his grandson 'William a Penne' was living there. In 1452 John Penne sold all his lands and tenements, both those acquired from the Faukes and those inherited from the Balles, to John Love, yeoman of Wigston, as we have already seen.

❧   CONCLUSIONS   ☙

The history of the Balle family and their property has been dealt with in great detail, so far as it can be unravelled, because it is so typical of the spirit of the peasant community of Wigston Magna in its sequence of small purchases of land – even single strips in the fields – both from the lord of the manor and from fellow-peasants, and in the care and forethought devoted to the disposal of their property, not only during the peasant's lifetime in providing maintenance for a widowed mother or for unmarried sisters or daughters, but after his death in ensuring an elaborate succession to avoid escheat to the lord, which was the fate of a free tenement for which the succession failed.

The continual buying and selling of land, mostly in very small parcels, between one peasant family and another, and somewhat larger transactions between the lord and a peasant family, is another fact brought out by a study of these medieval records. When we remember that the Balles, in two generations between about 1260 and 1304, made no fewer than twelve purchases of land, besides transferring property between each other frequently, and that they were only one of thirty or forty similar families of whose affairs we know nothing because no records survive, one begins to get some idea of the multitudinous small transfers of land that must have been going on all the time, all of which were witnessed by other peasant families and rarely by anyone more important. If the ability

---

[1] This is an interesting example, too, of how changes could occur in medieval surnames. Originally called William Balle (cf. the subsidy of 1327), William presumably moved to Penn in Staffordshire for several years. On his return he was known as 'William of Penne' or 'William a Penne', and the name stuck to him and his descendants ever afterwards.

[2] cf. *W.H.R.*, nos. 930 (1309), 977 (1393).

to enter into new contractual relationships based upon money payments is a fair test of peasant freedom as has been suggested by Professor Douglas, then Wigston was very largely a community of free men. The records show too the frequent use of money in the village even in the thirteenth century which, among the more substantial peasant families at least, must presuppose the sale of crops for cash on a not inconsiderable scale. In the case of Wigston the presence of Leicester only four miles to the north afforded a ready market for such sales, especially as the village had no market or fair of its own, and there was no religious house dominating the village and drawing off the surplus crops for its own consumption.

The impression we get from the Wigston records of the thirteenth century is that of a vigorous, thriving free peasantry, but how far this activity was general or how far it was confined to a minority of thrusting, acquisitive peasants we do not know for certain. We have no manorial surveys or extents to give us a picture of the village community as a whole, which can be compared with the general statement of Domesday Book for 1086.

We have seen that in 1086 about three-fifths of the land in Wigston was unfree and two-fifths was free. In later generations, towards the end of the thirteenth century, some had come into the hands of substantial tenants like Sir Simon Friday, Knt., who held nine virgates of the earl of Winchester, and the Wykyngeston family who held perhaps 10¾ virgates, though much of these holdings was regranted to smaller free tenants. We do not know how many free tenants there were in Wigston at the end of the thirteenth century, nor what (with a few exceptions) their holdings were. We can trace about forty names of free peasant families between 1250 and 1350 and there may well have been some others not known to us. And we have seen that there were thirty-seven free tenants of various descriptions in 1086. From these meagre facts we may, in default of any more precise evidence, deduce that the free tenants of Wigston had probably lost little ground between the late eleventh century and the late thirteenth.

On the other hand, at Galby, in the upland country a few miles east of Wigston, there was a recorded population in 1086 of thirty families in addition to the five slaves and two bondwomen on the demesne land. Of these thirty families, fourteen were free (eleven sokemen, two knights, and

one Frenchman) and sixteen were unfree. Yet in 1279 an inquisition reveals
only two free tenants in the vill, and the poll tax of 1381 records none at
all. Nearly half the population had been tenurially free in 1086; by 1381 all
held land 'at the will of the lord'. And yet at Illston, only a mile or two from
Galby and, like it, an almost purely Scandinavian settlement, fourteen of the
enumerated Domesday population of nineteen households were sokemen;
and nearly three hundred years later, in the poll tax of 1381, there were still
18 free tenants as against nine tenants who held at the will of the lord, and a
number of cottagers and servants. Why there should have been this striking
difference in the economic and social history of two villages hardly two
miles apart is impossible to say; and the same contrast is to be seen between
Wigston and Foston, two or three miles to the south.

Foston, like Wigston, was dominated by the Danes from the late
ninth century and had a Scandinavian overlord (Fotr's *tun*). In 1086,
nearly half the recorded population of twenty-three households outside
the demesne were sokemen (eleven sokemen, eight villeins, and four
bordars), yet an extent of 1314 speaks of two free tenants and twenty-
four villein families (*nativi*). The surviving records throw no light at all
on this remarkable change, parallel to that at Galby in its implications
for the later history of the village. With no substantial number of free
tenants to bar the way, Foston was half enclosed late in the sixteenth
century (*c.* 1575) and wholly enclosed a generation or so later, so that
by Charles II's time it had disappeared altogether as a village. At the
levying of the hearth tax of 1666, there were in the parish only the
squire's house, the rectory, a substantial farmhouse and two cottages.
Nichols wrote, at the end of the eighteenth century, that 'there is a
tradition that twenty teams were formerly kept in this now nearly
depopulated village' and the tradition was true. There had been twenty-
four or twenty-five households in the village as far back as Domesday,
twenty-seven or more in the early fourteenth century, and twenty-one
families as late as 1563. A hundred years later there remained only
the squire, the parson, a large farmer, and two labouring families. But
at Wigston the free tenants were still numerous in the middle of the
seventeenth century, perhaps stronger than they had ever been, and
enclosure did not come until the age of parliamentary acts and awards
in George III's time. The body of free peasantry were too strong for

any enclosing landlord, nor could any one man get a solid grip on the village lands and engross them.

All this, however, is well into the future. Before we speak of the economic and social changes of the later centuries we must say more of the medieval village as distinct from the purely tenurial organisation we have been discussing at such length. It only remains to say of the latter that in the absence of manorial records of any kind we know nothing of the customary tenants of the village lands. That they existed in considerable numbers is evident enough from the sixteenth-century records. A law suit of 1588 speaks of thirty-one customary tenants or copyholders at that date; and when the two manors were dismembered and sold off in 1586 and 1606 we find some 1750 acres of land being disposed of by the respective lords. As the total area of Wigston was 2944 acres, this leaves us with rather less than 1200 acres already held freely in the village. Thus the demesne and customary lands in the sixteenth century covered nearly sixty per cent of the total area, and must have done so in medieval times.[1] We shall not be far wrong if we estimate the customary tenants to have numbered about one-half the medieval population; and of this large and important class we know nothing until the time of Queen Elizabeth I.

[1] A rough estimate (see p. 29) suggested that in 1086 the free tenants had held about forty per cent of the land while the remaining sixty per cent consisted of demesne and unfree 'village land'. But this agreement between 1086 and 1586-1606 is deceptive and may conceal all manner of changes in the intervening centuries.

IV

THE MEDIEVAL VILLAGE AND ITS FIELDS

Medieval Leicestershire

In 1086 Leicestershire had a total population of between twenty-four and twenty-five thousand, with an average density of about twenty-eight persons to the square mile. Suffolk and Norfolk were the most densely peopled counties in England with between forty and fifty persons to the square mile. Leicestershire was 10th among English counties in order of density, but as in every other county the population was not evenly spread.[1] The areas of closest settlement were the middle Soar valley (in which Wigston lay), the south-eastern quadrant towards the rich meadows of the Welland valley, and the north-eastern side towards Lincolnshire. It is better perhaps to express densities in terms of *recorded* population rather than total population, since this removes all difficulties about the size of the eleventh-century household, and to say that these favoured regions had about twelve persons to the square mile, as compared with only two to five persons in the western half of the county beyond the Soar.[2]

By 1377 the East Midland counties had increased in population considerably more than the country as a whole. Both Leicestershire and Northamptonshire had slightly more than doubled in population, and Rutland had trebled. Norfolk was the most closely settled county as a whole with an average of 65.5 persons to the square mile, and Bedfordshire (which had more than doubled its numbers) had risen from seventh place in 1086 to second with 63.4. Northamptonshire, with its generally fertile soils and its numberless quarries of fine building stone, which were being increasingly exploited from the middle of the

---

[1] Russell, *British Medieval Population*, gives the total population figures for the counties, based upon an assumed average of 3.5 persons per family. The recorded population for Leicestershire was slightly more than 6,500. See Darby, *The Domesday Geography of Midland England*, 333.

[2] Darby, op. cit., Fig. 116.

twelfth century onwards, had risen from the eighth place to third (60.3 to the square mile). Suffolk, first in 1086, was now fourth (59.7), having added fewer to its numbers in the intervening period than any other county except Devon and Herefordshire. Rutland, also fertile and rich in building-stone, came fifth in 1377 (59.1), very little behind Suffolk; and Leicestershire had risen from tenth place among the English counties to sixth, with an average density of 58.1 persons to the square mile.[1] The borough of Leicester had multiplied its numbers by about 2½ times between 1086 and 1377, having risen from 1278 people to 3152; but the increase had in fact been more rapid than this, for in 1327, before the repeated devastations of the plague, the population is estimated to have been 4800 – almost a four-fold increase since Domesday.[2]

The increased population of the county, and its rise to one of the most densely peopled regions of medieval England, must be attributed almost solely to its agricultural development during those three hundred years – two hundred and fifty years if we take the years before the Black Death as our terminus. For the county had no building-stone worth mentioning – none, at least, that was known or sold outside its borders, like Rutland and Northamptonshire – and only a few small and local industries.

The cloth industry of Leicester itself declined from the second half of the thirteenth century onwards,[3] and was not replaced, as in some other parts of England, by an industry scattered over the surrounding countryside and based upon rural fulling-mills. In the west of the county, a small coalfield was being exploited in the last quarter of the thirteenth century; slate quarries had been opened up at Swithland on the eastern edge of Charnwood in the middle decades of the century, which were to have a profitable life of more than six hundred years; and the quarrying of iron-stone for local building (and a little for iron-smelting) had gone on in and around the eastern uplands since the twelfth century. But all this was on a small scale, serving local needs entirely.

[1] Russell, op. cit, Tables 6.4 and 11.8.

[2] Russell, 51, 142, 285, 293.

[3] Carus-Wilson, '*An Industrial Revolution of the Thirteenth Century*' in *Ec.H.R.*, xi, no. 1, 39–60. The cloth industry of Leicester did not wholly disappear, however, as an analysis of the occupations of the freemen admitted between 1350 and 1380 shows 6 weavers, 3 fullers, 3 shearmen, and 6 dyers, a total of 18 in the woollen trade. This is exceeded only by the numbers engaged in the preparation and manufacture of leather.

Leicestershire lived almost exclusively by its tillage. It owed its high density of population in the thirteenth and fourteenth centuries (and later) to its arable farming on the heavy but generally fertile clays, which were late in being cleared but were coming into full production from the second half of the thirteenth century onwards. Almost everywhere it was the traditional mixed husbandry of the open-field system, though here and there in the eastern hills (especially where the oolitic limestone crossed over the boundary from the Lincolnshire side) monastic sheep-farming on a considerable scale was already known.

All the evidence points to the growing prosperity of Leicestershire during the second half of the thirteenth century and the first half of the fourteenth, until the Black Death began its work of depopulation and disruption. The great period for the rebuilding and enlargement of the parish churches, in town and countryside, falls in Leicestershire (as in its neighbour Nottinghamshire to the north) in the two generations between about 1280 and 1349.[1] Grants of fairs and markets to towns and villages all over the county come thick and fast in the late thirteenth century and the early fourteenth; and at the same time we hear of a number of bridges in the county for the first time, as the growing traffic along the roads called for something better than a dangerous ford or a makeshift wooden structure.

In this small county of barely more than 500,000 acres, there were in medieval times some two hundred villages possessing parish churches, with 170 or so dependent hamlets. All over Leicestershire (except in the Charnwood district, the only substantial area of waste), villages and hamlets succeeded one another at intervals of a mile or a mile and a half, very rarely as much as two miles apart. It was a rich and thickly settled countryside by medieval standards, especially again the eastern half of the county, which continued to overshadow the west until Georgian days. It was in the eastern half that most of the medieval fairs and markets were to be found, and where, in general, the largest and most beautiful parish churches stood, serving the smallest parishes.[2]

---

[1] Hoskins, The *Heritage of Leicestershire*, 43–8.

[2] This medieval wealth and density of population is even more striking when one continues eastward over the border into Rutland. Here, in the twelfth-fifteenth centuries, 52 parish churches served fewer than 10,000 people (8,991 in 1377). Rutland had fewer than 3,000 people in 1086 and cannot have had more than 6,000–9,000 when most of its churches were going up between 1150 and 1250. In general, too, the churches of Rutland are large and handsome buildings, some of them superb – out of all proportion to the size of the community they at any time served.

It is necessary to say a little about the social structure of the county also, before we conclude this short account of the economic background against which the development of the village of Wigston must be considered. No great estate dominated the economy of the county, which was distinctively marked by 'a class of thriving middling gentry'. On the great majority of manors the demesne was small in extent. Another conspicuous feature of the social structure of the county was the existence of a large class of free tenants. A sample of 73 vills in the hundreds of Guthlaxton and Gartree, which covered the whole of the southern half of the county, shows that in 1279 no fewer than 39 per cent of the tenant population were free tenants. Of the remainder, 55 per cent were villeins and six per cent were cottagers. Viewed in another way, 43 per cent of the tenant population were not attached to the manorial demesne; and, of the 57 per cent who were, one-third were free tenants.

In the medieval period, too, 'Leicestershire [was] a region of light labour services' and as a consequence wage-labour was important in the economy of the county. We find, then, 'a large proportion of the peasantry ... comparatively independent of seigneurial agriculture; and that on many manors the labour services of those customary tenants that owed them were not heavy'.[1] Although the return of 1279 is not complete for Guthlaxton Hundred, and does not include Wigston as it should, it is certain that the social pattern at Wigston would have been very similar to that of the district in which it lay. Certainly, it repeats the most fundamental characteristics of its region in having a substantial class of more or less independent peasantry in the medieval period, and in being a village in which the ownership of land was divided among a large number of small men.

In this predominantly arable, and densely populated, countryside Wigston remained, from the eleventh century up to the late fourteenth at least, the most populous village community. In 1086 it had a recorded population of 86, representing in all probability some 83 households. In 1377 it had a population of at least 110-120 households,

---

[1] These summary paragraphs are based on the Introduction to Hilton, *The Economic Development of some Leicestershire Estates in the 14th and 15th Centuries.*

after four major visitations of plague. Even the market-towns of Melton Mowbray and Market Harborough show a smaller taxed population at this period.[1]

At an intermediate date – 1334 – the fixing of quotas for the fifteenth and tenth gives us valuable information about the relative economic importance of the village in the years before the Black Death. Leicester, naturally, had the highest quota. Its population of about 4800 was called upon to pay £26 13s. 4d. when the tenth should be demanded. Melton, the economic centre for the north-eastern quadrant of the county, paid £14 0s. 0d.; and Wigston came third on the list with a quota of £8 8s. 0d.[2] Bottesford, far up in the north-eastern tip of Leicestershire, had been a populous village in 1086, and in 1334 was still second only to Wigston with a quota of £8 5s. 0d. The next most important centres were Great Bowden, a large agricultural village (£7 13s. 4d.) and its flourishing offspring, the market-town of Harborough (£6 8s. 0d.); and Ashby de la Zouch, the market-town for the north-western side of Leicestershire (£7 5s. 0d.). The large village of Hallaton, centre of economic life in the south-eastern quadrant of the county, with its four annual fairs and two weekly markets, had a quota of £7 2s. 0d.; and a number of large agricultural villages like Great Easton, Barrow-on-Soar, and Medbourne, and small market-towns like Loughborough, all had tax quotas of between five and seven pounds. The assessment of 1334 brings out clearly the continued dominance of the eastern half of the county over the western, which was already evident in the eleventh century; and especially of the Soar valley and the Welland valley, which had been the most thickly populated areas in Domesday Book. Many purely agricultural villages in the south-eastern quadrant of Leicestershire were considerably more populous and wealthy than the market-towns of the western side, where Ashby de la Zouch was the only place of more than local importance.

When we remember that in 1377 Leicestershire was sixth among English counties in density of population (and probably much the same

---

[1] See Hoskins, 'The Population of Wigston Magna 1086-1810', T.L.A.S., xxxiii.

[2] Wymondham, a large village on the eastern border of the county, was assessed at £9 6s. 0d. but this included the separate village of Edmondthorpe, a mile or two away. In the sixteenth century the two villages were of equal size, so we are safe in assuming that in 1334 Wymondham's quota alone was substantially less than that of Wigston.

forty years earlier, before the plague came), it is evident that the eastern half of the county must have been one of the most thickly settled and, on the whole, prosperous regions in medieval England, particularly as it depended entirely on agriculture for its livelihood and had no industries whatever beyond those that served the needs of a confined neighbourhood. This belt of a dense agricultural population stretched away eastwards through Rutland, across south Lincolnshire, with Boston as its rich centre, to reach the eastern block of Norfolk and Suffolk; and southwards it extended down through Northamptonshire into Bedfordshire.[1] It is no accident that it is in this region, by and large, that we discover the finest medieval churches in England, thickly grouped together, mile after mile of them in a rich farming countryside.[2]

ഏ   MEDIEVAL WIGSTON   ൙

Although Wigston lay on the western edge of the most densely populated region in medieval England, and one of the most generally prosperous, its high quota for the fifteenth must be attributed, in part at least, to its numbers rather than to its prosperity. It lived entirely by arable farming – or, more correctly, by the mixed farming of the open-field economy which was largely arable – and it had no industries beyond those of the rudimentary kind that every medieval village of any size found necessary. Nor had it ever a weekly market or an annual fair, unlike many places only a half or a third of its size in the neighbouring countryside. Even with the powerful overlordship of the earls of Leicester, and later of the earls of Oxford, it could not escape the fact that it lay only four miles south of the borough of Leicester. That being so, it could never hope for the benefits and profits that medieval traders brought to village fairs and markets.[3]

---

[1] See the map in *An Historical Geography of England before 1800*, ed. Darby, 232.

[2] In the compact piece of country which includes the northern third of Northamptonshire, the whole of Rutland, the fenland of south Lincolnshire and the adjoining marshland of west Norfolk, we have what is probably the highest concentration in England of fine medieval churches. Possibly one might add the small county of Huntingdonshire to this rich galaxy.

[3] The much smaller village of Arnesby, four miles farther south down the road to Northampton, had a weekly market and an eight-day fair, granted in 1292; the village of Great Glen, three miles east, had a weekly market and a three-day fair, granted in 1348; and Narborough, four miles west, had a weekly market as early as 1219.

Wigston lived by the land alone, and by the early fourteenth century, with a steadily rising population, the pressure upon the available acreage must have become acute. It was a purely peasant community, whose farming was mostly on a subsistence scale and no more. It never had a resident lord at any time; no large estate dominated its fields. Nor did any monastic house overshadow its economic life, drawing off large surpluses of agricultural produce to sell for cash, as in many villages round about. Only one virgate out of the 92¾ in the township belonged to a monastery. From Domesday onwards, it was a large village whose dominant class was the peasant landowners themselves, who owned, so far as we can tell, about 1200 acres of land out of the 2900 or so in the village fields – rather more than forty per cent of the total throughout the medieval period. We can trace the names of some forty peasant landowning families in the village records between about 1250 and 1350, who existed in any one generation in this period. The great majority of these were small men owning and working a virgate or half a virgate of land, or something between. Of the numbers and status of the customary tenants we know nothing until the latter part of the sixteenth century when (in 1588) thirty-one are mentioned as the total number then occupying land. In the medieval period the free tenants were at least as numerous as the customary tenants; they may even have been slightly greater in numbers.

❧   THE VILLAGE FIELDS   ❧

The vill of Wigston had been divided between two manors since the latter part of the twelfth century, a division which was confirmed by the partition of the earl of Leicester's lands in 1204-7. But no such division showed itself in the village fields. The lands of the earl of Oxford's manor, and those of the Champayne (later the Turvile) manor lay intermingled everywhere in the three fields. There was no separate field-system for each. Such an arrangement would have been unworkable; and the field-system of the vill in any event ante-dated by centuries the division of the Domesday manor into two separate parts. In other Leicestershire villages there were three or more manors but only one field-system. The village and not the manor was the essential form of rural organisation in the Danelaw. There was no separation of different fees (like the Winchester and Leicester fees at Wigston) in the village fields; no seigneurial authority controlled the economic life of villages under divided lordship.[1]

The earliest Wyggeston Hospital records, which fall into the late twelfth century and the first half of the thirteenth, give no specific information about the number of open arable fields at Wigston. By 1269-80 we can say, however, that there were three fields: the west field is referred to in a grant and confirmation in 1269, the north field in a similar document of 1271, and the east field in an undated grant of *c.* 1280.[1] No surviving record suggests the prior existence of a two-field system.

The expansion of the fields up to Domesday seems to have been fastest on the north-eastern and south-eastern sides of the parish, where the frontier had been reached along a line of several hundred yards by the late eleventh century. To the north and south the frontier of cultivation still fell short of the parish boundary, as it did to the east and south-west also.

By the middle of the twelfth century it is probable that the south-western frontier had been reached, as we hear of a watermill at that point (now Crow Mill on the Sence) for the first time, but of the remainder of the work of clearing and colonisation we know nothing beyond the indirect hints given in the Wyggeston Hospital charters of the thirteenth century. These suggest that by the year 1300, as we might have expected from the considerable increase of population in the village and from what we know of agricultural expansion elsewhere, the fields of Wigston had been cleared and opened up for cultivation as far as the parish boundaries on all sides. In 1280-90 we read of 'two selions upon Mokilhow'; in 1272-3 of 'one selion at the foot of Goldehil'; and in 1305 of 'a rood upon Thythornhull'. All these points can be identified as lying on the boundaries of the parish. In the course of the fourteenth century the north, west, and east fields were named more specifically after these boundary points – Mucklow Field, Goldhill Field, and Thythornhill Field,[3] names which survived unchanged up to their extinction by the enclosure award of 1766. Small unreclaimed patches may still have remained here and there by 1300, but in the main the work of clearing

---

[1] Stenton, *Danelaw Charters* (1920), lxi-lxii.
[2] See Hoskins, 'The Fields of Wigston Magna', *T.L.A.S.*, xix, 169.
[3] 'The Fields of Wigston Magna', loc. cit., 170-1.

seems to have been completed by the end of the thirteenth century at Wigston.

In the meantime, the village population had grown by at least fifty per cent. We have a probable Domesday population of 83 households; in 1377 there were at least 110-120 households, and it is inconceivable that the population in 1300-48 was any less than this. It may well have been substantially greater. Whatever the precise figure may have been, there was a much faster rate of increase in the village population than in the taking-in of new land in the twelfth and thirteenth centuries. The 'land-hunger' of the thirteenth century must have had a real meaning at Wigston, and in many other villages round about; and it is not surprising that a Leicester tallage roll of 1271 should reveal that one-third of the borough population at that date had originated in villages all over the county. With such a high percentage of free peasants among the rural population, and especially of peasantry unattached to any manorial demesne, movement from the country into the borough was comparatively easy. Younger sons, for whom the peasant economy made little or no provision in the way of succession to land, migrated in considerable numbers, not only into Leicester but into the smaller towns also. An examination of the tax-list for Market Harborough in 1327 shows, even on this restricted information, that the new town (created about 1160-70) recruited its growing population largely from among the peasantry of villages for some miles around.[1]

As to the arrangement and lay-out of the fields in the medieval period, there is little new that can be said. Wigston lay in the centre of the parish where the three fields met, so that the farmers and cottagers whose homesteads lay on the streets, and in the back-lanes and 'ends', were as advantageously placed as they could be for the cultivation of their scattered lands. We have no knowledge of the extent of the arable fields, in the absence of any early map or survey; but even allowing for the meadows which fringed them on the north, south, and west, and the built-up area with its crofts and gardens, they cannot have been far short of nine hundred acres each. This area must be regarded as no more than a rough indication of their size, and it included an unknown area of 'sikes', or permanent grazing land along the sides of the smaller

---

[1] Hoskins, 'The Origin and Rise of Market Harborough', *T.L.A.S.*, xxv, 56-68.

streams with which the parish was laced. Such *sikes* were Blackwell sike, Hungerton sike, Cleyhill sike, and Boyter sike, all of which appear in late thirteenth-century records. All the sikes which can now be identified in the fields of Wigston lie on either side of a small stream (the word, from the Old English *sic* or Old Norse *sik*, means 'a small stream in marshy ground'). Their function in the general economy of the open fields has been well described by Orwin.[1] They provided useful grazing, and they acted also as occupation roads, giving access to a number of furlongs on either side of them. The larger streams, flanked by low lands that flooded every winter, produced the meadows; but the minor streams, hardly a foot or so across, were not large enough to flood and acted as drains for the adjacent furlongs, whose 'lands' or selions ran down the slopes towards them.

The medieval documents for Wigston tell us little about how the lands appurtenant to a particular farm were distributed in the three fields: we have to wait until the late sixteenth and the early seventeenth centuries for that information. Such fragments as we derive from the numerous grants and charters suggest an equal distribution among the fields as, for example, John Fawkes's grant and confirmation in 1417 of eighteen roods of arable to Thomas Smyth: here we find 1½ acres in each field, though the number of parcels in each field varies.[2]

So far as the size of the arable strip is concerned, the medieval charters give a good deal of information. A grant of *c.* 1300 shows a small tenement of 6½ acres 3½ roods divided into twenty-three parcels, of which two were only half a rood in size, twelve were a rood each, seven were 1½ roods, and two were two roods each. A half virgate in 1393 contained forty-nine parcels, of which twenty-one were a rood each, fourteen were 1½ roods, and two were two roods each. In addition, there were two headlands and ten butts, of unknown area. A virgate *c.* 1300 was made up of thirty-seven selions and three headlands. Twenty-two selions lay singly, twelve were two selions together, two were three selions each, and one consisted of seven selions all lying together.[3] Thus the 'strip' varied in size from half a rood to half an acre, but in the three examples quoted 45 per cent of the strips contained a single rood or selion, that is a single land in all probability.

[1] Orwin, *The Open Fields*, 123–4. [2] *W.H.R.*, no. 995.
[3] Ibid., nos. 913, 979, 926.

A strip of 1 rood or 1½ roods was by far the commonest. In the two tenements above, where the ground is described in roods, no fewer than thirty-three out of sixty measured parcels were of one rood, and twenty-one others of 1½ roods. Only four out of sixty were as large as half an acre.

The selion is more difficult to discuss. The earlier medieval Wigston records describe the specific parcels almost invariably as *selions*; but after about 1300-10 by roods. Very occasionally a document refers to both *selions* and roods in the same tenement.

The selion varied in size according to the quality and topography of the soil, but there are indications that at Wigston it averaged about ⅕ to ⅙ of an acre over the whole parish. A late thirteenth-century grant speaks of twenty-seven acres divided into 133½ selions, which gives almost exactly five selions to the acre, while an acre in the east field (about the same date) is seen to consist of four strips of which one was a single selion, two were of two selions lying together, and one is described as half a rood.[1] Here the five selions amounted to 31 roods, so that one selion was approximately one-sixth of an acre. We cannot therefore equate selions and roods, and the marked change in the terminology of the charters in this respect after about 1310 is very curious.[2] Nor can we equate the selion, land, or ridge with the strip. In the two examples quoted above, fourteen out of forty-one strips consisted of two selions together and twenty-three consisted of a single selion.

One further comment on the medieval field arrangements is called for. Nowhere in Wigston, either in the records or on the ground today, is there any evidence that the strips were separated from each other by unploughed balks. Such balks as there were in the fields were occupation roads giving access to particular furlongs, often running out from the village in a continuous (though possibly winding) course towards the boundaries of the parish, and acting also as footpaths to the next village. The later Wigston records speak of 'the town balk' and 'the common balk'

---

[1] *W.H.R.*, nos. 894, 901.

[2] In later records (of the sixteenth and eighteenth centuries) the expression 'an old rood' occurs together with simple 'roods', another change of terminology which I cannot explain. Does it reflect some rearrangement in part of the older lay-out? Possibly a rearrangement arising after much land had gone out of cultivation in the fifteenth century and a consequent reshuffling when cultivation was resumed at a later date?

when referring to these common ways, grassed over and left unploughed. Furlongs were sometimes separated by balks; but such balks as existed were mostly spaced at much greater intervals, wherever the need for access required it. Headlands also acted as small balks giving local access to a furlong, and were generally left unploughed. The grass upon them was not wasted, however, and most tenements had a number of headlands carefully specified as part and parcel of them. In most cases these headlands were necessarily ley ground.[1]

The clear evidence, from the sixteenth-century records and later, of ley strips dispersed among the arable is not forthcoming from the medieval records in an unambiguous form. A lease in 1464, which speaks of '3 yardlands and a quarter of land, and 7 acres of land, with meadows, pastures and leazes in the fields of the same town'[2] suggests the existence of leys as distinct from the meadows and the common pasture of the *sikes*. Another document in 1466 concerns 'a messuage, 6 acres of land, and 4 Pastures';[3] but these are only hints. The intermixture of arable and ley strips is, however, so well developed in the sixteenth-century fields at Wigston, and is known to have existed elsewhere in Leicestershire in the early fifteenth century, that we cannot doubt it had appeared here well before 1500.

Some of the medieval charters reveal that pasture rights appurtenant to particular farms, to particular virgates or half-virgates, were being separated from the arable to which they had of old time belonged and were being granted, or bought and sold separately, or added to the appurtenances of the other holdings. For example, the grant of a virgate of land *c.* 1300-10 carried with it 'a virgate and the fourth part of a virgate of pasture'.[4] In 1357 we find the Balle tenement described as 'half a virgate of land with half a virgate of pasture and a virgate of meadow' and in other documents we find small pieces of meadow changing hands; but in general, as we should expect, the common pasture rights and the

---

[1] Headlands and butts could sometimes be ploughed for crops, however. A lease in 1308 of a headland and a butt lying against it, for a term of 14½ years, allows the lessee to have 'ten crops of the said selions'. (*W.H.R.*, no. 928.)

[2] *W.H.R.*, no. 1045.

[3] Ibid., no. 1046.

[4] Such expressions as 'a virgate of meadow' or 'a virgate of pasture' appear repeatedly in the charters. They are to be interpreted, of course, as the amount of meadow (or of common pasture) rightfully going with a tenement of one virgate in the fields.

meadow properly belonging to a tenement of a certain size were kept intact at all times. Such parting of meadow and common pasture rights from the parent tenement as we find may be the result of the breaking-up of 'normal' tenements of a virgate or half a virgate of which there is good evidence in other Leicestershire villages and some slight evidence at Wigston.[1] In 1333 the tenement of Henry son of Adam of Wykyngeston is described as '17 acres of land, 6 pieces of meadow, and the moiety of a virgate of pasture', and in 1338 Simon Randolf granted to Richard, his brother, '11 acres of land, a plot of meadow, and half a virgate of pasture in Wikingiston, whereof William of Wisshton sometime held 4 acres and Richard Simon sometime held 7 acres and the meadow and pasture'.[2] One suspects that at Wigston too 'the great danger remains that the actual variety of village life may be concealed by the rigid categories of the manorial formulary'.[3]

By the time, too, that the Wigston records become sufficiently detailed in the second half of the thirteenth century – any evidence there may have been that the strips in the fields once followed the order of the homesteads in the village streets has vanished. The records throw no light on this matter, nor could we reasonably expect them to in the light of the incessant small sales and grants that appear from the earliest records onwards. Here, too, any rigid pattern that might once have existed, perhaps in pre-Conquest times, had been dissolved and the actual lay-out of the village and its fields was more various than any formula could embrace.

❧ THE MEDIEVAL CROPS ❧

Little can be said about the medieval farmer's crops at Wigston, though what we know of peasant farming elsewhere in the county is sufficient to tell us what it was like here. A lease of the rectory in 1402 to three local peasants refers to 'all manner of grain, pease, hay, hemp, and flax,

---

[1] Cf. Hilton, 'Kibworth Harcourt' (in *Studies in Leics. Agrarian History*) for a detailed account of such breaking-up in the thirteenth and fourteenth centuries. A fourteenth-century rental for Anstey also reveals this process at work (Farnham, i, 21-3). Rentals provide the best evidence of this, but none survives for Wigston.

[2] *W.H.R.*, nos. 948, 951. There are many small grants or leases among the Wigston records of pieces that must have been lopped off from larger tenements, e.g. 4½ acres, 3¼ acres, and numerous grants of a few selions.

[3] Hilton, loc. cit., 18.

which, on the day of making of these presents are stored there in the granges and houses of the same rectory and are forthcoming from the lands and demesnes of the same'.[1]

A grant early in 1347 by William Betrich of Wigston to Adam his son, and Joan and Felice his daughters, of a part of his house and 7½ roods of land, reserves to them also 'free entry and exit through William's gates for their wheat and other their necessaries'. Two peasant farmers of Quorndon, in the north of the county, had between them in 1386[2] 45 quarters of crops, of which wheat amounted to 4 qrs., barley to 21 qrs., and peas to 20 qrs. – much the same proportions as we find at Wigston or anywhere else in Leicestershire in the sixteenth century. It seems likely that one whole field was devoted to peas (and beans) at Quorndon in the late fourteenth century, as was done at Kirby Bellars, in the Wreak valley near Melton Mowbray, at the same date.[3]

All we can safely say about the cropping at Wigston in the fourteenth and fifteenth centuries is that in all probability a whole field was devoted to peas and beans, as it was throughout the sixteenth century; that the other sown field was largely under barley, together with a not inconsiderable amount of wheat sown in the previous autumn; and that the furlong was probably already an independent unit for cropping purposes, and not the field. Whether any rye and oats were grown at the time we have no knowledge. Nor can we speak with certainty of any period earlier than the mid-fourteenth century, for Hilton's figures of the tithe corn and demesne corn receipts of Leicester abbey show a marked rise in the cultivation of leguminous crops in Leicestershire during the second half of that century at the expense of barley and wheat.[4] These changes in crops must reflect a fundamental change in the working of the open fields in the same period.

The Leicester abbey figures for 1363, while not wholly satisfactory because of their lumping together of demesne and tithe returns, suggest that in the first half of the fourteenth century (and perhaps

---

[1] *W.H.R.*, no. 983.   [2] Farnham, *Quorndon Records*, 108.

[3] Hilton, *The Econ. Development of some Leics. Estates*, 152-6.

[4] Ibid., 63-5. In 1363 peas constituted 17 per cent of the total receipts (by qrs.), rising to 32½ per cent in 1401 and 30 per cent in 1470. Barley fell from 57 per cent of the total in 1363 to 45 per cent in 1399 (only 40 per cent in 1393) and to 42½ per cent in 1470. Wheat fell from 21½ per cent in 1363 to 14 per cent in 1393 and 1399, and 14½ per cent in 1470.

earlier) it was barley which had occupied the whole of one field, and that spring-sown peas and beans followed autumn-sown wheat (with a little rye) in the other field. In any even, the cropping of the second field must have been arranged by furlongs even at that period, in order to fit in wheat, rye, peas and beans, and possibly some oats, in the required proportions, and in proportions which doubtless varied somewhat from village to village.

The hemp and flax which are mentioend in 1402 at Wigston were grown by most farmers on small plots of land, often called *plecks* in the records. These produced enough hemp and flax to supply the peasant household with its linen cloth, but left nothing over for sale, and the acreage involved is so small that it never appears in the farmers' inventories when these begin in the sixteenth century. There is no doubt, however, from the frequency with which flaxen and hempen sheets and other household articles appear in the inventories from about 1500 onwards that these crows were grown all over Leicestershire by the peasantry; and it was probably so all over the midland counties. Finally, the minor names of the landscape in the medieval period amply demonstrate that the peaant was well aware of the variety of soils within his fields and of the crops best suited to them. There can be little doubt that he sowed small crops, at least with particular reference to the quality of soils available in any one year; and, indeed, that the open-field system as a whole was much more flexible in its cropping arrangements, even in the medieval period, than we have generally been led to understand.

Of the medieval peasant's livestock we know very little as yet in Leicestershire. We can only suggest in general terms that, as the rotation of crops which we find in the early sixteenth century appears to have been established in the late fourteenth or early fifteenth, so the livestock which we find on the Leicestershire farms in Henry VIII's time is probably what we should have found in the days of Richard II.

❧ PEASANT FAMILIES ❧

What little we know about the peasant families of the twelfth and thirteenth centuries at Wigston – in this instance only the free tenants – has already been discussed in the previous chapter. The assessment to the twentieth in 1327 tells us a little more. Of the thirty-nine names on the list, possibly only a third or less of the total number of families, the largest payers were William, son of Simon (Wykyngeston) 6s., William Balle 7s., Agnes Swan 13s., Henry Swan 15s. 6d., Richard Gylemyn ?18s. 6d., Isold Bek ?9s. 6d., Richard Godewyne ?6s. 6d., John Fryday 5s. 6d., John Hutte 8s., John Faucous (Faukes) 6s., John de Evynton 9s 10d., and one Nollynge ?6s. 6d. These are the twelve largest taxpayers, of whom ten can be certainly identified as free tenants. The other two (Nollynge and Evynton) almost certainly were also. Below them come two payers of 4s. each, and one at 3s. 6d.; five paying 3s. or 2s.; and fourteen paying between 6d. and 18d.[1]

The tax was a twentieth of movable good or personal property in town and country, with exemption up to 10s. worth of property. Thus the lowest amount of tax payable was 6d. and there should normally be a considerable number of taxpayers at or just above the exemption limit. In fact there are only two payers of 6d. at Wigston, and three at 8d. It seems clear that a number of peasant families who should have paid at or near the bottom of the scale escape assessment in some way, besides all those who were legitimately exempt. Indeed, we notice many remarkable omissions from the list even with our limited knowledge of the free tenants alone. Where are the Randulls and the Herricks, and a dozen others whose names we know from other records at the date?

The tax was assessed upon personal property and therefore offers very little guidance about the real estate of the peasantry. William, son of Simon Wykyngeston, possessed in 1334 a messuage, 8¼ virgates and three roods of land (with the appurtenant meadow and common pasture rights), and a windmill, all in Wigston; and other smaller property in two other villages – Ullesthorpe and Burton Overy. John Fryday, in 1344, owned a messuage, three virgates and five acres of land (with appurtenances), and 22s. 2d. chief rents per annum from other free tenants in the village. John Hutte was a member of a family who appear as owning 2½ virgates in inquisitions between 1444 and 1457.[2] Of the other leading taxpayers we know nothing beyond the

---

[1] See Hoskins, 'Wigston Magna Lay Subsidies, 1327 to 1599', *T.L.A.S.*, xx, 57-8.

[2] See Chapter III above for the Wykyngestons and Frydays. For the Huttes, use *Cal. Inq. post mortem*, iv, 223, 279.

fact that some of them appear in the Wyggeston Hospital Records as holding free tenements of a half, three-quarters, or a whole virgate. But these records relate to a very limited area of land – certainly less than a tenth of the whole vill – and all of them may well have had other property elsewhere in the village and its fields.

The Swans we know next to nothing about, though two of them between them dominate the tax-list in 1327. Roger Swan appears in a charter dated 1273; his son Ralph in charters of 1305 and 1324; Agnes Swan appears in the charter of 1324 and as the third largest taxpayer in 1327. Possibly she is Roger's widow. Of Henry Swan, the second largest taxpayer, the Wyggeston Hospital Records make no mention: he must have lived elsewhere in the village for he does not appear even as a witness to the numerous charters made during his lifetime. Robert Swan witnessed a Wigston lease in 1462, and that is the last mention of their name in their ancestral village. No Swan appears in the subsidy lists of 1524-5. By a piece of good fortune we discover what had happened to them, for a record of 1445 shows that 'William Swanne of Coventre in the county of Warwick *hosyer*, Humphrey Swanne of Coventre ... *hosyer*, Thomas Swanne of Coventre ... *hosteller*, John Swanne of Coventre ... *laborer* and John son of Henry Faukes of Wykyngston in the county of Leicester *laborer* were attached to answer John earl of Oxford in a plea whereby with armed force they broke into the earl's close at Wykyngston and consumed his grass growing there, to the value of ten marks, by depasturing certain beasts on it' and had committed other enormities to the serious damage of the earl and against the King's peace, on 14 July, 1431 – nearly fourteen years earlier.[1] At the time of the offence the Swans had apparently all been living in the village, so that their migration to Coventry may be dated as somewhere between 1431 and 1445.

The tax list of 1327, for all its imperfections, reveals that by the early fourteenth century a class of large, comparatively wealthy, landed peasants had already emerged in the village. The exact total of the tax for the village is indecipherable but is probably 161s. Of this total,

---

[1] P.R.O. Chancery Miscellanea, C. 47. Bundle 66, File 5, no. 163. The Swans were a turbulent family for in 1302 and again in 1352 a John Swan was pardoned for causing another man's death on each occasion. See Hoskins, 'Murder and Sudden Death in Medieval Wigston', *T.L.A.S.*, xxi, 176-86.

just under seventy per cent was contributed by eleven taxpayers, or by ten different families out of 120 or more in the village. Economic inequality was already very strongly developed, even in this largely peasant community, both in real and in personal property. The fact, too, that the closing years of the thirteenth century and the first forty years or so of the fourteenth were a period of comparative prosperity, for the minority of large peasants if not for all, is well evidenced by the complete rebuilding and enlargement of the parish church in these years, as well as by the foundation and building of a chantry chapel by the Wykyngeston family in 1301, who endowed it with 3 messuages and 2½ virgates of land in Wigston, and 40s. in rents per annum in Burton Overy. The whole of the present church – apart from the usual Perpendicular clearstory and minor structural changes of later date can be assigned to the period *c.* 1290-1340, a generation, indeed, in which a great number of Leicestershire parish churches, in town and country, were also being enlarged or entirely rebuilt.

The peasant freeholder's arrangements for the disposal of his property after death, and for the maintenance of younger sons and unmarried daughters during his lifetime, have already been touched upon. So far as the succession of the tenement went, it seems to have been usual for the peasant to vest all his property in a trustee, generally the chaplain[1] or the priest, who then reconveyed it to the owner and his wife for the term of their lives, with more or less elaborate remainders which dictated the succession as far ahead as one could see. It also appears that a landholder could convey his property to the chaplain who then granted it back, in order to strengthen his existing title. Thus in 1318 Richard Randulf, son and heir of Adam Randulf of Wigston, granted to Richard Haudekyn of Wigston, chaplain, 'a toft called Tenement, the fourth part of a virgate, and 11½ acres of land, and a pennyworth of rent issuing from a virgate of land which Richard Palmer holds, and three-halfpenceworth of rent issuing from three-quarters of a virgate of land in the same town which Simon Balle holds'. Six weeks later Richard Haudekyn regranted the property to Richard Randulf, most of the witnesses being those who had witnessed

---

[1] The chaplain at Wigston was often a younger son of a peasant family, e.g. Richard Haudekyn in 1318, John Swan in 1334, William Dicoun in 1357, and John Smyth in 1378.

the earlier grant.[1] There are similar transactions relating to the Huttes, the Godwins, and the Harcourts, all in the fourteenth century.[2]

As regards ensuring the succession to a property, the arrangements made by William Wykyngeston before 1334 and by John Fryday in 1344 have already been mentioned. In 1334 we find John Swan, chaplain, of Wigston, releasing to Symon, son of William of Wykyngeston, all his right in the family property which William had delivered and demised to Symon and John jointly, 'to hold and have for the term of life of the said William'.[3]

A generation or so earlier, Simon son of Henry of Wykyngeston, grandfather of the Simon involved in the transaction of 1334, had disposed of his estate in similar fashion. By a fine in 1301 between John de London, parson of the church of Whitwick, and Simon son of Henry of Wigston, John granted a messuage and four virgates of land in Wigston to Simon and Elena his wife and their issue for ever. In default of issue to Simon and Elena, the property should go to William, son of Nicholas, son of Alexander de Harcourt, and his issue; in default of issue from William, to Richard son of Adam Randolf and his issue; in default of issue from Richard Randolf, to William the brother of John and his issue; and in default of issue from William, then to the right heirs of Simon Wigston for ever.

By another fine in 1307 Simon Wigston received back from John de London another estate consisting of 4 messuages, a mill, and three virgates of land in Wigston, which had apparently been conveyed earlier to John for the purpose of this fine.

Similarly by a fine in 1344, Thomas Lewyn of Wigston reconveyed to John Fryday and Emma his wife a messuage, 3 virgates and 5 acres of land, and 22s. 2d. rents in Wigston. No record survives of the previous conveyance of the Fryday estate to Thomas Lewyn, but this clearly had taken place. Thomas granted the premises to John and Emma, with the reversion to John son of John and Eleanor his wife and their issue, and in default of such issue to the right heirs of John Fryday for ever.[4] In these elaborate and rather tortuous arrangements, the free tenants were

[1] *W.H.R.*, nos. 936, 937.   [2] Ibid., nos. 940, 945-7, 970, 972.
[3] Ibid., no. 949.
[4] The fines of 1301, 1307 and 1344 are given in Farnham MSS. For yet another example of this process, ensuring the succession to the Balle tenement in 1357, see above p. 67.

taking good care that their lands should not return to the lord's hands for want of an heir – an escheat *propter defectum sanguinis*, for 'want of the blood'.

It seems clear that at Wigston, as in most medieval villages, the custom of primogeniture prevailed. The tenement should go unbroken to the eldest son and his wife, and to their issue, as the normal rule; then to the second son, his wife and their issue if the eldest line failed; and so on. The Balle charter of 1357 also shows that daughters could inherit before the line of sons had been exhausted. Here the tenement of a messuage and half a virgate (with meadow pertaining to a whole virgate) was to pass to the eldest son and his heirs; in default to the second son and his heirs; in default again, to the two daughters and their heirs; and in default of this, to yet another son, for the term of his life, with reversion after his death to the rightful heirs of Richard Balle, the father of them all.

Provision was often made, however, for the widow's estate and for the maintenance of younger sons and unmarried daughters, almost invariably with a life interest only, so that the ancestral tenement was not impaired in size.

Some time between 1260 and 1272 Ralph Balle gave to Alice, one of his three daughters, a toft and a croft together with a single selion of land and the third part of the meadow belonging to a certain half-virgate. Five other selions and the other two-thirds of the meadow had been given by Ralph to the other two sisters. 'The grantor wills, however, that Hysenda his wife shall have her habitation for the whole of her life in the said house with the said Alice his daughter, and shall have moreover victual and raiment from the whole land and meadow given to his three daughters, as she ought to have of right'.[1]

In 1419 John Smyth gave to Beatrice his wife a messuage, with a horse-mill, and 3¼ acres of arable land in the fields for the term of her life, with reversion after her death to the said John and his heirs. This was a peasant's dower. Back in 1395, William Smyth – father of John – had given this house and piece of land to his daughter Alice 'and the heirs of her body lawfully begotten' for her maintenance, but it had evidently come back into the family on Alice's death.[2] If Alice had married, this would have been her dowry, and the small property would have descended

[1] W.H.R., no. 881 (n.d.).   [2] Ibid., nos. 979, 1000.

with her children. Usually, however, a peasant provided that any such gift to unmarried sons and daughters should revert to the main estate upon their marriage. In 1347 William Betrich granted to his son Adam and his two daughters Joan and Felice a specified part of his messuage and 7½ roods of land in the fields to hold for their lives in survivorship by the yearly rent of a rose-flower at Midsummer. 'If Adam, Joan or Felice or any of them be married, they shall altogether withdraw thereafter from the said tenements and claim nothing therein by reason of any right; but the said tenements shall remain entirely to those only who are not married, with reversion, in case of the marriage of all three, to William, his heirs and assigns'.[1]

In 1330 we find a younger son of the Godwin family holding 5½ roods of land from his eldest brother for the term of his life, with reversion to the latter and his heirs after that term, and a little later we find that the 5½ roods have duly returned to the family tenement.[2]

Such younger sons who were provided with two or three strips in each of the fields must have formed a pool of wage-labour in the village, possibly on the family farm, or possibly on someone else's, since no man could live off such a minute holding. Such a holding was merely a supplement, though a most valuable supplement, to a daily or a weekly wage, enabling the possessor to live in a cottage economy without being entirely dependent on a money-income. In some instances too these younger sons became the craftsmen of the village.

Several women had land of their own, though possibly only small parcels in many instances, We find a number of charters at Wigston in which daughters receive pieces of land from their fathers, and dispose of other pieces for money; and there is some suggestion that occasionally a woman may have held a more substantial tenement. In charters of about 1250-60 Richard Mabile often appears as a witness, and once he appears as 'Richard son of Mabel'. For the next century or two the family continued in Wigston as the Mabiles and seem indeed to have given their name to a part of the fields in 'Mablowe felde' (1417). Similarly, another part of one of the fields was *Gonewarehil* or *Gunwarhill* after some Scandinavian woman of the name of *Gunnvor*. The Moulds, another ancient family in Wigston (who still survive there), seem to get their

---

[1] *W.H.R.*, no. 954.   [2] Ibid., no. 945.

name ultimately from one Maud, back in the twelfth century. But in the main the women of the village, in the more well-to-do peasant families at least, had to be specially provided for with a cottage and a small piece of land, whether as widows or as unmarried daughters.

The peasant was tenacious of his rights: his land meant everything to him. He was even prepared to commit murder for it on occasion. On Sunday night, 13 November 1390, Richard Baker, clerk, of Wigston, met Adam Sutton in the street (now called Bushloe End) coming away from the inn. Richard 'because of various quarrels which had arisen between them, struck the said Adam on the head with a staff worth a penny, whereby the said Adam within a short while afterwards died without the rites of the church'. Emma Baker first discovered the body, but Richard had fled. Richard was later pardoned for the crime (in March 1392) but a record made fifty years later tells the story behind the murder. A record among the Hastings manuscripts[1] recites:

> The yearly rent paid by the hands of Robert Hutt, to wit one penny at Christmas from Alice Grendon, kinswoman and heir of Richard Mabyll, now deceased, for a certain tenement and four acres of land which Richard Hutt and Amice his wife, the daughter of Richard Mabyll, lately held of Roger Mabyll in chief at a rent as aforesaid besides foreign service to Sir John Fryday, knight, which said tenement lies in Bysserow streete in Wikingeston between the cottage of Henry Harcourte on the east and the common way called Hawthornegate on the west, and know ye that Richard Hutte and Amice his wife, the daughter of Richard Mabyll, had issue Thomas and John, and Thomas had issue John, which John had issue Robert, the now tenant. And Richard Mabyll the son of Roger had issue Emma and Amice. And Amice the wife of Richard Hutt being dead, a certain John Baker took the said Emma to wife and so had the capital messuage and virgate of land and 13½d. yearly rent, which messuage lies between the said cottage of Henry Harecourte on the west and the capital messuage of Richard Friday on the east. And John Baker and Emma his wife had issue Richard and Alice. After John Baker's death a certain Robert Levy married Emma and after Robert Levy's death a certain Adam Sutton took the said Emma to wife. Afterwards the said Emma died and the

---

[1] A version of this record may be found in *H.M.C.*, Hastings MSS., i, 95-6. The whole document is a good example of the importance of peasant family pedigrees at their own level.

said Adam enfeoffed a certain John Weston chaplain in the lands, etc., to the disinheritance of Richard Baker, the eldest son of the said Emma, for which the said Richard Baker by night killed the said Adam; for which reason the chief lord Sir John Fryday recovered the said messuage and virgate of land by the writ of estreats against Alice Grendon, widow, the sister of the said Richard Baker, made 20 May, 20 Henry IV [1442].

One wonders how many more murders there might have been for the same motive: why Adam Herrick killed Simon the clerk of Wigston, a crime for which he was pardoned in May 1299. Or why John Swan killed John Symon a few years later; and why Alice, the daughter of Roger de Walton of Wigston, killed Adam Godwin about the year 1343. And in July 1336, Richard Astel had killed William de Kylby of Wigston in the meadows of Newton Harcourt. William, with an accomplice, had attacked Richard, by reason of 'an ancient grudge' he bore him, but the latter had struck in self-defence and had killed his assailant. In all these instances, without exception, the protagonists in each incident were members of peasant landowning families.[1] Normally, things did not reach this pass; but there were many lawsuits concerning pieces of property. The Plea Rolls are full of them, not only squabbles over whole virgates, or over 'waste and destruction' of tenements demised for life, but over single acres or even less. Thus in 1316 'the assize came to recognize whether John Fryday and Adam Fryday of Wigston disseised Amabel Fryday of Wigston of her free tenement in Wigston, to wit a messuage and three roods of land. Amabel recovered her seisin'.[2] And in 1318, Rose, widow of William de Whetstone, demanded in the King's Bench, against Henry Balle of Wigston and his wife Emma, one acre of land and half a rood 'as her right by a writ of entry'. There are dozens of such suits for one village alone, buried in the mountains of the Plea Rolls.[3]

The life of the medieval villagers did not consist entirely of work; nor were their lives entirely wrapped up in their tenements and all the legal wrangling that they involved. Wigston lay on the main road in medieval times between Leicester and Northampton, with great men constantly passing through its streets on business far beyond the wit of the peasantry who watched them ride by.

[1] 'Murder and Sudden Death in Medieval Wigston', *T.L.A.S.*, xxi, 175–86.
[2] Assize roll, Hilary 10 Edward II (Farnham MSS.)   [3] Farnham MSS.

Sometimes the king himself passed through; and there was the memorable Tuesday morning of 13 December 1300 when King Edward I actually halted in the village and transacted some royal business.[1] Edward II also came this way and doubtless other monarchs on their way to and from Leicester.

Every year there was the Rogationtide procession of all who could walk round the village fields, blessing the growing crops at intervals, and traversing once more the boundaries of the parish so that they should never be in doubt. The Rogationtide procession is vouched for in the earliest surviving church-wardens' accounts (early seventeenth century), but was ancient even then, going back to pre-Conquest days in open-field country.[2] In Whitsun week there was another great procession, as far as the streets of Leicester itself, which led to trouble with another village in the year 1313. 'In Whitsun week the men of Wigston and [*blank*] came to Leicester with their procession and in the lane which leads to St. Margaret's a quarrel broke out between the said townships. Blows were struck with swords and with ash-sticks made like fists. The offenders fled. Chattels unknown'.[3] One would give a good deal to know more about this procession and the details of the fight.

Then there was the annual pilgrimage to the shrine of St. Wistan in the smaller of the two churches at the top end of the village. This we only learn about by chance in an Elizabethan enquiry into 'concealed lands'.[4] George Amery and William Pawley, both villagers with a long ancestry in Wigston, deposed before the commissioners that St. Wistan's church had been largely, if not wholly, maintained by the annual pilgrimage. 'There was an image called St. Wistans,' said Amery, 'to which men used to come on pilgrimage,' their offerings being delivered to the churchwardens, presumably on St. Wistan's day (June 1st).

Apart from the regular excitement of these annual processions and pilgrimages (and doubtless others of which we now have no record), there

---

[1] Edward reached Leicester on 6 December 1300 and stayed a week. He left on 13 December, sealed various documents at Wigston the same day and probably stayed the night at Mowsley, a few miles farther on.

[2] Homans, *English Villagers of the Thirteenth Century*, 568.

[3] Bateson (ed.), *Leicester Borough Records*, i, 375.

[4] P.R.O., Exch. Special Commissions, E. 178. no. 1230. Dated June 14 Eliz. (incomplete). Wistan was a local saint, grandson of Wiglaf, King of Mercia. He is said to have been murdered in 849, probably at Wistow (Wistan's *stow*) only three miles or so from Wigston.

were the occasional excitements of violent deaths in the village or in its fields. Some of these have already been referred to. The coroners' inquests which survive for the period 1390-1405 refer to others – to the death of John Haldenby on that July midnight in 1394 when 'certain men of Wigston were keeping watch for the aforesaid town as was the custom' and were throwing their staves in play to while away the hours; and Thomas Draper's stave struck John on the shin, so that he died four days later 'with the rites of the church'. Or there was the Saturday evening, at six o'clock, the day before Easter 1395, that John atte Hall was thrown from his mare in the street when two dogs ran at the mare and bit her, so that he fell from the rearing animal and fractured his skull. And William Swan, a boy of fourteen, who went to a well called Carewell to wash his hands one Wednesday afternoon (April 1397) and fell in and was drowned. The village was ordered by the coroner to block up the well within forty days under a penalty of forty shillings. The last inquest to survive among the records is that on Margaret Roost, aged eleven, who was driving her mother's cart in the fields on a May morning (1405), and, jumping from it in order to mend the harness of the horse, fell on her head and broke her neck, dying immediately without the rites of the church. But of all the others who died peaceful deaths, the anonymous multitude on whom no enquiry was held, 'the greater part must be content to be as though they had not been, to be found in the register of God, not in the record of man'.

❧   THE CHURCH AND THE RECTORY   ☙

Towards the end of the thirteenth century, the parish church of All Saints was considerably enlarged, indeed almost rebuilt. The church which survives today was so thoroughly restored in Victorian days that some of its structural development has been obscured; but it seems fairly certain that a north aisle was added to an older building *c.* 1290-1300, or, more probably, that the north aisle was rebuilt on a larger scale since it is unlikely that such a densely populated village could have made do with an aisleless Norman church.

Shortly after this, probably about 1320-30, the south aisle was added or rebuilt on a larger scale; and the handsome tower and spire completed the new work within a few more years. Thus the parish church was substantially rebuilt between about 1290 and 1340, a period in which a great number of Leicestershire town and country churches were wholly rebuilt. About the same time, probably in the last quarter of the thirteenth century, the second church, dedicated to St. Wistan, was built or rebuilt at the other end of the village to serve the Champayne or Leicester manor.[1] It was served by a chaplain from the parish church, and had the right of baptism and burial.

From the time of Henry I (probably *c.* 1110-15), Lenton Priory had possessed the advowson of the rectory and had appointed influential clerks to this wealthy living. Few if any of these rectors came near the parish: at any rate not one of them witnessed a medieval charter in the village; and some of them had more important offices elsewhere, such as William Newport (instituted in 1409) who was also Chancellor of Lichfield Cathedral. John de Hale, who was instituted in 1349 (by an exchange of benefices with Robert de Stretton) was also dean of the free chapel of St. Buryan, in far-away Cornwall. All these absentee rectors appointed chaplains to perform their spiritual duties in the parish, often the sons of local peasant families as we have seen.

More important than that, however, their absence from the parish involved the leasing of the glebe (three virgates in extent), and of the rectorial tithes, to men on the spot. Only one record of such a lease survives: an indenture drawn up in London (significantly) on 29 October 1402 between Robert Gowe, rector of Wigston (from 1399 to 1409), and John Nightingale, Thomas Grendon, and Richard Lufe. Grendon and Lufe (or Love) can be identified as Wigston farmers at this date; Nightingale may have been a Leicester man. This indenture annulled a previous agreement between the parties 'touching the farm of the church and rectory', but the rector 'granted anew to the same farmers all manner of grain, pease, hay, hemp, and flax, which, on the day of making these presents, are stored there in the granges and houses of the same rectory and are forthcoming from the lands and demesnes of the same', reserving a portion of the hay to the rector. For this the three

---

[1] Three undated documents among the Wyggeston Hospital Records (nos. 876, 879, 904) refer to the church directly or indirectly. The two earlier records may be *c.* 1260-70 but the tower of the present building (which is the only part of the original structure remaining) suggests a date *c.* 1290-1300. It has been suggested in Chapter I that St. Wistan's church already existed in 1086.

farmers were to render to the rector 'at his lodging in London' 110 marks sterling in five instalments at stated dates – three instalments of £20 each and two of 10 marks each. 'The same farmers shall also find a fit chaplain and deacon to do divine service for the parishioners' and also pay all pensions and other burdens on the rectory until next Michaelmas, while the rector 'shall repair all the houses of the said rectory and shall warrant the premises until next Michaelmas'.[1]

This was a lease of the rectory (tithes and glebe) for one year from Michaelmas 1402 to Michaelmas 1403 at a rent of £73 6s. 8d. A transaction of this magnitude must have been of great significance in the economy of the village and it is a pity that we have no further records of this nature. Elsewhere in Leicestershire, in the late fifteenth century, we find large capitalist peasants leasing the local tithes and demesnes of Leicester abbey properties in the surrounding countryside, and laying the foundations of large yeoman fortunes in the sixteenth century.[2] At Wigston the monastery of Lenton appropriated the rectory for itself in 1506 (as well as the right of presentation, which it had exercised from the beginning) and thenceforth made its own leases of the rectorial demesne and tithes; but we find that the peasant farmer is pushed out of the picture. In 1518-26 Sir Richard Sacheverell, kt., was leasing the rectory from the priory; and in 1536 Symon Catesby, a Nottinghamshire gentleman, took the lease for a term of 45 years, from five years to five years, and was in possession at the Dissolution. Thus at Wigston the farm of the rectory passed out of the hands of the capitalist peasant just when, in many other villages in the county, he was on the verge of reaping the unearned increment of rising prices in contrast to a long-term fixed rent. This characteristic feature of peasant economy in the early sixteenth century had no place at Wigston, which produced no outstanding yeoman family as so many other villages did.[3]

---

[1] *W.H.R.*, no. 983.

[2] Cf. Hilton, op. cit., 93-105.

[3] The early appropriation of the rectory of Wigston, and the subsequent ordination of a poorly endowed vicarage, is illustrated to this day by the physical site of the Rectory Farm, which stands between the vicarage and the parish church.

⬦ THE FIFTEENTH CENTURY ⬦

Our sources for the fifteenth-century history of Wigston are exceedingly meagre, but such as they are they call for a brief discussion. The primary fact in this century is the severe economic depression which is revealed by the cut in the quota for the fifteenth in 1446. In 1334 the quota had been fixed at £8 8s. 0d.; only the towns of Leicester and Melton had a higher assessment. Until 1433 this figure remained unaltered, as did the quota of every other town and village in the country, although all over England economic conditions had changed and were changing so drastically that these quotas were out of touch with reality in a great number of places. In 1433 a cut of £4000 was made in the national yield of £37000, Wigston's own yield being reduced by 19s. 3d. to £7 8s. 9d., but this was still not enough to meet the reduced taxable capacity of the country. In 1446 the national yield was, therefore, reduced by a further £2000, and within each county the reduction was applied more equitably than that of 1433, with minute regard to the particular circumstances of each township.

In Leicestershire, the total yield of a fifteenth and tenth had been fixed at £757 12s. 10½d.; in 1433 this had been reduced by £79 8s. 3¼d. In 1446 it was reduced by £119 2s. 5d., leaving £628 10s. 5½d. to be raised when a fifteenth and a tenth should be demanded. The national cut of about sixteen per cent seems to have been uniformly spread among the various counties, but inside these counties there was a careful apportionment of the county rebate. Some twenty-five places in Leicestershire had no cut at all: at the other extreme the village of Humberstone had its quota reduced by sixty per cent, and two other places were reduced by more than fifty per cent. The borough of Leicester was cut by twenty-one per cent, Melton – the second town – by as much as thirty-eight per cent. On the other hand the small market-towns of Loughborough, Market Harborough and Ashby de la Zouch were only cut by 2½ per cent, 5 per cent, and 7 per cent respectively. Wigston was among the villages most heavily reduced – by forty per cent. Altogether, twelve villages were cut by forty per cent or more. No fewer than 27 were cut by thirty per cent or more: that is, by twice the average for the county as a whole.[1]

---

[1] The list printed in Nichols (i, lxxxix-xci) is not entirely accurate. There is another contemporary copy of the record in L.R.O. (ref. 71-22).

Thus the revised assessment of 1446 gives a good picture of the changing economy of the county in the middle of the fifteenth century, a picture which reveals new places rising in local importance and older places failing behind. Occasionally the eclipse is only temporary, but sometimes it is permanent. Both Leicester and Melton kept their lead among the towns, despite their heavy fall in taxable capacity, but in the north of the county Loughborough had emerged as the economic centre; and in the south-east the new town of Market Harborough had effectively supplanted the older centre of Hallaton, which was henceforth to fall farther and farther behind, back to the level of an out-of-the-way village. Wigston, too, though it was never an economic centre for any district, with its new quota of £5 5s. 0d. was now well down the list: a dozen other places now exceeded it in size or importance.

The depression of the first half of the fifteenth century was a combination of both a diminished population, as a result of repeated outbreaks of plague, and of economic stagnation in town and countryside. The latter was partly, at least, the result of the former. In Leicestershire we can find plenty of evidence of agricultural depression. At Newton Harcourt, adjacent to Wigston, the value of the arable had fallen from 18s. a virgate in 1265 to 6s. a virgate in 1436. The assized rents of the free tenants had fallen from 60s. 11d. to 26s. 5d., the revenue from pleas and perquisites of court had halved, and the manor-house and its buildings were in decay. At Groby, to the west of Leicester, similarly, the value of the demesne arable had fallen from 6d. an acre in 1288 to 2d. in 1445, and the meadow from 2s. an acre to 8d. The fishing in the two ponds had been worth 40s., but had fallen in 1445 to only 2s. The two mills had been worth 46s. 8d. yearly; in 1445 only 20s. And the assized rents of the free tenants, too, had nearly halved from £7 5s. 2d. down to £4 per annum.[1]

The bailiff's accounts for Beaumanor in 1406 show the Beaumanor and Quorndon mills still working, but there were signs of gathering depression even then: against fern, flags (from the mill-pond), and willows, all of which had formerly produced a revenue, the bailiff notes that none were sold 'for lack of buyers'.[2]

[1] For Newton Harcourt, see Farnham, iii, 258, 263; for Groby, see Farnham, *Charnwood Forest and its Historians*, 100, 106.

[2] Farnham, *Quarndon Records*, 125-6.

Inquisitions post mortem for the first half of the fifteenth century reveal abundant evidence of depression and decay. An inquisition in 1413 on Henry de Beaumont's Leicestershire lands speaks of 4 messuages in Loughborough decayed for want of repairs and tenants. They were formerly worth 80s. a year, but now worth nothing. The site of the manor at Loughborough used to be let for £5, but now only for £2. The watermills of Beaumanor and Quorndon, working only seven years earlier, were now in decay and in the lord's hands for want of tenants: they used to render £4 a year, now they are worth nothing. At Arnesby, to the south of Leicester, a capital messuage, three meadows, and demesne pasture used to render 12 marks a year, but now they render only 5 marks. And at Whittington, the same inquisition records 4 messuages in decay for want of tenants: formerly rendering 106s. 8d. a year, and now nothing.

An inquisition of 1427 reveals the water-mills of Quorndon and Beaumanor still 'ruinous', and at Quorndon there were 12 houses in decay also. At Woodhouse, parcel of Beaumanor, 17 messuages were reported in decay and worth nothing for want of tenants. In the large manor of Whitwick, bordering upon Charnwood, the same inquisition reveals decaying farmhouses and unoccupied land in all the townships within the manor. At Whitwick itself, 12 of the 31 houses were vacant for want of tenants and rendered nothing, and 289 acres of land were described as *vastate*. In Swannington there were 2 ruined farmhouses and 2 virgates 'lying adjacent' were in the lord's hands for want of tenants. At Markfield 12 of the 29 houses were in ruins and at Donington-le-Heath 16 houses were in decay and lacking tenants. No other messuages are mentioned here. In the manor of Hugglescote, at the same time, there were 12 messuages in ruins and 10 others in the lord's hands for want of tenants. Finally, at Bottesford in 1440, no fewer than 22 messuages were returned as worth nothing because they were ruinous.[1] The fact that in 1446 the yield of a fifteenth at Bottesford was cut by only 12 per cent – less than the average for the county – is perhaps some indication of the severity of the decay and depopulation in villages where the cut was 30, 40, and even 50 per cent.

---

[1] Beaumont inquisitions, 1413, 1427, in Nichols, op. cit., *West Goscote Hundred*, 1115-6 and Farnham, *Charnwood Forest*, 137. For Bottesford, Farnham, vi, 202.

Thus, though there is no direct evidence of agricultural depression and depopulation at Wigston in the early fifteenth century, other than the tax cut of 40 per cent in 1446, there is overwhelming evidence from all quarters of the county in these years as to the existence of widespread depression in the countryside and in some of the towns. There can be little doubt that the population of the village fell markedly even after 1377. In the following chapter it is suggested that it may even have halved between 1377 and the bottom of the depression, and a considerable area of the village was certainly left derelict. Aerial photographs of a number of Leicestershire villages (e.g. Burton Overy) show a very considerable shrinkage of the village area, with all the signs of former habitations in the fields at one end of the present built-up area; and exploration on the ground (e.g. at Illston-on-the-Hill) shows clear traces of the village having once extended considerably farther into what are now green fields. The documentary evidence leaves little doubt that a good deal if not most of this shrinkage occurred before the end of the fifteenth century.

At Wigston there are only minute traces of possible former habitations on the edge of the old built-up area, on nothing like the scale which would be suggested by a halving of the medieval population, but here it seems clear that the abandoned area lay in the middle of the present village, or, more correctly, in the middle of the older part of it. The map (see p. 91) will make this clear. This map, by restoring the lines of the former streets of the central area – marked today by more or less straight lanes, hedged on either side – bears a remarkable resemblance in its general plan to air-photographs of wholly abandoned sites such as Ingarsby. This abandoned area at Wigston is occupied today by gardens, allotments, and small orchards, and is still wholly open.

It is possible that by the 1440's some recovery was taking place. A number of new surnames – perhaps a dozen in all – appear in the records of the middle decades of the century.[1] Some of these may have escaped earlier record, it is true, and may therefore be older than they appear: but there is no doubt about most of them. The village population was changing noticeably during the whole century: old families leaving, new ones coming in (perhaps after

[1] Court rolls, 1444, 1467 (B.M.), and contemporary Wyggeston Hospital Records.

an interval of stagnation and decay). The Randalls disappeared from the village about 1430 when Richard Randull migrated to Leicester and became a prosperous grocer, leasing his substantial inheritance to residents in the village like the Clarks. From another record we learn that the Swans, one of the most substantial peasant families a hundred years earlier, had migrated to the growing industrial town of Coventry, where in 1445 two of them were 'hosiers', one an inn-keeper, and another a labourer. A Herrick departed for London where he became a citizen and a skinner, leaving considerable legacies to his relatives back in Wigston when he died in 1494, and 10 marks towards the building of an almshouse in the churchyard of St. Wistan, the family church where Herricks had been baptised and buried since the late thirteenth century.[1] In the closing years of the fifteenth century we find John Wallys, son and heir of John Wallys of Wigston 'gentilman', at Southampton, where he also is described as 'gentilman'.[2]

The Harcourts, the Hutts, and the Fridays disappear, too, during the second half of the fifteenth century, but we do not know where; and a considerable number of lesser medieval families vanish from the village. Many of them, in the years of agricultural depression, must have walked the four miles down the road to the borough of Leicester, which, depressed though it was also, offered a greater variety of employment than an overcrowded village with no local industry. But the Leicester borough records, so voluminous for both the earlier and later periods, are almost entirely missing for the years between 1380 and 1465 when most of this migration was taking place. Some Wigston families apparently migrated to other villages: thus the Hutts are entrenched at Stoney Stanton and Sapcote, a few miles to the south-west, in the sixteenth and seventeenth centuries.

A solid core of middling peasant freeholders lasted right through this century of change and movement. They had accumulated no substantial estates (like the Wigstons in the early fourteenth century and the Randulls and the Swans in the early fifteenth) and were therefore not big enough to move away and start life elsewhere as town merchants or traders; but they had sufficient land to keep them in the village and to withstand the long depression. In general it was the wealthiest and the

[1] Will of John Eryke, 1494 (P.C.C., Somerset House, London.)
[2] P.R.O., Early Chanc. Proc. (1529-32) 686/47-9.

poorest who tended to leave – whether in good times or bad – and the middling peasants who tended to stay through thick and thin. Among these persistent families, who bridge the fourteenth century and the fourteenth, are Astill, Smith, Herrick, Palmer, Simon, Mould, Stanton and Clay, while Shepherd and Cook are doubtful cases. In all we cannot assume that more than ten families in Henry VIII's reign had come through from 1377. In Leicestershire as a whole about ten per cent of the village families of 1524-5 had persisted in the same place since 1377-81,[1] and our detailed survey of Wigston families agrees roughly with this figure. Here, in 1524-5, eight or ten families out of seventy had persisted since the fourteenth century; about six out of every seven had come in since 1377. Even if we allow generously for persistent families whose surname had changed in the interval, so that they appear to be newcomers but in fact are not, we are safe in saying that by the early sixteenth century more than two families in three had come in during the preceding four or five generations. During the fifteenth century there was an almost complete change in the village population, such as perhaps no other century could show until the nineteenth. After this great re-shuffle, with its accompanying changes in the social structure – the 'gentilman', for example, is a new phenomenon in Wigston – the pattern crystallised and the life of the peasant community resumed, by and large, its massive stability, conservatism, and continuity, until the industrial changes of the late seventeenth century and the early eighteenth began to break it up once more.

---

[1] Hoskins, *Essays in Leicestershire History*, 132.

V

THE MANORS AND THE LAND, 1500-1606

The Village and its Fields

The year 1500 is an arbitrary date, but it marks the opening of the sixteenth century in the strictly chronological sense and, more important, it also sees the beginnings of a greater volume of records which give us a fuller picture of the village after the comparative dearth and silence of the fifteenth century. We therefore begin where the thin trickle of record material resumes its flow, growing into a steady stream as the century goes on; and we end it in the year 1606, the year which saw the final break-up of the manorial system in Wigston and the selling-off to the inhabitants of all the lands that still remained in the lords' hands.

Wigston in the year 1500 was still a large village, one of the largest in Leicestershire, though much smaller in numbers than it had been in the fourteenth century. It now had a little more than half the population of four generations earlier. In 1377 there had probably been 120 households in the village; now there were not more than 70.[1]

Leicestershire was still, as it had been since the eleventh century, one of the most thickly peopled counties of England, with villages and hamlets scattered over the landscape at intervals of less than two miles, often not much more than a mile apart; though already a number had vanished from the scene and only a crumbling church spire, rising above new pastures, marked where they had stood a generation or two before. But these were exceptional: the great majority of villages and hamlets recorded in Domesday Book survived. Even by the middle of the sixteenth century, when the depopulating enclosures had mostly done their work, only about one village or hamlet in five had perished. Something like sixty villages and hamlets had gone by 1650, out of a total of three hundred or so. Of those that survived, some were hardly more than hamlets (though

[1] See 'The Population of Wigston Magna, 1086-1801', in *T.L.A.S.*, xxxiii.

they might have a parish church) with eight to a dozen families, but generally they numbered between 25 and 50 households and there were half a dozen villages like Wigston with 70 families or so. The county town of Leicester, still greatly decayed, may have had 500 households in 1500, possibly fewer; Loughborough, in the north of the county, was now emerging rapidly from its medieval obscurity and had probably over 200 households;[1] Lutterworth, Shepshed, and Hinckley were all approaching the landmark of 100 families. The market-towns of Melton Mowbray and Market Harborough, for they could no longer be called villages despite the fewness of their inhabitants, were no larger than Wigston, which was undoubtedly a village, and no larger than Kibworth, Great Bowden, Wymeswold, Sileby, Bottesford, and Husbands Bosworth. Wigston had been, from the eleventh century to the early fifteenth, the largest village in the county: by 1500 it was surpassed by half a dozen places on their way to becoming market-towns, and it was one of half a dozen others that were simply large villages and always would be.

The village of Wigston lay along two main streets which met at the May Green, the hollow where Moat Street and Bullhead Street meet today. One street ran eastwards from the parish church of All Saints towards the green for a distance of about six hundred yards: the other ran northwards from the green for a similar distance as far as St. Wistan's church. The two churches, about half a mile apart if one traversed the back-lanes rather than the streets, marked the limits of the built-up area in the sixteenth century, one at the south-western corner of the village, the other at the north-eastern, as they had probably done since the early thirteenth century.[2]

---

[1] Leicester had 591 families in the return of 1563; but in 1492 'the householders on whom the King's tenth was levied did not amount to 250'. (Billson, *Medieval Leicester*, 146.) Loughborough had been ninth in size when the tax quotas of 1334 were fixed, had risen to sixth place by 1446 when the taxable capacity of other places had been severely reduced, and was second only to Leicester in population by the early sixteenth century.

[2] There are no traces of any building to the west of All Saints' church earlier than the eighteenth century. It is possible that a few houses lay beyond St. Wistan's church in late medieval times, but only a few if any at all. In 1467 the common pasture adjoined St. Wistan's churchyard and John Carter was presented at a manor court for making an enclosure at that point (B.M. Add. Ch. 46139).

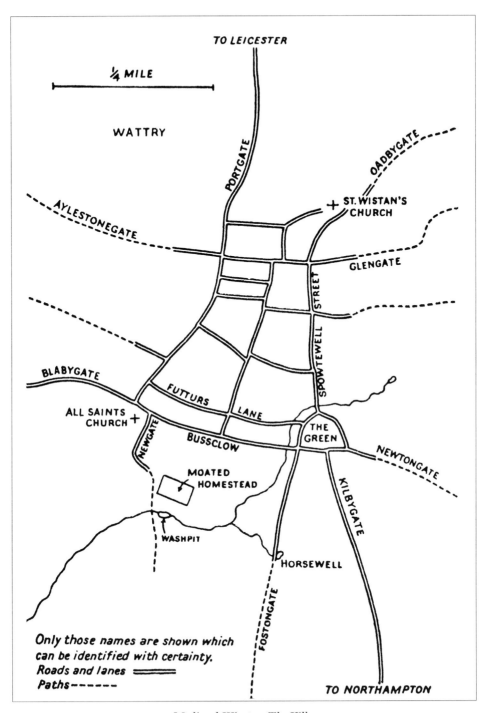

Medieval Wigston: The Village

Most of the farmhouses and cottages of the village lay along these two streets, some facing the street with their barns, stables, and outhouses at the back and their crofts at one side; others presented their gable-ends to the street and ran back along a narrow piece of ground at right angles to it, first the house, then the farm-buildings, and lastly the croft, or small enclosed pasture, over the hedge of which the open arable strips began. Farmhouses of this type represent the phase of the expansion of the village into its own fields in the twelfth and thirteenth centuries, their plan and lay-out conditioned from the first by the pre-existence of the arable selion; whereas in the heart of the original village, between the parish church and the green, we tend to find farmhouses and buildings whose plan first took shape while there was still plenty of room to spare on the street. Here therefore they occupy a squarish plot of ground rather than the narrow elongated plot of a later phase of building expansion.

Well before the sixteenth century and probably as far back as the early fourteenth, there had been building on either side of short narrow lanes, known to this day as 'ends', which ran off the two main streets for a hundred yards or so and then entered the fields. Newgate End, running south from the parish church, existed in the first decade of the fourteenth century and housed from the first some of the more important village families. Mowsley End (though not under that name) was probably opened up about the same time on the other side of the village, off Spowtewell Street,[1] and Church Nook, beside St. Wistan's church, likewise. These were all little *culs-de-sac*, ending in a gate that opened into the village fields, and each contained a small group of farmhouses and cottages.[2]

The majority of the village houses, farmhouses and cottages alike, were built of a timber frame consisting essentially of pairs of curved timbers known as forks, resting on a low plinth of rubble masonry, the space between them filled in with wattle that held the soft mud walls until they had dried out sufficiently to receive a coating of plaster inside and out. Roofs were thatched either with wheat-straw or reed,

[1] Now Bullhead Street. Also called 'the street of *Moseho*' in medieval deeds.

[2] Newgate appears in a grant of 1301 (Nichols, 379) when Simon de Wykyngeston granted a house there, with certain other property, for the foundation of a chantry in the parish church. Certain fourteenth-century Wyggeston Hospital charters suggest that houses had also been built in what are now Mowsley End and Church Nook.

mostly the former, though suitable reed was probably found in one or two places within the parish. One or two of the larger farmhouses – the 'capital messuages' of the records – seem to have been built of stone, probably unwrought stone brought from the medieval quarries of Enderby and neighbourhood, only a few miles away, the same kind of stone that was used for the rubble walls of the two churches and for the water-mill when it was rebuilt about the year 1300. Such houses were roofed, not with the common thatch, but with slates from the Swithland quarries seven miles the other side of Leicester, which had been busy ever since the middle of the thirteenth century. A lease of such a capital messuage by Richard Randull to William Clerke and Margaret his wife for a term of twelve years provides *inter alia* that 'the said William and Markett shall uphold all manner of repairs except laying of slate and great timbers.' But such houses were few: most were mud-walled, cruck-framed, and thatched: cottages of one bay generally, farmhouses usually of two bays, but occasionally three; all detached and set apart from each other, among their gardens and orchards, and for the farmhouses, their crofts.[1]

Outside the built-up area, immediately over the hedges of the village gardens and crofts, the strips of the three great open fields of the village began. Unlike many village field-systems in the Midlands, the three fields of Wigston remained undivided and uncomplicated from the time they first appear in the thirteenth-century records up to their disappearance under the parliamentary enclosure award of 1766.[2] Their names had now become fixed after some earlier changes: the north field was Mucklow Field, the east field Thythorn Hill Field, and the west field Goldhill Field. The exact boundaries of these three fields are not known, in the absence of any pre-enclosure map; but they can be roughly ascertained with painstaking research on the enclosure award (see p. 94). As to their size we cannot speak with any degree of accuracy, but since the total area of the parish was 2944 acres, and the common pastures were probably not very extensive by the sixteenth century, we may envisage each field as somewhere between

---

[1] A fuller account of the houses of the village, their plan, structure and furnishing, will be found below, pp. 283-310.

[2] The great majority of Leicestershire villages retained this simple three-field system to the end.

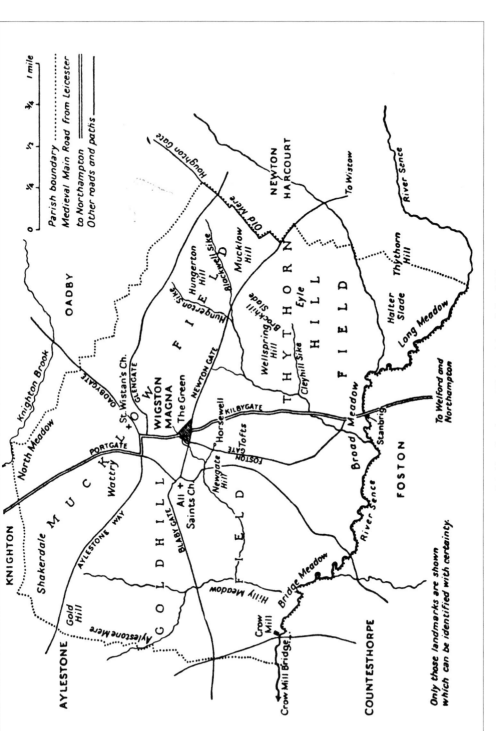

Medieval Wigston: The Parish and the fields

eight and nine hundred acres in extent, having made due allowance for the considerable meadows that lay along the streams on the north, south, and western fringes of the parish.

Scattered throughout the open fields at Wigston were strips of pasture or *leys*, intermixed with the arable. This intermixture of pasture and arable strips was found throughout the whole of Leicestershire in the sixteenth, seventeenth and eighteenth centuries and was indeed characteristic of a wider area throughout the Midlands. In addition to these separate pastures, there were remnants of the common pastures along the Old Mere, on the north-eastern frontier of the parish, but apparently little anywhere else. It seems probable that the development of *ley* strips in each of the three arable fields had largely superseded the common pastures that were still characteristic of some neighbouring parishes at least, but that some common pasture survived in Wigston is clear from seventeenth-century schedules and terriers. Meadow, too, was held separately and not in common. There was no enclosed land to be seen throughout the entire parish except the little crofts of permanent pasture, averaging half an acre to one acre in size, which adjoined every farmhouse. These are the 'ancient closes' of the enclosure award. But scattered throughout the arable fields there were probably numerous temporary enclosures of arable strips to be seen, a practice which will be referred to later in a more detailed discussion of the Wigston farmers' husbandry. Before we enter upon this discussion, however, it is necessary to say something of the manorial framework, the foundations on which the economic life of the village rested: the legal shadow behind the reality of crops and buildings, cattle and sheep, ploughs and carts.

❧ THE BREAK-UP OF THE TURVILLE MANOR ❧

The two churches whose steeples at either end of the village gave the place its distinctive name by Henry VIII's reign – 'Wigston with two steeples'[1] -were visible symbols of the two manors into which Wigston had been divided since the early years of the thirteenth century: All Saints in the earl of Oxford's manor, and St. Wistan's in the Turvile manor. In 1500 the lord of the larger manor, held of the honour of

[1] So called in a Chancery suit between 1529 and 1532, and for three hundred years afterwards.

Winchester, was John de Vere, thirteenth earl of Oxford, who had been attainted in 1475 but restored to all his former estates and manors, and more, ten years later when he fought at Bosworth as captain-general of Henry's army – 'a most valiant soldier'. The smaller manor, once held by the Champaynes, was now held by John Turvile, esquire, descendant of a family who had held lands in Leicestershire since the twelfth century.

The Turvile estate was by now substantial. They had been ancient neighbours of the Champaynes in Normanton, Croft, and Thurlaston (parishes only a few miles to the south-west of Wigston), where both families had held lands since the thirteenth century at least; and in the middle of the fifteenth century Margaret Everingham, John Turvile's grandmother, had united the Champayne and Turvile properties. Before her time the Turviles had possessed the manors of Normanton Turville (their ancestral home), Walton-on-the-Wolds in the north of the county, and Aston Flamville, which had come to them by marriage with the last of the Flamvilles towards the end of the fourteenth century, besides lesser properties. The Champaynes had held the manors of Thurlaston (Newhall), Croft, Stoke Golding (where they had built that beautiful church in the second quarter of the fourteenth century), and Wigston. Thus John Turvile had succeeded in 1474 to a handsome estate of seven manors in Leicestershire, and was one of the richest of the old Leicestershire squirearchy.

In Wigston his manorial rights were concentrated in the north-eastern part of the village: that is, most of the farmhouses and cottages that lined the east side of Bullhead Street (to use its modern name), or that lay in the *culs-de-sac* running off it, were appurtenant in one way or another to the Turvile manor, whether as freeholds or copyholds. Similarly, the farmhouses and Cottages along the street (now Moat Street) up to All Saints' church and on the west side of Bullhead Street, where some of the demesne lay, were mostly appurtenant to the earl of Oxford's manor, though in both streets there were houses, with lands going with them in the fields, that had been far removed from the original manorial nucleus by successive grants and re-grants. The manorial structure of Wigston was exceedingly complicated, as one finds in proceeding from house to house along the streets, and as one would expect from the continual subinfeudation of properties in medieval times. Fortunately, however, the economic and social history of the village can be written largely in terms of the two principal manors and it is to these that we shall confine our attention.

A manor can only be defined geographically up to a point, and when we say that the Turvile manor was centred upon Bullhead Street and its 'ends' there are clearly further considerations involved. For the farm, of which the dwelling-house, barns and stables, yard and croft, lay on the street itself, had arable, meadow, pasture, and common pasture going with it, or appurtenant to it to use the language of the legal records, all over the parish and not just in one particular part of it. The farmlands were scattered more or less uniformly throughout the three fields and in the meadows around them, so that, as we have already seen, the actual lands, as distinct from the homesteads, of the two manors lay intermingled everywhere.

No seigneurial authority, it has already been said, controlled the economic life of villages under divided lordship.[1] The men of the village had to control their own economic affairs, make their own rules for the management of their fields, appoint their own officers to administer the rules and to deal with offenders. Such a village meeting is well evidenced at Wymeswold in the north of Leicestershire. Here the regulations for the management of the fields were made 'with the common assent of the whole vill' in the presence of the three lords between whom the village was divided, and fines for infringements of the rules went to the parish church.[2] Such a village meeting existed at Wigston also, certainly in the sixteenth century, and probably earlier though we have no earlier record of it. In an Exchequer suit over the tithes of wool in Wigston in 1602 it was deposed by several villagers that it was 'an ancient custom and order' for the inhabitants or the greater part of them to meet together yearly 'and agree upon divers and sundry orders and bylawes for the good orderinge and preservacions of the proffitts of their lands and Commons within the ffields of Wigston'.[3] The fact that the village and not the manor was the essential unit of organisation at Wigston is one of profound importance for its social history: and when the manors were

---

[1] See above, p. 63.

[2] *H.M.C. Lord Middleton*, 106-9. The regulations are not dated but are assigned by the editor to *c.* 1425.

[3] P.R.O. Exchequer Depositions by Commission (E 134),44–45 Eliz., Mich. 16.

dismembered between 1586 and 1606, and manor courts ceased to be held, the village and the village officers became even more important as the only government on the spot.

The Turvile manor was the first to go, sold off between 1586 and 1588. Of its structure we know very little, in the absence of any court rolls, extents, or surveys. When John Turvile died in 1506 his Wigston property was described as the manor and 23 virgates of land. If this figure is accurate, and it bears some signs of exactitude, it may tell us a little. The 23 virgates probably relate to lands other than those already granted away in freehold farms and subject only to a small chief rent, of which we know incidentally from the Wyggeston Hospital records there were several.[1] They represent the copyhold lands only.

Sir William Turvile, son of John, ruled over his seven manors and other lands from 1506 until his death in 1549, whereupon the estate was divided. Normanton, Thurlaston, and Croft went to John, his eldest son; and Aston, Walton, Stoke, and Wigston went to George, his second son. George Turvile ruled from 1549 until 1562, when his son Henry succeeded him in his four manors and also at Normanton, which had previously gone to the elder branch. What happened next we do not know. The Turviles died out at the end of the eighteenth century and the family papers have vanished. But the Leicestershire fines of the 1570's and 1580's reveal Henry Turvile selling the ancestral lands at a great pace. In 1572 he sold off the manor of Walton-on-the-Wolds, where his family had owned land since the twelfth century, to Nicholas Sayvyle; in 1586-7 he sold off the manor of Wigston to his tenants; in 1591 he parted with Stoke Golding to Sir John Harington; and in 1601 he apparently mortgaged his home manor of Aston Flamville to Walter Hastings, esq., for £500. Only Normanton Turvile was apparently left untouched.[2]

In the absence of detailed information from family papers we can only surmise that the reason for Henry Turvile's dismemberment of most

---

[1] For example, a farm of about 32 acres (one virgate) with a house and buildings that can be identified as having stood on the north side of Mowsley End, had been granted away by the chief lord at a very early date and came to the Wyggeston Hospital in 1521, subject only to a chief rent to the Turviles of 1½d. per annum. The Hospital owned other farms in the Turvile manor which had belonged in earlier centuries to peasant families.

[2] Fines recorded in Farnham, *Leics. Medieval Village Notes*, for Walton-on-the-Wolds and Aston Flamville; in Farnham MSS. for Wigston; and in *T.L.A.S.*, xiv, 217, for Stoke Golding.

of his handsome estate was that common to many landed families in the second half of the sixteenth century: a rapidly rising price-level which increased the household expenses inordinately, coupled with an income derived largely from copyhold lands, which were subject to customary medieval rents that could not be raised or converted to more profitable leasehold (the copyhold tenants at Wigston would have been tough opponents for him, judging by what happened on the Oxford manor). And possibly there was the usual Elizabethan extravagance to add to the score. The building of a fine house at Normanton, probably by Henry Turvile, helps to account for the sales no doubt, but other squires were building, too, and did not get into this mess.[1]

Whatever the reason, the farmers of Wigston benefited: several hundred acres of land came into the market all at once. The two largest purchasers were men from outside – Ralph Freman, gent., and Robert Hall-and another smaller purchaser, Robert Wylde, was a newcomer also; but the remaining thirteen purchasers listed in the fines between Michaelmas 1586 and Michaelmas 1587 were Wigston men. Some were fairly recent arrivals, it is true, but most of them were of some long standing in the place (Vann, Johnson, Dand, White, Frere, Langton, Browne and Pawley).

There are fifteen fines and sixteen purchasers are recorded in them: but the other information yielded by the fines is wholly misleading and must be handled with great caution. The acreages recorded in each transaction are greatly exaggerated; the purchase price recorded is clearly a token sum as it is the same (£40) whatever the size of the farm;[2] and one suspects that in some instances two separate fines recording identical acreages of arable, meadow and pasture may refer to a joint purchase of one and the same property.[3]

[1] The old hall at Normanton, now wholly destroyed by fire, was said to have been 'a fine Elizabethan mansion' (White's *Directory* (1863), 718). As Henry Turvile reigned over the estates from 1562 to 1616 he was presumably its builder.

[2] The 'consideration' given in a fine was twenty times the annual value of the property as stated on the writ of covenant. But 'although it is safe to say that the fictitious consideration represents twenty times the maximum sworn annual value', one cannot assume that the sworn annual value is highly accurate (*Abstracts of Survey Feet of Fines, 1509-58*, ed. by C.A.F. Meekings, Surrey Record Society, xix, Introduction, xxii-xxiii).

[3] There are other grave defects in fines as a class of record. Though they usually relate to a straightforward sale of property they very often conceal mortgages, marriage settlements, or settlements in trust and not a sale, especially in families owning a good deal of landed property. They must always be read therefore in the light of subsequent documents, when their true purport may become apparent.

If we add together the acreages of arable, meadow, pasture, furze and heath recorded in the fifteen transactions we arrive at a total of nearly 1,700 acres disposed of by Henry Turvile. This is clearly an impossible figure. We know that he sold at the most the twenty-three virgates which had belonged to his great-grandfather at the beginning of the century.

A clue comes to hand, fortunately, in two wills – those of Maurice Bloxsom (1590) and John Whyte (1587). Maurice Bloxsom leaves to his son Richard 'all this my house and homsted and all the Three Quarterns of the yardland with all the appurtenances unto them in any way belonging which I lately bought of Mr. Henry Turvyll of Aston Flamvyle Esquiere'.[1] Now we are dealing at Wigston with a virgate or yardland of thirty-two acres. Maurice Bloxsom's will suggests therefore that he purchased about twenty-four acres from Mr. Turvile. The fine speaks of 25 acres of land, 5 of meadow, 14 of pasture, and 10 of furze and heath and common of pasture, a total of 54 acres, but only the first figure is relevant to the transaction. Similarly, John Whyte in his will dated 5 November 1587 asks his son Thomas to 'make a release of one half yardland which I sold last to Thomas Boulter', and the subsequent fine speaks of 15 acres of land, 2 of meadow, 3 of pasture and common of pasture in Wigston – 20 acres in all. Here too we see that the half yardland is accounted for in the fine by the acreage of 'land' alone.

To clinch the matter, the marriage settlement made 4 November 1592 'between Robert Freer the elder of Wigston, husbandman and Suzan Brabson widow late the wife of William Brabson of Boseworthe husbandman, deceased', in consideration of a marriage 'already had and solemnised' between Robert Freer and Anne, daughter of Susan Brabson, refers to 'the yardland lately purchased' by Robert Freer from Henry Turvile, esquire, 'as appears by deed dated 14 June 28 Elizabeth [1586]'.[2] Turning to the fines again, we see that the transaction is recorded as 30 acres of land, 6 acres of meadow, 16 of pasture, 10 of furze and heath and common of pasture. Here, too, we have the yardland accounted for in

---

[1] L.C.R.O., wills 1590. Wherever wills and inventories are quoted hereafter it should be understood that they are the MS. records lying in this Office.
[2] L.R.O., 9 D.43/192.

the acreage of 'land' alone, bearing in mind that in dealing with a 32-acre unit we cannot expect a mathematical exactitude from any record.

Whatever the explanation may be of the acreages of meadow, pasture, furze and heath inserted in the fines, it is clear from the above remarks that we shall be near the truth if we take account only of the 'land' acreages recorded in the fifteen fines. We have then a picture of fourteen farms sold off, totalling 711 acres. This agrees fairly closely with the assumption that Henry Turvile sold the twenty-three virgates recorded in the inquisition of 1506, which, at thirty-two acres to a virgate, would have amounted to 736 acres in all.

To sum it all up, Henry Turvile sold off his manor of Wigston in 1586-7 to sixteen purchasers, nearly all men on the spot and some of them probably sitting tenants, as we know they lived and farmed on this side of the village.[1] The actual property disposed of consisted of fourteen farms, covering 711 acres between them, and ranging in size from the 20-acre farm sold to Thomas Pawley to the 120-acre farm sold to Ralph Freman, gent. The complete list is as follows:

Purchasers of Turvile lands in Wigston, 1586-7

Ralph Freman	120 acres
Robert Hall	120 acres
William Johnson	80 acres
Robert Wylde and Robert Browne (joint)	70 acres
John White	60 acres
Thomas Boulter	40 acres
John Cartwright and William Langton (joint)	36 acres
John Vann	30 acres
John Dann	30 acres
Peter Ragg	30 acres
Robert Frere	30 acres

---

[1] Of the thirteen local men who bought, Pawley, White, Vann, Johnson, Langton, Bloxsam, Browne, and Ragg are all names that appear in the Duchy of Lancaster court rolls between 1562 and 1587, and Frere probably lived on this side also. Eight or nine of the purchasers therefore may have been sitting tenants.

Maurice Bloxsom. .. .. 25 acres

Robert Cartwright .. .. 20 acres

Thomas Pawley .. .. 20 acres

So ended the Turvile manor in Wigston. Its sale brought two or three new families into the village who had not previously lived there (Freman, Hall, and Wylde); added to the small estates of families who were already freeholders such as the Freres, the Pawleys, and the Danns; and raised some tenants to the status of small freeholders for the first time as far as we can discover. The ranks of the peasant proprietors received a further accession of strength in time for the final phase of the struggle in the other manor.

❧ THE BREAK-UP OF THE OXFORD MANOR ❧

The history of the Oxford manor in the sixteenth century is not as straightforward as that of the Turviles. A number of changes occurred in the middle decades of the century (between 1540 and 1577) which are not entirely clear. Indeed, it seems that they may have been confusing to men at the time, in view of the statements made in two Chancery suits between the lord and his tenants, as we shall see.

The thirteenth earl of Oxford died in 1513 and was succeeded by his nephew, who married Anne, daughter of Thomas Howard, duke of Norfolk. He died in 1526 without issue, leaving two surviving sisters and co-heirs.[1] This failure to produce male heirs ended, among much else, the long tenure of the manor of Wigston by the Veres, for the two sisters took all or some of their great estates into other families. Elizabeth, the elder, married Sir Anthony Wingfield of Letheringham, co. Suffolk, and Dorothy married John, third Lord Latimer. On March 13, 1531-2 an award was made as to the Vere inheritance, and an act of Parliament in the same year settled the manor of Wigston upon Anne, widow of the fourteenth earl, as part of her dower. On February 6, 1540-1, John Nevill, son and heir apparent of Lord Latimer and son and heir of Dorothy (Vere) his wife, had licence to

---

[1] The following account of the descent of the principal manor of Wigston is based in the main on the articles in the *Complete Peerage* on the earldom of Oxford and the barons Latimer (Nevill), and on the article in *D.N.B.* on Sir Anthony Wingfield.

enter on his mother's inheritance, she being dead. This inheritance by now included, apparently, a moiety or half of the principal manor of Wigston, the other moiety having gone to Elizabeth, wife of Sir Anthony Wingfield, a partition of interest which helps to explain some of the confusion which is apparent in the affairs of the manor about this time.

The fourth Lord Latimer succeeded his father in 1543 but died without male heirs on April 22, 1577, leaving four daughters and co-heirs, one of whom, Elizabeth, carried her moiety of the manor of Wigston to Sir John Danvers of Dauntsey, co. Wilts., in marriage. Meanwhile, Sir Robert Wingfield, eldest son and heir of Sir Anthony and Elizabeth his wife, had recovered possession of the other moiety in 1577, and in 1585 sold it to Sir John Danvers, who already held a moiety in the right of his wife. Thus the two moieties, separated more than forty years before, were united once more.[1]

The fine of Michaelmas 1585 describes the property as a moiety of the manor of Wigston, 30 messuages, 12 tofts, 1 watermill, 1 windmill, 4 dovecotes, 40 gardens, 800 acres of land, 140 acres of meadow, 300 acres of pasture, 40 acres of wood, 120 acres of furze and heath, 30 acres of moor, 100 acres of alderbed (*alneti*), £7 rent, and common pasture in Knighton, Belgrave, Laughton, Wigston and the town of Leicester, for a consideration of £320 sterling.[2] Again, the acreages cited and the consideration are wholly misleading, but it is possible to arrive at a truer estimate of the area involved in the sale from later documents and this will be discussed in due course.

The frequent changes of lordship in the principal manor of Wigston between about 1540 and 1585 – Vere, Latimer, Wingfield, and Danvers – are not solely of interest for manorial history, that stronghold of the antiquarian. They are of importance also for the economic historian, inasmuch as they introduce into the manor, for the first time for several

---

[1] Cf. Nichols, 375, who says that 'in 1577 the escheat was directed to be taken off a moiety of the manor of Wigston, which was to be delivered back to Sir Robert Wingfield and his wife'. We do not learn why the Wingfield moiety had escheated to the Crown. Nichols misprints the date as 1557, but it is clear that it should be 1577.

[2] L.R.O., 9D.43/192. The same bundle of deeds contains a conveyance dated 12 May 1585, by Edmund Bedingfield of Oxborough, co. Norfolk, esq. to Sir John Danvers, of a moiety of the manor of Wigston. The significance of this document is not clear. Possibly Bedingfield had some claim on the manor through his wife which required a formal release.

centuries, a series of changes which challenged the ancient customs of the manor and produced confusion and strife between the lords and the customary tenants. Whether or not this confusion was deliberately exploited by the tenants, as one lord succeeded another, for their own ends, or whether it was the new lords who were trying to upset the ancient customs of the manor for their own profit – for Wigston, as we shall see, was decidedly medieval in its rents and wholly undervalued in the eyes of a sixteenth-century landowner – we cannot tell with certainty. The legal records of the disputes are not complete and even if they were one does not arrive at the final truth about human motives in the law courts: and we have no sixteenth-century court rolls for the Oxford manor which might have illuminated the obscurity.

The main issue was joined in 1588 between eight of the customary tenants and copyholders, representing the whole thirty-one on the manor, and Sir John Danvers and Dame Elizabeth his wife.[1] It was a battle over the most vital question for all customary tenants: the nature of their copyholds and thence of the rights that flowed from it, a battle fought over so many manors in the Tudor law-courts. There had indeed been a preliminary skirmish at Wigston several years earlier, when John, lord Latimer, brought a suit in Chancery some time between 1558 and 1577 against two of the customary tenants[2] over a piece of property which he claimed was part of the old demesne land of the manor and which they claimed to occupy by copy of the manor court roll. The defendants asserted that the custom of the manor extended over the former demesne lands as well as over the indisputable copyhold lands, that they could hold such land by copy like any other, and that they could surrender it and get it regranted in the manor court to whomsoever they pleased as they could their other copyholds.

Whatever the upshot of Lord Latimer's dispute with his two tenants the trouble persisted and grew, and when Sir John Danvers bought the manor in 1585 he found himself faced with the same claims by all the customary tenants. For two years they wrangled over the customs of the

---

[1] *Chancery Proceedings in the Reign of Elizabeth.* (P.R.O. C.2/W.12/no. 60.) Dated 1585 in the calendar, but the Chancery Decree Rolls show that it was put down to be heard on 24 November, 31 Elizabeth [1588].

[2] P.R.O. Chancery Proceedings, Series II, 1558-79, C.3/109/32. The suit is undated but cannot be later than 1577 when Lord Latimer died.

manor until in 1588 the thirty-one customary tenants banded together, nominated eight of their number to speak for them, and commenced a suit in Chancery against their new lord and his wife.

The bill of complaint recites that the copyholders had enjoyed their tenements according to the custom of the manor from time out of mind. The custom at Wigston was that copyhold tenure was copyhold of inheritance with a fixed entry fine. This fine amounted to only one-quarter of the yearly rent. There were two sorts of land on the manor—bond land and berry land, in other words village land and demesne land. Bond land paid a yearly rent of 13s. 4d. a yardland, berry land only 10s. a yardland. Both bondland and berry land could be demised by copy of court roll, and had been from time beyond memory, to any persons willing to take them. The complainants gave several instances in detail of this ancient custom, by which among other things a customary tenant could transfer a copyhold farm to his son-in-law as part of a marriage settlement, or a widow could transfer such a farm to her second husband. All these lands, bondland and demesne land alike, were taken *sibi et suis* and enjoyed practically as freehold. As a consequence of this belief, copyholders could transfer any such lands in the manor court to any other person, whether resident in the manor or outside it, as though they were their own to dispose of. As a result also, copyholders claimed and had exercised the right to fell trees upon their farms in order to repair their buildings, and also to take the small wood for the repair of farm implements (ploughbote, cartbote, etc.). They also claimed to take freely the loppings of willow and thorns upon their farms for burning and other use. They claimed, too, the right to enclose their customary lands in the open fields with hedges, ditches, or quick-sets, and to keep them in severalty until Lammas Day when they were thrown open again for the exercise of common pasture rights. Widows enjoyed their husbands' estate on the same terms as their husbands had done, and could surrender it to the use of any other person to hold *sibi et suis* as 'a perfect estate in fee simple at the will of the lord'.

Sir John Danvers, it was alleged, was seeking to upset all these ancient customs of the manor, and was refusing to admit fresh tenants on these terms. He denied that copyholders had any such estates and had leased the surrendered lands, or part of them, to two outsiders who had begun to evict some of the tenants and had begun a lawsuit in the court of Queen's Bench against others.

The answer of Sir John Danvers and his wife was to assert that the Wigston copyholders had not 'an estate of inheritance in fee simple' but an estate for one life only, even in the bondland or customary land. As for the berry land, this was the old demesne land of the manor and was demisable only at the will of the lord and not otherwise, though the defendants admitted that a practice had recently grown up of demising berry land by copy of court roll and that the words *habendum sibi et suis* were recited on such occasions. Nevertheless, all this was 'contrary to the custom of the manor as heretofore used'. As for refusing to admit new tenants into the surrendered lands, they recited several breaches of the custom – such as letting customary lands for more than a year without licence from the lord, the unlicensed exchange of lands, temporary enclosure of lands in severalty, tenements in disrepair, trees felled without permission, and all the usual allegations of that kind – which allowed them to seize the customary tenements into their own hands again and to lease them as they pleased. It was even alleged that customary tenants had sold considerable parcels of demesne and customary land to each other. The defendants also said that the form of surrendering and regranting copyhold land as recited in the bill of complaint was not lawful or valid unless made before the bailiff of the manor. Nor was the entry fine a certain one; it was arbitrary at the will of the lord. Since the customary tenants had no estate of inheritance in the bondland, they also had no right to cut timber and enclose their copyhold lands in the open fields.

The struggle at Wigston has most of the familiar features of the widespread struggle that was going on all over England between lords and tenants in these years. On the one hand we have customary tenants who claim copyholds of inheritance with all the rights that flow therefrom, who pay a fixed and ancient rent more appropriate to the thirteenth century, and who claim to pay only a small and ancient fine. On the other hand we have a new lord who has purchased the manor (no doubt at a price appropriate to the rising price-level of the 1580's but we do not certainly know this) and who is anxious to sweep away this rabbit warren of medieval rents, customs and services, and to exploit its full economic possibilities in the form of leases at rents that bear some relation to the real annual value of the land. For the customary rents paid at Wigston had been fixed long before and represented a value per acre such as one finds in medieval inquisitions and extents. The rent of 13s. 4d. for a yardland of bondland appears as far back as a court roll of 1467[1] and was no doubt fixed long before that. It represents a rent of a fraction over sixpence per acre, which is the average valuation of arable land in late thirteenth- and fourteenth-century inquisitions and extents in Leicestershire.[2] So far as the 'Berry land' was concerned, the rent alleged to be payable by tenants was even lower: only five-pence an acre. Moreover, the Wigston tenants made a much more extensive claim on these lands than even the general run of copyholders of inheritance, for they claimed estates of inheritance by copy of court roll not only in the ancient customary lands of the manor but in the former demesne as well.

There can be little doubt – and the customary tenants half admit this in their Replication – that the berry lands represented the ancient demesne of the manor. Their very name, a corruption of *burh*, would suggest this, even if we had no other evidence; but we also know from the solitary court roll of 1467 that the Hallcroft, in dispute in both the Chancery suits we have been considering, was part of the demesne lands at that date: 'John Sherman rector of the church comes and takes of the lord a croft called Hallecroft of the demesne lands late in the tenure of William Clerk at 8s. a year. He does fealty and pledges William Clerk and William Palley and gives 12d. fine.' It seems clear that in the terms 'berry land' and 'bond land' we have the fundamental distinction between the former demesne land of the manor and the village land, and that by the middle decades of the sixteenth century this distinction had become obliterated, at least in the eyes of the customary tenants, and to some extent, apparently, in the eyes of the lord's officers on the spot who had done things that the lord found difficult to explain; and

---

[1] At a court held November 1467 'William Normanton comes and takes from the lord a messuage and one virgate of land late in the tenure of Roger Normanton at 13s. 4d. a year and one virgate called "le Beryland" late in the tenure of John Chapman. He does fealty and pledges William Drene and Roger Wodehale and gives 20d. as a fine'. (B.M., Add. Ch. 46139.)

[2] Farnham, vols. i-vi *passim*. An inquisition ad quod damnum in 1301 valued four virgates held by Simon de Wykyngeston in Wigston at '13s. 4d. for each virgate in all issues'. (Farnham, i, 274.) In 1412 a messuage and virgate of land in Wigston were leased for three years at an annual rent of 13s. 4d. (*W.H.R.*, no. 989).

it seems likely, too, that the frequent changes of lordship in the manor after 1540, after centuries of comparative stability at the top, helped to make the confusion worse.

There are other points of interest arising from this suit of 1588 which may be dealt with more appropriately in discussing the farming practice of the Wigston peasantry in the following chapter: our present purpose is to follow through the manorial struggle to its end, which came within the next twenty years. It is most unfortunate that we do not know the legal decision in this suit. The decree of the court, made 14 November 1588, dismissed the suit out of the High Court of Chancery as being 'more meete to be tried and decyded by the course of the common law than in this courte' and it was referred to the assizes at Leicester, of which no record has survived. Whatever the decision may have been, it does not seem to have been satisfactory to the Danvers family, for in 1606 they sold off the manor to the tenants. The mechanism of this transaction, and the extent of it, are known to us from another suit in Chancery in 1623 between Sir William Faunt of Foston (who had bought certain manorial rights in Wigston) and twenty-eight of the villagers, over their refusal to do suit to the mills any longer and other troubles which we need not enter into here.[1]

By 1606 the principal manor had descended to Henry, lord Danvers of Dauntsey. He, together with Sir Edmund Carey of London, Knight, lady Elizabeth his wife, and John Danvers of London, esquire, 'being seised of the manor'[2] agreed with the copyhold tenants that they should purchase the freehold and inheritance of their copyhold farms, cottages and mills 'with all the ancient rights customs (etc.) to the same belonging in as large and ample a manner as had always been enjoyed'. For this purpose the copyholders were advised by counsel that all the property in question should be conveyed 'unto four indifferent men and theire heires in speciall truste and confidence' who should afterwards

---

[1] Chancery Proceedings. Series II. James I. P.R.O. C/3. 348, No. 5. This suit is referred to more fully in Chapter VII. In this suit the 28 defendants reiterate their assertion that they had always been 'tenants of inheritance by copy of court roll' before the sale of the manor, which suggests that they had been successful in a substantial part of their case, if not all of it, in the suit of 1588.

[2] Elizabeth, widow of Sir John Danvers (d. 1594) married, as her second husband, Sir Edmund Carey. Hence the appearance of his name in the fines and conveyances. She is the Dame Elizabeth Carey whose superb tomb by Nicholas Stone is to be seen at Stowe Nine Churches, Northants.

convey to each of the copyholders the freehold and inheritance of his tenement 'with all the ancient benefits, priviledges, usages and customs thereof according to the said trust'. By a deed dated 10 July 1606 the property was conveyed by Lord Danvers and the others to Thomas Lawe, gent., Robert Fryer, William Johnson and Walter Chamberlain- all of them substantial farmers living in the village. The fine, made in November of that year, describes the property as 'the manor of Wykingeston alias Wygston Magna, and 40 messuages, 20 tofts, 3 mills, 10 dovehouses, 40 gardens, 1200 acres of land, 300 acres of meadow, 400 acres of pasture, 4 acres of wood, 100 acres of furze and heath, 100s. rent and common of pasture for all kind of cattle and view of frankpledge in Wygeston', and the consideration is given as £800. The acreages given are again unreal; nor does the consideration bear any relation to the purchase price.[1]

Twenty of the copyholders purchased their farms from the trustees, farms which varied from a quarter-yardland (going with a cottage) up to 2, 2¼, 2½, and 3¼ yardlands, a total of exactly 30 yardlands in all. Some of these may have purchased by means of a mortgage as the record speaks of 'collaterall conveyance' in some cases. Seven other copyholders did not buy their holdings but remained leaseholders, their estates assured to them by the trustees. Their total holding amounted to only 2½ yardlands. It is possible that Walter Chamberlain, one of the four trustees, represented a twenty-eighth copyholder, but he had sold his interest in the matter to Sir William Faunt in 1613. At any rate the total of twenty-seven or twenty-eight copyholders in 1606 agrees fairly closely with the thirty-one who had fought the suit nearly twenty years earlier.

It is certain that some of these copyholders were freeholders before ever they purchased their copyhold farms in the principal manor, just as some of the men who purchased land at the breakup of the Turvile manor were already freeholders in their own right. But it is difficult to be precise about this: some members of the same family might be freeholders,

---

[1] The Chancery suit of 1623 shows that 32½ yardlands were involved in the sales to copyholders, or about 1040 acres at thirty-two acres to the yardland. The 'consideration' is calculated on a sworn annual value of £40 (see above, p. 23), which is itself unreal. £40 was the value assigned to the manor when the countess of Oxford received it on her marriage *c.* 1240.

others not, and we cannot always be sure which men we are dealing with among these obscure peasant families. Of the twenty copyholders who bought their farms in 1606, at least five can be identified as being already freeholders and there may well have been several more.

Our information about the freeholders of the manor in the sixteenth century is meagre. For the period 1200-1500 the Wyggeston Hospital records supplied a considerable amount of information about this class of tenant at Wigston, but this source dries up very early in the sixteenth century with the endowment of the Hospital, as we shall shortly see, and the grants and conveyances of the medieval free peasant are replaced by leases from the Hospital. No comparable source of information about the free tenants exists for the sixteenth century. On the other hand, our medieval sources were singularly barren in references to the customary tenants and it is not until the middle decades and later of the sixteenth century that we learn anything about these as a class. The fact is that after 1500 there is a complete change in the nature of our sources for the economic history of the village and we must be careful not to allow this to alter unduly the character of our history. The free tenants loomed large in the medieval manor and it is quite certain that they were still a numerous and important class in the Tudor village though they have left less trace in the surviving records.

We know that certain families of free tenants either died out (like Ball, Godwin, Fawkes and Hutte) or moved elsewhere, like the Randulls and the Swans, but others took their place. There is no reason to believe that the amount of land held freely by peasant families diminished during the prolonged depression of the fifteenth century, when the records are scanty and our information correspondingly meagre, though it seems likely that the freehold land may have become concentrated into the hands of fewer families. If we look at the total sales of land involved in the break-up of the two manors in 1586 and in 1606 we find that about 1750 acres were sold off, representing all the customary and demesne lands. Henry Turvile sold off about 711 acres, Lord Danvers about 1040. The total area of the township was 2944 acres, according to the earliest accurate measurements of the nineteenth century, so that we are left with about twelve hundred acres of land already held freely in the two manors and hence not included in these sales. Of this about one hundred acres (three virgates) had belonged of old to the rectory glebe, and another 173 acres had passed from peasant ownership in 1521 to the Wyggeston Hospital, henceforward to be leased out. Thus, in the early sixteenth century (before the endowment of the Hospital) about eleven hundred acres of the township were held freely by native peasant families for the greater part; 100 acres belonged to the church; and the remainder, some seventeen hundred and fifty acres, represented the old demesne lands and the customary lands of the manors. After the break-up of the two manors, in 1586 and 1606, the peasant freeholders received an enormous accession of strength, for most if not all of this new freehold land came into the hands of the resident families of the village, the existing copyhold and free tenants.

As to the names of these peasant proprietors we can only use the few Wyggeston Hospital records that fall into the first quarter of the sixteenth century,[1] and such other occasional pieces of evidence as we find elsewhere (fines, conveyances, etc.). We may assume, as we did for the medieval charters, that the peasant witnesses to the early sixteenth-century charters are free tenants, especially as in several instances there is other evidence to prove this. In this way we recover the names of some twenty families who hold land freely in the village at this date and in some families (such as Herrick and Pawley) there are two or three such freeholders, making the total number of free tenants something well over twenty. Of this total of twenty families, about ten (Herrick, White, Smith, Astell, Clerk, Pawley, Wallis, Symon, Milner and Palmer) could be regarded as of long standing-going back the best part of a hundred years, that is – and five of the ten (Herrick, Smith, Astell, Symon and Palmer) go back as free tenants to the early fourteenth century. Four of them indeed go well back into the middle decades of the thirteenth century when the village records begin. The remaining ten of the twenty peasant landowning families were, so far as we know, comparative newcomers to the village.[2] These were Langton, Frere, Watts, Ferres, Mereman, Pailton,

---

[1] *W.H.R.*, nos. 1050-1071.

[2] The absence of a complete poll tax return for either 1377 or 1381, and of a series of court rolls or other manorial records for the fifteenth century, must make one chary of statements like this, but certainly it seems to be true of most of the ten families in question.

Burgess, Catton, Leed and Wraske, who do not make their appearance in Wigston before the second half of the fifteenth century.

The consolidation of tenements by free tenants of the manor had been going on, as we saw, throughout the fourteenth and fifteenth centuries. When William Wigston of Leicester, merchant of the Staple and remote descendant of the Wykyngeston family who had left their native village for the town in the 1340's, desired to found and endow a hospital for twelve poor people in Leicester he bought two blocks of property in Wigston, one of a farmhouse and cottage together with 1½ virgates of arable and meadow, and the other of three messuages, four crofts, and four yardlands of arable belonging thereto. The former property represented the union of the old Balle and Faukes lands, inherited by John Penne, who in 1452-3 had sold them to John Love, resident bailiff of the earl of Oxford in Wigston. From him they came to Joan his daughter, who in 1501 sold them to William Bulwardyne of Claverley in Shropshire. He in turn sold the property in 1516 to William Wigston for £24.[1] The second of William Wigston's purchases had been the Randull or Randolf accumulation. Richard Randull of Leicester, grocer, who died about 1480, was a direct descendant of Rannulf the clerk who had bought two virgates of land from Hugh de Champayne in Wigston *c.* 1200. Besides his capital messuage and four yardlands, with tofts and crofts to the same messuage belonging in the duchy fee, Richard Randull also possessed another messuage and half a yardland in the Winchester fee, which did not come into William Wigston's purchase, All this property descended to Elizabeth, Richard Randull's daughter and heir, who married Richard Kent of Kirby Muxloe, co. Leics. In 1509 she released all her lands in Wigston to Thomas Kent, her younger son, who in 1514 sold all but the messuage and half yardland to William Wigston for £37. To complete the transaction, William Wigston put both his purchases in trust in 1521 for the use of the hospital, which thus acquired a holding of 173 acres 35 perches in the village and fields of Wigston.

Just as the Bulwardyne purchase represented the accumulation of the Balle and Faukes lands, united in the hands of John Penne, so Richard Randull's capital messuage and farm – the largest farm in the village – seems to have been the result of the throwing together of three or

---

[1] *W.H.R.,* nos. 1026 1028, 1030, 1050 1067 and 1068.

four medieval farms and a number of smaller parcels of land. The description of his property in 1514 as 'three messuages and a croft with the tenements, and another croft called Morwde Randyles Crofte, and a croft called Redlys Crofte with another croft called Swetynggs, and four yards lands arable in the fields … to the said messuages and crofts pertaining' strongly suggests that besides uniting with another Randull property (possibly bringing together again the two virgates separated in the early thirteenth century) the Randulls had acquired the farms, each of the 'normal' yardland, belonging to the Swetyngs and the Redleys. Not all this was farmed together, however. The 'capital messuage' had 3¼ yardlands going with it and continued to be leased as such by the Hospital throughout the sixteenth century: a farm of about one hundred acres.

At the other end of the scale there were farms, or small holdings, of a quarter yardland or even less (perhaps 5 to 8 acres) going with cottages and often held by the village craftsmen in conjunction with their businesses. Between these two extremes there is some evidence from the sixteenth-century wills and inventories to suggest that the 'normal' farm of one yardland was still fairly common in Wigston,[1] as indeed it was in a great number of Leicestershire villages. The medieval framework of landholding was still plainly visible, though becoming increasingly obscured as the sixteenth century went on: and the break-up of the two manors at the end of the century, with the opportunities of purchase that it afforded to the more acquisitive and energetic peasant families, finally wiped out the old pattern.

The Chancery suit of 1622-3 gives us a list of the twenty men who had bought their farms from the Danvers:

William Lawe	2	yardlands
Robert Fryer	3¼	"
Henry Fox	2½	"
William Abbot the younger	2	"
William Johnson the younger	2½	"
John Evans	1¾	"
Robert Cartwright the younger	1	"
William Johnson medius	½	"

[1] Robert Wheteley's will (1560) speaks of a house and 'a yard of byrre land'; John Browne's inventory (1583) refers to the 'Croppe of an yard land'. John Cartwright's inventory (1572) which shows 16 acres under crops suggests a farm of one yardland also.

William Noone	2¼	,,
Robert Pynder	½	,,
William Ridley	½	,,
Thomas Cleay	¼	,,
Thomas Astill	1	,,
Thomas Holmes	¼	,,
Robert Clerke	2	,,
Isaac Fryer	1¾	,,
William Pynder	2	,,
Robert Smyth	1½	,,
William Holmes	½	,,
Francis Smyth	2	,,

Further, seven copyholders 'remained tenants by lease and occupy part of the lands included in the sale, assured to them by the trustees':

William Abbott the elder	- tenant for life of a house and ½ yardland.
Robert Cartwright the elder	- tenant for life of a house and 1 yardland.
John Holmes	- tenant for life of ½ yardland.
John Smyth	- tenant for life of a house only, with reversion to Robert Fryer.
Robert Johnson	- tenant by lease for years to Francis Johnson of a house and ¼ yardland.
James Awswyn [Oswin]	- tenant by lease for years to Mr. Deacon of a house and ¼ yardland.
Thomas Wynter	- 'saith he is a very poore man and tenant of a Cottage onely to one William Noone.'

It is not clear whether the 2½ yardlands occupied by the seven leaseholders are already included in the 30 yardlands listed as sold to the trustees, but I have assumed they are not in the light of the two small farms of ¼ yardland each, rented of Francis Deacon, who does not appear in the first list. The total of 32½ yardlands was made up of 25 farms, of which there were four of ¼-yardland, four probably going with a cottage rather than a farm proper; six of ½-yardland; three of one yardland; eight of 1½ to 2 yardlands each; and four ranging from 2¼ to 3¼ yardlands each. This wide variation in the size of farms is equally apparent from the sales on the Turvile manor twenty years earlier, where the fourteen farms ranged in size from about 20 to 120 acres (probably from ¾ yardland to 4 yardlands), although seven or eight of them fall into the ¾ to 1 yardland group. The pattern of land-ownership was changing rapidly at the end of the sixteenth century: one can discern the change even between 1586 and 1606 if one looks at the criterion of the normal one-yardland tenement.[1]

∽   PEASANT BUYING AND SELLING OF LAND   ≳

There was, too, and always had been, as far back as the records go, a good deal of buying and selling of land between the peasant-farmers of Wigston. The Wyggeston Hospital deeds record a multitude of such transactions, mostly involving small parcels, though very few of these peasant sales are concluded by fines. Thus, although we have occasional sales of land between Wigston peasants recorded in the sixteenth-century fines we can be quite sure that the majority of sales escape notice, except perhaps in the closing years of the century when the practice of recording transfers of land by means of fines seems to have spread: partly no doubt because the size of the average transfer between peasant families was itself increasing appreciably, no longer selions and acres as in medieval times, but half-yardlands, one yardland, sometimes even two yardlands, or more.

A cursory search of the fines before 1558 reveals little evidence of land-sales in Wigston in this period, and a more detailed search year by year after that date shows no recorded selling until 1570. That land was being bought and sold during the period 1500-70 is certain enough and we occasionally have direct evidence of it[2] but there is no doubt that before 1570 the amount of buying and selling was small compared with the great wave which broke over the village in the last quarter of the century (1577-1602). An analysis

[1] The list drawn up in 1622 – sixteen years after the sale of the Danvers manor – conceals some changes in itself, however. A grant dated 15 June 1608 by the four trustees to William Fryer (or Freer), junior, shows that he bought a farm of 1¾ yardlands (L.R.O., 9.D.43. Bundle 184), but his name does not appear in the later list. Presumably his farm is incorporated in Robert Fryer's 3¼ yardlands by that date. Similarly, John Evans is listed in 1622 as owning 1¾ yardlands, but in 1608 a release by Lord Danvers to Evans covers 1½ yardlands only (Moulton MSS., Bernard Halliday, Leicester).

[2] Thus in 1512 Robert Freer bought a messuage and half a virgate of land going with it from William Ashby of Lowesby, esq., who had probably acquired this morsel in Wigston by marriage (L.R.O., 9.D.43, bundle 184). A fine in 1525 records the purchase of a messuage and 16 acres of land, and 2s. 8d. rent by John Dand from John Prikke alias Richards. There must be many peasant transactions of this nature for which no record has survived.

of the Wigston fines for the whole of the reign of Elizabeth shows that
for the years 1558-69 there were no fines; 1570-79, 7; 1580-89, 25; 1590-
99, 9; 1600-3, 4 – a total of 45 fines. During the 1580's, of course, the
Turvile manor was dismembered and sold off in parcels. If we exclude
the fines recording these sales we still have ten transactions recorded for
that decade.

Although two transactions are recorded in 1570 – one the sale of 60
acres of land and other property by Everard Pawley to Thomas Walton
and Michael Walton[1] and the other of a messuage, a rood of arable and an
acre of pasture by Anthony Tyghe and his wife Agnes to John Bardesley
– the real wave of buying and selling begins rather abruptly in 1577 and
continues until 1602 without a check. It is true that the twenty–eight fines
for the period 1577-1602 (excluding the Turvile sales, that is) do not mean
twenty–eight different sales. Some represent settlements or transfers within a
family of the same property. Thus the property bought by the Waltons from
Everard Pawley in 1570 (all except the windmill) appears again in a fine of
Easter 1577, apparently sold by Thomas and Michael Walton to Clement
Brytten and John Goddard; but it was in fact for the purpose of settling
the property on Michael Walton and his wife and their heirs, probably on
Michael's marriage. And in 1590 we find Thomas Walton apparently buying
back the same property from Michael and Elizabeth for £61, again probably
some family arrangement. Thus three fines between 1570 and 1590 relate
to one property, only one of which may be an actual sale. Similarly, the
Pawleys, or their kindred the Tyghes, are involved in many transactions
between 1577 and 1588, some of which are undoubted sales to other village
families, while others appear to be the final record of previously agreed
family arrangements. Once more we see how cautiously the fines must be
handled if we are to arrive at the truth about their meaning. Nevertheless,
even allowing for the transactions which are really family arrangements
of one kind or another, there is clearly a remarkable outburst of buying
and selling of land in Wigston in the last quarter of the sixteenth century
which continues unabated up to the outbreak of the civil war. Not that

---

[1] The property is described as one messuage, two cottages, one windmill, one dovecote, three gardens,
60 acres of land, 50 acres of meadow, 40 acres of pasture, 2 acres of wood, 6 acres of furze and heath,
and 20d. rent in Wigston (Fine, Hilary 12 Eliz). I am assuming that the 60 acres of 'land' describes the
actual size of the property, as I have shown above for other fines.

this remarkable expansion in the land-market was peculiar to this one village. The fines recorded in Leicestershire as a whole show that the expansion was common to the whole county, as indeed it was throughout England at large. During the period 1570-9 we find 451 Leicestershire fines enrolled; thirty years later the number had more than doubled (1008 for the decade 1600-9).[1]

If we analyse the Wigston fines for the period 1570-1603, grouping them according to the families who are doing the buying and selling, we shall see more clearly what was happening:

Pawley (and Tyghe)[3]

Hilary, 1570	Everard Pawley sold 1 messuage, 2 cottages, 1 dovecote, 3 gardens, and 60 acres of land to Thomas Walton and Michael Walton.
Easter 1570	Anthony Tyghe and Agnes his wife sold 1 messuage, 1 garden, 1 rood of arable, and 1 acre of pasture to John Bardesley.
Mich. 1577	Anthony Tyghe and Agnes his wife sold 1 messuage, 1 garden, 1 orchard, and 13¼ acres of land to Richard Danne.[4]

[1] P.R.O. Index to Fines, In Leicestershire as a whole the land-market began to expand in the late 1570's, but the real boom occurs in the years 1586-91. After a passing slump in 1592, the market becomes very active again for ten years (1593-1602). In 1595, 1598, 1601 and 1602 the number of fines reaches or exceeds a hundred in each year, twice the annual average of the 1570's. From 1604 to 1641 this high level of activity continues almost unchecked. The depression of 1620-1 produced a temporary contraction of the market but nothing of note.

[2] In order to make the meaning of the fines more intelligible I have assumed throughout that the acreage given as 'land' represents the whole acreage involved in the transaction, as was demonstrated above. I have accordingly omitted the recorded acreages of meadow, pasture, furze and heath, as it is difficult to reconcile them with reality, except where the sale relates only to specific pieces of meadows and pasture. Similarly, where specific rights of common are stated in the fine, as against a general reference to 'common of pasture for all cattle', I have included them in this analysis.

[3] Anthony Tyghe of Seaton, co. Rutland, husbandman, married Agnes, the only daughter and heiress of Giles Pawley of Wigston, who had been seised in fee of 1 messuage, 5 cottages, and 60 acres of land in Wigston. All this descended to Agnes (cf. Chanc. Proc. Series II. 1558-79. C3/181/no. 40 n.d.). Thus all the Tyghe transactions in Wigston relate to Pawley land and are best treated under that head.

[4] Described as 'a cottage and half a virgate of land' in the grant, which survives (Leicester muniment room). The fine describes the property as '13 acres 1 rood of land, 1½ acres of meadow, 4 acres of pasture and ½ acre of wood' but the detailed schedule attached to the grant makes it clear once more that the figure of 13¼ acres includes arable, meadow, and pasture. There were actually 38½ roods of arable, 8½ roods of pasture, and '3 doles' of meadow, which probably accounted for the six roods required to make up the total of 13¼ acres (53 roods). This schedule is referred to in more detail later (p. 150).

Easter 1578.	William Pawley and Walter Pawley put in trust with Everard Pawley and Robert Hall 1 messuage, 1 garden, 1 orchard, and 40 acres of land, for the purpose of a grant to Walter Pawley for a term of 40 years from Mich. 1577 at a yearly rent of £20-6-8, with reversion to William Pawley and his heirs forever.
Easter 1579.	Anthony Tyghe and Agnes his wife put in trust one fourth part of 2 virgates for the purpose of a grant to William Frere (and 3 others named) for the term of 21 years from Mich. 1578 at a yearly rent of 4d., with reversion to Anthony and Agnes, and to one heir of Agnes for ever.
Mich. 1583.	William Pawley the elder sold 9 acres of land to Richard banne.
Mich. 1583.	William Pawley the elder granted 1 messuage, 2 cottages, 1 garden, 1 orchard, and 30 acres of land to Walter Pawley.
Mich. 1587.	Thomas Pawley bought 1 messuage, 1 garden, 1 orchard, and 20 acres of land from Henry Turvile, esq.
Easter 1588.	William Pawley sold 30 acres of land to William Freer.
Trin. 1588.	William Tighe and Bridget his wife (and 2 other men and their wives: all three men had married Pawley heiresses) sold 15 acres of land to Thomas Astell.
Mich. 1590.	William Tighe bought 3 messuages, 4 cottages, 6 gardens, 6 orchards, and 30 acres of land from John Greisbie and Agnes his wife.
Mich. 1590.	William Tighe sold 4 messuages, 3 cottages, 4 gardens, 4 orchards, and 20 acres of land to Ralph Freman, gent.

Freman

Mich. *1586.* Ralph Freman, gent. bought from Henry Turvile, esq. 1 messuage, 1 toft, 1 garden, 1 orchard, 120 acres of land, and free fishing in the water of Wigston.

Mich. *1590.* Ralph Freman, bought 4 messuages, *3* cottages, 4 gardens, 4 orchards, and 20 acres of land from William Tighe.

Mich. *1593.* Ralph Freman sold 1 messuage, 1 toft, 1 garden, 1 orchard and go acres of land to Matthew Waldram, gent.

Easter *1599.* Joan Freman (widow of Ralph) sold:

  (a) 2 messuages, 1 cottage, 2 gardens, 2 orchards, and 4 acres of pasture to William Dann.

  (b) 2 messuages, 2 cottages, 4 gardens, 4 orchards, and 24 acres of land to Richard Davenport.

Dann

Mich. *1577.* Richard Danne bought 1 messuage, 1 garden, 1 orchard, and *13,1* acres of land from Anthony Tyghe and Agnes his wife.

Mich. *1583.* Richard Danne bought *9* acres of land from William Pawley the elder.

Trin. *1586.* John Dann sold 2 cottages, 2 barns, 2 gardens, 2 orchards, and *3* acres of pasture to Thomas Astell.

Hil. *1587.* John Dann bought 30 acres of land from Henry Turvile, esq.

Mich. *1594.* John Dann sold 1 messuage, 2 cottages, and *60* acres of land to Robert Hall.

Easter *1599.* William Dann bought 2 messuages, 1 cottage, 2 gardens, 2 orchards, and *4* acres of pasture from Joan Freman, widow.

Whyte

Hilary *1587.* John Whyte bought 1 messuage, 1 garden, 1 orchard, and 30 acres of land from Henry Turvile, esq.

| Trin. 1587. | John Whyte sold 21 acres of meadow to William Goddell clerk and Zachary Goddell. |
| Hilary 1588. | John Whyte sold 15 acres of land to Thomas Boulter. |

Boulter

| Hilary 1587. | Thomas Boulter bought 40 acres of land from Henry Turvile esq. |
| Hilary 1588. | Thomas Boulter bought 15 acres of land from John Whyte. |

Astell

Trin. 1586.	Thomas Astell bought 2 cottages, 2 barns, 2 gardens, 2 orchards, and 3 acres of pasture from John Dann.
Trin. 1588.	Thomas Astell bought 15 acres of land from William Tighe (and others).
Hilary 1597.	Seraph Astill, Francis Astill, and William Astill sold 1 cottage, 1 garden, and 1 acre of pasture to Thomas Bennett.
Mich. 1601.	William Astell sold 1 messuage, 1 garden, 1 orchard, and 12 acres of land to John Freer.

Freer

Hilary 1587.	Robert Frere bought 30 acres of land from Henry Turvile, esq.
Easter 1588.	William Frere bought 30 acres of land from William Pawley.
Mich. 1601.	John Freer bought 1 messuage, 1 garden, 1 orchard, and 12 acres of land from William Astell.

Johnson

Hilary 1587.	William Johnson bought 1 messuage, 1 garden, 2 orchards, and 80 acres of land from Henry Turvile, esq.
Mich. 1597.	William Johnson the elder sold 2 acres of land to William Lawe Hall
Mich. 1583.	Robert Hall bought 1 messuage and 30 acres of land from Rice Page.[1]

[1] Described in 1659 as 'a yardland called Pagesland heretofore the land of Robert Hall', confirming once more that the acreage described in the fines as 'land' is the true acreage involved.

Mich. 1586.   Robert Hall bought 1 messuage, 1 garden, 1
                   orchard, and 120 acres of land from Henry
                   Turvile, esq.

Mich. 1601.   Robert Hall sold 10 acres of land, and common
                   for 4 cows and 20 sheep to Nicholas Wylde.

Easter 1602.   Robert Hall sold 1 cottage, 1 toft, 10 acres of
                   land, and common for 4 cows and 20 sheep to
                   Thomas Richardson, clerk.[1]

The above analysis covers all the Wigston fines up to 1602, with some unimportant exceptions, and excepting some of the Turvile sales which require no further comment. By grouping them under the headings of the nine families who are most frequently involved in all this buying and selling we begin to get a clearer picture of the land-market at Wigston in the last quarter of the sixteenth century. In the first place it is noticeable that all the families save one – Ralph Freman, gent. – are native peasant families, yeomen and husbandmen. Secondly, most of the properties involved are small farms of twenty to forty acres, and there is a good deal of trafficking in smaller parcels still, down to an acre or two. Very occasionally there are large farms in the market: Ralph Freman's 120 acres, Robert Hall's 120 acres, William Johnson's 80 acres, and John Whyte's 60 acres. But in the main the market is mostly in the 'normal' farm of one yardland, or the typical cottage tenement of a half- or quarter-yardland, with odd pieces of meadow and pasture changing hands here and there; and it is confined almost entirely to Wigston men themselves.

Thirdly, we notice the not infrequent buying and selling by the same family, and sometimes by the same man. And while the process of consolidation is still going on – the Freers, for example, are beginning to build up an estate that will be substantial in the seventeenth century – we also see a certain amount of breaking-up of larger farms into smaller holdings again. Thus it is by no means a one-way process: some peasant estates are being built up, but others are disintegrating again. The Pawley lands, a fairly substantial property earlier in the century (60 acres), are apparently being sold off in bits and pieces here. William Tighe acquired in 1590 a block of three farmhouses, four cottages (with

[1] These are the commons for a farm of half a yardland according to 'the old stint' (see later).

their gardens and orchards) and thirty acres of land from one side of the Pawley inheritance, and immediately sold the lot (except for ten acres of land which he kept back) to Ralph Freman, gentleman. In 1599 Freman's widow sold this property (with a few extra acres) in two parcels, some to William Dann and some to Richard Davenport. Other small pieces of Pawley land passed to Richard Dann (13¼ acres and 9 acres), to Thomas Astell (15 acres) and to William Freer (30 acres). It is this contrary process going on simultaneously with that of consolidation which preserves the balance in the peasant economy, checking the tendency to the formation of a small group of families owning the bulk of the land, and of a large class who own little or no land. This is the nineteenth-century system, but peasant society did not further its growth.

The peasant landowner took great pains to keep his modest property intact once he had amassed twenty, thirty or forty acres; and even cottagers and labourers made careful provision for the future disposal of their holdings. We see these elaborate precautions at work in their wills and in their marriage settlements, as well as in the fines we have just been studying. The Leicestershire peasant, even the labourer, is as careful as the squire in these matters.

Thomas Vanne, who died in 1577, left his farm to his wife and his eldest son to occupy 'jointly together during the natural life of them both for the bringing up of my children'; and if either of them should die then the farm is to remain to the longer liver of them as long as the lease lasts. Further, 'if Johan my wief do marrie' she shall have £20 'and go her waie'; but if she do not marry 'I will that on her death she shall leave to John my son the whole croppe, cart and all thereunto belonging as horse and mares and all other goods movable and unmovable two kine only excepted and half the household stuff as brass, pewter, and bedding'. Everything necessary for the working of the farm is therefore kept with the farm: the widow is allowed to will away nothing but two kine, and half the household goods as distinct from the farm-stock, live and dead.

John Whyte directed (in 1587) that his widow should have half the fruits of his land and half the rest of his goods during her lifetime 'not to be devyded or taken away from this farme but to occupye them loyntly together with my sonne Thomas to the payeing of my detts and legacies and mayntaininge of this famelye and at her latter ende not to give away above XIS.' Robert Browne (in the same year) left to his wife half the household stuff, half 'the fruits of my lande', half the team, cart, plough and gear of all kinds, half 'the hoemsted', and half the livestock, but she was to occupy and use all this jointly with Thomas the eldest son, who took the other half. At her death her half share of everything must return to Thomas to keep the farm intact, except an acre of barley and an acre of pease 'to give where she pleaseth'.

As regards the peasant's real property, for we have been speaking only of his personal estate so far, its disposition was usually governed by legal arrangements made in the testator's lifetime, frequently by a marriage settlement drawn up when he married so many years before. That is why the disposal of the farm and other real estate is rarely mentioned in the peasant's will, and why, though provision is made for all the other sons and daughters, the eldest son is frequently not mentioned at all except perhaps as an executor. Henry Abbott (1580) speaks of 'all those thinges which are specified in a paire of Indentures made betwixt him and me according to the meaning thereof' in referring to his eldest son William.

The marriage settlement governed the disposal of most of the yeoman's and husbandman's land and aimed at keeping the property both unimpaired and within the family. We have, for example, a bond binding Sampson Wase of Rotherby, gent. (dated 1597), reciting that in consideration of a marriage to be had between Henry Fox, son of Thomas Fox of Wigston, husbandman, and Margaret, daughter of Thomas Wase of Rotherby, gent., Thomas Wase has covenanted to procure the payment of £200 to Thomas Fox before the celebration of the marriage; and that Thomas Fox on his side has made over to Margaret Wase an estate in a farm of two yardlands, and apparently other property of his. Sampson Wase, brother of Margaret, binds himself in the sum of £200 to Thomas Fox that Margaret 'shall not hereafter at any time surrender, yield up, or otherwise depart with her estate or interest (or any part thereof) in that messuage or tenement and two yardlands with the appurtenances and all other the customary lands and tenements of the said Thomas Foxe in Wigston Magna aforesaid now being in the tenure or occupation of Thomas Foxe or his assignee or assignees, or any parte thereof unless it be to some or one of the children of the said Henry

Foxe ... ' If Margaret should keep her side of the bargain the obligation on Sampson Wase to pay Thomas Fox £200 shall be void.[1]

The marriage settlement drawn up in 1592 between two yeoman families of Wigston makes somewhat similar provisions for the preservation of the Freer property. Robert Freer the elder, husbandman, had married Anna, the daughter of Susan Brabson, widow of William Brabson of Bosworth, husbandman. He covenanted to make an estate unto Susan Brabson, or to Miles Brabson her son, and Richard Chamberlain of Wigston, husbandman, before the following Christmas of half a yardland of arable, meadow and pasture in Wigston (the moiety of a yardland he had bought from Henry Turvile, esq. in 1586). Of this yardland the other moiety had already been sold to William Chamberlain and Robert Noone, also husbandmen in the village.[2] The half yardland made over in the marriage settlement was to the sole use of Robert Freer and after his death to the sole use of his widow as long as she remained 'sole and unmarried'. If she should die or marry again then the farm reverted to the use of the male heirs of Robert and Anne, and failing male issue to the rightful heirs of Robert and Anne. On her part Susan Brabson covenanted to pay Robert Freer forty marks in money 'in full satisfaction of the Mariage goods of the said Anne'. If Robert should die and Anne marry again, the heirs of his estate should pay forty marks in money to Anne's second husband, or goods and cattle to that value.[3]

The fines frequently show the same elaborate precautions to ensure the succession of a peasant property. They are often, as we have seen, not outright sales between one family and another but a settlement of a family property on trustees with detailed instructions as to its future uses. This is evident, for example, from some of the Pawley fines and those of the Waltons, and there is no need to labour the point.

---

[1] L.R.O., 9.D.43. Bundle 184. Bond dated 4 March 39 Elizabeth.

[2] No fine records this transaction. It is another illustration of the fact that the land-market in Wigston in the last quarter of the sixteenth century was probably much more vigorous than even the fines disclose.

[3] L.R.O., 9.D.43. Bundle 192. Marriage settlement dated 4 November, 34 Elizabeth.

✑ WIGSTON LEASEHOLDERS ✑

So far we have discussed the customary tenants and the freeholders of the sixteenth-century village. There remain the leaseholders, of whom we catch only occasional glimpses apart from those who leased the Wyggeston Hospital property after 1521. It is clear from incidental remarks in various lawsuits that the customary tenants of Wigston often sub-let their holdings or part of them for a term of years, but of the terms of such leases we know nothing. We also saw in the fines that leases for long periods (21 years, and even 40 years) were not unknown. On the Wyggeston Hospital lands, which came to the Hospital in 1521, long leases were the rule from the beginning, with a large fine on entry and a nominal annual rent thereafter. There were, throughout the sixteenth century, four farms belonging to the Hospital, amounting in all to 173 acres 35 perches. These consisted of houses and buildings in Bullhead street together with the lands appurtenant to them in the three fields, containing respectively 3¼ of yardland, 1 yardland, ¾ yardland, and ½ yardland, a total of 5½ yardlands.

The largest farm was the old 'capital messuage' of Richard Randull and its lands, whose history we have already traced; and in 1522 (when the rental-books begin) it was in the occupation of 'ye gud wyff Watts', paying a rent of forty shillings per annum in two equal instalments at Lady Day and Michaelmas.[1] The farm of ¾ yardland was leased out to William Wallis at an annual rent of ten shillings. This, with the Watts farm, made up the four yardlands that had come to the hospital by way of the Randulls. It can be identified with the messuage and 'three quarters' of land, meadow and pasture which was leased on 10 November 1462 by Richard Randull of Leicester, grocer, to William Clerk and Margaret his wife, for a term of twenty years at an annual rent of fifteen shillings.[2]

The other two farms represent the property which had once been the medieval farms of the Balles and the Faukes, which had come to John Penne, and whose subsequent descent, until they came to the hospital

[1] Wyggeston Hospital rentals, etc. (L.R.O.).

[2] *W.H.R.*, no. 1040. The history of this property can be traced continuously from 1462 to the present day, though the lands belonging to it were, of course, reshuffled at the enclosure. The site of the farmhouse is plot no. 197 (O.S., 25-in. map, 1930 edn.), on the east side of Bullhead street.

Wigston Magna (Above): Parish Church and Rectory Farm: The Rectory Farm stands between the church and the vicarage, a physical arrangement which reflect the history of the advowson.

The Old Mere (Left): The ancient boundary between the open fields of Wigston Magna and those of Newton Harcourt. This green lane was never ploughed but was grazed as part of the common pasture. (Courtesy of Dr Richard Jones).

Canal Settlement at Kilby Bridge (Above): The Union Canal reached Wigston by 1795, and this small settlement grew up as a consequence on the southern edge of the parish.

Framework-Knitters' Workshop at Wigston: Such a workshop, intermediate in type between the knitter's cottage and the true factory, had appeared by the 1830's. It housed up to twelve frames.

in 1521, has also been traced. In 1522 Richard Herrick occupied the messuage and one yardland with a dovecote, at an annual rent to the hospital of 18s. 8d. This property was subject to a chief rent of 1½d. per annum to 'Master Turvell', which serves to identify it with part of the Balle property as far back as the middle decades of the thirteenth century.[1] Henry Eyryk, probably a direct ancestor of Richard, was occupying the farm in 1463, possibly by a lease from John Love who was then lately dead (*W.H.R.* no. 1041).

The fourth farm, consisting of a messuage, a close and half a yardland in the fields of Wigston, was held by John Freer in 1522 at a yearly rent of nine shillings. It can be identified with part of the medieval farm of John Faukes, which came eventually to the Pennes and from them to John Love, bailiff of the Oxford manor, whose daughter and heir sold it to William Bulwardyne, who resold to William Wigston. In 1442 it was described as 'a tenement and lands of the said Richard (Penne) situated in the street of Moseho in the town of Wykengeston, and lately called Faukes land or Gudwyns land ... '[2] Its history can be traced more or less continuously, as we have seen, from the late twelfth century.

Whether or not the four leaseholders under the Hospital in 1522 were farming any lands in addition we do not know for certain. We know that Herrick, Wallis, Watts, and Freer were all names of freeholders at this date, but there were two or three related families under each of these names and one cannot assume that the freeholder was identical with the leaseholder. In the case of Richard Herrick there is a possibility that he was both, for

---

[1] A grant dated 9 November 1318 speaks of 'three halfpence worth of rent issueing from three parts of a virgate with the appurtenances (in Wigston) which Simon Balle and Joan his wife hold.' (*W.H.R.*, no. 937.) The rent can be traced back to the third quarter of the thirteenth century, when Ralph Balle granted to his daughter Alice a toft and croft, together with a selion of arable and a small piece of meadow, she rendering 3s. a year to Nicholas de Champayne, the chief lord, for the toft and croft, and for the land 'a halfpenny at Michaelmas, saying as much foreign service as appertains to the said land, and a penny for relief if it is appurtenant'. (*W.H.R.*, no. 881, n.d. but 1260-74 from internal evidence.) This apparently became consolidated as a chief rent of 1½d. per annum and was subsequently paid to the Turviles as the inheritors in due course of the Champayne property in Wigston. As a matter of antiquarian interest the rent can be traced yet another stage farther back (docs. 8769) when Ralph Balle bought five selions of arable and a piece of meadow from Alexander, son of Thomas of Wykingeston, who held his lands of the Champaynes.

[2] *W.H.R.*, no. 1022.

he was one of the witnesses of a grant in 1516 but of the others we cannot be sure.

In the early years of the Hospital leases these farms changed hands fairly frequently; later they tended to become the prerogative of one family which hung on to them for generations. Thus the large farm occupied by 'gud wyff Watts' in 1522 continued in the hands of Richard Watts between 1526 and 1539. Then for a few years John Sawford (not a native) had it; then, for about ten years (*c.* 1547-57) Harry Hugglescote, followed by William Mould (1557 to his death in 1574) and his widow up to the late 1580's. Thus the Moulds farmed it for close on thirty years: when he died in 1574 William Mould left the largest personal estate in the village next to Robert Freer (died 1557). It is possible that the Freers took the lease when 'widow Molde' died and sub-let to Thomas Sampson (again not a native) as in 1589 the rental records 'Thomas Sampson for freers' under this property. Thomas Sampson, gent., who held a lease for three lives, sold his interest in the estate to Francis Brett in 1602. The Bretts occupied the farm for more than thirty years until Francis Brett, yeoman, sub-let it to a newcomer, William Lewis, late of Foxton, yeoman, in 1636.

The Wallis farm, on the other hand, showed great stability of tenancy. William Wallis occupied it until his death in the 1530's, followed by 'mothar Walles' – presumably his widow. In 1565 a new lease was made to another William Wallis, husbandman, 'of a messuage, a little close, and three farthings of land with meadow, pastures, and commons appurtenant in Wigston', he to allow his mother Margaret Wallis to enjoy half the messuage during her life. He also agrees to replant hedgerows and spinneys as needful and to fetch one cart-load of wood and coal each year for the hospital in Leicester. William Wallis died in 1605, having farmed there for forty years, and the lease passed to the Jacksons after more than eighty years in the Wallis family. Dennis Jackson had married Elizabeth Wallis in 1603 and probably acquired the lease of the farm as part of the marriage settlement. We find other leases being transferred for this reason, the property being treated almost as if it were a freehold possession. The Jacksons held the farm, generation after generation, until they finally surrendered the lease in 1823.[1]

---

[1] Wyggeston Hospital rentals and leases, loc. cit.

The Herrick farm had probably been leased by them in pre-Hospital days, Henry Eyryk holding it as far back as 1463. The family continued to occupy it until 1540 or shortly after; then, in 1543, the Cartwrights appear in Wigston and take the farm which they occupied for over half a century, up to 1596. They also held Hospital property in Oadby, the neighbouring village to the north-east, where they originated: no doubt this was the cause of their coming to Wigston to settle. In 1594 William Johnson married Joan Cartwright, and three years later William Johnson held the lease, again probably as a result of the marriage. By 1610, however, the farm had come to Richard Davenport.

Both the Wallis and the Herrick farms, under the Hospital, showed on the whole great stability of tenure, but the last of the farms, that occupied by John Frere in 1522, passed through a rapid succession of tenants until 1596 when it came into the hands of the Brabsons who continued to occupy and farm it down to 1755. There is no point in tracing the early succession of tenants in detail. For about twenty years (1539 to c. 1559) William Herrick occupied it; then it came to Harry Smyth for ten years (1559-69). Gilbert Becket, a newcomer, had it during the 1570's, and Robert Whyte alias Smyth from 1580 to 1587. The lease by the Hospital to Robert Frere, dated 8 March 29 Eliz. (1587) is still extant and its provisions became common form in all the Hospital leases subsequently. The property is described as a messuage or tenement 'wherein one Robert Whyte als Smyth now dwelleth', a close of pasture and half a yardland in the fields, with all the appurtenances belonging thereunto except great trees and timber trees, which are reserved to the Hospital. The term of the lease is for the three lives of Robert Frere, yeoman, Elizabeth his wife, and Alice their daughter, and the longest liver of them. The rent is nine shillings a year, payable at the two usual feast-days of Lady Day and

---

[1] There is no mention of a fine in any of these leases up to the nineteenth century, nor do any records survive among the Hospital muniments of the fines received from their properties, which extended into several parishes. It is quite certain that large fines were paid by leaseholders on entry. The reason for the silence of the records on the subject is known. Although under the original statutes of the Hospital all fines and profits arising from the leasing of its properties were to go to the use of the Hospital, by Elizabethan days the Master was appropriating the fines on renewal of leases or insertion of new lives to his own use and no record was, naturally enough, ever kept. The income derived from fines by the Master (who eventually became non-resident also, in spite of the statutes) eventually reached a prodigious level. One Mr. Selwin, Master from 1793 to 1823, appropriated £24,440 during that period, an average income of over eight hundred pounds a year.

Michaelmas,[1] and there are the usual clauses of re-entry if the rent is 28 days in arrear and regarding repair and maintenance of the property. Further, the lessees are to fetch and carry at their own costs and charges, with William Wallis and his assigns jointly – he occupied the adjoining house to the south – one load of coals measuring three 'quartrons' from the Leicestershire pits at Cole Orton or Newbold, which are to be paid for at the pits and brought to and laid in the Master's house in Leicester. Lastly, the lessees are to plant every year 'two plants or setts of oak, ash, or elm in meet and convenient places' and are to yield two good capons yearly or two shillings in money at the feast of the Circumcision.[1]

In 1595 Miles Brabson, husbandman, married Alice, daughter of Robert Freer. The Freer lease was thereupon surrendered and a new one made to Miles Brabson, Alice his wife, and William Brabson (a kinsman of Miles) on the same terms and conditions, and thereafter the farm continued to be occupied by the Brabsons until 1755.

The Wigston Hospital lands formed a valuable reservoir of leasehold land, available to local men, over and above the freehold farms of the village, nearly all of which were occupied by their owners. Apart from the Hospital land the only other fairly substantial source of rentable land was that held by the Waldrams, who lived at Oadby. John Waldram owned two farms of one yardland each in Wigston, which in 1580 he was leasing to John Cartwright and one Coultman, both Wigston farmers, at a reserved rent of three shillings a year.[2] As we have seen, Matthew Waldram gent. of Oadby had bought a 90-acre farm in Wigston in 1593 from Ralph Freman, so increasing the Waldram estate there by another three yardlands and bringing its total area to rather more than 150 acres. In all then there were some

---

[1] Eighteenth-century leases dwell more lovingly on the capons, as we might expect. A lease of 1755 specified 'one Couple of good Fat and well Fed Capons'. By the same date, what is more important, the provision for the planting of timber had been tightened to 'six setts of oak, ash, or elm and six setts of willow every year', a reflection of the desperate shortage of timber and wood of all kinds in Leicestershire by that date.

[2] B.M. Add. MSS. 6702, fo. 110. These two yardlands formed part of the manor of Brokesby in Oadby which overflowed into Wigston. It can be identified in fact as the Domesday holding of Robert de Buci in Oadby and Wigston under the countess Judith. It was bought by John Waldram in 1550.

320-330 acres available in Wigston at the end of the sixteenth century for leasing, or about one-ninth of the total area of the parish.

✇ THE RECTORY FARM AND TITHES ✇

One other important piece of property in the village must be dealt with, and that is the rectory. The value of this lay, of course, in the tithes of grain, hay, wool and other smaller commodities growing or arising within the parish, and in the farm of three yardlands which constituted the glebe. Up to 1506 Lenton Priory merely exercised the patronage of this wealthy rectory. They did not enter upon and appropriate the rectorial tithe but contented themselves with receiving from the rectors appointed by them an annual pension of 100 shillings. The rectors in their turn were usually pluralists with other great offices in the church and did not reside in the parish. They farmed out the rectory and tithes to others, as we have seen in one instance, drawing the annual rent from the farmer who was left with the obligation of finding a suitable chaplain on the spot to attend to the spiritual needs of the parish.

In the year 1506, however, the priory entered into full possession of the rectorial tithe and made an agreement with the Bishop of Lincoln for the ordination of a vicarage. In the Valor Ecclesiasticus (1535) the rectory was valued at £33 0s. 2½d. in tithes, oblations and other profits, of which the vicar was allowed the modest sum of £9 per annum, and the bishop 13s. 4d. a year for agreeing to the appropriation. The last rector, Master John Edmondes, who had been instituted in 1498, conveniently resigned on 21 July 1507 and the first vicar of Wigston, William Reede, was instituted on 3 August following. From a spiritual standpoint the difference was perhaps hardly noticeable in the village: it had always been served by a resident chaplain or sometimes two, ill-paid but probably more or less conscientious: and the neglect by the priory of the fabric of the church and of the distribution of alms to the poor continued. But from an economic standpoint the change meant that a valuable piece of real property passed into lay hands within a few years, for the appropriation by the priory came within a generation of the Dissolution, just in time to present another plum to the scrambling local gentry who were picking up monastic rectories and tithes all over the county in the 1540's and 1550's. Wigston was one of the fattest rectories in the county at the Dissolution.

Between 1506 and 1539, when Lenton was dissolved, the rectory of Wigston was leased by the priory, first to Sir Richard Sacheverell, kt., on terms we do not know, and then, by a lease dated 25 January 1536, to Symon Catesby of Clifton in Nottinghamshire. Catesby paid £40 down for a five-year lease and a rent of £22 7s. 4d. a year, and was to hold the rectory from five years to five years for a period of 45 years on these terms. He was thus in possession when the priory was dissolved and the prior hanged above his own gates 'for divers rebellions against the King's peace' and he was left in undisturbed possession at the same rent now payable to the Crown. In 1549, so we are told in a Chancery suit,[1] he put the property in trust with Edmund Thurlond, parson of Clifton – 'his cosen' – Edmund undertaking to provide for the living of Symon 'as also for the advancement of his children'. Symon on his part undertook to pay the sum of £290 to Edmund but failed to do so, whereupon a writ was directed to the sheriff of Leicestershire to 'attach the body of Symon Catesby and all his lands, goods, and chattels'. By virtue of the writ, Sir Richard Manners, sheriff of the county, empanelled a jury to find the true value of the rectory and Catesby's other lands and goods, and amongst other things extended the lease of the rectory of Wigston at £60 a year over and above the yearly rent payable to the king. The lease was seized by Manners into the hands of Edward VI and thereafter became the subject of much dispute and litigation the full import of which is not wholly clear. It appears from this suit, however, and from other sources (such as the Particulars for Leases and Particulars for Grants) that the Manners family themselves acquired the lease of this valuable rectory very shortly afterwards.

For a time, however, the rectory was held by the notorious John Beaumont of Cole Orton, esquire, who became Master of the Rolls in 1550. He, shortly afterwards, was obliged to resign his judgeship by reason of many serious misdemeanours, and assigned most of his property, real and personal, to the king in satisfaction of all claims. It is probably at this point that the Manners family obtained their first lease of the rectory, but their tenure of

[1] Chancery Proceedings, Series II (1558-79). C.3/45/no. 32.

it, and that of their under-tenants, was complicated for some considerable time afterwards by the claims of Elizabeth Beaumont, widow of John Beaumont. She obtained a commission of enquiry into her rights in the rectory at Wigston and judgement was given in her favour in 1566. She was to recover as dower the third part of the rectory; divers parts of 'the mansion house and the glebe thereof'; and a third of the tithes belonging to the rectory. The farmers of the rectory under the Crown apparently held back a third of the reserved rent of £22 7s. 4d. due to the Crown in consideration of this judgment, but the decision periodically led to trouble. In 1581 Elizabeth Beaumont was suing Richard Stanford, at that time an under-tenant of the farm of tithe and glebe, over some default, and in 1587 the court of the Exchequer had to clarify once more the position of the farmer in keeping back a third of the rent from the Crown, as Elizabeth Beaumont was still alive and enjoying a third part of all the profits.[1]

During most of this period, Roger Manners, esquire – a younger son of the earl of Rutland at Belvoir – held the principal lease under the Crown. We know he held it in the 1550's and in 1574 we find it renewed to him for twenty-one years at the same rent of £22 7s. 4d. There is no mention of any large initial payment such as Simon Catesby had made to the prior of Lenton back in 1536, but such a payment must have been made as the rent is always spoken of as a 'reserved rent'. We also discover from proceedings in the archdeacon's court at Leicester, which are mostly disputes about tithes, that Roger Manners made a sub-lease to 'the bayley of Sawley', who in turn sub-let the rectory to one Richard Ward, who had married his daughter. Ward was the actual farmer of the tithe and glebe, therefore, and appears in that role between 1557 and 1574. In the years 1578 and 1579, we learn from another squabble over tithes, Thomas Clark – probably the Thomas Clark, innholder, who was mayor of Leicester on two occasions – occupied the rectory, i.e. took the tithes and the profits of the glebe, and he made a further lease of it in 1580 and 1581 to Richard Standord,

---

[1] The suit of 1581 (P.R.O., C.2. B.8. no. 4) is a mutilated fragment only, which does not tell us the real matter at issue between the plaintiff and the defendant, but it was probably some dispute over the sharing out of the proceeds of the rectory. The details of the 1587 judgement in the Court of the Exchequer are given in Nichols, 379-81.

a wealthy butcher of Leicester. The Stanfords were a rising family in Leicester in the second half of the sixteenth century, mostly butchers and graziers on a big scale. The rise of the butchers and tanners in Elizabethan Leicester is particularly noticeable in the town records: it is they, rather than the mercers and merchants of the earlier half of the century, who fill the mayoral chair and the aldermanic robes after 1550, reflecting in their rise the changing emphasis in farming in the Leicestershire countryside, especially round the town itself. The Stanfords were prominent in this new class and before the end of the century we find them buying substantial estates in the county, and having dealings in rectorial tithes as at Wigston.[1]

In 1587 a new family, and a family of a new type, arrived in the village – the Lawes, representative of the large class of traffickers and speculators in monastic properties who made their appearance after 1539. Back in 1553 we find Hugh and Thomas Lawe, described as haberdashers of London, purchasing monastic lands, rents, and rectories in Northamptonshire and Huntingdonshire.[2] A generation later, in 1581, William Lawe, probably of the same family, obtained a twenty-one year lease of Wigston rectory at the accustomed rent. We do not learn what had happened to Roger Manners' lease of 1574; possibly it had been surrendered. William Lawe himself did not take up his residence in Wigston immediately. There was further trouble, as we have seen, over the reserved rent, which was not cleared up until the judgement of the High Court in 1587, and it was after this that he arrived to look after his property in person.[3] He seems to have occupied the glebe farm of three yardlands himself and to have received the tithes of the parish directly, without farming any of them out again. It is possible that between 1581 and 1587 he built himself a new house, the largest that had yet been seen in the village, as the description

---

[1] The details about the Stanfords are taken from the *Leicester Borough Records*, vol. III (ed. Bateson), from the *Register of the Freemen of Leicester*, 1196-1770, ed. Hartopp (1927), and from the Farnham MSS. and elsewhere.

[2] Cal. Pat. Rolls, Edward VI, v, 42. Hugh and Thomas Lawe made a substantial purchase in 1553, paying £1,315 8s. 10½d. for the monastic properties in Northants. and Huntingdonshire.

[3] Lawe's coming to Wigston is dated by his own deposition in a tithe dispute in the archdeacon's court in 1601 (Court Proceedings, L.R.O.) wherein he says that he first came '13 or 14 yeares ago', i.e., in 1587 or 1588. The family continued to live in the village until the 1720's, but in very much reduced circumstances after the middle of the seventeenth century.

of it in his inventory, made in January 1603, is that of a gentleman's house and not that of an enlarged farmhouse. A reference also to various oddments of wood and timber 'in the parsonage yard' suggests that he was occupying the rectory or glebe farm. Almost next door to him the humble vicarage was occupied by Thomas Thornton, who scraped along on the residue of the once-large rectorial income and was almost a pauper. But this unequal division of income between a wealthy lay rector and an underpaid vicar, was of course a common feature – one had almost said a characteristic feature – of the English countryside, of which Leicestershire alone furnished many gross examples from the later sixteenth century onwards.

Tithes have been a source of bitterness and litigation in almost every English village for centuries, and Wigston was no exception. How could it be otherwise when in so many instances they had become wholly divorced from their original purpose, and had become a piece of lay property just like any other, a private levy by the squire on everyone else's land in so many parishes? Though even when the parson, as rector, continued to collect the levy the resentment was hardly less acute and the evasions hardly less ingenious. The details of these disputes are a somewhat arid field of enquiry but occasionally they throw a passing light on some aspect of the social or economic history of a village that we should otherwise not know about. At Wigston there had been the usual minor squabbles in earlier years in the archdeacon's court, but in 1602 a larger dispute developed out of a preliminary skirmish between William Lawe and Robert Freer or Fryer, now the largest farmer in the village, and reached the Court of the Exchequer in London. Not until 1605 was a judgement given and from the prolonged depositions by village people we learn a little that is worth recovering from the past.[1]

The dispute between William Lawe, as farmer of the tithes, and Robert Freer arose over the custom of tithing on sheep sold out of the parish before clipping time. Sheep which were 'going feeding and couchinge' within the parish from New Year's Day and remained there to be clipped paid every tenth fleece as tithe: that was agreed by both parties.

---

[1] The first tussle was in the archdeacon's court in 1601. The details of tile Exchequer suit are to be found in Exchequer Depositions by Commission, 44–5 Eliz., Mich. 16, continued in the same series, 2 James I, Mich. 7.

But Freer, who was brought into the archdeacon's court for detaining tithe on sheep sold in Leicester before clipping time, maintained that it was the ancient custom in Wigston to pay to the farmer of the tithe a halfpenny for every sheep so sold in full discharge of any tithe wool that would have been due at the shearing. Such a custom, if true, clearly lent itself to the defrauding of the farmer of the tithe, especially as it was also alleged by the villagers that if they bought sheep after New Year's Day, and brought them into the parish, no tithe wool was payable on these sheep when the next clipping time came round. By selling their own sheep between New Year's Day and shearing time and buying others in their place they could evade the wool tithe entirely, paying only a halfpenny on each sheep sold.

Freer brought various supporters into court to depose as to the ancient custom. Jasper Astill deposed that the payment of a halfpenny on each sheep sold before clipping time was the custom in his youth (1547 to 1553. when he had lived in Wigston) and John Spencer of Lutterworth, yeoman, who had lived in Wigston for forty years (between 1557 and 1597) said likewise. He remembered buying forty sheep from 'one Robert Fryer alias mynnibeard' about Whitsuntide thirty years ago and that Fryer had paid a halfpenny on each sheep to the farmer at that time. He had also heard 'old Robert Noone and old William Pawley who were anncyent men in Wiggeston at such time as he came' say that the custom had always been so within their remembrance. William Pawley, son of 'old Pawley' and now an old man of seventy-two himself, 'borne and upbrought in Wiggeston', said the same, provided that the sheep sold before shearing were 'sold for need and not to thend to defraud the farmer'. It had always been so in his father's time, who was born and lived all his life in Wigston, until lately 'some fewe' have paid more to Lawe for fear of being sued. Lawe, the record of whose answer is incomplete, denied this custom but we hear more of his side of the case in the Exchequer records.

The Exchequer suit, begun in 1602, covered a wider field and brought in more defendants. William Lawe cited Robert Freer, William Dande the elder, Francis Clarke, William Freer the younger, John Cartwright and William Johnson, and alleged that thirty-one other inhabitants of the village (named in the suit) had 'bound themselves by writing to the defendants' to maintain the suit and had contributed towards the cost of it by subscriptions and by levies of sixpence, eightpence, and a shilling a yardland. Not only was the tithe of wool and lambs brought into issue, but also the tithing of furze, willows, and 'shredding', and various other matters were touched upon in the interrogatories and depositions.

Once more John Spencer of Lutterworth turned up to depose on behalf of the defendants. Lawe, he said, had been farmer of the tithes for about fifteen years (i.e. since 1587) and before his coming they had always paid a halfpenny on every sheep sold out of the parish before clipping time, which halfpenny was paid at the same time as the tithe wool. Only in the last ten to twelve years 'some fewe that have byn new corners to the towne' have agreed to pay more on such sheep 'rather then they wold contend in lawe'. On sheep pasturing in the parish on New Year's Day and dying before shearing time the custom similarly was to pay a halfpenny for the pelt at the same time as the tithe wool was paid.

New Year's Day was 'the general ruleinge daye' by ancient custom when every parishioner keeping sheep within the parish was directed what tithe wool he should pay to the farmer for that year. Such tithe was therefore only payable on sheep which were in the parish on 1 January and were clipped by the owners in the same year; no tithe wool had ever been paid on sheep bought or brought into the parish after New Year's Day and clipped there in that year. As to the manner of taking the tithe, where it was due, the custom was that every 10th fleece was taken, but that if there were only seven fleeces to tithe the farmer took one nevertheless and paid the owner 1½d. as an offset.

As to lambs born in the parish and kept there till St. Mark's day (25 April), the tithe was paid in kind on that day, the owner choosing the first four and then the farmer choosing his tithe lamb from the remainder; but for lambs sold before St. Mark's day in the same year only a halfpenny was payable to the farmer.

John Spencer also deposed that no tithe had ever been paid on willows, furze and shredding, which were always used by the owners for hedging and for fuel. But there was a penny payable by every inhabitant to the farmer at Easter each year known as a 'smoke penny', and variously called a garden-penny, a hearth-penny and a house-penny by other deponents.

Lastly, he said that every year the inhabitants or the greater part of them met together and agreed upon 'divers and sundrye orders for the good ordering and preservation of the proffytts of there lands and Comons within the ffeilds of Wigston'.

The other deponents all said substantially the same. William Johnson the elder of Wigston, husbandman, aged eighty years or thereabouts, could speak of the customs of the past seventy years in the village, back to the time of Henry VIII. He supported with all the authority of his years what had been said as to the manner of taking tithe, adding that when tithe wool was taken the owner chose the best four fleeces and the farmer took one of the remainder; on nine fleeces the farmer took one, after the owner had made his choice of four, and paid ½d. to the owner; on eight fleeces the farmer took one and paid back 1d.; and on seven fleeces he took one and paid back 1½d. On six fleeces and less no tithe was taken.

William Pynder, husbandman, and John Ward, carpenter, both of Wigston, deposed that they had lately compounded for sheep sold away from the parish at a much higher rate than the ancient custom, the former at 20d. for every 10th sheep sold, and the latter at 18d. Both had been threatened with lawsuits unless they did so and had 'yelded for verye feare'.

There had been some other trouble over the impounding of Lawe's sheep which some of the deponents touch on. It was alleged by the defendants that at the annual general meeting of the inhabitants to discuss the regulation of the fields in the year 1601 it had been agreed that, after the corn had been 'inned' in Goldhill Field, the field should be eaten and depastured only with great beasts and not with any sheep until September 29th; and that Lawe had given his consent to that order and had nevertheless put his sheep in the field before the appointed day, whereupon they had been impounded by three of the defendants. The interrogatory for William Lawe puts the matter in another light: that an order had been made that Goldhill Field should be kept in several after harvest until September 29th, but 'how many of the inhabitants were present at the making of the same order if any such were?' The plaintiff had not been present, he said, and had not been made acquainted with the new order before the impounding of his sheep. To this John Holmes, husbandman, deposed that Lawe gave his consent to the order long before the impounding of his sheep, that the penalty 'sett downe in the lords Court' was 6s. 8d. for every default, and that this penalty had been published openly in the parish church in Lawe's hearing and he did not contradict it.

In the middle of the proceedings, William Lawe died (in January 1603) and the suit had to be revived by Katherine, his widow and executrix. Little new information emerges on behalf of the defendants. William Freer of Wigston, yeoman, aged 72 or thereabouts, 'beinge borne and bredd and dwelt there all his time', supported the claims already made by the earlier deponents, adding that where there were fewer than seven fleeces to be tithed the custom was to pay a halfpenny on each fleece, and similarly on lambs where there were fewer than seven. No tithes had ever been paid on furze, willows, and shreddings. Furze had always been used in their furnaces and ovens for brewing and baking, and willows and shreddings (loppings) for hedging and 'mendinge of there grounds'.

The first deponent on behalf of the plaintiff was Richard Stanford the elder, of Leicester, butcher, who had known the parties and the rectory for the past 20 years. He had been farmer of the whole rectory for a time, and for a time of part of it, and the custom always was that tithe wool was paid on all sheep going in the parish on New Year's Day whether subsequently sold before shearing-time or not. Only in the last two years had some of the inhabitants begun to break the custom, but he knew Lawe had received tithe wool in this form from several inhabitants, including 'old White, old Watts, and old Dand'. There was, he said, 'an ancient booke which they call a custom booke which is usuallie remaining in the hands of some of the inhabitants of Wiggeston' in which the customs of tithing in the parish are set down, and he had heard it read out that all sheep which were in the parish on 1 January were to be tithed in wool and lamb, whether or not they were afterwards sold before shearing. On the other hand, he had never heard of any composition for furze, willows, or shredding.

Various other deponents on behalf of the plaintiff say much the same. Thomas Lawe, son of William Lawe the farmer, said he had received 18d. or 20d. for every 10th sheep sold out of the parish, sometimes more and sometimes less according to when they were sold. He had received this payment from a number of the inhabitants during the past seven years, and only Robert Freer had refused, saying that it was not due. Every year on January 1st a note was taken by the farmer of the rectory, or by his deputy, of all such sheep as were in the parish on that day so that the farmer knew what tithe wool to expect, but several of the owners had willingly compounded for any sheep subsequently sold on the above terms. Shepherds and husbandmen deposed that until recently tithe had been paid on all sheep whether afterwards sold or not, until William Johnson[1] had come to the village from Desford and had stirred up strife.

The judgement of the court was given on 3 February 1605.[2] The court held that the custom set forth by the defendants was 'in some parts both unreasonable and against the law', namely that they could sell their sheep before clipping time and pay only a halfpenny for each sheep so sold, and that they could buy sheep after New Year's Day, keep them over clipping time, and pay nothing. By selling their own sheep and buying others in their place they would defraud his Majesty and his farmers of all the tithe wool of the rectory – 'which is conceived by the Court to be a very unreasonable custom and tending nearly to the defrauding of the farmer and disherison of his Majesty, his heirs and successors, in whom the reversion of the said rectory in fee is'.

It was therefore ordered that (1) where anyone has sheep in the parish on New Year's Day and sells or puts them away before clipping time, and buys or brings in others in their place, then such owners of sheep so brought in should pay the tenth fleece in kind to the farmers of the rectory; (2) if anyone buy or bring any sheep into the fields after New Year's Day, or do not sell or put away any others in their place, the owner of such sheep so brought in shall pay tithe on them in money or otherwise according to the time they remain in the parish 'any usage there pretended to the contrary notwithstanding'; (3) if anyone sell or put away sheep before clipping time with intent to deceive the farmer of his tithe, he shall pay tithe wool or lamb in kind or the reasonable value thereof, for all such sheep so conveniently sold or put away, any usage or custom there notwithstanding, but for a *bona fide*

---

[1] This is not the William Johnson already referred to as a deponent but a younger kinsman.
[2] Given in full in Nichols, 380-1.

sale the owner shall pay ½d. for every sheep in lieu of tithe-wool or ½d. for every lamb sold, in full satisfaction of the tithe thereof; and (4) no tithes shall be payable on furze, willows, or shredding, 'inasmuch as it appeareth not that there hath been ever any paid, but that they are used for fuel to burn in their houses, and for fencing of their grounds, for which grounds tithes are paid'.

VI

THE PEASANT FARMER IN THE TUDOR PERIOD

The Distribution of Wealth

During the fifteenth and sixteenth centuries there emerged at Wigston what may be called a peasant aristocracy, or, if this is too strong a phrase as yet, a class of capitalist peasants who owned substantially larger farms and capital resources than the general run of village farmers. This process was going on all over the Midlands during these years, but at a varying pace in different villages. At Wigston it was slower to develop its full force. Men are born with widely different energies and abilities, with an acquisitive instinct of very variable strength. Some have a flair for 'getting on' and fortune smiles upon them regardless of merit or ability, while others are dogged by inscrutable and undeserved bad luck. All these things tend to bring about inequality even in such a comparatively equal and stable society as the medieval village; and in the East Midlands, where so much land was held freely from early times, the energetic and acquisitive peasant had opportunities for amassing property denied to his fellows elsewhere, as for instance in South-Western England.

These natural forces making for inequality were accelerated by the general economic environment of the fifteenth century. The prolonged depression, beginning about the middle of the fourteenth century and lasting, with short respites, until the last quarter of the fifteenth, gave even greater opportunities to the men or the families who could hang on in the face of adversity, either because they had greater economic resources than their fellows to begin with, or because they were endowed with greater inborn staying power. We know next to nothing of the details of these processes at Wigston but we can safely surmise that they were at work. The depression was particularly severe in this crowded village; the tax cut of forty per cent in 1446 was almost as high as anywhere in Leicestershire and nearly three times the average cut for the county as a whole. During the three generations or so that this depression lasted, the population of the village was nearly halved. Elsewhere in Leicestershire manorial records we read of demesne land left untenanted, farmhouses and cottages left unoccupied by the dozen, mills in ruin, the value of land falling.

Undoubtedly, it was happening at Wigston, too, and the tougher peasants, like the Randulls for example, emerge from the struggle having acquired the lands of their weaker fellows like the Swetings and the Redleys; or as Richard Penne acquired the farm of John Faukes back in 1412. One can trace this strengthening and expansion of certain old peasant families over and over again in the Leicestershire village records between the late fourteenth century and the early sixteenth; and one finds as a result that by 1525 there are, in scores of villages, one, two, or three leading yeoman families who own a quite disproportionate share of the personal estate or movable goods.[1] In sample taken from forty villages all over the county, we find that 4 per cent of the rural population owned a quarter of the personal estate, and 15½ per cent owned a half of it, even if we omit the squires entirely from the calculation. This minority of well-to-do families in our sample consists almost without exception of yeomen, to give the capitalist peasant his new name.[2]

In certain villages, conditions had favoured this tendency to inequality and accumulation to a marked degree: at Mowsley, for example, the three Horton households (all yeomen) owned three-quarters of the personal estate of the village. William Horton, assessed at £50, was richer than some Leicestershire squires. But in other villages, of which Wigston was one, conditions were not so favourable to the emergence of such gross inequality in worldly goods, the most important deterrent being

[1] In some villages, though not at Wigston, the acquisition of a long lease of the rectory and tithes of the parish by a capitalist peasant helped greatly to enhance the fortunes of his family through the 'unearned increment' of these years of recovery and rising prices. Leases acquired on easy terms in the latter part of the fifteenth century became increasingly valuable pieces of property during the first quarter of the sixteenth. Thus Thomas Bent at Cosby leased the rectorial tithes in 1477 from Leicester abbey, which had appropriated them, and he also farmed the abbey's demesne lands there. Thomas Meryell farmed the abbey's demesnes at Bitteswell, as well as the hay and corn tithes; and Thomas Humberstone farmed the great tithes of Wymeswold under Beauchief Abbey. All were rising yeomen in these decades.

[2] Cf. *Essays in Leicestershire History*, 129-30, where fuller details are given. These calculations are based upon an analysis of the subsidy for 1524 and 1525, which taxed every adult on land, movable goods, or wages of £1 a year and more.

the continued existence of a large body of peasant proprietors whose ownership of land tended to act as a drag on the unequal accumulation of movable goods into fewer hands. Even in 1524-5, though there were obviously certain leading families in the village, they were all peasant families still and not so much better off than the average. There were not such great extremes at Wigston as in some villages. It was still, and it continued to be for a long time, a peasant village consisting essentially of a solid core of middling-sized farmers, with a few larger men at the top who were different only in mild degree and not in kind from their humbler fellows, and a sprinkling of cottagers and wage-labour below.

The 1524 subsidy list for Wigston contains 67 names. None paid on lands; 42 were assessed on movable goods; and 25 were assessed on wages.[1] The value of all the personal estate in the village was £204, made up of £179 in 'goods' and £25 in 'wages'. The highest assessments were William Chamberlain £16, Thomas Whyte £13, and William Astyll £10. Contrast this with the great number of yeomen elsewhere in Leicestershire whose assessments ranged from £20 to £60, the highest being Thomas Bradgate at Peatling Parva who was assessed on goods to the value of £110.[2]

An analysis of the Wigston assessment as a whole brings out the character of the village as a solid community of middling-sized farmers, small yeomen and husbandmen, with no overshadowing yeoman family at the top, dominating the place as the Bents did at Cosby, the Bradgates at Peatling Parva, the Hartopps at Burton Lazars, and the Chamberlains at Newton Harcourt and Kilby, to cite a few outstanding examples out of many from the Leicestershire records. Only three Wigston farmers were assessed on £10 or more; nine

---

[1] P.R.O., E. 179. 133/122. A man was assessed on lands or goods according to which produced the greater yield to the Exchequer. Thus the absence of any Wigston assessment on 'lands' has no significance except that no man had real estate of a greater annual value than his personal estate. 'Goods' included 'every pound in coin that he has, all plate, stock of merchandise, corn and grain severed from the ground, household stuff, and all other movable goods and all sums of money owing to him'.

[2] In 1527 a subsidy was collected from all persons with goods to the value of £50 and upwards. In Leicestershire (P.R.O., E. 179. 133/120) nineteen men were assessed on this basis, of whom none was a Wigston man. Another levy in 34 Henry VIII (P.R.O., E. 179. 133/134. Indenture of contributions to a loan) lists 33 payers of £10 to £26 13s. 4d., again with no Wigston name in it. Sir William Turvyle, lord of the smaller Wigston manor, was, however, one of the highest contributors (£20).

assessments fell between £5 and £9; thirty between £2 and £4. Of the forty-two farmers and craftsmen in the village, for there were no other classes among those assessed on movable goods, no fewer than thirty-three fell into the middle range of £2-£5: three households out of every four fell into this group.

Viewed in another way, it is true, three families between them (the Chamberlains, Astells, and Whites) owned nearly a quarter of the personal estate of the village, and one-fifth of the taxpayers owned a half of the wordly goods. But, even so, wealth was less unequally distributed in Wigston than in the county generally, and in this it is representative of a considerable number of midland villages where a substantial body of peasant proprietors still kept their hold on the land. Below this topmost dozen or so taxpayers, movable goods were fairly evenly distributed in the village; and, so far as we can tell, the village land was distributed roughly in the same way. At the top were a few men with two, or at most three, yardlands, but the great majority of men who owned any land owned half a yardland or a yardland and no more.

William Chamberlain, the most highly assessed man in Wigston, was a young newcomer to the village in 1524, closely related to the Chamberlains of Newton Harcourt and Kilby, two small villages only a couple of miles away to the south and south-east, where they were by far the most affluent inhabitants. William Chamberlain of Wigston was the son of Henry Chamberlain of Kilby, yeoman,[1] who was assessed on goods to the value of £30 in 1524, out of a total of £71 for the entire village, the next highest assessment being one of £8; and he was the nephew of William Chamberlain of Newton Harcourt who was assessed on £40 out of a total of £93 13s. 4d. for the whole village. In these two villages the Chamberlains owned more than forty per cent of the personal estate.

We possess no inventory for William Chamberlain of Newton Harcourt, who died in 1525, but Henry Chamberlain's inventory (taken in 1547) shows that he was one of the new type of farmer still uncommon in the county despite the noise about enclosures. The average Leicestershire farmer at this date kept rather more than thirty sheep and about six

---

[1] Cf. the will of Henry Chamberlain of Kilby, dated and proved in 1547, in which he appoints his son William Chamberlain of Wigston to act as his executor, for which pains he shall be rewarded with £4, 20 sheep, and a colt.

cattle of all kinds, only as many as he could feed off his farm and the
appurtenant common pastures, and his personal estate was worth
perhaps £20 in all.[1] Henry Chamberlain's estate was worth £71 7s.
4d. – between three and four times the average – and he had 180 sheep
and 26 cattle of all sorts (kine, bullocks, and calves). His farm-goods
accounted for six-sevenths of his whole personal estate, and of these
his livestock amounted in value to £50 8s. 8d. and his crops only
to £9 18s. 8d. He had gone a long way from the traditional mixed
husbandry of the open-field farmer, and was the forerunner of the
large grazier who was to become typical of so much of Leicestershire
farming within the next two or three generations.

William Chamberlain, his son, came to Wigston probably in the
second decade of the sixteenth century and established a family which
lasted just a hundred years. The occasion of his coming was almost
certainly his marriage with Joan, daughter of Thomas Pawley.[2] The
Pawleys were, as we have seen, one of the leading peasant families in
Wigston at this date, owning between them a number of farms; and
knowing what we do of the arrangement of yeoman marriages later in
the sixteenth century, and during the seventeenth, we can safely surmise
that there was a generous marriage settlement on both sides. Possibly
some of Thomas Pawley's lands passed to William Chamberlain and no
doubt Henry Chamberlain helped to stock his son's farm. At any rate,
although a young man and a newcomer, William Chamberlain headed the
subsidy list of 1524 in Wigston, well ahead of all the older men whose
families had been established there for generations. We know nothing,
unfortunately, of his farming – whether, for example, he represented the
new type of grazier as his father did at Kilby – since his will and inventory
have not survived; but whatever he was neither he nor his descendants
disrupted the immemorial economy of the village or its farming: they
fitted into the traditional pattern with their fellows, buying land like

---

[1] *Essays in Leicestershire History*, 173-4, 176. The average estate for the period 1500-31 was £14 to 15,
but prices were rising fast by the late 1540's and £20 would be a fair estimate then.

[2] William Chamberlain's name does not appear among those of the seventeen Wigston men 'of good
credence and reputation' who were called together in January 1515 to witness the delivery of peaceful
seisin of Elizabeth Kent's property in Wigston to Thomas her son (*W.H.R.*, no. 1065). We learn from
Thomas Pawley's will (dated 12 Sept. 1536) in which he left a red heifer to 'yonge William Chamberlayne',
that his daughter Joan had married William Chamberlayne the elder.

the rest of them on a modest scale and never rising above the rank of
yeoman. At Newton Harcourt, on the contrary, the parent branch was
acquiring land in substantial parcels in the later years of the sixteenth
century; they bought the manor in 1603 and built themselves a new
mansion to replace the timber-framed and mud-walled farm-house of
their ancestors.[1]

Thomas Whyte took second place in the subsidy list, assessed on £13,
and William Astell third at £10. In the £5-9 group we find the names
of Herrick, Pawley, Smith, Amory, Palmer, Hugglescote, and Catton. All
these names (except perhaps that of Thomas Hugglescote, of whom
we have no previous knowledge) are recognisable as those of peasant
freeholders, and of these all but William Catton (or Ketton) are of long
continuance in the village – several generations, if not several centuries.
As a family, the four Pawleys (spelt Palley at this date) who are named
would actually head the list with a total assessment of £21, and the two
Whytes (both freeholders) would come second with £19. The Palley
wealth – land and movable goods – was, however, fairly evenly distributed
among the various sides of the family. Thomas Palley, assessed on £8,
whose daughter William Chamberlain married, was the most affluent of
them, followed by Robert (£5), John (£4) and Henry (£4).

Below the £5 level came the bulk of the village farmers and
craftsmen – thirty of them, as we have seen. And lastly we have twenty-
five assessments, out of a total of sixty-seven, levied on 'wages'. It
would be wholly wrong to deduce from this that already, in the first
quarter of the sixteenth century, a considerable class of landless labour,
dependent on a wage-income, had come into existence at Wigston. One
of the great merits of studying a single village in detail is that one
comes to know all the individual families and a good deal about their
economic and social circumstances; one learns to observe the workings
of a small community in detail and not to generalise rashly. And as we
look through the names of the twenty-five men who are assessed on
'wages' at the lowly figure of twenty shillings per annum, we recognise

---

[1] This manor-house still stands, evidently a building put up in the late sixteenth century and the early
years of the seventeenth. The Chamberlains of Newton Harcourt furnish another excellent example
of the type of capitalist peasants who emerge in the fifteenth century to become wealthy yeomen in the
sixteenth. By 1630 we find the senior branch described as gentry.

the names of several sons of yeomen and husbandmen who will one
day succeed to their fathers' farms, and who, in the meantime, are
working and learning their apprenticeship on father's farm or someone
else's in the village. Nine of the twenty-five names are those of this
younger generation (such as William Whyte, William Astyll, John
Rydley, William Symon, Robert Frere) and one or two others look like
the younger sons of yeomen of neighbouring villages. Thus about ten
of the wage-labour group really belong with the farming class. Of
the remainder we can be reasonably certain that most of them were
dependent, in part at least, on wages, but here again nothing could be
farther from the truth than to regard them as wage-labour pure and
simple. They were – those who did not live in with their employers as
'servants' – cottagers first and foremost and labourers second: their
'cottage economy' fitted into the economy of the open-field village, as
we shall see, and their earnings were supplementary, albeit a necessary
supplement, to this mode of life. Money played only a marginal part in
this cottage economy as indeed it did for the whole peasant economy.
We shall return to this important point later.

Thus, though wage-labour was becoming necessary on some of the
larger farms that were now making their appearance at Wigston, the
labouring class did not bulk very large in the village during the first half
of the sixteenth century at least. There may have been a dozen men who
would have been described in contemporary records as 'labourer', out
of a total of some seventy households, but some of these would equally
well have been called 'cottager' and as such would enjoy an estate and a
standard of living equal to that of many a small husbandmen.[1]

✤ THE PEASANT FARM ✤

So far we have largely been concerned with the inhabitants of Wigston
in their legal capacity of freeholders, leaseholders, customary tenants

---

[1] The economy of the cottager and labourer is discussed more fully subsequently (pp. 171- 4). In
Leicestershire as a whole, assessments on wages amounted to 22 per cent of the total in 1524–5. Allowing
for those men who were sons of farmers, learning the trade, we may put the 'labouring class' at about one
in six of the total rural population in this county. By contrast, in Devon the proportion is something like
one in three. Here the peasant proprietor, too, is far less conspicuous, as a result of an entirely different
social and economic development.

and taxpayers, and we have been discussing the village and its lands
primarily from the manorial point of view. Now we turn to the people
of Wigston as farmers, to study, so far as the records permit, their
mode of farming under the open-field system, which is still far from
being rightly understood; to discover, if we can, what were their crops,
their livestock, and their implements, how they rotated their crops and
treated their pastures, how the craftsman and the cottager fitted into the
whole economy of the open fields; and how far we have a self-sufficient,
subsistence husbandry and how far a cash or money economy.

The Wigston farmer had his house and buildings on the village
street, never out in the fields. His house either faced the street, in the
oldest part of the village, or lay at right angles to it in that part of
the village which grew into a built-up area in the thirteenth century.
Besides the dwelling-house, there were the barn and the stable; the
yard, in which lay certain 'hovels' or roughly built out-houses, used
to store peas and other crops or implements and wood and coals; the
croft, an enclosed pasture varying from half an acre to an acre in size;
and a garden and a small orchard. In the middle years of the sixteenth
century, before the break-up of the manors had altered the pattern of
land-holding fundamentally, the typical farmer had ½, ¾, or 1 yardland
scattered throughout the fields in 'lands' or 'roods'. These lands were
always regarded as belonging to, or going with, a particular house in
the village. When Robert Frere bought a farm of half a yardland from
William Ashby, esquire, in 1512, it is described as 'one messuage in
Wigston situated between the lands of the earl of Oxford on all sides
and extending from the king's way to a lane (*venella*) called *ffutturs lane*
on the north side and half a virgate of land in the fields to the same
messuage belonging, with pastures, meadows and other commodities
belonging to the said messuage and lands'.[1] And when William Fryer
(or Freer), junior, bought a farm in 1608 from the Danvers manor, in
the same part of the village, it is described as 'a messuage with a croft
or close on the back side, between the common street on the south side

---

[1] L.R.O., 9.D. 43. Bundle 184. The site of the farmhouse may be identified as on the north side of what
is now Moat Street, extending back to the lane now called Blunts Lane (anciently Futturs lane: so called
in a court roll of 1467 when John Penne was presented for not having made a water-course there).

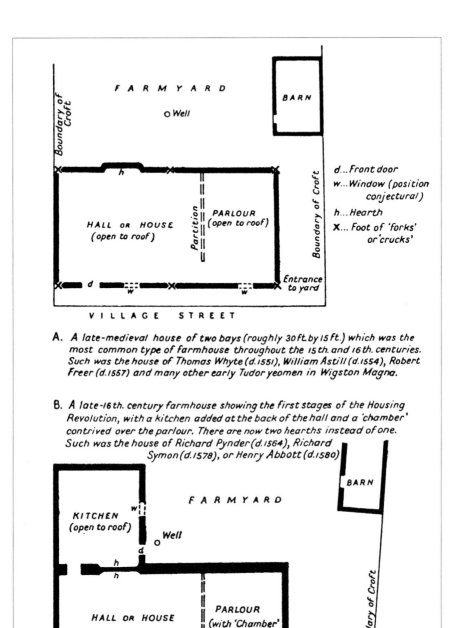

A. A late-medieval house of two bays (roughly 30 ft. by 15 ft.) which was the most common type of farmhouse throughout the 15th. and 16th. centuries. Such was the house of Thomas Whyte (d.1551), William Astill (d.1554), Robert Freer (d.1557) and many other early Tudor yeomen in Wigston Magna.

B. A late-16th. century farmhouse showing the first stages of the Housing Revolution, with a kitchen added at the back of the hall and a 'chamber' contrived over the parlour. There are now two hearths instead of one. Such was the house of Richard Pynder (d.1564), Richard Symon (d.1578), or Henry Abbott (d.1580)

Two sixteenth-century farmhouse types at Wigston.

and *le Hall Closse* on the north side, together with one virgate and three quarters of a virgate *anglice* A yard and three quarternes of land to the same messuage belonging.'[1] Nevertheless, there was no immemorial fixity about these lands: sales and exchanges, partitions among heirs, had all modified the regularity of the earlier pattern to some extent.[2]

The lands going with a particular farm were distributed throughout the three open fields, but not necessarily in equal proportions by the late sixteenth century, so far as we can judge from our limited information. Few early terriers, or schedules attached to grants and conveyances, have survived. The earliest is that of half a yardland bought by Richard Danne in 1577.

Richard Danne's farm was small: a cottage and half a virgate is how it is described in the conveyance: probably the 13¼ acres specified in the fine. Of this about 47 roods lay in the three fields (11¾ acres) and there were 'three doles' of meadow which probably made up the remaining 1½ acres.[3] Of the 47 roods in the fields, 12½ lay in Thythorn Hill Field, 16 in Goldhill Field, and 18½ in Mucklow Field.

Another terrier of 1582 relates to 26 roods, probably a quarter of a yardland. Of these, 10 roods lay in Mucklow Field, and 8 each in Thythorn Hill Field and Goldhill Field. Attached to this record is another (but incomplete) terrier of late sixteenth-century date, covering only Goldhill Field and Mucklow Field. There are 16 roods specified in the former and 19½ in the latter. Almost certainly this terrier relates to a farm of half a yardland containing some 55 to 60 roods in all.[4]

A terrier dated 1601,[5] relating to half a yardland sold by Robert

---

[1] The site of this farmhouse can he identified almost exactly in the present Moat Street, where the Primitive Methodist church now stands, extending back to close no. 193 (O.S. 25-in.map, 1930 edn.) which was anciently 'Hall Close' or 'Halcroft' in the fifteenth century.

[2] See also *Essays in Leicestershire History*, 136-7.

[3] The small uncertainty over the acreage in the fields arises from the fact that 'one hade land' is not measured and 'one ley' is similarly left undefined. Other leys are put down as 1 rood or 1½ roods. I have assumed here that the headland and ley together amounted to two roods. Similarly, the doles of meadow are not defined in area, but we cannot go far wrong in assuming that each was half an acre in extent, so making up the total of 13¼ acres of land specified in the fine.

[4] L.R.O., 12 D. 38/5.

[5] L.C.R.O., Court Book of Beaumanor, *c.* 1605-13. The terrier is complete. It is undated, but the fine relating to the transaction survives in the P.R.O.

Hall to Nicholas Wilde, shows that there were 16 roods of arable and ley in Goldhill Field, 13½ in Mucklow Field, and about 13 in Thythorn Hill Field, a total of about 42½ roods. An undated terrier of the early seventeenth century, relating to the sale of one-eighth of a yardland by William Wild to William Simpson, shows 6, 5½, and 6 roods respectively in the three fields.[1]

It will be noticed in these, and in later terriers and schedules, that the yardland at Wigston varied somewhat in size (as we know it did in other Leicestershire villages) though some allowance must be made for the difficulty of translating acreages into fractions of a yardland with any high degree of accuracy. The 'normal' yardland at Wigston was thirty-two acres and most measurements approximated closely to this.

On the whole we may say that no great irregularity in the distribution of strips among the three fields had appeared at Wigston even by the early seventeenth century, nor in fact could it ever do so under a simple three-field rotation or the whole balance of the farm would have been upset. There was a limit to the extent to which sales of single strips could take place, and the limit was soon reached. Exchanges of strips between two owners were another matter, for they did not alter the total amount of land in each field belonging to a particular farm, but only the size of the particular strip.

This consolidation of 'lands' into larger units had gone on to a varying extent on different farms. An analysis will show what had happened on three typical Wigston farms between 1577 and 1601:

Size of strip	Danne (1577)	Danne (1582)	Wilde (1601)
½ rood	0	4	4
1 rood	20	6	26
1½ rood	10	0	0
½ acre	4	7	8
over ½ acre	1 acre	1 (1 acre)	0
	35 strips	18 strips	38 strips
Total area excluding meadow	11¾ strips	6½ acres	11 acres

[1] L.R.O., 4 D. 38/25.

All three farms were still largely conventional farms of one-rood strips: nearly three strips in five conform to that size. It will be seen incidentally that the acre-strip is a text-book myth. Of the ninety-one strips listed above, twenty-one were half an acre or more, roughly a quarter of the total. Only two strips out of ninety-one were an acre in size.

We also discover from these early terriers or schedules an intermixture of arable strips and leys in each of the three fields, an intermixture which Gray rightly found to be a characteristic of Midland field-books. Of the 47 roods of ground on Richard Danne's farm in 1577, eight were leys, distributed unevenly among the three fields in the proportion of 1, 4½, and 2½ roods. Of the forty-four roods on Nicholas Wilde's farm in 1601, ten were ley ground, distributed in the proportion of 4, 3, and 3 roods in the three fields. On another late sixteenth-century farm for which we have some details, ten roods out of 38½ were ley ground. The amount of ground under leys in the open fields (that is, excluding any consideration of meadow ground) was 17 per cent, 23 per cent, and 26 per cent respectively. We shall refer to this aspect of open-field husbandry at greater length on a later page.

These leys were quite independent of the meadow ground which went with every farm and is separately listed in the terriers. The meadows were for hay, the leys primarily, if not entirely, for grazing of tethered beasts or animals enclosed within temporary hurdles. The meadow ground was not intermixed with the arable like the leys, but extended in great blocks that fringed each of the three arable fields. Thythorn Hill Field had Broad Meadow and Long Meadow, the largest stretch of meadow in the parish, along its southern edge bordering the little river Sence; Goldhill Field had Hilly Meadow along its western edge; and Mucklow Field had North Meadow which extended along the Knighton Brook.

✌ OPEN-FIELD HUSBANDRY ✌

The farming of Wigston throughout the sixteenth century was the traditional mixed farming of the open-field system in which the arable was by far the most important. On the average farm the arable acreage was just about three-quarters of the whole, rising to as much as eighty per cent in some cases. The main source of our knowledge about the mixed farming of the typical open-field village lies in the probate inventories, and in wills, and lawsuits. Wigston farming was typical of Leicestershire at least, if not of a wider extent of the East Midlands. It retained a simple three-field system to the end, and so did the great majority of Leicestershire villages. Four out of five had a three-field system until well on into the seventeenth century, if not longer.[1]

The wills and inventories have already been used elsewhere for a study of the Leicestershire farmer in the sixteenth century[2] and we shall draw upon the results of this study, and upon further inventories from other open-field villages in the county, to supplement our knowledge of the Wigston farmer and his husbandry. For Wigston alone we have fifty-six inventories covering the period between 1529 and 1603, together with twelve others for which only the totals, and no details, now survive. These inventories cover all classes in the village, from the cottager and labourer, the craftsman, the husbandman and the yeoman, up to a solitary gentleman in the person of William Lawe, the farmer of the tithes and the rectory, which had three yardlands going with it. They range in value from the humble 23s. of Alice Pallett to the £937 15s. of William Lawe, and give us a cross-section of the social classes of the whole village; but primarily, of course, they are the inventories of peasant farmers.

Although about thirty of the inventories tell us something of the farming of the village, only four are sufficiently specific as to the distribution of crops; but these, fortunately, are enough to tell us that (with certain qualifications which we shall notice) the distribution of crops in the fields of Wigston and the numbers of livestock kept were essentially the same as in Leicestershire as a whole. This enables us to draw upon our knowledge of the county as a whole, and of particular open-field villages in it, to supplement the deficiencies of the Wigston records without sacrificing the truth about this one village.

As in Leicestershire generally, the Wigston farmer's household goods accounted for only one-sixth or one-seventh, on an average, of his total personal estate. The remainder consisted of his farm-goods: his livestock, crops, implements and gear, and miscellanea such as 'hovels', dunghills, and 'pales' or hurdles, in that order of value usually.

[1] *Studies in Leicestershire Agrarian History*, 94.
[2] *Essays in Leicestershire History*, 123-83.

In this respect, too, the Wigston farmer is typical of the open-field farmer anywhere in Leicestershire.

In any given year two fields were sown with various crops and one lay entirely fallow. Of the two sown fields, one was reserved exclusively for peas and beans, which thus constituted fifty per cent of the acreage under crops. There is a very slight variation in this percentage from farm to farm but over the whole parish peas and beans accounted (to be precise) for 49½ per cent of the sown acreage.[1] For Leicestershire as a whole peas took up 43.3 per cent of the acreage in 1500-31 and 45.9 per cent in 1588. We have no such detailed figures for Wigston, but it is clear that peas and beans were somewhat more important here than in the county generally. It is also apparent from the Wigston inventories that they took the place of oats which, where they were sown, were almost invariably sown in the pease field and accounted for about 3 per cent of the sown acreage in Leicestershire in 1588. Not a single Wigston inventory mentions oats, either growing in the field or in the barns and ricks. The whole of one field at Wigston was therefore sown with peas and beans and nothing else in the sixteenth century.

The other field was sown with both winter and spring corn wheat, rye, and barley – all over Leicestershire. The wheat and rye went in the ground in the autumn and occupied rather less than 20 per cent of the sown acreage for the year. Towards the end of the century this figure fell to 12½ per cent.[2] In other words, rather more than a third of the corn field was sown with wheat and rye in the autumn, and the remainder was sown with barley in the following spring. By 1588 only a quarter of the field was being sown with winter corn, and three-quarters with barley. At Wigston the same rotation was observed in principle but the proportions under the three crops were different. Very little rye was grown, only about 1 per cent of the sown acreage as against 4 per cent in the county as a whole. Many farmers seem to have grown none, as it is not mentioned in the ground or in their barns. Wheat was also less important than in the county generally: most, if not all, farmers at Wigston grew some, except the cottagers

---

[1] Beans are never separately mentioned in the inventories: it is always 'pease', and the field was sometimes called 'the pease field'.

[2] Actually 18.8 per cent in the period 1500-31, 17.2 per cent in 1558, 12½ per cent in 1588. *Essays*, 162, 168, 171.

who concentrated on barley, peas and beans, but the acreage under wheat was 6 per cent of the sown area as against 8½ per cent in Leicestershire generally. Barley was correspondingly more important: 43½ per cent of the sown acreage as against 38½ per cent in the county. The differences are statistically slight but they represent an important fact, and that is that in the sixteenth century there were variations in cropping even within a small and apparently uniform area like Leicestershire. The land in Wigston is largely strong heavy clay land, excellent for peas, beans, and barley. There was little sandy land and consequently less scope for rye than elsewhere: the village was built over the largest tract of soil that might have grown rye: nor were the local soils suitable for oats. Once more we have testimony to the knowledge of the open-field farmer and to the flexibility of the system in which he worked.

These figures do, however, raise questions as to the rotation of crops practised in the fields. If only seven per cent of the whole sown acreage was under winter corn, how did the open-field farmer at Wigston get through the apparently overwhelming proportion of work left for the spring? The answer is that in the Midlands peas and beans were a winter-sown crop as early as the sixteenth century, even perhaps as early as the fourteenth. A record of 1343 tells us that on the demesne of William de Roos at Bottesford (in the extreme north-east of Leicestershire) twenty acres had been sown with peas before his death, which took place on 3 February.[1] Beans and peas could be sown, then, in January or February, and the bulk, if not all, of this seed got in before the sowing of the barley in March or April.

That wheat, rye, and barley were invariably sown in the same field, and oats (where grown) and pease and beans in the other, is abundantly clear from the inventories. Either the crops are valued in two groups ('all the wheate, rye, and barlie' and 'all the pease and oates') which clearly reflect the two separate fields as inspected by the appraisers, or else, if the acreages under the separate crops are specified, we can see that we must have this grouping to obtain an approximately equal acreage in each field.[2]

[1] Farnham, vi, 197-8. The inventory of Thomas Jackson, a Wigston yeoman, made on 27 January 1662, values *inter alia* 'pease sowed on the ground'.

[2] Cf. Cotesbach, where Exchequer depositions of 1616 tell us that the two fields under cultivation were known as the Barley Field and the Pease Field. At Cossington in 1610 we find the two fields under cultivation again called the Barley Field and the Pease Field.

Clearly, too, the unit of cropping, especially in the corn field proper, was the furlong and not the whole field, so making the cropping far more flexible than one could otherwise have got. In this way one can explain the adjustment in the wheat and rye area in Leicestershire between 1500-31 and 1588 from 18.8 per cent of the sown acreage to 12.5 per cent: it was simply a question of sowing fewer furlongs or strips with wheat and rye in the autumn and that many more with barley in the spring.

At Wigston the crops were distributed as to acreage:

Peas and beans.   ..   .. 49½ %
Barley   ..   .. 43½ %
Wheat and rye.   ..   .. 7 % (wheat roughly 6 per cent, rye
                                    roughly 1 per cent)

Values and yields would be more informative than acreages sown, but we cannot arrive at these figures. In Leicestershire as a whole, after the harvest of 1558, barley accounted for 47 per cent of the value of all crops (35.8 per cent of acreage); peas and beans 27½ per cent of value (38½ per cent of acreage); wheat and rye 24 per cent of value (17.2 per cent of acreage); and oats 1½ per cent of value (8½ per cent of acreage). The Wigston inventories do not lend themselves to this treatment as they almost invariably lump all the crops together, in the field or in the barn, and give a composite value. Nevertheless, one can see that at Wigston barley would have been by far the most valuable crop, with peas and beans a good second – far ahead of wheat and rye – but well behind barley in total value. It is significant perhaps that one part of the old fields got its name from the fact that it was excellent for barley; and that, unlike so many Leicestershire parishes, Wigston had no local spot called 'Ryelondes' or 'Ryehill'.

Apart from these major crops, one knows also that small crops of hemp and flax were grown at Wigston as in the majority of Leicestershire villages, though the acreage is always too small to appear separately in the inventories. *Flaxlondes* appears as the name of a furlong at Kimcote, in the south of Leicestershire, in the thirteenth century, and a record of 1402 at Wigston speaks of 'all manner of grain, pease, hay, hemp and flax … stored there in the granges and houses of the same rectory'.[1] The crops of

---

[1] Kimcote (*W.H.R.*, no. 268), Wigston (*W.H.R.*, no. 983).

hemp and flax were important enough in many villages in the county to be tithed in the sixteenth century. They were grown on small parcels of ground known as *plecks* and supplied the farmhouse with the raw material for its linen sheets, table cloths, napkins, pillow-cases, and towels, all of which appear abundantly in the sixteenth-century inventories together with one or more 'linen wheeles'. There is no evidence that they were ever cash crops.

Turning now to the livestock of the Wigston farm, we have thirty inventories, made between 1534 and 1602, which give sufficient details of the farms concerned, though all but three of these fall in the period 1550-1602. There is, however, very little change in Leicestershire as a whole throughout the sixteenth century except perhaps in the number of horses kept, and we can regard the Wigston inventories as typical of the whole century. We find that on six of the 30 farms no sheep at all appear, and these are not all inventories made in the winter months. Richard Herrick's inventory was made in October 1534: he had horses, six cattle, and four pigs. Thomas Whyte's inventory was made 10 April 1551: he had three horses, three cattle, three pigs. William Holmes' inventory is dated 28 October 1602, and lists six horses, six cattle, and two pigs, but no sheep. The other three inventories which show no sheep were made in the months of January and February and may indicate that the sheep had been killed off for lack of winter feed, though in fact the majority of Leicestershire farmers kept at least some of their flock in being all through the winter months. Innumerable inventories made between November and April reveal the number of sheep one would normally expect. Possibly a number of farmers sold off their sheep about Michaelmas and this may account for their absence in the October inventories.[1]

The great majority of Wigston farmers, however, kept sheep as an integral part of their mixed husbandry. One has only to read their wills, of which nearly a hundred survive for the period 1512-1603, to realise how important sheep were in the peasant farmer's mind. Practically every farmer made bequests of sheep or lambs–to the parish

[1] The inventory of Robert Freer, probably the largest farmer in Wigston in the early seventeenth century, similarly shows no sheep on 30 October 1626, though he had horses, cattle and pigs. But he had large sums of money 'due upon Bills and Bonds' and some of this may represent sheep-sales.

church, to his children, and his children's children, to his widow, his shepherd or his farm-servants, and to relatives of all kinds and degrees. It was almost as if a man was nothing without a few sheep: even labourers managed to keep two or three, and sometimes considerably more. On the twenty-four farms which carried sheep, the distribution was as follows:

1-19	sheep..	..	..	..	..	..	..6	farms
20-9	"	..	..	..	..	..	..9	"
30-9	"	..	..	..	..	..	..2	"
40-59	"	..	..	..	..	..	..2	"
60-79	"	..	..	..	..	..	..2	"
80-99	"	..	..	..	..	..	..1	"
100-180	"	..	..	..	..	..	..2	"

The median farmer had 25 sheep, as against 30 in the county at large. This reflects the greater division of property at Wigston among middling-sized farmers, whereas in the county as a whole the figure is pulled up by the existence of a top class of big farmers who carried flocks of 200-500 sheep. At Wigston two farmers out of three, among those who had any at all, carried fewer than thirty sheep: the average farmer had between twenty and thirty, as many as could be fed off a farm of a ½-1 yardland in the sixteenth century. At the other end of the scale we find the occasional farmer like William Astell (died 1554) with 100 sheep and Robert Freer (died 1557) with 180. William Astell, we know, occupied what was probably the largest farm in the village in his time – the old Randull capital messuage, with the three yardlands that went with it, and the Hall Close – by copy of court roll dated 29 Henry VIII (1537-8), and Stephen Astell his son still occupied it fifty years later. As for Robert Freer, we know little of the size of his farm, though it was evidently much larger than most. We know the Freers were buying land in Wigston early in the century and leasing other land from the Hospital as well, but beyond that nothing. They appear as the most energetic and acquisitive family in the village in the sixteenth century – as their kindred were at Burton Overy, not far away, at the same time.[1] Robert Freer,

---

[1] At Burton Overy they appear as freeholders from 1,428 up to the eighteenth century though they ceased to live there soon after 1600. In 1524 they were second highest in the subsidy list; in 1545 they were first. It is highly probable that the Freers came to Wigston late in the fifteenth century from Burton Overy.

when he died, left the largest personal estate that had been known in the village – £94 16s. 0d. in all, of which his sheep accounted for £40, his wool for £16, and his crops for £8. Cattle and horses were worth about £16 more, making a total of £72 for livestock as against £8 for crops. The average farmer's livestock was worth about twice the value of his crops. But Robert Freer and William Astell were exceptional. No other Wigston farmers followed in their path for a long time afterwards.

The remainder of the farmer's livestock need not detain us long. The number of horses of all kinds (horses, mares, foals, etc.) ranged from none to twelve. William Astell had twelve, but his waggon – the first to appear in the village – was pulled by six bullocks.[1] The average farmer had three or four horses, kept for cart, plough, and harrow. Cattle of all kinds were not numerous, ranging from the cottager's three milch kine to William Astell's twenty. Even a largish yeoman had only 10-14 cattle on his farm; the average farm carried about six or seven, enough for the milk, butter and cheese that were made and mostly consumed on the farm. As for pigs, nearly every farmer had three or four: again William Astell heads the list with sixteen, but even a yeoman-farmer only had 8-10 on an average. Poultry, of course, one found everywhere – hens, ducks, and geese – and many farmers and some cottagers kept hives of bees.

Farming implements and gear varied as much from farm to farm as anything else. The poorest husbandmen had no cart or plough: probably they were what we should call 'cottagers' though they might be farming up to half a yardland – say 10 to 15 acres in all. Such men presumably borrowed their carts, ploughs and harrows in return for their help on a larger man's farm, but some villages kept a 'town plow' at the church which one imagines was borrowed by the ploughless husbandman in turn. There are references in the Archdeacons' Visitation Books at Leicester to such ploughs. Or a sensible parson, like the vicar of Ashby Magna in 1558, might leave

---

A Freer of Burton witnessed a Wigston deed in 1428. Like the Chamberlains, the Freers came to Wigston, not as newcomers having to make their way from nothing, but already solidly established on land of their own in a neighbouring village. As with the Chamberlains, a marriage with another peasant landholding family may have been the occasion for settling at Wigston.

[1] He had 6 horses going with carts and plough, 2 'panneers' horses, 2 'myllne' horses, and 2 foals.

'to everyone of my paryshioners yt be occupeyed so mych tymber as shall make everyone of them a plow'.[1]

The average Wigston farmer, however, had a plough, one or two carts, and two or three harrows (usually 'one great harrow' and one or two little harrows). Only two farmers, out of all those fifty or so whose detailed inventories we have, possessed a waggon. William Astell (once more) had a 'wayne' in 1554, and John Cartwright in 1572. But waggons were uncommon all over Leicestershire before 1600: in some parts of the Midlands, indeed, non-existent. Only the big farmers had one or two, and only a minority even of these.[2]

'Iron-bound carts' are always distinguished in the inventories from the others which are sometimes described as 'bare'. Although the practice of putting iron strakes on the wooden wheels of carts goes back to the late thirteenth century, and possibly somewhat earlier, and represents a big improvement in a farmer's gear, just as waggons did when they came in the second half of the sixteenth century, only a minority of farmers could afford the extra cost involved. At Wigston, up to 1603, we find only five farmers possessing 'iron-bound' carts, and twenty-one 'bare' carts.

The only other farm-gear (other than implements like scythes and so forth) of which we hear anything in the sixteenth century are a 'draught rake' and a roller. Rollers were almost unknown in Leicestershire, certainly at Wigston. A draw-rake appears on Harry Huckyllscott's farm in 1557, and on the farms of Richard Boulter (1581) and Robert Coulson (1596). Harrows were apparently all made of wood: no iron harrows are mentioned in any sixteenth-century inventories.

Two further aspects of the Wigston farmer's practice call for comment: one is the practice of making temporary enclosures to which reference has already been made in passing, and the other, connected with it, is the difficult question of the treatment of the leys which every farmer had amongst his arable strips.

The customary tenants of the manor in 1587-8 claimed the right to enclose any of their customary or copyhold lands lying in the open fields

[1] Thomas Chamberlayne of Newton Harcourt, 'yowman', left by his will dated 29 September 1571 'to every poore neighbour in Wistowe [the mother parish] goinge with no plowghe' half a strike of malt.
[2] The inventories show that by 1558 there might have been one waggon in most villages in Leicestershire, but they remained rare for the next fifty years. Even after 1600 many big yeomen and farming gentry had none.

with 'hedges, ditches or quicsetts' and to keep these parcels enclosed and separate until August 1st in any year. That they had been doing this is clear from Sir John Danvers' answer to them: they had also exchanged parcels of their customary lands with each other and 'bothe geven and taken estates in cache others lands' and had enclosed these parcels in severalty, together with parcels of their own customary lands. We are not now concerned with the custom of the manor about this practice, but with its importance for farming practice at Wigston. What other evidence is there of this practice of making temporary enclosures, and were they solely enclosures of small separate pastures (leys) or did they go farther and enclose some of the arable lands?

It is difficult to come by information about the extent and purpose of these temporary enclosures. The by-laws regulating the management of the open fields have perished, though we know they once existed in writing, and we have only scraps of evidence on the subject from this and other Leicestershire villages. A quarrel between Henry White and William and Richard Boulter in the 1620's eventually reached the High Court of Chancery in London and throws a little light on the question.[1] After an exchange of three lands to settle disputes between them, Henry White 'at his own cost made a ditch and set a quicksett hedge' upon one of the lands which lay near the highway and was 'lying in destruccion', and fenced it off from cattle. He planted 'divers willowes and sallowes' upon it and greatly improved the value of the piece. 'But now that the thorns and trees be well grown, and the land which was formerly of little value because it was neare the highway is now worth three times such value before the hedging', Richard Boulter (son of the Boulter who had made the exchange) 'seeketh all the ways he can to avoid the said exchange'. He had cut and carried away some of the tops of the thorns and willow trees, had made a lease of the ground to someone else, and had brought a suit at common law to evict White and to take advantage of the improvement.

Another kind of enclosure appears in seventeenth-century terriers. Richard Davenport's half yardland in 1659 contained 'two Rood Leyes uppon the overend of Hungarton sicke … one of the Leyes haveing a

---

[1] Henry White v. Richard and William Boulter. Bill dated 16 May 1634 (Chancery Proceedings, P.R.O., C.3. 418/no 52).

hedge uppon it'. Thomas Coltman's half yardland in 1626 contained
one half-acre piece in Goldhill Field, now cutt into two with the hedge
thereon,' and in Mucklow Field 'one half acre ley in the closse called
the three leyes closse with the hedge on the same'.[1] Here we apparently
have small-scale enclosure of pasture. The reference in the Chancery
suit of 1588 is clear enough so far as it goes but gives no hint of the
purpose of the enclosures mentioned. I am inclined to think they were
enclosures of ley ground only, either for the purpose of growing hay or
for the grazing of cattle and sheep amongst the corn.[2]

The evidence we have is meagre enough and we shall need to study
other open-field villages in detail before we can arrive at the truth.
What is clear, however, is that the leys in the arable fields had formerly
been ploughed and cultivated. In a dispute over the tithe of hay on
certain parcels of land in Wigston in 1574, one deponent said 'that the
parishioners of Wyggeston have allwaies and at this present tyme dothe
paye tythe hey of all such lees and hades which hathe bene arrable unto
the parsonns and farmers of Wiggeston'.[3] It is also clear at Wigston
that some of the leys in the open fields lay in parts that were probably
never ploughed up, though they may have been under cultivation in the
'land-hunger' of the thirteenth and fourteenth centuries.[4] What we do
not know, but can only suspect, is whether some leys, at any rate, were
ploughed up again after a few seasons under pasture: in fact whether a
convertible husbandry was practised in parts of the open fields from an
early date. One strongly suspects that the open-field farmer in certain
parts of the Midlands, instead of sowing a grain crop, or peas and
beans as the case might be, on every one of his strips in the field,
chose to leave a varying number under grass for some years, either for

[1] L.R.O. (Wigston Magna docts: unclassified).

[2] Similar enclosure of leys in the open field occurs at Cossington, Leics. Among some lands exchanged
in 1609 we find 'three selions or leys of pasture ground enclosed in the field called little Rye Field'. In
1634 these are described as 'all those three selions of pasture enclosed in the little Rye Field'. (Skillington,
History of Cossington, 140.)

[3] L.R.O., Proceedings in the Archdeaconry Court, 1574. Richard Warde, farmer of the rectory of
Wigston v. William Clarke of Wigston.

[4] Thus we have leys in Watery Leys (1639) and Watry leyes (1704), which suggests permanent
pasture at that date on land really unsuitable for arable cultivation. But in documents of 1324 and 1393
we read of selions of arable land on *le Wattrie* or *Wattry*. Possibly this arable had reverted to pasture
in the fifteenth century when the population of the village was failing steadily, so easing the pressure
on the ploughland.

the purpose of growing hay as a crop amongst the other crops, or for grazing them with his sheep and cattle. If the latter, he would fence around the strip, either with hurdles if the enclosure was a temporary one, or by planting quick-growing trees like thorns and willows if he envisaged a long-term ley. After a few years some of the leys might be ploughed up again, and other strips let down to pasture in turn.

If sheep were grazed on temporary grass, hurdles were probably put up around or on the ley. Every farmer's inventory mentions 'pales' or 'peales' and 'fleaks' among his gear and tackle. If larger animals such as horses and plough-oxen were grazed in this way, they had to be tethered or otherwise held in check. This is made clear by the Wymeswold regulations again, which show that it was exceptional for the larger animals to be put on the separate leys. Only if his horse 'is febull and may not do his werke for faute of mete' was a man allowed to put him into his 'severyll grasse', taking precautions that 'he save his neighbour from harm'. Probably these regulations as to the feeding of stock on separate grass were fairly general. We know from eighteenth-century records that the larger animals were tethered or 'nogged' at Wigston.

There is yet another difficulty to face. In the sixteenth century these temporary enclosures were thrown open on Lammas Day (August 1st), in order that when the corn or the pease field was cut the whole could be grazed over freely. This was reasonable enough as the farmer would have gathered his hay from his separate pasture by then, or if he were grazing sheep on an enclosed pasture it made little difference to have it thrown open at that date. Such 'Lammas closes' are well known in many openfield villages. But it also appears that some of these enclosures of ley ground developed into permanent closes among the arable. Henry White's enclosure in the 1620's (not of pasture, it is true) was a permanent enclosure within planted hedgerows, and in 1740 we find Amos Simon selling a close called 'Thackasick Close' together with all the hades thereto belonging, lying in Mucklow Field. This had developed out of the enclosure of leys at some date in the past, and had become permanent. Similar small permanent enclosures of ley ground in the open arable fields can be found in other Leicestershire villages. It seems probable that these permanent closes may have lain on the edge of the arable field so that they did not constitute awkward little islands in the great sea of the fallow field, or that they lay together in a block in some out-of-the-way part. But by what arrangement a farmer could permanently hedge off a piece of the open field for his own benefit, and so diminish the amount of the common pasturage over the fallow, we do not know. A number of such small closes existed at Wigston by the time of the enclosure award, but their total area did not amount to much. The majority of the leys were only temporarily enclosed, and were thrown open on 1 August as common to all until some date early in the new year, when they reverted to separate pasture. The amount of land so treated varied from farmer to farmer and from field to field according to his special needs, but the total extent of land under convertible husbandry at Wigston was not negligible. On the three farms already noticed, the leys amounted to between seventeen and twenty-six per cent of the land in the open fields. Roughly speaking we may say that about twenty per cent of the open fields were subject to convertible husbandry by the closing years of the sixteenth century.

The practice was not of course peculiar to Wigston. It was followed in most if not all of the open-field villages in Leicestershire and probably over the Midlands as a whole. At Lutterworth the ley ground varied in extent from a sixth to a thirteenth of the whole farm, the average being rather more than ten per cent on the seven farms sampled.[1] At Arnesby, about four miles south of Wigston, a mid-sixteenth century survey of a farm of two yardlands shows 24½ acres of leys and meadow distributed among the three open fields out of a total area of 58½ acres. Here about three acres in every five were arable and two were under grass. The existence of separate leys among the arable is clearly evidenced at Wymeswold in north Leicestershire early in the fifteenth century. The open-field system was obviously a far more flexible system than has been commonly supposed, with its adaptation of crops to variations in soils and its treatment of the pastures, both of which allowed individual farmers a good deal of initiative and latitude in the management of their husbandry.

As to the meadows at Wigston, these lay on the north, south, and

---

[1] *Essays in Leics History*, 140.

western edges of the three fields but were regarded as coming within the adjoining fields for purposes of schedules and terriers. Each farm had certain pieces in one or other of the three meadows. Richard Danne's half-yardland in 1577 had three single doles of meadow in Long Meadow and Broad Meadow, going with Thythorn Hill Field; another quarter-yardland of his in 1582 had 'a piece' each in Long Meadow and Broad Meadow and two pieces in Hillow Meadow, all of unspecified size. Thomas Coltman's half-yardland in 1639 had one piece 'two swaeths' broad and three other pieces of undefined width, all in Broad Meadow.

In no instance is the area of the meadow pieces stated, and we do not discover anywhere what the acreage of meadow appurtenant to a yardland farm, for example, was reckoned to be. Specific pieces of meadow ground went with each farm, and exchanges of pieces were made as with the arable strips. In the hay-tithe dispute of 1574, Henry Abbott deposed that 'Walter Clarke hathe three hades in halterslade of whiche one belonged to his house all his tyme and the other two hades he had by exchange of John Androe and Thomas Smythe … ' Henry Abbott himself had three hades together lying next to Walter Clarke. Walter Pawley deposed 'that in somer when the(y) use to mowe there grasse the parisheners beinge togeather doe amongste theym. selves agrey and saye lett us begin and mowe longe medowe suche a day and soe that day they doe mowe longe medowe and halters slade togeather as one meadowe … '[1]

Unfortunately we can form little idea of the average monetary value of the hay crop on the Wigston farm. Almost invariably hay is lumped in the inventories with all the corn and pease. Only now and then do we get a separate valuation, and, even so, much obviously depends on the time of the year as to the value of the crops one finds in the barns and hovels. Richard Herrick in October 1534 had barley to the value of 40s., pease (with the hovel timber included here) valued at 35s. 8d., and hay 20s. In January 1543 Richard Burgess's wheat and barley were valued at £5, and his pease and hay at £8, but he was by way of being a bigger sheep farmer than the average in the village. Ann Evyns in March 1558 had 33s. 4d. worth of corn in her barn and 13s. 4d. worth of hay. Walter Clark in February 1581 had crops in the barn to the value of £18 – barley

---

[1] L.R.O, Archdeaconry Court Proceedings (1574).

£10, pease £6, hay £2. We have to take the Leicestershire inventories as a whole to get a better idea of the relative importance of hay as a crop, though this of course obscures what variations there might be between different parts of the county; and already, in the sixteenth century, one can see from the inventories that a certain amount of specialisation was beginning to develop in the farming of different districts.

Taking ten inventories at random from the large bundle for 1558 we find that the hay crop was worth more than the pease crop on three farms, though on an average it was worth just about a half. Occasionally the hay was worth as much as, or rather more than, the wheat crop on a particular farm. On all ten farms the value of the hay varied between eight and sixteen per cent of the total value of all crops and averaged twelve per cent. Hay was a most variable crop in the sixteenth century, as we might expect from the varying acreages of ley on typical open-field farms, though not more variable than the grain and pease crops from farm to farm. Thomas Knight, husbandman at East Norton, in the eastern uplands of the county, died in 1546 leaving 95 sheep, 23 cattle of all kinds, and 15 horses of all kinds. His crops were valued (just after harvest) at: wheat 40s., barley 80s., peas and beans 48s., and hay 60s. The hay on this farm was worth well over a quarter of the whole crop: already the famous pastures of High Leicestershire were exerting their influence on farming practice. But at Wigston, away from the upland country, our meagre information rather suggests that the hay crop took about the same place in the farmer's economy as it did in Leicestershire generally – fourth in value, after barley, pease, and wheat.[1]

❧   THE CRAFTSMEN AND TRADESMEN   ☙

There remain for discussion two classes of village society, the craftsmen and tradesmen, and the cottagers and labourers. Here our Wigston inventories alone are not sufficient to give us a detailed picture and we must draw upon what we find in the other open-field villages round about in Leicestershire. The pattern of economic and social life which the inventories reveal, in these villages that remained open and more or less untouched by enclosure, is so obviously a uniform one, a pattern indeed that one finds repeated

---

[1] *Essays*, 170, note 2.

over a much wider area of the Midlands, that we sense that we are
dealing with a peasant culture over a wide area with certain fundamental
characteristics in common, however much local variation there might be
in detail, arising from local differences of soil, building materials, past
accidents of history, and the like.

Among the craftsmen the smith, the wheelwright, and the carpenter,
were the most important in Wigston; among the tradesmen, for want of
a better term, we find the miller and the baker in the sixteenth century,
with the butcher and the tailor emerging early in the seventeenth. One
characteristic was common to all of them: they carried on their craft or
trade in conjunction with the ownership or at least the occupation of a
small farm. Just as the whole village had a balanced economy, with the
land as its basis, a balance of farming and of industry and trade within
its own narrow field of activity, so the individual craftsman or tradesman
kept a balance in his own economy, turning from his craft or his trade
back to his farm in slack times and in busy times performing a function
in the village economy which was indispensable. The village would have
broken down without him. But we must leave these larger aspects of
the peasant economy and describe, for the moment, the two classes as
we find them in Wigston.

The smith had always been the most important of the craftsmen. In
earlier centuries there had been a regular dynasty of Smiths in the village,
peasant landowners and witnesses of village charters for generation after
generation. Our information about the Smiths in the fifteenth century
is scanty and by the sixteenth, though they are still landowners in the
village and resident in it, we have no evidence that they carried on their
ancestral craft. In the 1530's Richard Redley was the village blacksmith.
He died in 1539, leaving his 'forge and shoope' to 'William my sone &
Richard together yf Ryc' be myndyd to yt occupacion', and if William
died without issue 'my wyll is that my forge & shoope shall remayne
& pertaine to the next of the name'. A third generation of Redleys
were still blacksmiths in 1603-4 (Exchequer depositions) but they seem
to have left the village and gone elsewhere before the middle of the
century. Richard Redley's inventory of 1539 amounts in all to only £6
18s. 10d., of which 'the forge and smethey shoope the stythey [anvil]
tongs hammer butt^r w^t the appurtenances' were valued at 16s. and all the

farm goods at £5 6s. 10d. His modest household goods were put down at a few shillings only. It is clear that his farming was at least as important as his smithing, just as it had been for the Smiths in the thirteenth and fourteenth centuries.

One finds this combination of farm and forge in many other Leicestershire villages in the sixteenth century and later. The personal estate of Robert Cawnte, blacksmith of Ab Kettleby, was valued in 1588 at £20 1s. 4d., of which 'a Stithie w^t bellooes & hammers & other furniture for a Smith' were worth 40s., but his two kine, fourteen sheep, and an acre of winter corn were altogether valued at £6 13s. 4d., or one-third of the total inventory. The inventory of Richard Cockin of Muston in 1588 totals £46 exactly, of which the smithy and its furniture are valued at 26s. But the barley and pease growing in the field on that 16th of April were worth £10, malt and barley £5, wheat and pease unthreshed 26s. 8d., and his pigs, cattle, and lambs £11 in all. Here the farm goods were worth well over a half the total personal estate. One could find similar examples for any other Leicestershire village in any other year, and probably in any other Midland village judging by the Bedfordshire inventories for the years 1619-20.[1] The most notable example one could take in the Midlands is that of the Franklins in the Northamptonshire village of Ecton, forebears of Benjamin Franklin who tells us that for three hundred years his ancestors farmed their own freehold of thirty acres and bred up the eldest son in each generation as a smith. We do not know how much land the smith at Wigston owned or farmed, but in general the Leicestershire inventories give the impression that he had considerably less than a thirty-acre yardland, usually a small holding of ten acres or so, sometimes less than this.

Of the other craftsmen at Wigston we know little. Edward Twychell (died 1559) seems to have been a carpenter, and Robert Freer (died 1529) also. Edward Twychell left various carpenter's tools to his son Richard, and he also bequeathed twenty sheep, a cow, and a calf to various children. Robert Freer's inventory mentions various carpenter's tools (axes, an adze, wimbles, chisels, and iron saws) and also considerable quantities of barley (10 qrs.) and pease (8 qrs.) in the barn, besides a load of hay. He

---

[1] *Jacobean Household Inventories*, ed. Emmison (Bedfordshire Historical Record Society, vol. xx, 1938).

had, too, a horse, a cow, and six sheep. Here again the picture is a familiar one in any Midland village.

Among the tradesmen of Wigston in the sixteenth century the miller was pre-eminent. There was one water-mill, on the Sence, which had been there since the twelfth century, and a number of windmills, dotted about the high ground of the parish, had come into existence at various dates since the early years of the thirteenth century. We do not know exactly how many windmills there were in the parish but there seem to have been at least three or four in the seventeenth and eighteenth centuries.[1]

In 1531 Thomas Savage held the water-mill, and appears in the miller's usual role of taking excessive toll. Later court rolls, beginning in 1562, show Roger Langton as 'the common miller' (again taking excessive toll). In 1565 he is described as holding a horse-mill, in 1564 and 1571 as holding a windmill also. By 1584 the name of William Langton, the son of Roger, who died in 1577, appears at the mills. He died in 1602 and was followed by his eldest son William who was miller in 1623, at the time of a Chancery suit. At least three generations of Langtons therefore were millers at Wigston. The Chancery suit tells us that William Langton, who probably held the mills from his father's death in 1577 to his own death in 1602, held the ancient water-mill called 'Crowemille' and an ancient windmill by copy of court roll to him and his heirs for ever, according to the custom of the manor, and we may reasonably assume that his father had held the same mills on this tenure as far back as 1562. William Langton also erected another windmill near the water-mill, but upon his own ground. At the selling-off of the Danvers manor the Langtons bought the freehold of their copyhold mills, and the two windmills and the water-mill descended to William Langton the younger, who sold one windmill and the water-mill to Sir William Faunt, squire of Foston, on 9 October 1612, retaining the ancient windmill for himself and continuing to grind there.

---

[1] The map in Nichols (frontispiece to *Guthlaxton Hundred*, 1810) shows the watermill on the Sence, with a windmill a little to the north of it (presumably the one 'newly erected' by William Langton before his death in 1602). A windmill also stood near the Welford Road, on the brow of the hill to the south of the village; and there is at least one windmill mound out in the fields to the east of St. Wistan's church, and possibly two. These were presumably the mill, or mills, grinding for the Turvile manor just as the Crow Mills beside the Sence ground for the Oxford manor.

The Langtons were peasant proprietors in the early years of the sixteenth century; Roger Langton (possibly the grandfather of Roger the miller) witnessed charters in 1504 and in 1515. How much land they held we have no means of knowing. But in 1587 William Langton purchased, jointly with John Cartwright, a 36-acre farm from Henry Turvile and probably occupied some of this himself as we know he built his windmill on his own ground. His father's estate in 1577 had been a very modest one (£16 4s. 0d.: but no details have survived) and his will tells us nothing of his affairs. William Langton's inventory in 1602 is much more informative. He left estate to the value of £87 13s. 1d., substantially more than that of the average farmer, which was between £60 and £70 by this date. Of this nearly £35 consisted of debts due. But he had also a sizeable farm and his farm-goods were worth in all £28 6s. 4d. or about one-third of his whole estate. He had no cattle or sheep (the date of the inventory is 3 February 1602-3) but three horses, five pigs, and a good deal of corn and hay. He may well have been farming half the yardland bought with John Cartwright: the inventory is about what one would expect for a farm of that size.

Similarly, the Whites, who appear as innkeepers in the second half of the century, were ancient freeholders in Wigston. Henry White appears in the court rolls as a common brewer of beer between 1562 and 1565 and his son Robert followed him in the trade, appearing in court rolls for 1584, 1585, and 1587. By his will dated 18 June 1565 Henry White left 'my shoppe to one of my children that will be of my occupacion and yf two of them be of the occupacion then they shall parte my shoppe betwixt them. lie too farmed in a small way, but his total estate amounted only to £17 1s. 8d.

William Dent, who kept the Angel in the High Street of Hallaton in Elizabethan days, is more typical of the bigger innkeeper. He owned a small freehold, including his inn. The inquisition post mortem of 30 April 1584 says he was seised of 'one messuage or common inn called the Angel, and of the shop to the same messuage adjacent, with the appurtenances, lying in a certain street called the High Street in Hallaton, and also of three acres and one rood of arable land belonging to the same messuage ... ' His personal estate, valued on 22 March 1583-4, amounted to £104 14s. (rather more than twice the estate

of the average farmer at this date), of which his farm-goods came to
£69 6s. 8d., or about two-thirds of the whole. There were 14 cattle
of various kinds, nine horses, nine pigs, and no fewer than a hundred
sheep. Amongst his personal belongings we find 14 silver spoons and
six pieces of gold.[1]

No innkeeper in Wigston lived on this scale, and indeed it is true to
say that the Wigston farmer, craftsman, and cottager are only typical of
the open-field Midland village up to a point: wherever we can compare
them with their fellows in other villages they appear on a noticeably
smaller scale. The fact is that Wigston was much more populous and overcrowded than the great majority of villages and this was beginning to
show itself by the later years of the sixteenth century. When the hearth
tax returns of the period 1662-74 enable us to measure the poverty
of the village, in a rough and ready way, we find that Wigston was
indeed a poorer village all round. Its soil was fertile enough, and little
of it was too poor to cultivate, but there were too many people in the
place. The second half of the sixteenth century saw a steady influx of
new families which continued into the seventeenth century: by 1605
there were probably between 130 and 140 families in the village. The
population had been reckoned at 80 families in the return to the Bishop
in 1563: it had increased by sixty or seventy per cent within 40 years,
and it had just about doubled in a hundred years.[2]

☙ COTTAGE ECONOMY ❧

The cottager, apparently called 'cottager' or 'labourer' indifferently
in the wills and inventories, lived by an economy of his own, a house
and a few acres of land, supplemented by work for wages or kind on a
larger man's farm. How far there was payment in money and how far
an exchange of services is difficult to tell: there are indications of both
systems. Probably much depended on the size of the cottage-holding
in the fields. The larger it was the smaller the part, in all probability,
played by money in the total economy. Where a cottager had from five
to ten acres going with his house, he probably tended to exchange his

---

[1] The Angel can be identified with the Royal Oak today, and much of the Elizabethan inn survives.
[2] For the basis of the 1605 estimate, see *T.L.A.S.*, xxxiii.

services on a larger farm for the use of cart, plough, and harrow on his own holding, and it is possible that he sometimes exchanged his labour for crops such as hay, of which he could not grow enough. Money played only a marginal part in such economy. But some cottages carried very little or no land in the open fields, and here the occupier, more truly a labourer, found it necessary to work more consistently for a money-wage, without which he could not live at all. His small piece of land merely supplemented, though in a vital way, his money-income. We find hints of both systems side by side in Wigston, as it must have existed to a varying degree in most villages.

The extent to which money entered into his economy, then, was largely determined for the cottager by the size of his holding, and it is not easy to discover any general rule at Wigston. At Saxelby and Grimston, two villages not far from Melton Mowbray, we find a series of leases between 1600 and 1615 relating to cottage property on Robert Brokesby's estate. There are ten such leases. Only one is of a cottage without any land attached; the remaining nine have from five acres up to a virgate going with them. Four cottages had a bovate (probably twelve acres here) going with them; four others had 5, 8, 10 and 10 acres respectively. At Grimston and Saxelby, then, a cottage usually had attached to it a holding in the open fields ranging from 5 to 12 acres.[1]

At Wigston we find leases and conveyances of cottages with a 'quartern of land', i.e. six to eight acres according to the size of the yardland. Richard Danne's 13¼ acres in 1577 went with a cottage (so called in the conveyance) but as a general rule the cottage holding was a quarter-yardland and could be anything down to an acre or two, or even no land at all. Again, one gets the impression that cottage holdings at Wigston were generally appreciably smaller than they were in less populous villages in the deep country farther out from Leicester.

Let us, however, examine such evidence as we have for the Wigston cottager in the eighteenth century. We have only three inventories of people who can be certainly identified as cottagers or labourers: Robert Jarvice (1581), William Bradshaw (1586), and John Winter (1603). The first left an estate valued at only £4 2s. 8d., mostly his meagre furniture. He had no land in the fields as the inventory, taken on 14 March, does not refer to any crops either growing or sown; but we find

---

[1] Farnham, ii, 82–4, 348.

a pig, 4 hens, and a little hay and straw. There is not much doubt that Robert Jarvice was a wagelabourer on someone else's farm. William Bradshaw was a similar sort of man, though even poorer: his total estate came to 35s. 10d. But he had half an acre of barley and half an acre of pease in the two fields, worth 13s. 4d., and to that extent he was better off than Jarvice.

John Winter, on the other hand, though he is described as 'labourer', was much more the sort of prosperous cottager or labourer one finds in a number of villages in Leicestershire. It is true there are not many of these flourishing labourers in any one village; they are not typical of their class, but they do show, nevertheless, what possibilities were open to the man who was modestly ambitious, however lowly his start in the village. John Winter's estate in 1603 amounted to £17 13s. 8d. His two-roomed cottage, with outhouses attached, was altogether more comfortable than the cottages of Robert Jarvice and William Bradshaw: there were hangings on the walls of the hall, pewter and brass on his cupboard shelves, flaxen sheets and towels in the parlour (the Leicestershire name for the bedroom from the early sixteenth to the early nineteenth century); and in the outhouses there were peas and hay, and all the hurdles, rails, cowstandings, pig-sties, and other gear of a smallholder. He had a heifer and 15 sheep (though it was the depth of winter – early February – when the valuation was made) and he had sold sheep to John Cartwright, a large farmer, who owed 40s. 'at May Day next'. We do not discover whether he had any strips in the fields, since none is mentioned in the inventory. It is possible that John Winter had no land going with his cottage. If this is so, he must have been supplied with grazing for his stock and with winter feed for them by the man for whom he worked.[1]

There are various hints in the Wigston records of this kind of exchange between master and man. William Herrick of Queniborough deposed in the tithe dispute of 1574 that 'when he was of the age of xvj yeares dwelling wᵗ his father (Richard Herrick of Wigston) he dyd carrye one lode of tythe hey in cokes out of halters slade for one Thomas

---

[1] He may also have rented another man's commons from time to time. In 1642 for example, we find that William Kerkham of Muston, labourer, had let his sheep commons to Thomas Warren for that year for 10s. (Inventories, 1642, no. 14).

burgis his fathers shepherde'. Richard Pinder left to his shepherd by his will in 1564 a 'lande of barley' and 'a whete land at the water milne'. But in the main we are driven back on inference: where a cottager had no plough, cart, or harrow among his goods and chattels he must usually have borrowed his implements in return for his own labour, and we can hardly expect a contemporary record of what must have been an everyday arrangement.

Some of these Leicestershire labourers were remarkably well off, as well off in worldly goods as many a farmer. Richard Spencer of Long Clawson, who describes himself as 'labourer' in his will of 1560-1, left personal estate to the value of £32 18s. 8d., of which £18 0s. 6d. consisted of debts due to him. He had a cottage, 1½ acres of wheat ground, an acre of pease ground, and presumably an acre of fallow also – probably 3½ or 4 acres in the fields, going with his cottage. Equally important, this gave him certain rights over the common pasture, which he would have needed for his 20 sheep and 6 cattle; and he kept a couple of pigs and six hens.[1] At Wigston 'the old stint' was two kine and ten sheep to a quarter-yardland.[2] This was theoretically the limit of a cottager's livestock. But few at Wigston had a holding of this size or stock in that quantity. Where, however, a more ambitious labourer had more stock than he could put on his own commons, he could rent from others, or alternatively his employer might help him out.

---

[1] Such cases are, of course, exceptional, but they are not rare. One finds a few examples in every year covered by the inventories. A remarkable example is that of Thomas Bryan of Barkby Thorpe, labourer, whose estate was valued in 1642 at £110 13s. 10d., of which £103 1s. 2d. consisted of debts due to him. In the same year Robert Plummer of Braunston, labourer, left £106 17s. 5d., of which he was owed 'upon specialty and without' £60 12s. 5d. But he had as well 25 sheep, 4 kine, 1 pig, and a flitch of bacon all valued at £19: the growing crop was valued at £4 10s. 0d.; and the corn and hay in barn and yard (together with gorse, wood, and fuel) was worth £6 13s. 4d. Lastly, he had two hives of bees.

[2] Leases of 1629 and 1709 (Wyggeston Hospital MSS.) speak of commons for two kine and ten sheep going with a quarter-yard land 'according to the old Stint', while Simon Brett in his will (1600) left to his wife four kine and twenty sheep 'and the commons of half a yardland for her beasts and sheep'. Thus 'the old stint' goes back to the sixteenth century at least. A Great Glen deed of 1606 shows that in that village, not far from Wigston, the stint was the same: commons for '3 kine, 1 follower, and 20 sheep' going with a farm of half a yardland.

❧ Subsistence Farming ❧

Although Wigston lay so near the town of Leicester, its farming was still very largely subsistence farming. Indeed, Leicester itself, though the county town and an ancient borough, was hardly more than an average market-town with about six hundred families at the beginning of Elizabeth's reign, and its own open fields, so that it exerted little influence as yet on the surrounding villages as an urban food market. Some of the larger Wigston farmers, like Robert Freer in the 1540's and '50's, sold their sheep and wool in the Leicester markets and possibly some of the smaller men disposed of their surplus butter and cheese in the town, and to a lesser extent their meat. But the wills and inventories make it clear that, up to the closing years of the sixteenth century, money played but a small part in the economy of the village. Few farmers left more than trifling sums in ready money at death, and the list of debts owing to them (if any at all) is similarly a list of small amounts owed mainly by neighbours in the village.

The largest inventory of the sixteenth century, that of Robert Freer who died early in 1557 leaving personal estate to the value of £94 16s. included only £9 9s. 4d. in debts owed by nine people, ranging in magnitude from 4s. 4d. owed by Harry Herrick, a fellow-farmer in Wigston, to forty shillings owed by a kinsman of Enderby and a similar sum 'for shyppe whyche Russell dyd take for the queries behoffe'. The longest list of debts is shown in the inventory of Richard Burgess (1543), in which they totalled £38 out of the entire personal estate of £63 2s. Most of the twenty-six debtors, however, owed only small sums – sixteen of them under £1 – which ranged from the two-pence owed by William Symon to £13 15s. due from one Edmund Sadler. Twelve of the debtors were Wigston men; the remainder were drawn from nine different villages in the county (one just over the Northants border). In 1551, Thomas Whyte refers in his will to over £26 in ready money, a substantial sum indeed for Tudor Wigston, including 'xix ponds x^s the whyche mony I toke Wyllam my sone and he toke yt to one robart ffraar to kyppe yt' and another £6 13s. 4d. 'the whyche robart Whyte my sone bath yn Costody'. There are other indications even earlier in the century that the larger farmers were accumulating not inconsiderable sums of money and laying them out in purchases of small properties, such as William Symon's purchase of Enderby windmill, a few miles away, from William Bent of Cosby – a rising yeoman – for the sum of £8 13s. 4d. The Freers, too, were buying small parcels of land in the village fields early in the century; and from 1522 onwards the leases of the Wigston Hospital lands called for substantial fines on entry for which ready money was necessary. But for all these signs to the contrary, the picture drawn for us by the hundred wills and inventories is essentially one of a subsistence economy: only here and there did a Wigston farmer march in the vanguard towards the eighteenth century: nearly all his fellows trod an older and familiar path, their farming as medieval as the houses most of them still lived in, living in a true peasant economy with only small surpluses to dispose of in good years.

In the last ten or fifteen years of the sixteenth century, the pace of economic life quickened noticeably, it is true, even at Wigston. The breakup of the Turvile manor in 1586-7 threw several hundred acres of land on to the market and most of it was snapped up by Wigston men in small parcels of twenty to eighty acres for ready money. It may be argued that this in itself is an indication of something more than subsistence farming but it is not necessarily so. For the price of foodstuffs had been rising rapidly since the 1540's – had indeed doubled between 1540 and 1560 – while the farmer's expenses remained the same (above all his rent, whether the chief rent of a freeholder or the quit rent of the copyholder); and even a peasant farmer with only marginal surpluses to sell in good years could not fail to accumulate twenty, thirty or forty pounds or so in ready money in as many years. There is no evidence in Wigston of any substantial development of farming for a market among the great majority of the peasant farmers, though it is clear from wills and inventories that the use of money was becoming more common by the end of Elizabeth's reign. There had always been a class of larger farmers in every generation, but the difference was only one of degree. William Mould died in 1574 leaving personal estate to the value of £91 3s. 4d. and distributed £74 in money by his will, though not all of this had to be found at once for nearly one half was payable on the respective marriages of his three daughters. And when Simon Brett died in 1600, leaving £218 17s. 1d.

– the largest estate yet seen in the village – he was owed, of this total, about £71, or a third of his total estate, and he had £16 in silver and gold in his coffer. William Johnson, another large farmer, died in 1602 leaving personal estate to the value of £239 7s. 0d. of which he was owed £27 in smallish sums. William Langton, the miller, was owed nearly £35 in 1602, when he died, out of a total estate of £87 13s. 1d., but that is only what one would expect.

There is a marked increase in the value of personal estates left by Wigston farmers during the second half of the sixteenth century, which is readily explained by the rapid rise of their selling-prices (especially of foodstuffs) for some sixty years before 1600, and by their almost complete freedom from direct taxation during the same period. The subsidy of 1524-5 had fallen upon nearly seventy of the village population, probably upon every household and able-bodied man in the place except for a few poor widows. But later subsidies fell upon only seven or eight of the principal farmers. In 1545 there were ten names upon the subsidy list, in 1549 only four. From about 1553 to 1571 seven only were taxed, and from 1571 to 1599 only eight. In the second half of the sixteenth century only about one household in every eleven or twelve at Wigston paid any direct taxation, and even they paid upon a quite unreal valuation of their estates. Thus at Leicester we know that by the end of the sixteenth century assessments 'on goods' were about a thirtieth or a fortieth of a man's personal estate; and rural assessments were probably no less unreal. Assessments 'on lands' were similarly based upon ancient valuations for inquisition purposes that bore no relation to the improved values of Elizabethan days.[1]

Apart, however, from two or three of the larger men in the village whose monetary transactions were on a bigger scale than the average, the fact is that Wigston farming was fundamentally still peasant subsistence farming in which money played only a marginal part: sales of intermittent surpluses on the one hand and intermittent purchases

---

[1] For the Leicester valuations, see Hoskins, 'An Elizabethan Provincial Town', in *Studies in Social History* (1955), 44. The remarks upon the scope of Wigston subsidies during the sixteenth century are based upon all the lay subsidies that survive in the Public Record Office. The seventeenth-century assessments for Wigston show a widening of the tax-collector's net. In 1611 and 1612 there were twelve on the list; in 1621, thirteen and in 1626, sixteen. In 1641, eighteen, and in 1664, twenty. But even in these later years only one household in every eight paid to the subsidy and still upon a fictional valuation.

of leases or small freeholds on the other; or the purchase of a new cart from the wheelwright or of new implements and tools from the blacksmith and the carpenter. And at death the bequests of most farmers still were, not of sums of money, but of furniture, linen, 'the best brasse pot' or 'the greate pann', and of ewes and lambs or a heifer. It is clear that nearly everybody in the village, at the end of the sixteenth century, still thought in terms of goods rather than money, the chief exception being that most men, whether large or small farmers, tried to provide dowries for their daughters on marriage or a few pounds for younger sons on their coming of age, if they were not to have a share of the farm or the family trade or craft. Elsewhere in Leicestershire the old peasant economy was being shattered by large-scale enclosures for sheep and cattle pastures, or by the engrossing of many farms into the hands of vigorous yeomen with substantial capital, who seized every opportunity as readily as any town merchant and often became lords of the manors on which their forebears had been tenants-at-will two or three generations earlier; but nothing like this happened at Wigston or in scores of other villages throughout the county where neither large-scale enclosure nor large-scale engrossing took place. In these villages, still the majority, the traditional mixed farming of the open fields by a score or more of middling yeomen, husbandmen, craftsmen, tradesmen, and better cottagers still went on, though not entirely unchanged or unchanging; and the peasant economy remained unimpaired by the commercial ideas of the outer world. It was indeed even strengthened in many places by the acquisition of lands from improvident local gentry (as at Wigston), extravagant peers, or the needy Crown (as at Anstey, on the other side of Leicester, where several yeomen bought old monastic property from the Crown in 1609). No picture of sixteenth-century England would be true which failed to take account of the fact that, even in those parts where change was most noticeable and the outcry the loudest and longest, as it was in the Midlands as a whole throughout the entire Tudor period, life went on in much the same way as it had done for centuries past. Superficial changes, not unimportant by any means, were indeed occurring in every village; but beneath them the unchanging traditional life of the peasant system flowed on uninterrupted like a deep, underground river 'with noiseless current strong, obscure, and deep'. It had flowed already for something like a thousand years in open-field England and would continue to flow for another two hundred. The vast output of pathological literature by royal commissions, committees, pamphleteers and preachers during the Tudor period, though it arose from real and undoubted evils in the English countryside, must not blind us to the existence of that other side of English country life which passes mostly unnoticed because of its very stability. Even in Leicestershire, where some sixty villages and hamlets disappeared as a result of enclosure and engrossing, mostly between 1450 and 1600, some three hundred or so still remained. Only one in six at the most had gone – a great enough evil, it is true – but five out of six were still left at the end of the Tudor period, and much the same is true of all the other midland counties where depopulated and deserted village-sites are numerous.

✎ Church and School ✎

We have referred in passing to the superficial changes which were apparent in the Tudor village, in Wigston and in many others in Leicestershire; and these are none the less important for the economic and social historian though they did not shake the rock-like stability of the traditional peasant society.

The principal changes were the marked improvement in the standard of housing and of living generally during this period, including the beginnings of format education; the equally marked rise in population and the vicissitudes of fortune among village families, some rising, some falling in wealth and importance, though all were subject to the same economic forces, and the religious changes, in so far as they can be detected in the absence of any churchwardens' accounts for the whole of the sixteenth century.[1] The first of these changes is best dealt with separately (see the excursus on Peasant Houses and Interiors, 1400-1800) while the last – the religious changes of the sixteenth century – must be disposed of briefly for lack of material relating specifically to Wigston.

[1] Nichols quotes a few sketchy extracts (op. cit., p. 385) from a volume of the churchwardens' accounts from 1591 onwards, but the surviving accounts begin only in 1615. They continue without a break up to 1718 but are missing thereafter.

From 1506 onwards Wigston had a resident and ill-paid vicar, as we
have seen, receiving a stipend of only nine pounds per annum while the
profits of the fat rectory, principally the tithes of corn and hay, wool and
lambs from nearly three thousand acres of rich land, were diverted into
the hands of Lenton Priory. An archidiaconal visitation in 1510 reveals
that the vicar was not receiving his proper maintenance from the priory,
that the chancel of the parish church, which was the responsibility of
the priory, was defective in many respects, and that the priory had not
distributed alms to the poor as they were bound to do as one of the
conditions of their appropriation of the rectory.[1] In 1517 and again
in 1518 things were no better. Hamilton-Thompson observes of the
latter visitation that 'the prior and convent of Lenton near Nottingham,
the proprietors of the church of Wigston, had allowed the chancel
to fall into such disrepair that the high altar was open to the rain and
its ornaments were rotting. The rectory house and its premises, their
special care, were in bad condition; no vicarage house had been built
since the comparatively recent appropriation; the prior and convent
had neglected their obligation to supply a silken cope; the distribution
of alms among the poor, which was a condition of appropriation, was
omitted'.[2] At another visitation taken on 1 June 1526 the churchwardens
presented that the glass of the great window above the high altar was in
disrepair so that pigeons and other birds flew in and fouled the high altar
itself, to the serious damage of the goods and ornaments of the church.
They also presented that the churchyard, which was the responsibility of
the parishioners, was not sufficiently enclosed. The archdeacon ordered
that the prior and convent of Lenton should be cited to show cause why
the profits of the church should not be sequestrated by reason of the
notorious disrepair of the chancel, and the parishioners were given until
the feast of St. John to repair the fences of the churchyard under penalty
of 3s. 4d. The priory seem to have made the necessary repairs to the
fabric of the chancel under this threat to confiscate their revenues, as
the visitation of 1531 makes no reference to their deficiencies but only

---

[1] Fletcher, *Documents at Lincoln relating to Leicestershire*, 39. Details of the later visitations referred to
in the text may be found in *Reports and Papers of Associated Archit. and Arch. Soc.* (1905), 122, 137, 155.

[2] Hamilton-Thompson, *Visitations in the Diocese of Lincoln*, 1517-31. (Lincoln Record Society, xxxiii)
I. xxvii.

to the continued failure of the parishioners to enclose their churchyard properly: and the churchwardens were instructed also to see that the seating in the nave of the church, the responsibility of the parish, was repaired and made good, much of it being in a broken condition.

The parishioners compare well with the priory in the matter of caring for their parish church and in looking after their own poor. A number of pre-Reformation wills show that the fabric of both churches was a matter of concern to them. William Freer in 1520 left 6s. 8d. to 'the reparacion off the rode loft off Wygeston' besides ten shillings for 'a trentall of masses to be sting for my soul'. William Pawley in the same year left 'an pece of wode to mak the timber off a porch at the kyrk off all Saints in Wegeston' and Agnes Wyllys in 1524 left 6s. 8d. towards the rebuilding of our Lady yle' at the parish church. In 1518 Thomas Leyd had left a sheep towards the maintenance of 'the lyght befor the crucyfyxe' in the parish church and in 1529 Robert Freer left sixpence 'to ye ymage of Saynct John'. Even where there was no specific bequest, all parishioners who made wills left a small sum of money to the parish church or to both churches, or more often a bushel of malt, over and above the 'principal' of their best beast or their best good of any other kind, 'after the manner and custom of the country'. We notice, too, the expected bequests of masses and bread for the purpose of praying for the testator's soul and for all good Christian souls. Besides a sum like ten shillings 'to an honest prest' to sing masses for a month, the testator often left twopence in money or in bread 'to every houshold in Wygeston to pray for my soull and all crystyn soulles', a bequest which in Elizabethan times becomes a colourless gift of twopence or fourpence 'to the poor man's boxe' at the church. Even in 1551 Thomas White was making the pious Catholic bequest of twopenny-worth of bread to every house in Wigston to pray for all Christian souls, and the reign of Mary saw a renewal of gifts to the church itself: John Redley left a bushel of malt to the rood loft in October 1558 and in March of 1558-9 Anne Evans left to the altar of Our Lady in the parish church a linen table cloth.[1] No doubt the conservative parishioners of Wigston did not hasten to obey the edicts about their fabric and furnishings in the first place and, as in so many country places, merely removed them at the

---

[1] L.C.R.O., Wills.

last moment and stored them in a safe place until better times; but in the absence of the churchwardens' accounts we shall never know the details of change and counterchange in this parish during these years. Judging by their wills, which is all the evidence we have, the people of Wigston accepted the final settlement of the Elizabethan church without any fuss one way or the other. During the 1560's they still continued to bequeath a bushel or a strike of malt to their parish church for the upkeep of the fabric, but this dropped out, too, and by the 1570's and '80's they usually contented themselves with the bequest of a few pence to 'the poore man's boxe of Wygeston'. The gift of a pennyworth or twopennyworth of bread to every household in the village also disappeared as a custom, and was replaced by the more impersonal charity of a church levy or a gift from the box in the church.

At the other end of the village the ancient church of St. Wistan, which had baptised the children and buried the dead of the Duchy manor since at least the thirteenth century, ceased to be used as a church. We do not learn the exact manner and date of its disuse but it may have come about as a result of the act of 1547 supressing chantries and confiscating their lands, although it was not founded as a chantry but was a dependent parochial chapel. Nevertheless, a special Exchequer commission was taken in June 1572 concerning 'concealed lands' at Wigston and depositions were taken at Quorndon, some fragments of which survive to tell us a little of the old church in its last days.[1] George Amery of Wigston, aged fifty-four years or thereabout, deposed that he knew St. Wistan's church and had known it since he was a child: he had heard it called a parish church for as long as he could remember. William Pawley of Wigston, the only other deponent whose answers have survived, did not know whether it was a parish church or not, though he knew All Saints to be so. The north wall of the chancel of St. Wistans had fallen down for lack of repair and the rest of the chancel was pulled down with the consent of the whole of the inhabitants to repair All Saints' church and to rebuild St. Wistans anew. Some of the lead, timber, and stone from the church had been sold, but the earl of Huntingdon, hearing of this, had ordered the villagers to fetch the lead back from Aylestone, where it

[1] P.R.O., Excheq. Special Commissions, E. 178. No. 1230.

had been sold, and to put both their churches in repair, 'and the churches are now accordingly repaired'.

The deponents tell us what had happened to the bells of the church: one had gone for recasting as a new bell for the parish church, another had been sold in aid of the rebuilding of St. Wistans itself, while the whereabouts of the sanctus bell was uncertain. Some of the timber and stone had gone to mend the bridges in the fields of the village. At the dissolution of the church four marks in money remained in the coffer, which the churchwardens of All Saints had spent on church books. The chalice and other ornaments had been sold by the churchwardens in Edward VI's time. Nevertheless, the chapel of St. Wistan remained in use, or came back into use, as between 1557 and 1561 various parishioners left malt to the church in their wills. After 1561 there is no bequest to the chapel until 1572, when we know the fabric had been put into repair again. It seems likely therefore that after a temporary suppression in Edward VI's time, probably after the act of 1547, it had come back into use in Mary's reign and had continued for a few years into Elizabeth's, falling into disuse and disrepair after 1561. Many years later, in 1633,[1] when further depositions were being taken in the archdeacon's court over the final pillage of the building, old Mary Hay said that 'about threescore yeares since as she now remembreth she being 10 or 11 yeares old and dwelling in Wigston with her mother' she went and heard Sir John Savage, then minister, read prayers 'upon a Christmas morning a litell before day by a torch at St. Wistans but whether the said prayers were in English or lattine this deponent doth not now remember and then after it was day the said Sir John went and read prayers at All Saints church… ' This recollection takes us back to about the year 1573.

When Thomas Thornton became vicar in 1577 he gave up using the old church and read no services there, according to other deponents. The building was thereupon put to use as a free school, certainly by the early 1580's as we learn from a deposition by Sir William Faunt, squire of the neighbouring village of Foston. Sir William deposed that he knew Wigston well: he had gone to school in St. Wistans 47 to 50 years ago (i.e. about 1584 to 1587) when he was between ten and thirteen years of age. In his will dated 10 July 1583 John Browne, husbandman, who

---

[1] Archdeaconry of Leicester, Court Proceedings, 1633, loc. cit.

farmed a yardland in the village fields, left twenty shillings to his young son Francis 'and my will is that he be kept to scoole tyll he cane wrytt & reade'. So, among all the other evidence of increasing comfort in sixteenth-century Wigston and of a rising standard of living, we have the beginnings of formal education for the children, boys and girls alike, whether the squire's son or the cottager's. This free school, held in the nave of the chapel of St. Wistan, was the only schooling provided in Wigston from the early 1580's up to 1839. Only when the National School opened in the village in the latter year did the old free school close its doors, after teaching the children of every generation to read and write over a space of more than two hundred and fifty years.[1]

[1] We learn quite by chance from Sir William Faunt's deposition that girls attended the school from the first. 'There was an hower glasse stood neere unto the font upon a piller and one Bell came druncke or distempered into the church and brake the said hower glasse and when this deponents schoolemaster named Mr. Carter came in he gave this deponent one end of the hower glasse and gave the other to one Halls daughter'. (Archdeaconry Court Proceedings, loc. cit.)

VII

THE PEASANT SOCIETY, 1600–1766

The Village in 1625

When the sale of the second and larger manor was completed in 1606, life at Wigston settled down again slowly. It was now entirely a peasant village, without a lord, a community which consisted mostly of middling and small peasant landowners, farming the three open fields that still lay unimpaired all around; and so it remained up to the revolution of 1766 when the enclosure award altered the face and the whole economy of the parish for all time. It is this peasant society, the way it worked and the way in which it developed between the early seventeenth century and the middle of the eighteenth, which is the theme of the chapters upon which we now embark.

Before doing so, however, we shall obtain a clearer picture of what the village looked like, and what all the detailed changes of the preceding century had amounted to, if we pause at the year 1625 and compare the village of that time with that of a hundred years earlier: for, while in fundamentals it was much the same as it had long been, in some important respects it was very different.

The most obvious change was that the population of the village had doubled: from about seventy households in 1525 it had grown to a 140 or so by 1625. It was now considerably larger than it had been at the end of the fourteenth century, possibly slightly larger in numbers than it had been before the first visitation of the Black Death. This doubled population was accommodated in a built-up area no larger than that of the older village, by putting more houses into the remaining open spaces in the village area – on corners of crofts and gardens or round the edge of the green – or by enlarging and otherwise improving some of the existing houses, which generally had ample room to expand on their own crofts, gardens, or orchards. But the village as a whole could not expand: its land was too precious to cover with houses, as it had been also in the fourteenth century. There was not enough land to go round as it was, and so houses were packed more closely together on the available space. The consequences of this overcrowding were not as disastrous as they might have been: the yeoman with ten or twelve children in many instances built himself a new and a larger house on the same site.[1] Nevertheless, the village as a whole was more closely packed together than it had been since the fourteenth century and health suffered as a consequence. The epidemic of 1609, which killed about forty people in the village, was the worst for more than half a century and was the prelude to generations of sporadic sickness of one sort or another.[2]

And yet, though the village was more populous, more crowded, and becoming more unhealthy again, the standard of living of all classes was markedly higher than it had been three generations earlier. Houses, in general, were larger, with more rooms and rather more privacy; they had glass in their windows and more of them had two or three fireplaces in place of only one; furniture and household goods of all kinds were more varied and numerous in all households except the very poorest; the average personal estate of all classes at death was something like five times as high as it had been, and though some of this great increase in monetary value merely reflects the rise in the general level of prices there is no shadow of doubt, when one examines the inventories of peasant estates in detail, that much of it represents, too, a higher level of household comfort and a greater command of implements, tools, and stock-in-trade of all kinds.[3] This marked improvement in the rural standard of living between about 1540 and 1640 is common to the whole of the Midlands, and indeed to the greater part of England, judging by the evidence of rural building, both inside and outside.

There were other important respects in which the Wigston of 1625 differed from that of 1525. It no longer had any lord: the manorial organisation had for all practical purposes melted away, leaving the village as the supreme, indeed the only, organ of government. It is true that the lords of past centuries had always been absentee lords, and that Wigston

---

[1] See below, pp. 285-94.

[2] See 'The Population of Wigston Magna, 1086-1801', *T.L.A.S.* xxxiii.

[3] See below, pp. 296-8 and *Essays in Leicestershire History*, 135. The average farmer in 1524 left personal estate to the value of £14 to 15; in 1603 his great-grandson's estate was worth rather more than £67. The estates of cottagers and labourers scent to rise equally strikingly.

had never had a resident squire; but the villagers had been subject to the various burdens, payments, services and irritations incidental to manorial organisation and now they were free even of these.[1] Only two years

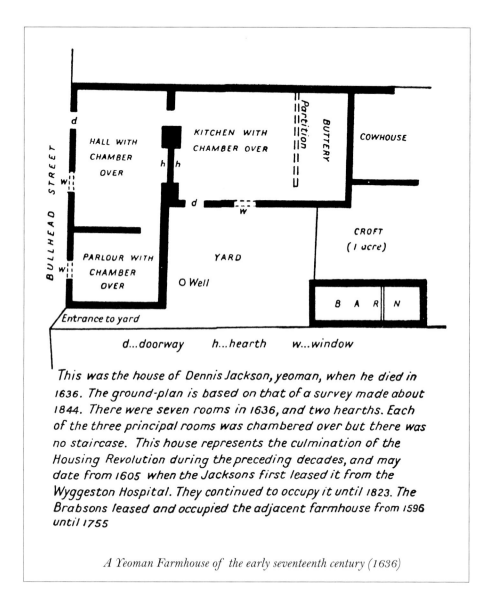

d...doorway   h...hearth   w...window

This was the house of Dennis Jackson, yeoman, when he died in 1636. The ground-plan is based on that of a survey made about 1844. There were seven rooms in 1636, and two hearths. Each of the three principal rooms was chambered over but there was no staircase. This house represents the culmination of the Housing Revolution during the preceding decades, and may date from 1605 when the Jacksons first leased it from the Wyggeston Hospital. They continued to occupy it until 1823. The Brabsons leased and occupied the adjacent farmhouse from 1596 until 1755

A Yeoman Farmhouse of the early seventeenth century (1636)

---

[1] For example, when Thomas Watts committed suicide in his farmhouse in 1594 all his good and chattels were forfeited to the lessee of the royalties of the Duchy manor in Wigston, at that time Henry Turvile, esquire. The attempt by the bailiff to seize the 20 or 30 sheep belonging to the farm was resisted, however, by the widow and a dozen others, 'being all armed and arrayed in warlike manner', who set on him and beat him. (Duchy of Lancaster Pleadings, P.R.O., D.L.I., Vol. 167, A.8. and Vol. 108, 28A.)

before, it is true, Sir William Faunt, who had bought a fourth part of the manor (for what this was worth after the great dismemberment), had tried to exercise the last of the manorial rights. He had brought a law-suit against twenty-eight of the former copyholders who refused to do suit to the two mills which he had also bought. The twenty-eight defendants replied that suit to the mills was extinguished in law by their purchase of their freeholds in 1606; and they also said that the mills themselves were formerly copyholds of inheritance, like all the rest of Wigston copyhold, and not parcel of the demesne, and that they had ground there out of courtesy only, since they could not do suit to another tenant who was their equal and not their lord.[1] We do not learn the result of this argument, but one suspects that the tenacious, hard-headed peasants of Wigston had their way again.

The dismemberment of the Danvers manor also meant that the thirty or so copyholders of Henry VIII's time had ceased to exist by 1625: copyhold tenure had gone for good, and there only remained freehold and leasehold. By far the greater part of Wigston's 2944 acres now belonged to the peasantry of the village, large and small. It was they who had bought most of the farms at the Turvile sale of 1586 and at the Danvers sale twenty years later. Such leasehold land as there was, owned by absentee landlords, was mostly accounted for by the 173¼ acres belonging to the Wyggeston Hospital in Leicester, and by one or two other absentee landlords with tenant-farmers in Wigston whom we shall come to later.

There were, in 1625, two more differences from the village of a hundred years earlier which were only just beginning to make themselves felt and which were to become more conspicuous during the second half of the seventeenth century. One was the increasing part coming to be played by money in the village economy: it is very noticeable in the peasant inventories and marriage settlements, not only in Wigston but in all Leicestershire villages as the seventeenth century goes on. Money had been known and used in the Tudor village but it had played only a marginal part in the peasant economy: few sums of money of any size appear in the sixteenth-century records. It is a difference of degree in the following century, not one of kind: but it is a sharply marked difference.

---

[1] P.R.O., Chancery Proceedings, C.3/348/5. (1623).

The other difference is also one of degree rather than of kind, and that is the growing incidence of poverty in the seventeenth-century village. There had been poor in the medieval and the Tudor village, but one gets the impression from peasant wills, in the Tudor period at least, that they were few and that the problem of their relief was manageable by small acts of private charity – bequests of bread or money to all 'cottage households' in pre-Reformation wills, or in later wills simply of money to 'the poore man's boxe' at the parish church.

Most poverty in the sixteenth-century village was incidental, a matter of individuals (the old, or the orphaned, the maimed or the sick) rather than of *the poor* as a class. Most such poverty, especially that arising from old age and infirmity, was relieved within the family, too: as witness the provision made by medieval peasants for their dependants – aged parents or unmarried sisters – and by the Tudor peasant also, where many a modest inventory of a yeoman or his widow discloses that the old man or old woman had 'his parlour' or 'her parlour' in the house; and here they rested in quiet among a few possessions while the rest of the ancestral house was given up to a son and his wife and the clamour of another infant generation. This is often the explanation of the very small personal estate left by a man who is described as 'yeoman', whom one knows to have been a considerable farmer. He had handed over his farm and live and dead stock to his eldest son, retaining only a few personal belongings in his parlour, and possibly a strip or two in the fields to potter over in his declining years.

By the second half of the seventeenth century it is clear that we have 'the poor' as a permanent feature in the village community. They were emerging as a class, and a considerable class at that; and the problem of their relief was becoming more and more unmanageable by acts of private charity or by family self-help. Nearly everyone enjoyed a higher standard of living than that of a century or even fifty years earlier; but the division between the better-off as a class and the poor as a class was also beginning to appear more sharply.

These were the differences that had emerged in the course of a hundred years of growth and change, and they were all important differences. And yet, in its fundamental way of living, the village had not changed: it was the same as it had been for centuries: and if the peasant of Henry VIII's day could have returned to the streets and lanes and fields to visit his great-grandson, he would have felt at home, back in a timeless world in which all the fields had their familiar names; in which many of the families that he had known still carried on the remembered trades or cultivated the ancestral acres as of old; and in which all the familiar boundaries and landmarks were still to be found where he had always known them, the same mills, wells, springs, lanes, and hedges. There were the immemorial sights and sounds that he had always known, and the rich smells of living in a busy arable-farming village. The smells alone, most nostalgic and evocative of all our senses, would have set his mind at rest almost at once, would have told him that nothing had really changed: the sweet mild scent of the great field of flowering beans, the astringent dry smell of straw in barns and yards, the heavy summer scent of the hawthorns that enclosed the little crofts and orchards, and of the hay in the meadows by the Sence and the Knighton Brook. And in the village street, the smell of the smithy, of the wheelwright's shop, and the bakehouse; and the ancient sounds of timber being sawn, of iron being hammered, of the creak of laden carts. In the fields the wind still seethed through the wheat and shook the barley. This was the ancient, unchanging life of the village, whatever else had happened in the meantime.

The three great fields – Mucklow, Thythorn Hill, and Goldhill – were still unenclosed and unimpaired in any way, cultivated under 'the open-field system', though the old men in 1625 could probably remember when there were rather fewer grass leys among the arable. But it was still an agrarian society, with no industry beyond the local crafts and trades, living by the traditional rules of mixed farming in the open fields; and the peasant owner was still the typical figure in the fields, the most numerous single class in the village. It was still fundamentally a peasant society, living almost entirely by its own resources, and by its own skill and physical labour, living in an economy in which nothing was wasted, in which every trifle had its value.

❧   THE PEASANT ECONOMY   ☙

Wigston produced all its own food, clothing, light, power, and building materials, and nearly all its own heat, out of the most commonplace natural resources; for the parish was not specially endowed by Nature in any single respect beyond the fact that its clays, with constant hard labour, were capable of producing good crops. For its buildings – houses, barns, and boundary walls – it had its own clay, used in the preparation of the long-lasting 'mud walls'. The boulders in the clay, of every size from pebbles upwards, provided the necessary footings for all these mud walls, and the mortar that bound them came from Wigston's own lime-pit. Wheat-straw or selected reeds from some special corner of the parish[1] provided the material for thatching houses and copings for mud walls. The parish had its own sand-pits and gravel-pits, the latter especially valuable when the coming of turnpike roads in the eighteenth century made better surfaces necessary; and when the general use of bricks for domestic building came in in the last quarter of the seventeenth century good brick-earth was found right in the village.

The willows that fringed the streams of the parish provided wattles for sheep-hurdles and other temporary fences, besides the framework for 'wattle-and-daub' farmhouses, a more substantial construction than mud alone. The furze of the common pastures, though there was not much of it, was burnt in bakehouses, brewhouses, and kitchen fires, as were the 'shreddings' or loppings off the hedgerows also.[2]

As for its crops, the parish grew enough flax and hemp to meet its own needs for linen sheets, napkins, towels, and clothing; it produced enough wool from its own sheep to keep the five or six village tailors well supplied. Its barley, grown over several hundred acres every year, supplied food and drink; and its wheat, rye, oats, peas, and beans provided food for all men and beasts. Every cottage and farmhouse had its own poultry (chiefly geese, but ducks and hens were numerous), and most kept pigs and bees. All had herb-gardens and many had small orchards: so the village had meat, bacon, eggs, cheese, butter, milk, honey, apples, and herbs of all kinds. The parish generated its own power: for the wind did not blow to waste but was harnessed to two or three windmills: and the waters of the little river Sence were not allowed to flow unused across the parish boundary.

---

[1] 'Thatchers' hill' and 'Thatchers' *sike*' appear as local names in Mucklow Field from the thirteenth century onwards.

[2] Tithe suit of 1602-3. P.R.O., Exchequer Depos. by Commn. 44-45 Eliz.

Since the middle of the twelfth century they had turned the waterwheel at Crow Mill, and from time out of mind they had yielded a few precious fish, the only fishing water in the whole parish.

Wigston was not exceptional in practising this high economy of all its natural resources, nor was it by any means exceptionally endowed. It was, indeed, less fortunate than a great number of other parishes, for it lacked building stone, coal, a sufficiency of large timber for building purposes, iron for farm implements and gear, and the inevitable salt; and most of these things had to come in from elsewhere, though usually not far.

Where stone was required for more important buildings, for which wattle-and-daub or plain mud were not suitable, the tough granite-like rubble of Enderby was brought in from about five miles away. The two churches and the water-mill were mostly built of this, and so, too, were one or two of the larger houses in the village.[1] The local fuel supplies of the village were also inadequate, and the larger farmers had long been in the habit of fetching coal in their carts and wagons from the Swannington and Coleorton pits, about eighteen miles away to the north-west.[2] Wood was much too scarce all over Leicestershire to burn: the poor used furze, 'shreddings', and dried bean-haulms, and so, too, did the bakers and ale-brewers who found coal unsuitable for their purpose. As for the lack of large timber, which was felt all over the eastern side of the Midlands by Elizabethan times, it was met by economising strictly in the use of what was available, and by the sensible provision in some leases that tenants should plant timber every year. Thus the Wyggeston Hospital required all its tenants at Wigston, from the sixteenth century onwards, to plant 'two plants or setts of Oake Ashe or Elme like to grow and prosper' and to 'nourish and presurve them'.[3]

---

[1] The Davenports' 'manor-house', which formerly stood on a moated site to the south-east of the parish church, was said by Nichols to have been built largely of unwrought stone. This can only have been rubble masonry of Enderby stone.

[2] Swannington coal was reaching Leicester before the end of the thirteenth century, and was being burnt in villages all over Leicestershire by the early sixteenth century. *Calpit* appears as a name in Goldhill Field at Wigston in 1393, and in later records as Coalpit Way. It is safe to conclude that some coal was reaching Wigston from the Leicestershire pits before the end of the fourteenth century, though possibly only for the use of the village smiths at first.

[3] Wyggeston Hospital lease dated 30 November 1596 to Miles Brabson, husbandman. A lease of the same farm in 1755 to George Ross, hosier, of Wigston, specifies 'six setts of Oak, Ash, or Elm, and six setts of Willow' to be planted every year.

The local shortage of fish worried no one: it was not a diet for people with hard physical work to do, and there were few in the village outside this category. But the blacksmiths had to buy all their iron from outside: there was no substitute for it and no going without it, especially as the use of iron in farming implements and carts was extending greatly in the seventeenth century. Most of the iron was bought in Leicester, coming perhaps from some great fair like Stourbridge.[1] Some of the ironmongers of Leicester, from the later years of the sixteenth century onwards, were men in a large way of business, who made not insubstantial fortunes and rose to high civic rank.[2] They must have regularly supplied hundreds of village blacksmiths over a wide area round about.

Much of what has been said above may seem obvious, a great deal about trifles; but these trifles, down to the pebbles under the clay or the beehives in the garden and the feathers on the goose's breast, were the very foundation of that old peasant economy which thought all the time in terms of goods and services and not of money. And unless one has a proper understanding of this peasant or thrift economy, of the foundations on which it was built up, the way they thought about it and the way it worked in practice, one cannot begin to understand the economic and social history of a good deal of rural England between the sixteenth and the nineteenth centuries. It was this economy, which lived almost entirely off its own resources, that enabled the peasantry of all classes from the yeoman down to the cottager and labourer not only to stand up to the catastrophic rise in prices of the later sixteenth century but even, for many of them (labourers included), to improve their position; and it was this same economy which enabled the village to withstand for so long the disintegrating effect of parliamentary enclosure and not to collapse at the first blow. The tenacious cement that bound it together, compounded of local resources, of traditional

---

[1] The earl of Rutland's iron for the resident farrier at Belvoir was, however, bought at Boston at this time. It was Danzig or Spanish iron at £18 a ton. (Hist MSS. *Comm.*, *Rutland* MSS. vol. IV, 484. Treatise on the Provision of Supplies at Belvoir, 1611.)

[2] Most notable of these were the Herricks, who were ironmongers for about a hundred years 1534–1633). They provided mayors for the town on six occasions in that time – 1557, 1572, 1584, 1593, 1605, and 1619. A younger son of the second generation of ironmongers was William Herrick, who became a wealthy goldsmith in London, and returned to buy the Leicestershire estate of Beaumanor from the representatives of the earl of Essex in 1595. He was knighted in 1605, and his descendants continued to hold this estate until 1915.

knowledge of those resources and skill in making use of them, of living in a place which had meaning and significance for its inhabitants, of work that still, for the great majority, completely satisfied their creative impulses, of governing themselves through their fellows – such a cement was not likely to give way at one blow, however formidable. Parliamentary enclosure was indeed the most formidable blow ever felt in the Midland village, but, as we shall have occasion to see, the village was slow to feel its full effects. Even well into the nineteenth century much remained of the old peasant system, of the self-sufficient village and its self-contained society. The cement still held, though it was crumbling faster as the Railway Age added its pressure to the disruptive forces.

These changes were, however, far into the future, and in the early seventeenth century Wigston, like thousands of other villages up and down England, was still deeply embedded in an ancient peasant economy. Like the physical landscape of the parish, which all knew by heart, this mental and spiritual background had subsisted so long that all took it for granted: they were indissolubly linked with it. They did not merely live in it; they were part of it and it was part of them. And in the early years of the seventeenth century it all looked more solid than it had ever been. Rural England had been rebuilt, much of the medieval poverty and squalor removed, and there was a general air of well-being, if not indeed of prosperity. One has only to look at the villages of almost any county in England, above all perhaps in the counties of the Stone Belt, to see how many of them were rebuilt in the years between 1580 and 1640, and how well they were built, with what profound assurance and serenity of mind; and to see that the builders were part of a home-made rural civilisation that was to them eternal, satisfying, and unquestionable.

❧ THE VILLAGE IN 1670 ❧

The materials for writing the history of the village during the seventeenth century, though incomplete, are still overwhelming in their bulk. The fines, conveyances, mortgages, leases, and marriage settlements alone

for this period, in such an incessantly active land-market as Wigston are
bewildering in their detail; the parish records proper grow in volume;
the number of peasant wills and inventories for this century runs to
hundreds, each document adding something to our knowledge of the
village and its past life. If we are not to lose our way in this mass of
detail, it will be best to take our stand at some particular point of time,
to view the village as it was at that time, and thence to trace backwards
the origin and course of such major changes as we perceive. For this
purpose we may choose the year 1670, when an exceptionally full hearth
tax assessment, together with certain of the parish records, gives us the
completest picture of the village society that we have yet had.

The hearth tax assessment reveals to us a large village of 161
households, of whom 114 were taxable and 47 were exempt. One
perceives a greater tendency to differentiation between social classes in
this record than in, say, the records of the early sixteenth century: at
the top of the social pyramid we have five substantial and comfortable
houses with five hearths each, inhabited by Mr. John Pochin, Mr. John
Horsepool, Mr. Francis Smyth, and Deliverance Freer, the fifth being
'the parsonage house' (i.e. the rectory farm) probably occupied by one of
the Davenports who farmed the rectory for some considerable time. At
the other end of the scale we have 73 houses with only one hearth each,
or no fewer than 120 if we include the exempted households. Between
these extremes were 25 houses with two hearths, nine with three, and
two with four, occupied in the main by the larger yeoman-farmers of
the village. The social pyramid was well developed in the village of
Charles II's day.

Before we pursue this theme, however, there is another point which is
worth notice, and that is the longevity of family residence in the village.
The 161 households represent about 82 different family-names,[1] since many
families had branched out all over the village as the generations went by.
Most remarkable were the Boulters who in the hundred years they had lived
at Wigston had established no fewer than eight different households. The
Freers in about two hundred years had formed eight branches also. The

---

[1] The exact total is impossible to ascertain as a few entries on the record are rubbed, but the figure
of 82 is not likely to be more than one or two removed from the truth.

Smiths, Vanns, and Wards numbered six households each; the Johnsons five; the Langtons, Holmeses, Noones, and Abbotts four each; and several others had three branches. Moreover, as all these families persistently inter-married with each other (rarely going outside the village for a bridegroom or a bride) the degree of inter-relationship must have been beyond belief, and the number of 'cousins' beyond accurate computation. In this blood-brotherhood lay another of the great hidden strengths of the peasant community. By one marriage whole dynasties of peasant families were brought into relationship with each other.

Of the eighty-two different families who made up the village population, about thirty-six had lived in Wigston for at least a century, and fifteen or sixteen had been there for two hundred years. That is, about 44 per cent had been there a hundred years, and about 20 per cent for two hundred. This is in marked contrast to the village of Henry VIII's reign, in which only about one family in seven had been there for five generations. The fifteenth century had seen an almost complete change in the village population; but after this great re-shuffle the community settled down, stabilised itself, and the peasantry proceeded to re-establish the roots that had been torn up by the Black Death and the long agricultural depression, and to strike those roots even deeper into 'the cultural humus' formed by generations of ancestors on that spot. This was another of the outstanding characteristics of the peasant system in the seventeenth century: its deep roots in one place, and all that that meant in terms of social cohesion.

To return to the social classes of the village: there was indeed a growing economic gulf between the richer and the poorer. For the first time we have a class of 'gentry' appearing, partly alien gentry superimposed on the village by some accident of marriage or purchase, but for the most part native gentry sprung from the minority of successful peasantry. The gentleman was not an entirely new phenomenon in Wigston: the Wallyses were so described in the late fifteenth and early sixteenth centuries: but they were an isolated example. But in the latter part of the seventeenth century we find a number of such families – the most well-to-do branches of the Davenports, of the Freers, the Smiths, the Deacons, and a little later the Pawleys.

Others, like Thomas Mawson, John Lawe, and John Pochin, all described as 'gentlemen', were of different origin. Thomas Mawson was

a successful Leicester tanner who bought a small property in Wigston
from the Lawes in 1642 (probably twenty-two acres) and a much larger
property of three farms covering 110 acres from the same family in
1655. He seems to have taken up his residence in the village with the
first purchase.[1] His total estate would have been about four yardlands,
and this he farmed himself.

The Lawes, on the other hand, were a decaying family by this time.
They had come into Wigston with the long lease of the rectory by
William Lawe in the 1580's and had occupied the rectory farm and other
land. From the beginning they were styled as gentry; but the succeeding
generations saw them selling out bit by bit and by 1670 they were of
little consequence in the village. The Pochins, squires of Barkby, on the
other side of Leicester, were an old county family. A younger branch of
them had come to Wigston after the Restoration, when (in 1663) 'Mr.
John Puchin of the parish of Barkby, gentleman' married 'Mistress Jane
Fryer of Wigston gentlewoman' and again, five years later, when Mr.
George Puchin of the city of London married Mistress Mary Fryer. Jane
and Mary were probably co-heiresses to the substantial estate which one
branch of the Freers (or Fryers) had built up in Wigston since the early
years of the sixteenth century and much of this property passed to the
Pochins by these two marriages. A marriage settlement of 1696 reveals
that by that date, a generation after their arrival in the village, John Pochin,
gent., possessed a large farmhouse and six yardlands belonging to it in
the fields of Wigston, a fourth part of the manor of Wigston (for what it
was worth), and a small estate in Glen Parva, to the west of Wigston.

Thus, from the early seventeenth century, substantial estates in
Wigston were passing into the hands of families from outside, not
native to the place, some of whom came to reside in the village and to
cultivate their own lands, while others were merely absentee landlords.
Walter Rudinge, gent., of Westcotes, just outside Leicester, bought
the Waldram property in Wigston in 1613, anciently described as two
virgates and going back to the Domesday holding of Robert de Buci
under the Countess Judith: now described as 66 acres of land in the fine.

---

[1] The acreages are taken from fines (P.R.O.) in which I have assumed that the first figure ('land') is the
true one. Thomas Mawson was admitted to the freedom of Leicester in 1598-9 after his apprenticeship
to Mr. George Tatam, tanner. The Elizabethan tanners of Leicester were a wealthy class, producing
several mayors for the town.

The Waldrams had bought this property back in 1550, and had leased it out to Wigston men as two farms of a virgate each. At the time of the sale to Walter Rudinge, gent., who continued to lease it out, the two farms had been consolidated into one.

One more example of the absentee landlord will suffice. In 1634 John Major, gent., bought from Robert Clarke the elder of Wigston, representative of a fifteenth-century peasant family, a farm of 60 acres; in 1656 he bought 2 messuages, 4 cottages, and 110 acres of land from Sampson Davenport, clerk, of Wigston; and in 1669 Antony Major, gent., his son, bought a messuage and cottage, and 56 acres of land, from the Lawes. They bought about 226 acres in all in Wigston. Other Leicestershire fines show John Major buying lands in seven other parishes, all over the county, between 1653 and 1658. The Majors, whose origin is obscure before this date – they certainly do not appear to be a Leicestershire family – took up their abode in Leicester for the next hundred years or so. At Wigston their substantial estate, now one of the largest in the village, was leased out. The large tenant farmer – large by peasant standards, that is – was also making his appearance in seventeenth-century Wigston.

Thus the peasant community, despite its apparent solidity and stability, was in fact being subjected to steadily increasing pressures from within and without, and the familiar features of nineteenth-century farming were beginning to make their appearance: the absentee landlord with property in a number of parishes, of which Wigston was only one, exploiting his lands to the full through tenant-farmers; the consolidation of farms, so that units of fifty to a hundred acres and more were becoming increasingly common; the growth of a native gentry in the village, of peasant families who had been successful in accumulating largish estates – three to six yardlands, or a hundred to two hundred acres which they had managed to retain intact. By the end of the seventeenth century there were about half a dozen such 'peasant gentry', if such a term may be permitted, who lived in the largest houses, cultivated the largest farms, and were slowly beginning to spread into the professions in Leicester and the county as parsons, lawyers, and surgeons. In a way, the peasant community was breeding its own downfall, by producing a class of successful landowners, both native and strangers, whose interests and whole way of thinking gradually became estranged from the peasant system under which their ancestors had lived and prospered in earlier times. The new peasant gentry, and the absentee gentry, were far removed from the pebbles and the mud walls, the beehives and the goose-feathers, that had occupied the thoughts of the older peasantry. In the thriving town of Leicester they had frequent visions of a less earthy life, more comfortable, and civilised in a different way. They were losing the homely rural culture for a wider, more sophisticated urban culture – books, silver, mirrors and china, carpets and curtains, cushions and conversation.

But we must not hurry: the peasant system was not breaking up as rapidly as these words might imply: it was still vigorous in the year 1670 and far from decay. There were a number of factors which mitigated the effects of this emergence of a class of gentry. The first, and perhaps the most important, was that the economic standing of the Davenports, Freers, Pochins, Pawleys, Smiths, and Horsepools did not represent a social gulf. For one thing nearly all these families had less well-off relations in the village, middling farmers and even cottagers, and this helped to bridge any social differences that might have arisen. But, more than that, they all farmed their own land and were still largely dependent on its yield, on the weather and on the communal management of the open fields. 'The small owners of the parish,' said George Bourne of his own Surrey village, 'might occupy more land than the labourers, and have the command of horses and waggons, and ploughs and barns, and so on; but they ate the same sort of food and wore the same sort of clothes as the poorer folk, and they thought the same thoughts too, and talked in the same dialect, so that the labourer working for them was not oppressed by any sense of personal inferiority. He might even excel in some directions, and be valued for his excellence … '[1] That is well said, and I cannot say it better. There was no social gulf while these things were so.

And again, a great part of the population of Wigston in 1670, of almost any peasant village at that date, still consisted of the middling farmers, the true peasantry, and the freehold cottagers, men with ten to thirty acres of land, some with none at all but a cottage, a cow or

---

[1] Bourne, *Change in the Village*, 119.

two, and certain rights upon the common. That there was such a cottage husbandry the records leave us in no doubt. The inventories of labourers in earlier years demonstrate it, as we have seen, and such inventories are still as frequent in the 1670's. A Skeffington labourer in 1670 left only £10 7s. 0d. worth of personal estate: he had a humbly furnished cottage: but he had also 'two old cows and a yearling calf', a small quantity of barley and peas, and a load of hay. Another Skeffington labourer in the same year left personal estate to the value of £22 19s. 4d., including three sheep, three cows and a yearling heifer, peas, hay, barley, and malt.[1] Robert Arden of Sutton Cheney, in the west of the county, left estate valued at £24 17s. 2d. His cottage was by no means badly furnished: the parlour (bedroom) contained 'a joined bedstead' and a feather bed, and a great deal of linen napery – napkins, sheets, tablecloths, and ten yards of (new flaxen cloth'; and in the hall (the livingroom) pewter, brassware, and more linen. Well over half his total estate lay in two cows and a yearling, four sheep and three lambs, one hog and two store-pigs, five loads of hay, one load of winter corn, and three loads of peas.[2] Such men as these were not poor. They lived in a self-reliant cottage-economy, producing as much as they could for themselves and using money only to buy such necessaries as they could not produce by their own efforts; and they were to be found in every village throughout the length and breadth of the Midlands. It may be objected that these men were exceptional, that many others were poorer, and left no will and no inventory. So they may have been, but inventories such as this show what was possible to a man, however humble his start, if he had the will and the ambition to 'get on' in a modest way. No social system is perfect, but if it offers the possibility of well-being to the majority of men able and willing to work it can be called good; and the peasant system did that. It made it possible for men to get on in a modest but satisfying way, to enjoy well-being, to acquire a standing and some measure of respect in their own community by reason of the quality of their work. If all men did not reach this level, the fault lay largely in themselves in a relatively closed economy.

---

[1] L.C.R.O., 1670 Inventories, nos. 230, 270. Skeffington is a small village in the east Leicestershire hills.

[2] Ibid, no. 202.

Such a cottage husbandry, which we have illustrated from villages elsewhere in Leicestershire, was well developed at Wigston. A considerable number of cottages belonged to their occupants: many had small parcels of land going with them – perhaps only half an acre to an acre in each field, others had no land but certain common rights. Thus, when the constables of the village collected their levy of so much per yardland from all who occupied any land at all in the year 1670, they also raised the sum of 9s. 6d. 'of them which did pay for noe land', at the rate of 2d. a cow and 4d. a score of sheep.[1] In other words, the cottagers who neither occupied nor owned any land possessed the equivalent of 57 cows or 570 sheep. We do not know the exact numbers of sheep and cattle they may have had, but in the village as a whole the number of sheep was roughly six times as large as the number of cows in any one year and if the cottagers followed the same proportion they would have had about 35 cows and about 220 sheep between them.[2] Thus even those who lived in one-hearth houses, who constituted the bulk of the population at the time of the hearth-tax assessment, were far from being poverty-stricken.

At the bottom of the assessment, we have, it is true, no fewer than 47 householders out of a total of 161 in the village – nearly thirty per cent – who are exempted from the hearth-tax by reason of poverty. But at least 19 of these are described as 'widow', and are poor only in that sense, and a few others – like Samuel Pawley, Patience Abbott, Francis Deacon, and others – are probably old yeomen ending their days in a small cottage to which they had retired, or in their 'parlour'.

Amongst the names of those exempted from the hearth-tax, for example, is that of 'Widow Cley'. It so happens that the documents relating to the provision for her old age survive, and they are worth quoting briefly as illustrating another aspect of the life of the village. On 17 November 1658 Thomas Cley of Wigston, weaver, and Joan his wife, conveyed to their son Zachariah the cottage house, yard, garden, orchard, croft, and backside 'now set forth and divided from the ground

---

[1] Constables' Account-book, 1653-1714 (Parish chest, Wigston Magna).

[2] These numbers would have produced a total levy of 9s. 6d. as was in fact raised. The proportion of six sheep to one cow is derived from the churchwardens' accounts for the period 1678-1714 which give the respective totals for rating purposes in each year.

of Robert Smyth of Wigston, weaver', together with 1¾ acres of arable in the fields, and common pasture for one cow and five sheep, the consideration being a payment of ten shillings yearly during the life of Thomas Cley 'for and towards his Livelyhood and mentenance'. On the same day, Thomas and his wife also conveyed to their neighbour Robert Smith, weaver, two lands in each of the village fields and five doles or pieces of meadow in Hilly Meadow, 'for the consideration that Robert Smyth and his heirs and assigns shall from time to time and at all times hereafter during the natural lives of Thomas Cley and Joan his wife and for the life of the longer liver of them or either of them well and sufficiently provide for mentayne and keepe the said Thomas Cley and Joan his wiffe with good wholsom meat drinke lodginge fyre washinge starchinge Cloathes both Lyninge & Woollinge hoose shooes and all other nesessaryes and things Convenient and fittinge for people of their qualletys and Condicion'.[1] It is clear from these two records that the original cottage-holding carried with it a total of three acres of land in the fields, some meadow, and common pasture for a cow and five sheep – the stint for a holding of one-eighth of a yardland. This small holding, combined with weaving by Thomas Cley, was sufficient to maintain him during his working life, but with the approach of old age it was split up and sold in order to provide a small money income for himself and his wife, and maintenance for the rest of their lives *fitting for people of their quality and condition.* This is the sort of pride and self-help that would have delighted Cobbett.

Thus, many of those exempt from the hearth tax are not the genuine able-bodied poor. We should be nearer the truth if we put the number of able-bodied poor – 'the poor' in the true sense – at about one-half of those exempt from the tax, at about one-sixth of the population at the most.[2]

There is one other matter calling for comment before we leave the hearth-tax assessment, and that is the change in the personnel of the

---

[1] L.R.O., Wigston deeds etc., 9 D. 43. nos. 191, 192.

[2] This would agree roughly with the figure we get for 1698-1701 when, for a brief period, the occupation or status of those named in the parish register is given. Out of 75 for which the information is given, 12 are described as 'poor man', 'poor woman', 'poor maid', or 'poor widow' – about 16 per cent, not a large class but perceptibly greater than it had been, and about to grow more rapidly.

leading families of the village since the year 1524. In that year William Chamberlain, Thomas Whyte, and William Astyll had headed the tax-list, and the Chamberlains, Astells, and Whites had owned nearly a quarter of the personal estate of the village between them. Now, in 1670, the Chamberlains had gone, and both the Whites and the Astills, though still living in the village, were much less important than they had been. Walter Chamberlain, who had been one of the four trustees for the sale of the Danvers manor to the tenants, had sold out soon afterwards. In 1613 he had sold his fourth part of the manor, and a messuage, to Sir William Faunt, the squire of Foston; in 1616 he sold ten acres of land to Simon Pawley; and in 1623 another thirty acres to George Buswell, gent., an outsider who was buying other small properties in the village. The name of Chamberlain then disappears from the records after a stay of three or four generations.

The Astills still survived, represented by 'Widow Astill', who was exempt from the hearth tax in 1670. Some of them had moved away, to farm elsewhere (at Bagworth and Rearsby); those who were left were middling farmers-husbandmen – like Robert Astill, whose inventory in 1612 totalled £59 14s. 10d., and Thomas Astill whose estate was valued at £35 18s. 8d. in 1616. William Astill in 1626 was probably a poor cottager, with an estate of £5 3s. 4d. In 1642 Richard Astill is described in the parish register as a labourer, and fifty years or so later, in 1698, John Astill is called labourer, and Katherine Astill 'poor woman'. They were evidently a decaying family throughout the seventeenth century and the eighteenth, but they still clung to a little of their land. In 1765 John Astill was rated upon a quartern of land in his occupation (about eight acres) and at the enclosure award in the following year was allotted 7¼ acres.

The Whites, too, still remained in the village, to which they had come early in the fifteenth century. A marriage settlement of 1615, when Henry White, yeoman, married Judith, one of the daughters of Robert Hall, yeoman, of Wigston, shows that Henry then owned a messuage, two cottages, two yardlands of arable, meadow, and pasture, and two further pieces of meadow called 'the Baylie pieces'. When he died in 1638 his personal estate amounted to £377 17s. 0d. – one of the largest estates in the village of which £300 was money owing to him by Francis Pawley, yeoman, of Wigston. Possibly this was part of a marriage settlement, of which no record now remains. The Wigston yeoman families were continually marrying with each other, the greater with the greater, the lesser with the lesser, and considerable sums of money changed hands on these occasions. Another Henry White was a yeoman-farmer in the 1660's and occupied a farmhouse larger than the average in 1664 (hearth tax assessment). The Whites, then, had maintained their position since 1524, neither rising like the Freers and Davenports nor decaying like the Astills, but remaining solid yeoman-farmers of fifty or sixty acres of their own land.[1]

Of the next group of farmers in 1524, below the most affluent, several had disappeared from the village within the next three or four generations. The Herricks seem to have gone by the 1630's; and so, too, had the Amorys, Palmers, Hugglescotes, and Cattons. But the Pawleys and the Smiths still survived. They had been substantial yeomen in 1524; and since then they had added steadily to their estates and were, by 1670, either recognised 'gentry' or about to become so. A Pawley marriage settlement of 1698 speaks of two messuages, a cottage, 3½ yardlands in the fields and a small close, and this may not have been all that belonged to the family.[2]

There were in 1670 a number of other substantial yeoman families in the village, farming one to three yardlands each, most of whom had been there for several generations – the Clarkes, Raggs, Johnsons, Jacksons, Abbots, and Rosses. All of these had consolidated their position by the end of the seventeenth century. They were all biggish farmers by peasant standards, though not quite gentry yet. And, not least, there was a considerable class of craftsmen and tradesmen, of whom the butchers (like the Brewins who were butchers and graziers here from the early seventeenth century to the late eighteenth) were the most important, and the tailors and shoemakers the most numerous. There were at least half a dozen tailors in Wigston in the late seventeenth century and nearly as many shoemakers. Almost without exception, they combined their trade with the cultivation of some land.

---

[1] They had mostly sold out, however, by 1766. The enclosure award of that year allotted them only 13½ acres.

[2] But by 1766 they were reduced to 4½ acres.

❧ PARISH GOVERNMENT AND PARISH OFFICERS ❧

At Wigston we hear only of the two churchwardens, the head constable, and the two petty constables during the seventeenth century. There were two overseers of the poor also, but the surviving accounts of these officers do not begin until 1728; and in the eighteenth century also we hear for a brief period of the field-reeves and the eveners, who kept separate accounts from 1750 to 1764.

The churchwardens were the most ancient of these officers, though the head constable ran them close.[1] Before the suppression of St. Wistan's church, about the middle of the sixteenth century, there had been four churchwardens at Wigston; but by the end of the century there were only two. From the earliest surviving accounts we discover that the churchwardens drew their income from the letting of closes and other grass in their possession and, very largely, from a levy which varied slightly in form and magnitude from time to time.[2] Thus in 1615 William Noone and Thomas Coltman drew about 32s. from the rent of various closes (such as Hall close and Balldike close) and certain grazing in the fields, probably ley ground that belonged to the church from old time. William Dann paid 14s. in that year for 'parting grasse' and William Clarke 9s. 'for part of Foston Gate'. But the bulk of the income came each year from a special levy, which in 1615 took the form of eightpence from every yardland, and a penny on every horse, cow and communicant, bringing in a total of £6 10s. 9d. A similar levy in the following year produced £6 9s. 8d. A second levy of 12d. on every yardland produced £4 1s. 11½d.[3] The total income for this year was £20 19s. 4½d., the expenditure £20 3s. 10½d., and the credit balance handed over to the succeeding wardens 15s. 6d.

The expenditure of the churchwardens in every year was almost entirely on repairs and other necessary work about the church, the purchase of bread and wine, costs of visitations, and other matters

---

[1] The poll tax returns for many Leicestershire villages in 1377 are headed by a man called *constabularius*.

[2] Nichols prints extracts from a book of accounts from 1591 onwards, but this is now lost. The present accounts, in two books, cover the period 1615-1715. (Parish chest, Wigston Magna.)

[3] The parish was always reckoned at 92¾ yardlands, but there were always small arrears carried over from year to year, as in this instance.

connected with the church, besides the usual payments to 'poore men havinge a passe' or to those who 'had greate losse by fire'. There is nothing unusual in all this and we need not be detained by these accounts any further beyond remarking that the church-wardens also looked after several matters relating to the fields which the field-reeves later took over. They paid for innumerable moles, hedgehogs, and other vermin, and for two men 'to keepe the fields'. Indeed, throughout the seventeenth century as great a part of the churchwardens' duties arose in the fields as in the church: every year's accounts shows a number of such items. In 1628 we find 'spent at Thomas Boulters [one of the four village inns] when we mad out the fild 5s'. In 1632 there was a comprehensive levy: 'rec. of the parrish by a peny a communicante tow pence a cow and xii^d. a yardland for ye Church viii^d a yard land for mold catching and viii^d a yard land for feild keping 14^{li} 18^s 0½^d'. This dual function of the churchwardens goes on until the surviving accounts end in 1718.

About the overseers of the poor we know nothing, as their accounts do not survive before 1728, but they were certainly in existence from the act of 1601 onwards.[1] Even so, the churchwardens still performed a number of functions in connection with the relief of poverty as they had done before the passing of the act. They administered at Wigston the 'coal money', the 'bread money', and a fund called 'the poore stocke', besides 'the freeschoole money', for all of which except the poor stock they kept separate accounts.[2]

The coal stock had been started by William Lawe, the farmer of the rectory, in 1595, and had been added to often in subsequent years by the more well-to-do yeomen like Simon Brett and William Langton the miller. A considerable number of farmers (sixteen in all) gave the carriage of the coal from the pits gratis.[3] Similarly, John Evans and Zachariah Pawley left money in 1618 for wheaten bread to be distributed every Sunday to the poor; others in the parish left money from time to time for 'the poor stock', out of which in 1618 the sum of £14 was taken, 'the interest thereof to pay for poor children's learning for ever'.

---

[1] The churchwardens' accounts for 1615 refer to Robert Freer senior and Robert Freer junior as the overseers of the poor in that year.

[2] The accounts of coal money, bread money, and freeschool money survive for the period 1663-1718, and are kept in the parish chest.

[3] Nichols, loc. cit., 384, for a list of the parish charities to 1755.

This was the origin of the freeschool money, the annual interest going towards the payment of the Schoolmaster.[1] As late as 1755 Henry Clarke gave £20, the interest to be given to the poor by the churchwardens and overseers. Thus the churchwardens continued to administer a good deal of the poor relief through the parish charities.

By 1674 the accounts show that the coal money had reached a total of £117; the freeschool money remained at £14, and the bread money at £40. All this money was lent out, in sums of varying amount, at six per cent interest, and out of this interest the coal and bread charities were administered and some of the school-master's salary paid. Of the £117 coal money, £100 was lent to Mr, James Oliver and Mr. Coleman, both of Tur Langton, a village some miles away, but the remainder was out on loan in small sums to a number of Wigston people. The total income in 1674 amounted to £13 0s. 10d., the total expenses were £8 6s. 1½d., and the balance of £4 14s. 8½d. was handed over to the succeeding churchwardens.

During this year the churchwardens bought 179 cwt. of coal at 9½d. a cwt. which they resold to the poor at 4d. a cwt. and this system continued up to the end of the accounts. The price of the coal to the churchwardens varied between 8d. and 9½d., but they always re-sold it at 4d. Bread was distributed weekly, on Sundays, and again at Christmas; and at Easter there was a distribution of money to the deserving poor. By 1714 the income of the churchwardens for these purposes came to £21 3s. 6d.,[2] their expenditure to £16 9s. 5d., and their credit balance to £4 14s. 1d. In that year they bought 280 cwt. of coal at 7¾d., and sold 264 cwt. at 4d. The great increase in the quantity of coal needed, between 1674 and 1714, is some measure of the increase in the poor as a class in the village; and yet these accounts were always healthy. They generally showed a credit balance and at the same time relieved a great deal of distress with bread, coal, and money, and educated the village children. The philanthropic impulse was no less strong in Wigston than in England as a whole; and private

---

[1] The school was held in the old St. Wistan's church as it had been since Elizabethan days.

[2] In 1679 the old system of lending out sums of money at interest was abandoned. The churchwardens bought a close in the neighbouring township of Glen Parva ('the poor's close') and let it annually.

charity continued to be important in the relief of poverty in England long after the State had set up its own machinery and instituted compulsory rates.

The constables' accounts show the same mixture and overlapping of functions as the churchwardens', for they, too, devoted some of their revenue and time to 'field-keeping'. There was the head constable, who served for several years at a time, and two petty constables who were chosen annually. Webb says that the office of Petty Constable was the one most objected to, 'either abandoned to humble folk, attracted by its perquisites, or else invariably filled by a substitute';[1] but there is no evidence of this at Wigston in this period. Year after year we read the names of all the leading yeomen, husbandmen, and craftsmen of the village; there is not a cottager or a humble householder among them. The 'head Constable', when the surviving accounts open in 1653, was Mr. Robert Freer, but some time about 1660 Mr. Francis Smith succeeded him and remained in that office until 1690, to be followed in turn by Mr. John Noone. The head or chief constable was chosen from among the leading families in the village, as William Astill was in 1524, and the petty constables were drawn from the upper half of the village population as a whole.

Unfortunately, the constables' accounts begin after the civil wars were over, but they show throughout the 1650's what a heavy burden of taxation the war had left behind, heavier than anything known before. The subsidies of the period 1600-41 had fallen on only 12 to 18 households. On an average only about one in every ten households paid the subsidy. The monthly assessments of the war period fell much more widely and heavily. In 1644 Wigston had to raise £1 6s. 6d. a month; by 1647 the assessment was up to £2 11s. 0d. a month, or £30 12s. 0d. per annum.[2]

In 1653-4 the constables levied three taxes, of six shillings, four shillings, and eightpence per yardland, raising £61 10s. 8d. in all, of which all but is. 10d. was spent (no details are given). In the following year they raised £70 8s. 4d., of which three assessments totalling twelve shillings per yardland (as against 10s. 8d. the year before) were described

---

[1] *English Local Government: The Parish and the County*, 18-19.
[2] P.R.O., E.179. 269/22 (1644) and E.179. 134/312 (1647).

as a tax, and the fourth as 'a levy' of 1s. 4d. a yardland.[1] Altogether the occupier of a yardland paid 13s. 4d. in this year and the lesser men proportionately. The 'lainges forth' show that the national exchequer took £59 16s. 6d. of the total revenue for this year; the burden of national taxation had nearly doubled since 1647.

This high rate continued until 1662-3, when as much as £97 7s. 2d. was raised and £94 19s. 8d. spent. This was the heaviest year of all; in the next year the burden fell to less than one-third. The accounts for 1662-3 were delivered up on 20 October 1663 by Peter Ragg and William Johnson before 'Mr. Francis Smith head Constable' and Mr. Francis Smith senior, Mr. William Lewis, Francis Pawley, 'and many more of the inhabitants of the towne then there present'. They are worth quoting in full to show how heavy and all-embracing the burden had become:

Receipts		
for the 4th 3 months Tax	Rec^d a Tax after 4^{sh} the yard land & the Tithe valued att 17 yard & a halfe & Mr. Fawnts mills att one yard & Ten shillings & eight pence of divers that was Taxed for stocke which is	23- 5- 4
for the 5th 3 months Tax	Rec^d allsoe the like Sume of	23- 5- 4
for the 6th & last of the eighteen months Tax	Rec^d allsoe the like Sume of	23- 5- 4
	Rec^d for a Tax after 1^{sh}-4^d the yard land for the militia which amounts to the sume of	7-11- 8
	Rec^d another Tax for the militia after 8l the yard land which amounts to the sume of	3-15-10
	Rec^d another Tax for the pensioners after 8d the yard land which amounts to the sume of	3-15-10

[1] This last was probably the constables' rate for the village's own business.

Rec^d a Levye after 1^sh-4^d the yard land & 4^d a
schore of Sheep & 2^d a Cowe which amounts
to   12-7-10

The whole Sume of our Receipts amounts to   97-7-2

Disbursments

paid to Mr. Thos Mawson Colector for the 4th
months Tax of the Eighteen the Sume of   21-12-9
paid to the same Colector the sume of   21-12-9
for the 5th of the eighteen months
paid to the same Colector the like sume of   21-12-9
for the 6th and last of the eighteene months Tax
paid to Mr. Smith the Sume of   3-7-00
paid to him allsoe the Sume of   1-16-1
paid to him allsoe the Sume of   1-16-1
paid to Mr. Huckle of Leicester the Sume of   7-3-3
paid to Mr. Smith for Gaole & quartridge & aquit-
tances for the quarters   1-19-4
paid to him allsoe for 6 bills for Assizes & Sessions   00-3-0
paid for poore passengers & other Expences &
for Tho: Johnson for writeing our yeare the Sume
                                                          of   13-16-8

the whole Sume of our Layings forth is   94-19-8
they are indebted to the towne the Sume of   2-7-6

By far the greater part of the constables' income went to the national exchequer: in this year just about two-thirds of the total. A considerable part was passed on to the Head Constable as a sort of county rate; while the residue – about one-seventh of the total was spent on the 'townes business', as it is elsewhere described, of which no details are given.

After 1664-5 the constables raised less than £20 annually in several years – as little as £11 4s. 0d. in 1670-1 – but the level of payments began to rise again throughout the 1680's, reaching a peak in 1692-3 of £37 5s. 6d.[1] By the late 1690's and the early 1700's, however, the total had dropped again to between £15 and £25, averaging about £20 a

[1] Much of this was due, however, to expenditure on 'the old Church', which had ceased to be used as a church. It is not entirely clear what the constables were doing there, but they may have been converting it into cottages as in 1702-3 they received eight 'house rents' from it of 6d. each. It must have been turned into an almshouse at one end and a school at the other.

year. As the total fell, so more of the constables' income – for which they levied a special rate of their own – went on town business, chiefly the management of the fields; the repairing of the local bridges in the parish, including those in the fields; the cleaning and repair of the town wells; mowing rushes and trenching the meadows and pastures; and paying for sparrows, moles, foxes, badgers, and hedgehogs. The constables apparently appointed field-reeves for 'keeping the fields', and pinders to look after the stock and haywards; and by the middle of the eighteenth century the field-reeves and others known as 'the eveners' were keeping separate accounts. The mixed and overlapping administration of the seventeenth-century parish was beginning to sort itself out into clearly defined officials and functions.[1]

❧ SUMMARY AND CONCLUSIONS ❧

In this chapter we have been mainly concerned with the social structure of the village, the peasant economy within which it worked, and the parish government. Throughout the century Wigston was a true peasant community, with no lords of the manor, and no manorial organisation. The village had triumphed completely over the manor. The peasant landowner, from the yeoman down to the freehold cottager, was the typical figure, and the village or parish was the sole unit of government through the churchwardens, the petty constables, and the overseers of the poor, and their specialised deputies like the field-reeves and the eveners.

The village had doubled its numbers in a hundred years before 1625, and was one of the largest and most populous villages in the Midlands. But the exuberant growth which began about 1570 had largely exhausted itself by 1620. Thereafter births and marriages tended to fall and the crude death-rate to rise. From 1620 to 1675 or so there was comparative stagnation, or very slow growth at the most. In the last quarter of the century there was a renewed growth of population, mainly due to the inflow of new families looking for work rather than to any substantial changes in the birth-rate or the death-rate.[2]

---

[1] The work of the field-reeves and the eveners is dealt with in the following chapter, as also is that of the overseers of the poor.

[2] *T.L.A.S.*, xxxiii. In 1670 there were 13 villages in Leicestershire with more than a hundred households, Wigston being the third largest (161). It was exceeded only by Mountsorrel (168) and Hallaton (165). In addition there were seven little market-towns (excluding Leicester) ranging in size from 104 to 413 households *V.C.H. Leics.*, iii, 170-2.

This inflow is probably connected with the contagious enclosure of Leicestershire parishes throughout the century, and their almost invariable conversion to pasture for large-scale grazing. The displaced people of these parishes drifted to towns like Leicester and Hinckley where the framework-knitting industry was growing rapidly after 1670, or to large open-field villages like Wigston where labour was still needed in the fields. Wigston itself was becoming industrialised also. A brief record of the occupations of the village appears in the parish register between 1698 and 1701. It is only a sample of those who happened to have children, to marry, or to die, in those years, but it is a useful indication of the occupational structure of the village within its limits. If we count all the eleven labourers as engaged in farming (which they mostly were), we find 36 per cent of the sample dependent on agriculture (including nine yeomen and six husbandmen); 30 per cent in various crafts and trades, who also depended on agriculture to a varying degree; 17 per cent dependent on framework-knitting; and 16 per cent described as 'poor'. About one-sixth of the population by the end of the seventeenth century had broken the immemorial tie with the land and were earning their living in industry. It is to this cottage industry, and the employment it offered, that we must attribute the greater part of the inflow of new families into Wigston in the last quarter of the seventeenth century; and these families were recruited largely from the displaced population of the one-time arable parishes round about.[1]

One of the most striking characteristics of the economic and social history of the village during the seventeenth century was the incessant buying and selling of land in the parish, mainly by native peasant families but to a growing degree by prosperous and successful men from Leicester and elsewhere. Small parcels of land, an acre or so at a time, still changed hands., but the average transaction was considerably larger than it had been fifty or a hundred years earlier with the consolidation of farms. Hence we find, too, the growing importance of the absentee landlord and of the tenant-farmer.

---

[1] For a list of pre-Parliamentary enclosures in Leicestershire, parish by parish, see *V.C.H. Leics.*, ii, Appendix I, pp. 254-9.

One detects, also, the increasing part played by money in the seventeenth-century village, which is very evident in the peasant marriage settlements, wills, and inventories. Sums of £100 to £300 change hands between these families at times. Alongside this we have the emergence of a rudimentary

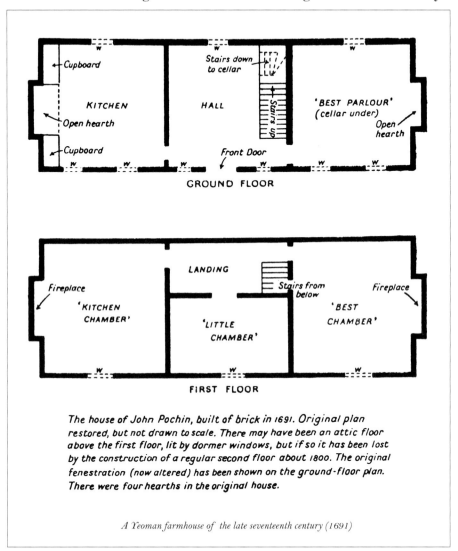

The house of John Pochin, built of brick in 1691. Original plan restored, but not drawn to scale. There may have been an attic floor above the first floor, lit by dormer windows, but if so it has been lost by the construction of a regular second floor about 1800. The original fenestration (now altered) has been shown on the ground-floor plan. There were four hearths in the original house.

A Yeoman farmhouse of the late seventeenth century (1691)

class-structure out of the hitherto rather amorphous and generalised peasant community of earlier days. A number of the successful peasant families had in the course of time accumulated up to two hundred or so acres of land in the parish and by the second half of the seventeenth century constituted a small class – perhaps half a dozen families in all – of 'peasant gentry'. Such were, for example, the Freers and the Davenports. Moreover, these sizeable accumulations of landed property began to attract attention from outside, and old gentry like the Pochins married their younger sons into the Wigston peasant-gentry and settled in the village.

Parallel with the emergence of an 'upper class' in the village we have the growth of the able-bodied poor as a class, who amounted to perhaps one-sixth of the total population by the end of the seventeenth century. The labouring class in general, with or without a small cottage-holding, was also growing.

There were three special reasons for the growth of such a class of labouring poor at the bottom of the social structure. First, the rapid growth of population between 1570 and 1620, of new families flooding in and of children being born in hitherto unparalleled numbers, was bound to have its effect in the succeeding generations in a village which had long ago reached the limits of its available land. Small holdings were even further divided to meet some of the need, and even the labourer with a cottage of his own and some common rights could do well for himself. But there were limits to this minute subdivision; and as the century went on we find an increasing number of landless labourers, poor weavers, and, towards the end, stocking-makers in the village. Moreover, farms were all the time being engrossed into fewer hands and this greatly aggravated the problem. The Pochins' or the Davenports' six yardlands[1] meant that some twenty or more other families who could have lived comfortably off a farm of half a yardland were altogether deprived of this opportunity. And when we add to this the numerous farms of two, three or four yardlands that now existed in the village we have no difficulty in seeing why the landless labourer grew so conspicuously in numbers in this century. Parts of these larger peasant holdings were, it is true, let to smaller men in half-yardlands or so – as we frequently discover from conveyances or marriage settlements – or the pressure of population on the supply of land would have been intolerable in this overcrowded village; but even so the consolidation of farms was depriving a great number of small peasants of the opportunity of acquiring some land

---

[1] In 1636 Sampson Davenport, clerk, levied a fine to put his property in trust. It was then described as three messuages, 11 cottages, and 198 acres of land. This is between six and seven yardlands.

just when the increased numbers born in the late sixteenth century and early seventeenth were growing up to manhood.

One wonders, too, how far the heavy taxation of the civil war and Commonwealth period helped to reduce the status and living standards of the smaller peasantry. The war itself flared up repeatedly in the Midlands and caused intense excitement in Wigston itself from time to time; but its more permanent effect was perhaps to make life harder financially for the smaller men. The more affluent families certainly paid heavily to the monthly assessments and their aftermath, and felt the burden keenly; but it was direct taxation of a regressive kind and it fell relatively hardest on those least able to pay. A tax at a flat rate of so much per yardland, or so much per cow or score of sheep, was in fact regressive in effect; and long years of this kind of heavy taxation – twenty years of it from the early 1640's to the early '60's – must have had a slowly depressing effect on the status of the smaller peasantry. These were the reasons, then, for the growth of the poor as a class: too many people on a fixed supply of land, the engrossing of what land there was into fewer hands, and heavy taxation for twenty years on end. The standard of living for a considerable part of the village population therefore fell in the course of the seventeenth century: nearly all the gains of the Elizabethan period were lost or diluted. More crowded, more unhealthy, less land available: the village was producing a class of landless labour ripe for early industrialisation.

For those not divorced from the peasant system, and these were still the majority – true peasant farmers of five to thirty acres of land or cottage-freeholders – for these life was still relatively comfortable and stable. Nearly a half of the population had lived in the village for at least a hundred years, a fifth of them for over two hundred years. The fields, and the open-field husbandry, were still unimpaired. Those with common rights still lived in a self-contained cottage economy. Despite all the forces that were slowly undermining it, the peasant system was still vigorous. If only there had not been so many people in the village, it would have been even stronger, perhaps even indestructible.

VIII

WIGSTON ON THE EVE OF THE REVOLUTION

Owners and Occupiers

The private act for the enclosure of Wigston Magna was passed in 1764 and the award was made 17 November 1766. This was one of the most momentous events in the long history of the village. It transformed the physical landscape of the parish within a few years, altered its farming almost beyond recognition, and changed the entire culture and habits of the peasant community. It was comparable, in the magnitude of its consequences for village society, with the introduction of Christianity in the Dark Ages, an event which coloured the whole life of the village for centuries afterwards. Indeed, the enclosure of the parish was perhaps a more dramatic event, for it took place suddenly and produced immediate effects, whereas the leavening of heathen life and the reshaping of a barbarian society by the coming of Christianity was a slow, an almost imperceptible process. And yet the full consequences of the enclosure award were not immediately apparent either. Sudden and dramatic changes there were almost at once; but the full impact was not felt for many years, during which it worked in hidden ways to undermine the old peasant society, as the Christian faith had once worked slowly in hidden ways to fuse it together.

Parliamentary enclosure has often been blamed for the destruction of village life over the greater part of England, for the disintegration of a traditional culture and society. It has, perhaps equally often, been absolved from blame. Let us see, therefore, what the peasant community of Wigston was like on the eve of this great revolution, so that we can determine, as far as may be, the extent to which enclosure was in reality a sudden, mortal blow, or how far it merely set the seal upon changes that had already gone a long way towards disintegrating the old form of peasant life.

We are fortunate in possessing an assessment, made by the field reeves on 30 January 1765, at the rate of eightpence a yardland in order to defray their expenses for the preceding year.[1] From this we can reconstruct a picture of the village on the eve of the enclosure, the way in which the land was owned and occupied. A poor rate assessment dated about eighteen months later (September 1766), tells us that 149 households were assessed to this rate and that about 50 were exempt on the ground of poverty,[2] giving a total of about 200 households in the village at that date. The field reeves' levy shows that there were 60 occupiers of land, excluding the tithe and glebe (which were assessed as equivalent to 20½ yardlands), whose holdings ranged from John Dand's two acres[3] up to William Johnson's eight yardlands and half a quartern – about 260 acres.

Thus two interesting facts emerge at once about the open-field village. By 1765 only three families in every ten occupied any land; seven families in every ten had none, but earned their livelihood as labourers in the fields, as framework-knitters, and as small craftsmen and tradesmen. Already, then, before enclosure had taken place, two families in every three had been largely divorced from the land. There were fewer occupiers of land in Wigston in 1765 than there had been in 1086, and the population of the place had more than doubled in the meantime.

There was, too, a great range between the smallest occupiers and the largest, another feature of nineteenth-century 'capitalist farming' which had already developed in the eighteenth-century open-field village. The complete list of occupiers is shown on page 218.[4]

The acreages given in the above list must not be regarded as mathematically exact as the original assessment is based on yardlands, quarterns, and fractions of quarterns, the smallest unit being a quarter quartern of two acres; but it is accurate to within a small margin of error. Its chief defect is that it excludes all occupiers of less than about two acres-for whom there was often a separate levy based on the number of their cattle and sheep-and therefore does not give a complete

---

[1] Field Reeves' Account Book, 1752-65 (Parish chest, Wigston church).

[2] Nichols, 387.

[3] Given as a quarter of a quartern. The quartern was a quarter-yardland, and the normal yardland at Wigston was 32 acres.

[4] I have translated yardlands, quarterns, etc., into acres for the sake of clarity.

Occupier	Acreage	Occupier	Acreage
Oliver Fox	46	Patience Abbot	8
Mr. Buszard	4	Daniel Ward	6
William Freer	18	John Pawley	4
Mrs. Holms	8	Henry Johnson	8
Luis Russell	88	William Gibbons	66
Richard Pochin	112	William Richardson	4
Thomas Coltman	4	Widow Darker	4
Mrs. Russell	32	Thomas Langton	4
Wm. Goodrich	12	Thomas Hurst	4
Armston Pochin	128	Mr. Burgess	44
Samuel Davenport	83	Thomas Willson	208
Tithe and glebe	–	Henry Branson	160
John Dand	2	Widow Langton	8
John Astill	8	Alban Aynge	14
Thomas Blockley	104	Widow Johnson	12
James Bingley	8	Joseph Johnson	10
Thomas Johnson	4	Thomas Goode	16
John Johnson	4	Thomas Horner	132
John Freer	200	Cornelius Darker	16
Simeon Brewin	88	John Phipps	8
Francis Johnson	4	Thomas Goodwin	28
Richard Abbot	4	George Boulter	16
Mr. Clarke	148	John Burdet	4
Mr. Ragg	44	Abram Hach	208
Robert White	4	Mr. Ragg	172
William Brewin	64	Joseph Langham	8
Sarah Simons	4	William Johnson	260
William Langton	6	Thomas Jackson	136
William Coltman	4	George Ross	117
Richard Coltman	20	John Cooper	8
William Blaksley	4	Richard Branson	4

account of the open-field economy, in which the cottager with his acre or so of arable and small common pasture rights was an important element. An analysis of the enclosure award in the following chapter, which reveals ninety-nine owners of land,[1] makes good this deficiency to a considerable extent.

[1] Excluding the Duke of St. Albans (in lieu of great tithes), the vicar (in lieu of small tithes), and three or four corporate bodies like the Wigston Meeting, Narborough meeting, etc.

Nevertheless, the 1765 list is very informative even as it stands. No fewer than eighteen occupiers farmed less than five acres, and thirty farmed ten acres or less. Twelve more farmed between eleven and fifty acres. That is to say, fully two-thirds of the occupiers at Wigston farmed less than fifty acres, and a half of them less than ten acres. At the top of the scale, five men farmed more than 200 acres each,[1] and eight more farmed between a hundred and two hundred acres.

The picture we get from these figures is one of a mixed economy. To a large extent the peasant economy survived, with thirty farmers of less than ten acres, and forty farming thirty-two acres or less, besides an unknown but appreciable number of cottagers. But the economy of the large 'capitalist' farm had also developed to a marked degree beside this peasant economy; developed out of it, we may say. Nearly 1100 acres of the available land were being cultivated in large farms of 200 acres or more, or roughly 37 per cent of the total area of the parish. Another 1037 acres – about 35 per cent of the total area – lay in farms of between a hundred acres and two hundred.

Wherever one draws the upper limit of the 'peasant farm' it is bound to be an arbitrary decision, but to put it as high as a hundred acres – in England, anyway – is to be fairly safe. Thus at Wigston we can say that, before parliamentary enclosure had begun, more than seventy per cent of the land had been withdrawn from the strict peasant economy. Though these larger men still enjoyed all the rights enjoyed by the remaining peasantry and managed their cultivation within the rules and limits laid down by the community as a whole, they were in other important respects fairly large-scale capitalist farmers. At any rate, we can no longer call them peasants. In 1765 we have a village in which the peasantry were still the largest class numerically, but in which also the greater part of the land had already passed out of peasant occupation.

Moreover, a good deal of land had also passed into the hands of absentee landlords who lived elsewhere and leased their Wigston property to tenant-farmers, some of them native to the village and owning land of their own; others are strangers to the village, the sort of migrant tenant-farmers who would take a good farm wherever it

[1] Mr. Ragg appears twice in the list, his total holding amounting to 218 acres.

was available. By comparing the levy of 1765 with the allottees in the
enclosure award of the following year, we can see who were the absentee
landlords and who the tenant-farmers.

Most of the land occupied by tenant-farmers was owned by five
absentee landlords: Thomas Wightman 247 acres, the Wyggeston
Hospital 173 acres, John Noone 150 acres, Sarah Norton 147 acres, and
John Darker 130 acres.[1] This gives us a total of 847 acres held by these
absentee landlords; but other smaller absentee owners are revealed by
the enclosure award, like Martha Bruin of Oadby, Simeon Brewin of
Leicester, and Richard Metcalf, a Leicester butcher, whose lands added
up to about 170 acres before enclosure. Thus rather more than 1000
acres of Wigston, or about a third of the whole, were in the hands of
the absentee landlord in 1765; and about two-thirds were in the hands of
the owner-occupier.[2] Of the total of sixty occupiers, about forty-seven
owned some or all of the land they were occupying.

The largest of the absentee landlords was Thomas Wightman, who
was a woolstapler living at the Castle View in Leicester, a freeman of
the borough, and descendant of generations of prosperous Wightmans
back to the middle of the sixteenth century.[3] We do not know how
or when the Wightmans acquired this substantial estate (nearly 250
acres) in Wigston, but it may have come by purchase or otherwise from
the Majors, who, as we have seen, acquired about 226 acres in three
purchases in 1634, 1656, and 1669.[4] This was the largest single estate
in the village in the late seventeenth century and it seems reasonable
to suppose that it is represented in 1765 by Thomas Wightman's
estate, since the Majors no longer appear as landowners by that date.
The greater part of Wightman's land, if not the whole, was let out to
one farmer – Abraham Hack – who was assessed on 6½ yardlands in

---

[1] I arrive at these figures by taking the acreage allotted to each in the award, and adding one-fifth to
each to allow for the proportion which was deducted from each landowner in order to provide land in
lieu of great and small tithes (see the next chapter, pp. 250-1).

[2] Richard Metcalf is a border-line case. He was a Leicester butcher, admitted to the freedom of the
town in 1743. He occupied no land in Wigston in 1765, but received an allotment of 74 acres in the
following year. In 1767 he was living in Wigston as a butcher, but still occupying no land.

[3] Hartopp, *Register of the Freemen of Leicester* (1927), I, 311. Many references to the family may be found
in this register, back to John Wyghtman, late of Branston, glover, admitted to the freedom in 1554–5.

[4] See Chapter VII, p. 198, above.

1765, He was not a native of the village, he had no land of his own, and he had disappeared again by 1781.[1]

On the other hand, the second largest estate – 173 acres held by the Wyggeston Hospital since 1521 – was let out in no fewer than six farms in 1765. Two were mere cottage-holdings of a quarter-yardland each; three were farms of ½, ¾, and ¾ yardland respectively; and one was a farm of three yardlands. From 1521 up to the 1620's, the Hospital had let its property as four farms of 3¼, 1, ¾ and ½ yardland respectively, each farm retaining its medieval identity as it had come into the hands of the Hospital.[2] Shortly before 1629, the largest farm had had a ¼-yardland lopped off it, which was then let to the Boulters for the next hundred years.[3] They were weavers, as the successive leases show, combining this small holding with their trade. In 1729 the lease passed to Henry Coltman, yeoman, who had married the daughter and heir of William Boulter. As so often happened the Hospital land passed with the marriage and a new lease was made to incorporate Henry Coltman's name. Shortly afterwards the land passed again by marriage to John Cooper, framework knitter, who married one of the daughters of Henry Coltman. Cooper was in possession in 1766, when the enclosure award was made, and he received a close of three acres 25 perches as lessee of the quarter yardland.

Towards the end of the seventeenth century, or very early in the eighteenth, the Hospital farm of one yardland became divided into ¾ and ¼ yardland respectively and from 1709 onwards these were let separately. Thus the original four farms had become six by Queen Anne's time, and were still so at the time of the enclosure. The farm of three yardlands – the Randull accumulation of the fifteenth century – was let to William Johnson in 1765 who received just under 74 acres for it at the enclosure, equivalent to about 89 acres before deductions in lieu of tithes. Two or three small homestead closes or crofts brought the total original area up to 93 acres or so, in other words to three yardlands of 32 acres each approximately.

William Johnson was the largest farmer in Wigston in 1765, farming some 260 acres. Of this 50 or 51 acres were his own land – the Johnsons

---

[1] L.C.R.O., Land tax assessments, 1773, 1781. These assessments cover the period 1773-1832. Hack was probably a Leicester butcher (see *Register of Freemen*, passim, for Hacks as butchers and graziers).

[2] See Chapter V, p. 125 *et seq.*

[3] Wyggeston Hospital MSS., loc. cit.

had been peasant proprietors in Wigston since the sixteenth century, and this probably represents 1½ to 2 yardlands – and about 93 acres were leased from the Hospital. This still leaves nearly 120 acres unaccounted for, which he must have been leasing from other landlords. Several of the larger peasantry at this date rented land in addition to their own and farmed both together.

Two Hospital farms still retained their ancient identity up to the eve of enclosure. The ¾-yardland farm leased by Thomas Jackson – in addition to 30 acres of his own freehold – had been in the hands of his family continuously since 1603, and had been one of the Randull farms back in 1462.[1] And the ½-yardland farm which was in George Ross's hands in 1765 – in addition to some 90 acres or three yardlands of his own – had been the farm of the Faukes's in the thirteenth and fourteenth centuries, if not earlier. It had been leased to the Brabsons continuously by the Hospital from 1596 to 1755, coming to George Ross in the latter year, and at the enclosure he received 16 acres 0 rood 28 perches for it in Thythorn Hill Field. Only in 1766 did these two ancient farms lose their identity for ever.

Of the other three absentee landlords, we need say little. John Noone's 150 acres represented the accumulation of many generations in the village, for the name of Noone had been on the 1524 subsidy assessment, and they had come up steadily in the seventeenth century. In 1670 they had been amongst the principal inhabitants of the village. In 1766 the executors of John Noone were allotted 124½ acres, representing an original estate of 150 acres or thereabouts. When Martha, the widow of John Noone of Oadby, mercer, married Robert Brewin the younger, butcher, of Wigston, she brought £1200 as a jointure and he settled £1000 on her.[2] Both were old peasant families, who had come up in the world.

Sarah Norton's accumulation of 147 acres or so represents the most substantial of the Freer properties, of which she was the sole heiress. She had married Cornelius Norton, a prosperous grocer of St. Martin's parish in Leicester, in 1749, and so carried this ancient peasant

[1] See Ch. V, p. 127. Thomas Jackson, yeoman, whose will is dated 1658, speaks of 'three quarters of the hospital land' and 'three quarters of free land'. (L.C.R.O., 1662 bundle, no. 98.)
[2] L.R.O., 15. D. 41/89. Marriage settlement of Brewin and Noone, dated 25 April 1739.

accumulation into alien hands, to be farmed by tenants and no longer by a peasant proprietor.

John Darker, the last of the absentee landlords, owning about 130 acres, was the descendant of a long line of butchers and graziers in Leicester, the earliest of whom had been admitted to the freedom of the borough in 1522-3. Richard Darker, also a butcher, had been mayor in 1560-1. The family remained as butchers in Leicester for a hundred years or so, and are then found, still as butchers and graziers, in the neighbouring villages of Evington, Oadby, and Stoughton during the seventeenth century.[1] In 1668 William Darker, of Oadby, butcher – son of William Darker of Thurnby, butcher – married Elizabeth, the daughter of William Johnson of Wigston, yeoman, settling upon her about four acres of land in the fields of Oadby. Marriage with the solid yeoman family of the Johnsons was an excellent start, and in the course of the years William Darker bought land from the Coltmans (15 acres in 1665 and 42 acres in 1668) and thirty acres from various persons in 1672-87 acres in all. This must have been the nucleus of John Darker's estate in 1765, which totalled about 150 acres if we include the small allotments made to two other Darkers resident in the village. John Darker himself had left the butchering to others in the family – one of them was still a butcher in Wigston in 1748 – and went to London where he made a large fortune. He entered Parliament as one of the two members for Leicester in 1766 and became a freeman of the borough in the same year. Rejected at the election of 1768, he was returned in 1775 and again in 1780. He died in 1784.[2]

If we turn from the absentee landlords to the tenant-farmers we find that, apart from the Hospital lands, the bulk of the property was let out in large farms to men who were not natives of the village: another breach that had developed in the old peasant economy. Strange landlords and strange tenants had invaded some nine hundred or so acres of the village lands. These large tenant-farmers are: Thomas Willson (6½ yardlands), Abraham Hack (6½ yardlands), Henry Branson (5 yardlands), Thomas Horner (4 yardlands), and Thomas Blockley (3¼ yardlands). All these were farming

---

[1] Hartopp, op. cit. See index under Darker.

[2] Darker marriage settlement, 1668 (L.R.O., 3 D. 36/97); Leics. Fines (P.R.O.); Thompson, *History of Leicester in the Eighteenth Century* (1871), 249; Greaves, *The Corporation of Leicester 1689-1836* (1939), 103-6, where he is wrongly called James Darker.

more than a hundred acres, two of them well over two hundred acres. Abraham Hack farmed all Wightman's land; Willson farmed some of Darker's, Noone's, and Clarke's; Branson farmed John Ragg's land (or some of it); Blockley farmed part of Darker's; and of Horner's landlord we have no trace. He may have farmed Sarah Norton's land. Besides these, who were all more or less strangers to the village, a considerable number of owner-occupiers rented additional land, as we have seen, notably John Freer and William Johnson, both of whom rented considerably more land than they owned.

So far we have only considered the absentee owners of land in Wigston, but two-thirds of the village land was still in the hands of owner-occupiers, most of whom were the descendants of peasant families of long residence. First we must consider the rectory, since the extinction of the great tithes in 1766 was to have the effect of creating in the fields by far the largest farm that Wigston had ever seen – nearly 400 acres.

The rectory had belonged, as we have seen, to Lenton Priory in Nottinghamshire since the early years of the twelfth century. At the Dissolution it had not been sold off like so much of ex-monastic property. It was a valuable rectory, and the Crown hung on to it until 1607, when it was sold, together with property in nine other counties ranging from Cornwall to Yorkshire, to two speculators, George Johnstone and Edward Bostock, the old rent of £22 7s. 4d. being still reserved.[1] The Lawes had been tenants of Wigston rectory under the Crown since 1581 and had taken up their residence in the village as a consequence. They were still tenants at the time of the sale in 1607, and John Lawe, gent., seems to have purchased the rectory from Johnstone and Bostock shortly afterwards. In 1626 he sold it to Sir James Stonehouse, knight, the consideration being stated in the fine to be £200. Another and a later record tells us, however, that the actual purchase price was £3000.[2] By the 1690's the rectory had come into the possession of Samuel Newberry, a London haberdasher, whose daughter and heiress married Sir Thomas Roberts of Cranbrook in Kent. The grand-daughter of Sir Thomas married George,

---

[1] Nichols, 381, quoting the Patent Rolls for 1607.

[2] *Cal. Ctte. for Advance of Money*, p. 775. See Feet of Fines, Hilary, 2 Chas. 1, for the fine, where the rectory is described as one messuage, 72 acres of land, eight of meadow, 12 of pasture, and common pasture for all manner of cattle in Wigston Magna, and the rectory of Wigston Magna and all manner of tithes.

3rd duke of St. Albans, and so by these changes, the rectory – that is to say, the glebe or rectory farm, together with the great tithes – was in the hands of the Duke when the enclosure award was made.

Of the other resident owners of property in 1765, the largest were Mr. John Ragg, the Pochins, the Clarkes, George Ross, and Joseph Burgess. The Raggs had lived in Wigston since the middle of the sixteenth century. Peter Ragg had bought a yardland at the Turvile sale in 1586, but his descendants made no spectacular progress in accumulating property as the Freers and Davenports did in the first half of the seventeenth century. Nevertheless, by 1765, John Ragg was farming about 218 acres, of which about twenty acres was leased from the Hospital and the rest was his own. He was allotted 250½ acres in respect of his own land at the enclosure, which means an original estate of just about 300 acres before deductions for tithes.

The Pochins we have already discussed in the previous chapter. In 1765 Armston Pochin was cultivating a 4-yardland farm and Richard Pochin one of 3½ yardlands – about 240 acres between them. The enclosure award shows that they must have owned about 162 acres in the open fields, so here, too, we have owner-occupiers who rented additional land.

Mr. John Clarke was farming about 148 acres in 1765. In the following year he got 94 acres in the award, representing about 113 acres in the open fields, but two other Clarkes also got 68½ acres in the award, equivalent to some 82 acres in the old fields. Thus the Clarke estate was about 195 acres in all. They, too, were a very old peasant family, who appear as big tenant-farmers as far back as 1462 when they leased the Randull farms. Since that date they had steadily bought property of their own, both in Wigston and in adjacent parishes.

Two other biggish owners were Joseph Burgess and George Ross, with about 100 acres and 91 acres respectively. Joseph Burgess had been one of the most substantial hosiers in the town of Leicester in the 1740's and '50's and had bought this Wigston estate about the middle of the century. In 1765 he was farming 1¼ yardlands (about 40 acres) of it himself, the remainder being let to local men.

George Ross was of a different type and origin. His ancestors had been

named in the subsidy of 1524. In the course of two hundred years or so
they had consolidated their position slowly and by 1755 were farming
about 117 acres: their own lands together with the old Hospital farm that
had been let to the Brabsons for so long. In the Hospital lease of 1755
George Ross is described as 'hosier'. A number of the larger farmers in
Wigston were becoming interested in the hosiery or framework-knitting
trade during the eighteenth century, at first as a side-line and later as a
full-time occupation.

To sum up the position as regards the ownership of land we must
have recourse to the enclosure award, which will be treated more fully
in the next chapter. Ignoring small defects of the record (e.g. the joint
ownership of some very small allotments in the award), and ruling out
the Duke of St. Albans and the vicar of Wigston, whose holdings were
only created by the enclosure, we can summarise the ownership of land
as follows.

There were nearly a hundred landowners in Wigston in 1765, but 70
of them owned only one-fifth of the village land between them. Well
over half the total number of landowners owned only one-tenth of the
land. Amongst this large group of free cottagers and husbandmen we
find the bulk of the old peasant families of Wigston; those, that is, who
still survived. Their holdings had been subdivided over and over again
as a result of the rapid increase of population since the 1570's, and the
original yardland or half-yardland that some ancestor had bought in
1586 or 1606, or about that time, had been split up among a number of
collateral branches of these prolific families. Fourteen landowners had
holdings of less than 3½ acres, 28 had less than six acres each.

A middle group of 21 landowners, again mainly old peasant families,
owned estates of 24 to 120 acres covering rather more than forty
per cent of the total acreage of the parish; and a top group of six
landowners, with more than 120 acres each, owned just under forty
per cent of the total.[1]

Such is the picture of land-ownership in Wigston on the eve of

[1] The Hospital lands have been distributed in these remarks among the lessees, as they were so allotted
in the award of 1766. This does not affect the broad picture that we get from these figures. Moreover,
lessees of Hospital lands treated their long leases (invariably for three lives) almost as their own property,
passing them on from father to son or sideways by marriage.

enclosure, a picture of extreme inequality already, with a crowd of about seventy small peasant farmers at the bottom of the scale owning less than one-fifth of all the land, and a select dozen families at the top who own three-fifths of it. Of this dozen, less than a half were native families of Wigston: the majority were outsiders, frequently well-to-do Leicester men like Wightman, Burgess, and Metcalf, of whom the last two, however, came and settled in Wigston.

Out of two hundred families, only sixty occupied two acres or more of land in 1765. There may have been ten or a dozen more households with an acre or so, and rights of common in proportion; but well over one-half the total population had been wholly divorced from the land (except as wage-labourers) before enclosure took place, probably nearer two-thirds. The majority of these worked as labourers on the larger farms that appeared from the early seventeenth century, increasingly so as the years went on. For others, weaving was a frequent stand-by, though the usual village trades absorbed many in such a large village as this. There seem, for example, to have been five or six tailors in the village at any one time in the seventeenth and eighteenth centuries, and shoemakers, carpenters and bakers, added up to perhaps ten or a dozen. By the end of the seventeenth century, however, frame-work knitting had come to be more important than any other non-agricultural occupation, and as the eighteenth century went on absorbed an ever-growing number of landless poor.

✎ THE FRAMEWORK- KNITTING INDUSTRY ✎

Introduced into Leicestershire about the year 1640 at Hinckley, framework-knitting did not reach the town of Leicester for another thirty years;[1] but thereafter its growth in the towns and villages of the western half of the county was very rapid. Almost from the first it was a rural and domestic industry. It could be carried on with a very minimum of equipment: a frame hired from a master-hosier at a few pence a week, knitting-wool supplied by the hosier or a middleman, the workshop little more than a mud-walled outhouse in the garden.

---

[1] For the early history of the trade, see *V.C.H. Leics.*, ii, 2 ff. There seems little doubt that the trade was not introduced into Leicester itself until about 1670.

It was an ideal trade for absorbing the poor and the dispossessed. The seventeenth-century enclosure movement in Leicestershire, which was still mainly for pasture, squeezed out large numbers of the old open-field population who drifted to the new 'hosiery' towns and villages, of which Wigston was one – so near to Leicester that the middleman or 'bag hosier' could walk into town.

The trade of framework-knitting was introduced into Wigston soon after it reached Leicester, certainly by 1675-80.[1] By 1698-1701, when the parish register specifies occupations for a few years, framework-knitters constituted over one-sixth of the occupied population (12 knitters out of 69 whose occupation is given). Such a rapid development of a new domestic industry is not surprising: it is what we should have expected from the size of Wigston's population, which had long ago outgrown the available supply of land, and would have done so even had there been no growing concentration of land into fewer and fewer hands. Indeed, the unrestricted growth of population probably favoured and accelerated this tendency to concentration of land-ownership.

The industrialisation of Wigston proceeded rapidly all through the eighteenth century. We have no statistics of its growth until 1801, when the first census revealed that out of 1658 people in the village only 113 were chiefly employed in agriculture and no fewer than 1020 in 'trade, manufacture, or handicraft'.[2] With all the imperfections of this early census, it is abundantly clear that even in 1801 the village had changed its character completely. About sixty per cent of its population were engaged chiefly in trade and industry. In the early eighteenth century the proportion of framework-knitters in the occupied population was approaching one in five. It is reasonable to assume that in 1765 the 'industrial' population must have formed at least a third of the whole occupied population. All over the western half of Leicestershire the dispossessed peasantry, whether dispossessed by their own proliferation or by private enclosure agreements between freeholders, found a living of a sort in the domestic industry of framework-knitting.

---

[1] The inventory of Mr. Daniel Vann, of Wigston, made in September 1680, includes four stocking frames 'with apurtenances', valued at no less than £40. (Inventories, 1680, no. 92)

[2] Nichols, 377.

By 1765, too, 'the poor' had become a prominent and permanent class in most Leicestershire villages, especially in those that were changing over from agriculture to industry as the major occupation of their people. Contemporary opinion always associated the coming of industry with a rise in the poor rates.[1] At Wigston, in 1766, as we have seen, one-quarter of the households were too poor to be assessed by the overseers: they were the recipients of relief, not the contributors.

THE RELIEF OF POVERTY

The overseers' accounts are wholly missing at Wigston apart from one book covering the period 1728-56.[2] When they begin they show that the village had three overseers of the poor who each served for four months and kept separate accounts. In 1748, however, this system was abandoned in favour of two overseers who served for six months each, still keeping separate accounts. A workhouse was already in existence when the surviving accounts begin – symptom of the new economy in which the problem of the poor had become permanent – administered directly by the overseers in turn. In 1743-4 the experiment of farming the poor was apparently tried for the first time, and an agreement was entered into with Mr. William Brabson, a largish yeoman-farmer, to take all the poor of the parish for a year, for a weekly payment of twenty-three shillings. 'The town' was to find clothing as the overseers thought necessary (except lace and pins). For every funeral 'under Mr. Brabson's care' the town was to allow eight shillings, and 'Mr. Brabson to be at all other expenses and Bury them in a Decent manner'. But 'Mr. Brabson Excepts ye small pox Broken bones and scald Heads except they should happen under his care before the misfortune'. The farmer was to find all meat, drink, washing, lodging, and all other necessaries except clothing, and was to have the free use of the labour of the poor in his charge. Finally, the town was to provide a workhouse.

William Brabson continued to farm the poor, year after year, at weekly sums which varied in the annual agreement from 23s. down to 14s. 6d., the usual sum being 17s. or 18s. a week. In 1748 the poor were apparently not farmed out, but were relieved directly by the overseers. It may have been

---

[1] See, for example, Nichols' remarks under Ullesthorpe, op. cit., 120.
[2] Wigston parish church, MS. accounts.

difficult to get local men to take on such a contract – pauper labour must have been as unsatisfactory on farms as anywhere – but late in 1748 another largish farmer, Robert Freer, agreed to take on all the parish poor for 20s. a week. The other terms of the agreement remained unchanged. In the following year he took them on again at 18s. a week, plus an allowance of 45 cwt. of coals; and so he continued until Lady Day, 1753, when Edward Smart took over the contract at 20s. weekly. In the following year Samuel Moor – another stranger – took the contract at 21s. weekly.

No certain indication appears in the accounts as to the number of those in the workhouse, or of those in receipt of out-relief. In 1746-7 seven were receiving out-relief, at rates varying from 6d. to 2s. a week, five of them being widows. As the workhouse contained ten pairs of sheets when an inventory was made in 1757, and the usual sum allowed to the farmer of the poor was 18s. to 20s. a week, we may perhaps estimate the normal number of inmates at nine or ten.

The sums spent by the overseers between 1735-6 and 1754-5 ranged from £52 2s. 7d. in 1741-2 to £107 6s. 1½d. in 1752-3, but there were fairly wide variations from year to year.

Expenditure on the Poor at Wigston, 1735-55

1735-6	£57 7s. 9d.	1745-6	missing
1736-7	£77 5s. 6¾d.	1746-7	£74 13s. 10½d.
1737-8	£75 6s. 10½d.	1747-8	£59 9s. 9d.
1738-9	£57 1s. 0½d.	1748-9	£71 5s. 7½d.
1739-40	missing	1749-50	£75 18s. 3d.
1740-1	missing	1750-1	£91 14s. 3½d.
1741-2	£52 2s. 7d.	1751-2	£73 18s. 0½d.
1742-3	£94 2s. 4¼d.	1752-3	£107 6s. 1½d.
1743-4	£81 12s. 8½d.	1753-4	£91 13s. 10¾d.
1744-5	£65 5s. 2d.	1754-5	£95 3s. 10d.

The money was raised by levies, usually of so much in the pound in lands, houses, and homesteads. A levy of 6d. in the £ in 1752-3 (one of three for that year) produced £28 13s. 6d., which gives a total rateable value of about £1147. Unfortunately the actual assessments do not survive.

The overseers' accounts show a fairly steady increase in expenditure on the poor between 1735 and 1755, but the worst was yet to come. Twenty years later, in 1775-6, Wigston spent £377 14s. 10d. on poor relief – over £390 if minor items like the cost of litigation is included. In twenty years the expenditure on the poor had more than quadrupled; and this was but the beginning of the complete breakdown of poor law administration.[1] In the meantime, the number of Wigston children apprenticed to Leicester woolcombers grew rapidly in the 1730's, '40's, '50's and '60's. Many others went as apprentices to Leicester fellmongers and tradesmen; but the hosiery trade absorbed the majority both in Wigston and in Leicester.[2]

❧ The Farmer and his Fields ❧

By 1765 the economic and social pattern of village life had been transformed from what it had been five generations earlier. How far does the cultivation and management of the open fields show any changes of comparable magnitude?

The size of farms can be observed growing steadily throughout the seventeenth century, until by 1765, as we have seen, nearly 1100 acres were being cultivated in farms of 200 acres or more, and just over 2000 acres – rather more than seventy per cent of the parish – in farms of 100 acres or more.

There were other ways also in which the open-field economy was changing: strips were being consolidated into larger parcels – we often find three or four strips thrown together in seventeenth- and early eighteenth-century terriers – especially, of course, by the larger farmers such as the Freers, the Davenports, and the Pochins. At the same time the percentage of 'grass ground' in the open fields was tending to increase, again among the larger farmers, who had wider opportunities for such changes in technique and farm management.

The following table, based upon terriers of eight farms between 1693 and 1745,[3] ranging in size from a cottager's holding of 2¼ acres up to 3 yardlands farmed by the Pochins, reveals in summary form something of what was happening:

---

[1] The figure for 1775-6 is given in Nichols, 377. The subsequent history of poor relief in Wigston is given in Ch. X, pp. 269-72.

[2] Hartopp, *Freemans Register*, I, *passim*.

[3] L.R.O. (various deeds).

Size of 'parcel'	1693 (1 yard-land)	1696 (3 yard-lands)	1697 (¼ yard-land)	1703 (2¼ acres)	1704 (¼ yard-land)	1712 (¾ yard-land)	1744 (1 yard-land)	1745 (¼ yard-land)
½ rood	4	1	1	-	-	4	-	-
1 rood*	19	66	11	7	4	7	24	8
1½ rood	-	2	-	-	-	12	-	6
2 roods	33	43	6	1	3	15	21	11
3 roods	4	17	2	-	1	9+	10	2
1 acre	5	8	-	-	1	2	5	-
Over 1 acre	-	17	-	-	2	4	2	1
Total no. of parcels	65	154	20	8	11	53	62	28
% ley in fields	20%	31%	18%	nil	20%	20%	25%	30%

* 'an old rood' has been counted throughout as '1 rood', since we do not know its exact area.

+ includes 4 parcels of 2½ roods each.

The total number of parcels of land on these eight farms was 401. Of these only 146, or slightly more than one in three, were still single strips of one rood, as against 60 per cent in the closing years of the sixteenth century.[1] In those years, too, only about one-quarter of the parcels of land had been half an acre or more; now the proportion was well over one-half (56 per cent). One-third of the parcels were of half an acre, and another quarter were more than half an acre. In 1577-1601, only two per cent of the parcels were an acre in size: in 1693-1745 there were 47 out of 401, nearly 12 per cent. We find, too, that many of these larger parcels in the fields were enclosed by the early eighteenth century, and turned over to permanent grass. Several terriers of the larger farms reveal such closes of from one to two acres in size, as, for example, in a schedule of half a yardland bought in 1669 by John Davenport from Mr. William Lawe: under the heading of 'Ley ground in Mucklow field' we read of 'One Close with the hedges, ditches, and Trees therein Blackwellsick-close containing 8 roods, the Close of Mr. Francis Smith on the N. side thereof.'[2] Most of the larger farmers seem to have possessed such closes.

[1] See Chapter VI, p. 152.   [2] Reference Library, Birmingham. MS. no. 242759.

Their total area made little difference to the open fields as a whole; but they were significant of the way things were going.

In the late sixteenth century, too, we noticed that, on an average, about 20 per cent of the open fields were in 'grass ground', most of which was probably temporary and part of a convertible husbandry. These leys would be broken up after some years, and sown for crops, but other arable strips would be laid down to grass to replace them. At any given time, one-fifth of the open fields would be in leys, mostly scattered throughout, and intermixed with, the arable. Seventeenth-century terriers and schedules of Wigston farms show that this proportion of one-fifth was generally maintained during that period,[1] though the smaller farmers carried much less ley and the larger farmers somewhat more. The sample of eight farms above shows that this was true of the period 1693-1745 also. Four of the eight farms had 18-20 per cent in ley, but a small holding of 2¼ acres had none. The 3½-acre Cley holding in 1658 similarly had no ley ground. The cottager relied upon a few small pieces of meadow and his stint on the common, where his holding of ¼-yardland gave him the right to pasture one cow and five sheep under 'the old stint'.

On the larger farms the tendency to extend the area under pasture in the open fields is very marked. William Abbott's yardland in 1744 had 41 roods of ley ground out of a total of 128 roods – practically 25 per cent – and George Pochin's three-yardland farm had 31 per cent under ley. Robert Freer's ¼-yardland was leased from the Hospital and worked in conjunction with his other lands, which were extensive, so that its proportion of 30 per cent in ley reflects a large farm and not the usual smallholding.

Moreover, the leys tended to be in larger parcels than the arable: William Abbott in 1744 had leys of an acre in each of two fields (besides several of two roods each) and one of five roods in the third field. In Mucklow Field he had the upper end of a pasture close, his share being one acre. Robert Freer in 1745 had a close of two acres in Mucklow Field called Lammas Close. George Pochin's farm of three yardlands in 1696

---

[1] For example, Richard Davenport's farm of ½-yardland in 1659 had 21½ per cent ley ground; John Davenport's ½-yardland had 20.7 per cent; Robert Freer's yardland had 20 per cent; and Thomas Boulter's ¼-yardland had 18 per cent (L.R.O., various deeds.)

shows this tendency in its most advanced form: in Goldhill Field he had 'Newgatehill Close containing six roods with the hedges, Clarke's Close containing one acre with the hedges, Little Dale Close containing seven roods with the hedges' and a number of smaller leys with hedges round them. In both Mucklow Field and Thythorn Hill Field he had closes of four acres and others of ¾-acre to 1¼ acres. Here we have a clear indication of the way the larger farmers were thinking some seventy years before the parliamentary enclosure.

The terrier of George Pochin's 90-acre farm also shows once again that arable land could be let down to grass for a number of years and then ploughed up again, as we saw was done in the sixteenth century. Under the heading of Long Meadow we are told of 'One peece in the same Shoote beinge a plough Land two thirds thereof is yearly exchanged with William Abbott for two thirds of another plough Land at the Elmes' and another piece of meadow is similarly described as 'a plough Land'.[1]

The problem of getting sufficient pasture was indeed the greatest problem of the open-field village during the seventeenth century and the early eighteenth. At Wigston it was as acute as anywhere and by 1707 had given rise to a revolutionary agreement between all the land-owners, large and small, which was enrolled in Chancery. But let us first of all dispose briefly of the arable farming of the village in this period.

The discussion of peasant farming in the sixteenth century, in an earlier chapter, was largely a discussion of arable farming. That indeed was where the main emphasis of Midland agriculture lay at that time, despite all the noise about enclosure for sheep and cattle pastures. We saw that at Wigston, as in the great majority of Leicestershire villages, the whole of one field was devoted to peas and beans, though on some farms we find a small proportion of oats sown in the same field, especially by the larger men who kept a number of horses. In the other sown field, wheat and rye were sown in the autumn, to the extent of about one-seventh

---

[1] Most of the meadow ground was fixed and always went with a particular farm, but some of the terriers (especially of the larger farms) show that a certain proportion of the meadow was exchanged yearly between different men. This seems to be the meaning of 'running peeces' of meadow which are sometimes referred to.

of the whole acreage; and the remaining six-sevenths of the field were sown with barley in the late spring.[1]

The inventories of the seventeenth and eighteenth centuries are much less informative about the crops than those of the sixteenth, mainly because as the personal estate of farmers grew in volume and variety less attention was paid to minute details such as we get in the earlier period; and so we almost invariably find all the crops, whether in field or barn, lumped together in the later inventories and valued as a whole.

Nevertheless, the picture of arable farming at Wigston emerges unmistakably enough. The whole of one field continued to be sown with peas and beans, with a few lands of oats on the bigger farms; and the other field continued to be sown mainly with barley, together with autumn-sown wheat. The chief change in the cropping is that rye almost disappears: only one farmer in a sample of thirty-three Wigston inventories for the seventeenth century had any rye among his crops in field or barn, and he was a late Elizabethan, dying in 1616. This change appears to be general throughout Leicestershire. Such rye as continued to be grown by a minority of farmers seems to have been used as early spring pasture for sheep, in the eighteenth century at least.[2]

The smallest farmers grew barley in one field and peas and beans in the other;[3] but some wheat was grown by the majority of husbandmen and yeomen. One cannot tell from the inventories, however, whether the acreage of wheat was growing at the expense of barley among the bigger men as is suggested by a few records of the last phase of open-field farming elsewhere in the county.[4] It appears to be so from the inventory of George Davenport, one of the biggest Wigston yeomen, who died in 1713. His malt and barley were valued together at £100, his beans and peas at £100, and his wheat as high as £80. The hay was worth £20. His personal estate was worth £795 5s. 6d. in all, of which crops in the barns and growing in the fields accounted for £420, or rather more than half the total. His livestock was worth £186 (horses £80, sheep £50, cattle £42, and pigs £14).

---

[1] See Chapter VI, pp. 152-6.

[2] Cf. *Studies in Leics. Agrarian History*, 141.

[3] E.g. Richard White, blacksmith, in 1640, had sown six roods of barley and six of peas and beans. Thomas Boulter, in the same year, had sown four acres of barley and seven of peas and beans.

[4] *Studies*, 135-6.

As a general rule, however, the Wigston farmer's livestock was worth nearly as much as all his crops. Here is a sample of farmers from the larger to the smaller:

Henry White (1638)	crops	£26 6s. 8d.	stock	£21 0s. 0d.
William Lawe (1636)	crops	£67 6s. 8d.	stock	£59 10s. 0d.
Robert Edgeley (1635)	crops	£10 0s. 0d.	stock	£8 6s. 0d.
Robert Freer (1626)	crops	£33 0s. 0d.	stock	£21 2s. 0d.
Richard Mould (1636)	crops	£4 10s. 0d.	stock	£4 10s. 0d.
William Symond (1633)	crops	£37 10s. 0d.	stock	£27 6s. 8d.
John Evans (1627)	crops	£40 0s. 0d.	stock	£34 0s. 0d.
Dennis Jackson (1636)	crops	£56 0s. 0d.	stock	£47 10s. 0d.
Robert Brabson (1642)	crops	£63 0s. 0d.	stock	£93 10s. 0d.
Richard Davenport (1635)	crops	£50 0s. 0d.	stock	£23 10s. 0d.
Robert Freer the elder (1625)	crops	£5 0s. 0d.	stock	£87 18s. 0d.

Although the average farm was about eighty per cent arable, and twenty per cent ley, the value of the livestock was generally two-thirds to three-quarters of the value of the crops. One cannot be too precise about this – so much depends on the time of the year when the inventory was taken – but the trend of the above figures is clear enough. Where the stock was valued at much above the crops, as with Robert Freer the elder in 1625, or Robert Brabson in 1642, we have the big farmer with more ley ground than the average and, of course, proportionately larger common pasture rights.

The churchwardens' accounts for the late seventeenth century, and the early eighteenth, give us some idea of the total number of livestock in the parish, since the churchwardens' levy usually took the form of a rate of so much on every yardland, on every communicant, on every cow, and on every score of sheep. Again one cannot press these figures too far since the accounts show that some farmers paid in arrears: their defection reduces the figures of livestock in one year and unduly swells the next.

Year	No. of cows	No. of sheep
1665	302	[not given]
1666	285	[not given]
1674	243	[not given]
1678	249	1780
1679	232	1320

Year	No. of cows	No. of sheep
1680	265	1488
1681	280	1180
1682	266	1170
1683	305	1710
1684	304	2020
1685	247	1580
1686	259	1730
1687	280	1545
1688	282	2170
1689	292	2175
1690	280	1705
1691	(account missing)	
1692	268	1590
1693	259	1490
1694	262	1765
1695	233	1835
1696	228	1815
1697	252	645
1698	245	1070
1699	252	2490
1700	255	1470
1701	259	1455
1702	312	[not given]
1703	251	940
1704	265	1545
1705	262	[not given]
1706	267	2132
1707	266	1815
1708	251	1670
1709	224	[not given]
1710	210	2015
1711	185	1830
1712	204	1945
1713	230	1873
1714	234	1898
1715	215	[not given]
1716	236	[not given]
1717	225	[not given]
1718	225	[not given]

Disregarding some of the more extreme fluctuations, the average number of sheep in a normal year was between 1700 and 1900, and the number of cows somewhere between 250 and 280. The number of cows shows a much smaller fluctuation than the sheep from year to year, suggesting that it is not the accounts which are irregular but that something occasionally happened to reduce the sheep to a half or a third of their normal numbers.[1]

Theoretically the stint of eight cows and forty sheep per yardland would have permitted about 740 cows and some 3700 sheep to graze on the common pastures at Wigston; but in practice the number of sheep was just about a half of this and the number of cows a little more than one-third. There are repeated hints in the records that the by-laws of the fields and common pastures required revision, and that new rules were promulgated from time to time, but no fuller record of these changes survives until the year 1707 when a comprehensive agreement was made concerning the entire management of the pastures, and enrolled in Chancery.[2]

For several years there had been disputes among the landowners as to who were entitled to enjoy grazing rights in the common pasture. There had been many costly law-suits and many persons had thereby been impoverished 'to the great disquiet of the whole Towne'. To prevent further disputes several meetings had been held in the village and finally articles of agreement were drawn up and duly executed.

These articles, numbering thirty-five in all, regulated the feeding off the open-field stubble and the common pasture in minute detail. The chief changes were that 'the old stint' of forty sheep per yardland, which had stood since the sixteenth century at least, was reduced to twenty-four, and that for cows was reduced from eight to four. Everyone was required to leave eight yards of grass-ground 'to amend the Cornon att every Lands end'; and it was further ordered that there should be 'one foot Baulke … betwixt every land to be Left within the Space of three yeares next Ensueing'; and that everyone with less than 2½ acres of grass-ground per yardland in each of the three fields should lay down enough grass to bring it up to this measure. No one should plough up any of this grass-ground unless he had, three years previously, laid down an equal

[1] It is quite clear that there was some disaster among the sheep in 1697 and probably again in 1703.
[2] P.R.O., Chancery Proceedings, Hamilton, C.7/248/10, dated 24 December 1707.

quantity to replace it. It was also ordained that 'the Eveners shall have the same Liberty to provide pastures for them that have none as Formerly and that poor men that want shall not pay for a single pasture above Fower shillings … ' Article no. 31 laid it down that everyone having a yardland should 'spare and Lett one single pasture every yeare if need be to bee for poor men that shall have occasion for them and have none of their own' at a price not exceeding four shillings. Those having a yardland and a half were required to let 'a double pasture' in this way.

We are confirmed in our belief that it had long been the practice to graze sheep on the winter wheat by one of the rules (no. 22) 'that the Wheat Feild shall be eaten every yeare with Sheep untill the day Commonly Called Twelfth day and no longer and all other Cattle shall keep the old tyme.'

The six defendants, all Wigston men, admitted that they had agreed to these articles but afterwards considered that some of them 'might be of doubtful Interpretation', and they wished to bring into the suit also the earl of Stamford, to whom the lordship of the honour of Winchester had descended in the course of time. The whole suit is apparently a collusive one for the purpose of clarifying some of the articles of agreement and getting legal authority for all of them through a decree in the Court of Chancery. This decree was duly obtained on 7 February 1707-8.[1]

The whole suit, and the details of the agreement, make it clear that the problem of finding enough pasture-ground in the township had reached the proportions of a crisis by the end of the seventeenth century. From 1707 onwards every farmer was to have about a quarter of his land laid down to grass, and the old stint was drastically reduced – for sheep by nearly one half, and for cows by a half. In fact the old stint had long been ineffective as the actual numbers of livestock showed by this time, and the revised stint merely brought the rules into line with the practice. Although Wigston, like all the other open-field villages, was still a predominantly arable farming community – practising the traditional mixed farming of the Midland Plain – the balance was tipping away from crops to stock, from tillage to grazing.

---

[1] P.R.O., Chancery Decrees and Orders, Hilary 6 Anne, C.33/310/f. 234.

The crisis over pasture was temporarily resolved by these elaborate new rules drawn up in 1707; but it was only a temporary solution. The shadow of the parliamentary enclosure act of 1764 was beginning to fall across the immemorial pattern of the open fields.

It is clear enough what had brought about this crisis in the farming of the open fields. There had once been common pastures, deliberately left untilled, sufficient to support a stint of eight cows and forty sheep per yardland in the fields. In the earliest days there had probably been no need for stinting at all: then the problem had been how quickly the commons and the 'waste' could be brought into tillage to support a growing population. But at some point a balance had to be struck between the further expansion of the arable, and the retention of sufficient unbroken common pasture to support the livestock that were an essential part of a mixed open-field husbandry. This balance had been struck at Wigston, at some date we do not know but probably by about 1550,[1] so as to leave sufficient common pasture for the stint above. But the population of the village had doubled between 1524 and 1603, and it had increased by a further 50 per cent between 1603 and 1765. There can be little doubt that this pressure had meant the steady breaking-up of common pasture throughout the sixteenth and seventeenth centuries in an attempt to get more land under crops. The problem of the rising population was much too large to be solved in that piecemeal fashion. An additional amount of arable had been squeezed out of the commons, but in the end the village had merely succeeded in upsetting the balance between arable and pasture that had been wisely struck before the pressure of population had begun to exert itself so fiercely. Hence the constant disputes that had led eventually to the formal and elaborate agreement of 1707. There had been a real crisis: the whole balance of open-field farming had been upset: and this was an attempt to rectify some of the damage that had unwittingly been done over the past several generations.

---

[1] I suggest this date on the grounds that much land must have gone out of cultivation during the greater part of the fifteenth century, judging by what happened elsewhere in Leicestershire, and there can have been no problem of pasturage then, especially with a falling population. The substantial recovery of population from the late fifteenth century onwards must have led to a renewed breaking-up of pastures which by about 1550 would have necessitated the striking of a balance once more.

The arable fields at Wigston were looked after by the field-reeves, of whom two were annually appointed. Their duties, as exemplified in their surviving account-book, were simple: they appointed and paid the pinder (who kept the pinfold), they rewarded small boys who arrived with sparrows by the score (young sparrows at twopence a dozen, old ones at threepence: the slaughter was tremendous); they bought powder and shot for the crow-scarer and rewarded the mole-catchers. They mended the gates leading into the fields, paid someone to guard the peas, especially as they began to fill out; and they let the 'town balks' for pasture. They kept a 'town plow' in the church for those who had none of their own, cleared out the ditches in the fields, and scoured 'Newgate pool' where the village women did their washing. They constructed plank bridges where required across the small streams that laced the fields, and kept the old ones in repair; mended the fences in the meadows; counted the sheep in the fields and laid out the sheep-walks; and they called meetings to fix the dates for mowing the meadows and anything else the village ought to be informed about. And they drank ale on every conceivable occasion, when they hired the pinder or the crow-scarer, when they took out the town plough or put it back again, when they wrote up their accounts. The covers of the account-book are ringed with the marks of ale-mugs – alas, there was leisure in those days to sit down and drink sociably on the slightest occasion. The eveners were just the same: when they hired the herdsman, sold the bull, bought a new one, wrote up the accounts, allotted the pastures, 'evened' the cows: all involved a shilling or two on drink.

The origin and functions of the 'eveners' are obscure. We have the casual reference to them in the Chancery agreement of 1707, and we have their account-book for the period 1748-64. They were closely associated with the field-reeves, their accounts being kept at the other end of the same book. In general they appear to have charge of all matters relating to the pasturage of the village, while the field-reeves dealt with everything pertaining title to the arable. It is not clear where the 'eveners' get their title from beyond the fact that they 'evened' the cows. This probably means that they were responsible for the stocking of the stubble fields and of the common, seeing that each man's stock did not exceed that proportionate to his holding. They also let certain cow pastures, hired and paid the herdsman, bought or hired the town bull, and, as we have seen, saw to it that any poor man who had no pasture of his own acquired some at a reasonable rent.

How far had the Peasant System been breached by the economic and social changes during the hundred and fifty years before enclosure took place?

On the eve of enclosure only three out of every ten families in the village occupied any land, perhaps rather more if we include those whose holding was so small that the field-reeve did not levy on it. About one-third, at the most, occupied some land; and two-thirds of the village population none at all. There were fewer farmers in 1766 than in 1086, and the population had more than doubled in the meantime.

One-half of the occupiers farmed less than ten acres; and at the other extreme farms of 100 acres or more accounted for some 70 per cent of the total acreage. It was a mixed economy by 1766: a small number of capitalist tenant-farmers at one end of the scale, and a large number of small peasant-farmers at the other. The peasantry – most of them old families in the village – were still the largest class numerically, but they owned and occupied only a small proportion of the land. Some of the large owners and farmers, it is true, were native to the village and had descended from peasant forebears; but they were now out of the peasant-class. They were gentry and were styled Mr. Ragg, Mr. Davenport, and so on.

The picture is much the same if we look at the ownership of land in the village. There were still some ninety-nine owners – a formidable army indeed compared with other enclosed villages round about where the squire shared the parish with perhaps two or three big yeomen – but, of this large number, about seventy owned less than twenty-four acres, less than one-fifth of the whole parish between them. A dozen men at the top owned three-fifths of the parish – more than half of them not native to the village. The poor had become a permanent feature of village society, and they were a slowly growing class, recruited from the landless labourer as well as the widows and children who had always called for relief. In 1766 one-quarter of the village population was too poor to be assessed by the overseers.

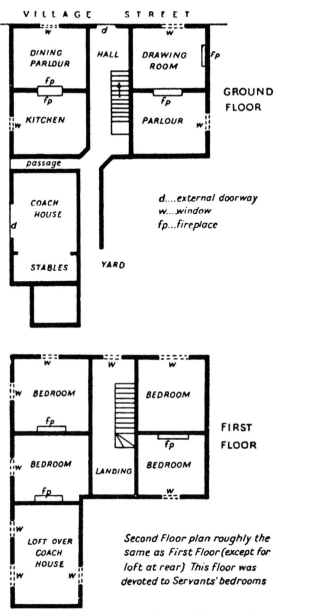

VILLAGE STREET

GROUND FLOOR

- DINING PARLOUR
- HALL
- DRAWING ROOM
- KITCHEN
- PARLOUR
- passage
- COACH HOUSE
- STABLES
- YARD

d....external doorway
w....window
fp...fireplace

FIRST FLOOR

- BEDROOM
- BEDROOM
- BEDROOM
- LANDING
- BEDROOM
- LOFT OVER COACH HOUSE

Second Floor plan roughly the same as First Floor (except for loft at rear) This floor was devoted to Servants' bedrooms

A three-floored house of brick built by Samuel Davenport in 1752, later known as The Elms, and now the British Legion Club. The Davenports came to Wigston in the 1570s. In 1664 one is described as 'gent.' in the hearth tax, and in the 1770s two are described as 'Mr.' They constitute one of the half-dozen families of peasant-gentry in the village in the eighteenth century, and their new house is a more or less sophisticated urban dwelling.

A peasant-gentleman's house (1752)

Again, if we look at the agricultural practice of the parish, we see changes that foreshadow the end of the ancient pattern of mixed husbandry that had always characterised the open fields. The largest farmers had more of their lands under grass than the small peasant – as much as a third, perhaps, in some instances. And the problem of feeding the livestock was more urgent than anything to do with the crops. The agreement of 1707 made several fairly drastic changes in an attempt to solve the problem, compelling all farriers to put about one-quarter of their open-field acreage under grass; but so long as the open-field system was retained the greater part of the acreage necessarily hid to remain in tillage.

So long as the open fields remained, the peasant economy itself continued to stand on a stable foundation even though its superstructure had been weakened. For we still must not, despite the important changes we have seen in the village and its fields between say 1625 and 1765, exaggerate the extent to which the old system had been destroyed or dissolved. We must remember all the time that the records do not tell us much about the greater part of the village population who still subsisted by this system, this culture, as we have called it; and that statistics can never tell us the whole truth about any historical problem, for there is more than one way of looking at the same figures.

If we turn back to the figures of land-ownership, for example, we find that 64 families still owned their tenements, ranging from a few strips up to a 24-acre farm (¾-yardland); and that 83 families owned up to 60 acres. Most of these families were natives to the village, of more or less long descent in the place; and most of them were owner-occupiers. The great majority of the landowners in 1765 were still peasants, even if they owned between them rather less than two-fifths of the land of the parish.[1] Though their relative share of the village land was small, they still lived, if we consider their individual economics, as their ancestors had done for the past two or three centuries. Many of them still lived in the same house and tilled the same strips.

Again, there were those with no land, who still lived within the peasant economy for all that. We have seen that in 1670, for example – and things

---

[1] This takes the limit of 'peasant' holdings at 60 acres. A fifth of the land was owned by men with less than 24 acres; about another fifth by those with 24–60 acres.

had not changed much in this respect even by 1765 – the cottagers with no land possessed about 35 cows and about 220 sheep between them, about one-eighth of the total for the village as a whole.[1] Such households often had a cottage of their own, even if it carried no land with it,[2] and they could rent single pastures at a low rate from the larger farmers. It was an obligation on the larger men to provide such pastures for men who had none, under a penalty of £5, and the eveners had to see that this obligation was observed. Moreover, if a man had only a strip or two in each field, he acquired a proportionate right in the common. The sixteenth rule of the 1707 agreement allowed everyone with a quartern of land or less to tether one horse or one cow on the common, and even at the new stint of 24 sheep to the yardland the small man with only a half-acre in each field could keep one sheep also. The 'town plow' was available to him to till his lands, free of charge; and in his cottage garden he could keep pigs, poultry, and bees, and get crops of apples and vegetables. The value of such an economy, eked out though it had to be by a money-wage at certain times of the year, cannot be measured statistically and so is apt to be lost and forgotten, or at the best under-estimated, by the historian who allows himself to be led away by large numbers. It cannot be emphasised too often that we are dealing here with a qualitative civilisation, with an economy that was also a way of living and therefore not susceptible to quantitative measurement. We have seen how well the cottager and the labourer could fare in the sixteenth and seventeenth centuries, even where he did not combine his holding with a small trade like that of shoemaker or tailor, as so many of them did; and the early eighteenth-century inventories show that this satisfying economy, founded on hard work and a desire to get on in a modest way, was still profoundly characteristic of the open-field villages all over Leicestershire up to the very eve of enclosure.

For all the changes that had taken place by this date, the peasant economy, as we have described it in an earlier chapter, still remained fundamentally solid and stable for most of those who lived under it. Its major characteristics were unchanged: its self-dependence, its self-

[1] See Ch. VII, p. 201.
[2] The land-tax assessments, when they begin in 1773, show that there were many such cottages in Wigston, owned and occupied by the cottagers themselves.

subsistence, its self-help, its thrift, its real savings – in goods, not money – its localism. There was still an essential relationship between the human spirit and its physical background. The old system still permitted a man to hope for well-being without seeking to escape from his own class into some other; and it gave him a life of manifold interest, a pride in his work even if it was hard and not too well rewarded, the respect of his fellows for a good workman; and there was too the general effect of working and living in the well-known landscape, something familiar to him all his life and to his ancestors before him. It was still a world in which a man felt at home, even if, as at Wigston, he had to spend a good bit of his day at the frame knitting stockings. At least he was in his own house, in his own village. 'Out of all this there proceeded an influence which acted upon the village people as an unperceived guide to their conduct, so that they observed the seasons proper for their varied pursuits almost as if they were going through some ritual … and thus a succession of recurring tasks, each one of which seemed to the villager almost characteristic of his own people in their native home, kept constantly alive a feeling that satisfied him and a usage that helped him.'[1] In its essence, Wigston was still like that. Though it had been more 'industrialised' than most villages by the middle of the eighteenth century, and other social changes had gone farther than elsewhere, it was still fundamentally a community of small peasants living in a familiar, almost timeless, world in which there was plenty of hard work and yet plenty of leisure, and in which a man could still have dignity and self-respect.

[1] Bourne, *Change in the Village*, 122-3, on which this whole paragraph is based.

IX

THE ENCLOSURE, 1764-6

The Enclosure Act

On 24 January 1764 a petition was presented to the House of Commons from several proprietors of the open fields of Great Wigston to the effect that their lands lay greatly inter-mixed and dispersed in the fields and that they were desirous of bringing in a Bill to enclose and divide these fields and to re-allot the lands of the respective owners in more convenient form.1 Before this stage had been reached, there must have been a public meeting of the interested parties in Wigston itself, probably in the autumn of 1763, with a view to preparing and presenting the petition. This required the signatures of a majority before it could go forward, but not of a numerical majority of land-owners. It was a majority by value – either by acreage or by annual value as expressed in the assessments for the land tax or the poor rate – and it had to include the signatures of the lord of the manor (where there was one) and of the tithe owners. The first step, therefore, which started the expensive and formidable machinery of enclosure moving, was far from democratic in the modern sense of the word. It is true that the consent of the owners of three-quarters or even four-fifths of the property was required;2 but at Wigston this meant a very small minority of the owners. Even excluding the two tithe-owners (the Duke of St. Albans and the Vicar), who subsequently received 476 acres in lieu of tithes and glebe, the consent of only 27 owners out of the total of 99 would have been sufficient to send the petition forward. If the property of the tithe-owners was reckoned in, the number of signatures required was even fewer: about 20 would have sufficed. At Wigston we may say that the petition could have gone forward with the consent of only a quarter

---

¹ *J.H.C.* xxix, 723.
² For fuller details of the machinery of parliamentary enclosure, see Curtler, *The Enclosure and Redistribution of our Land* (1920), 152 ff.

or even a fifth of the landowners; and there is some reason to believe it may have done so.

The promoters of the Wigston bill, which was introduced by Sir Thomas Cave on 24 February 1764 and read for the first time, were the Duke of St. Albans, the Rev. James Pigott (Vicar), John Darker, John Ragg, Armston Pochin, Thomas Wightman, John Clarke, Thomas Jackson, George Ross 'and others'. Not only were the promoters a numerical minority of the landowners, but they included too a strong representation of absentee landlords.[1] Thus the interests of the village as a community and as a society were even more likely to be overlooked or ignored. Whatever the general case for enclosure, the fact remains that the case against it on social grounds could hardly make itself heard and indeed failed to make itself heard at all in London.

On 6 March the Wigston bill was read a second time and sent on to the Committee; and on 21 March Sir Thomas Palmer reported back from the Committee that the allegations of the bill were true. The parties concerned had given their consent to the bill except 'the proprietors of about fifteen yardlands'. The whole lands intended to be enclosed amounted to about ninety-six yardlands. No person had, however, appeared before the Committee to oppose the bill, which was accordingly, with the Committee's amendments, sent forward to be engrossed. On 26 March it was read a third time and passed; on 18 April it received the assent of the Lords; and on the following day the royal assent.[2]

No records have survived locally of the proceedings at Wigston, either before or after the Act,[3] so that no further light can be thrown on the objections of the smaller proprietors. This is particularly unfortunate as this bare hint in the Journal of the House of Commons suggests a fundamental cleavage of interest between the minority of large owners and the numerical majority of smaller peasantry. Assuming that the objectors were recruited entirely from the smaller owners, as is highly likely, their fifteen yardlands (about 480 acres) represented the lands of

[1] Of the nine men named above as promoters of the bill, four were absentee landlords who received 796 acres between them in the award – well over a quarter of the total acreage allotted.

[2] J.H.C. xxix, 911, 969, 983, 1053, 1057.

[3] The parish has not even a copy of its own award. A copy survives (without its map) among the county records at Leicester. Another copy is enrolled among the Chancery records at the P.R.O. (C.P. 43/735, m. 212-m. 259.)

about sixty or so of the surviving peasantry of the village, men who owned from one acre up to about twenty. And it is significant that not one of these men appeared before the Committee in London to voice the objections they had evidently voiced so numerously on their native heath. How *could* they make a case, these humble village farmers who had, most of them, been no farther than Leicester on market-days? How *could* they travel a hundred miles and argue before a Committee of learned gentlemen in London, or even pay a lawyer to go and do it for them? They did not speak the same language as the gentry and the lawyers. They spoke the language of a peasant world that an old-fashioned Tudor squire might have understood but hardly a Georgian gentleman who spent a good deal of his time in the Metropolis. Once the undemocratic machinery had begun to revolve, started by a petition from a minority of the larger landowners, the small peasant and his little self-contained world were doomed to extinction. A quarter of the landowners at the most could have promoted the bill, and nearly three-quarters could have been, and indeed seem to have been, against it; but the machinery continued to revolve and the small peasant came out at the other end with a smaller piece of land than he had had before (about one acre in six had been deducted in lieu of tithes) and a larger demand for money than he had ever seen before in his life, the cost of doing something that he had not wanted done. The Commissioners appointed by the Act[1] no doubt acted fairly at all points: there was no overt injustice to anyone who could establish a legal claim. The bewildered peasant would have been hard put to it to point to any specific injustice or wrongful act; but he was inarticulately and profoundly aware that he had been caught up in machinery whose working he had not understood and that it had altered his life, the whole familiar landscape and economy in which he and his ancestors had always lived. It is necessary to labour this point, for in no other way can we understand why this peasant economy, whose creation and working we have traced so laboriously through the centuries, which had produced in turn a form of society that satisfied the creative impulses of most of its members, should

---

[1] They were William Beckwith of Lincolns Inn, esquire; Joshua Grundy of Thornton, co. Leics., esquire; William Wyatt of Seany Park, co. Stafford, surveyor; George Cooper of Great Glen, cc. Leics.; and John Stone of Quorndon, co. Leics., gentleman.

succumb to this formidable attack from outside without any apparent struggle. The peasants of Wigston had not lacked force and courage in earlier centuries, when they called their lords into court or opposed the lords' claims in court. They had not hesitated to attack when it seemed necessary, or to defend vigorously. But in 1764 the dice were too heavily loaded against them at the start. In 1588 they had fought their case over their copyhold rights in the High Court of Chancery; in 1764 they sent no one to the House of Commons to fight for their rights as peasant freeholders. The machinery of government had become too formidable, and, more important, was weighted against them. In 1588 it had, if anything, been weighted on their side, at least to the extent of ensuring that they got a full hearing before the judges.

⤙ THE ENCLOSURE AWARD ⤚

The award for Wigston was made on 17 November 1766. It dealt with 2887 acres 2 roods 14 perches. The total area of the parish at that date is not known with certainty owing to modern boundary changes, but it was stated at the time of the Poor Law enquiry in 1832 and again in 1836, before the Select Committee of the House of Lords on the state of agriculture, to be 2944 acres.[1] Thus only about 56 or 57 acres escaped the great redistribution, accounted for by the cottages of those who had no lands in the fields, and by the roads of the parish. We may say that the whole parish was involved in the enclosure award.

The Commissioners had caused to be made a detailed survey of all the lands in the common fields, and in the homesteads and ancient enclosures of those who had lands in the fields. Thus the only land that escaped reckoning was the minute area occupied by those in the village with freehold cottages who had no lands in the fields themselves.

The next step was the allotment to the Duke of St. Albans – 'Quantity and Quality considered' – of one-eighth part of the common fields (the meadows excepted) in lieu of the tithes of corn, grain, and hay arising in the parish. He was also entitled to four pieces of meadow ground and to several other pieces and parcels of land in the fields and certain

---

[1] The census reports of 1831 to 1851 give the acreage of the parish for population purposes as 2780, but this is incorrect. Early official estimates of parish acreages in general are quite unreliable.

rights of common therein. In all, the Duke's allotment amounted to 387 acres 1 rood 9 perches, or 13.4 per cent of the total area allotted. Of this 291 acres 2 roods 25 perches were in lieu of the great tithes. A further allotment of 21 acres 3 roods 16 perches of meadow was in lieu of certain meadow closes he had held before the enclosure, and 73 acres 3 roods 8 perches were in lieu of the glebe land which he possessed in the open fields as the proprietor of the rectory of Wigston. This last allotment represents the three virgates of land granted to the church of Wigston early in the twelfth century by the first and second earls of Leicester.

After the allotment to the Duke, the vicar's share was dealt with. He got in lieu of the small tithes such share of the residue as would be worth £62 a year when enclosed. This came to 88 acres 3 roods 37 perches. Between them the Duke and the vicar took 476 acres 1 rood 6 perches. Thus the extinction of the tithes involved the appropriation of about 380 acres or a little under one-seventh of the available land. Together with the settlement of the glebe, this preliminary allotment amounted to about 16½ per cent of the total, and every other landowner's share was reduced proportionately.

Moreover, as was customary in such cases, the allotments to the Duke and the vicar were 'to be mounded and fenced round by ditches and quickset hedges guarded or fenced with good posts and double rails' at the expense of the other proprietors. Not only this, but the Duke's land was to be subdivided into closes which were to be similarly fenced at the cost of the others. All this was to be done within four months of the sealing of the award. If any proprietor refused or neglected to pay his share of these and the other costs and charges, the commissioners had power to levy a distress and sale of his goods and chattels, or to enter upon the lands allotted to him and take all rents, issues, and profits until the full costs had been met.

Before we consider the allotments of the lesser proprietors, however, there are other features of the award to be mentioned briefly. Several pages of the award are taken up with precise directions as to the number and course of the public roads and carriage ways to be laid out within the parish. These were to be at least forty feet wide clear of the ditches and to be repaired and maintained by the village unless the owner of any adjoining lands should make a fence (other than a ditch) within fifty yards of such way, in which event the owner of that land was to repair and maintain that portion of the road.

As regards the great change-over from open field to enclosed fields, in which nearly everyone found himself with lands which had been occupied by someone else immediately before, the numerous occasions for disputes were settled by the commissioners. It was laid down in the award, for example, that such tillage parts of the fields as were fallow within the year of the division and allotment should be 'plowed in an Husbandlike Manner' and as often in that year between 2 February and 1 November as the Commissioners should order. If this were not done, the old proprietor was to pay the new six shillings per acre for every ploughing omitted. If, on the other hand, the old proprietor should not receive as much tillage in the new allotment as he or she had ploughed or folded with sheep then the new proprietor should compensate him or her as the Commissioners thought reasonable. A clause in the Act had given the Commissioners full powers to direct the course of husbandry in the fields between the passing of the Act and the making of the award. 'Every Person's estate in the said Fields shall, during that Space of Time, be liable and subject to such Directions as the said Commissioners or their Successors, or any Three or more of them, shall appoint, as well with regard to the stocking, as to the plowing, folding, tilling, sowing, and laying down the same.'

Turning now to the details of the allotments, there were 99 proprietors, excluding the Duke of St. Albans and the vicar, whose allotments varied from the quarter-acre going to Ann Ault up to the 267 acres that went to John Ragg. It will be best to consider this regiment of peasant proprietors, and how they fared, by beginning with an analysis of the award as a whole (including the Duke and the vicar for the sake of completeness).

The eight largest owners took one-half of the land of the parish between them, leaving the other ninety or so to share the remainder. More than half the allotments in the award were of less than ten acres; more than a quarter were less than five acres. The smallholders, those owning up to twenty acres, constituted nearly seventy per cent of the proprietors, but they held rather less than one-sixth of the total acreage. As we have already seen, this large class contained the bulk of the old peasant families of Wigston.

ANALYSIS OF THE WIGSTON ENCLOSURE AWARD, 1766

Area of allotmen	Number of allotments	Total acreage allotted A. R. P.	% of total area enclosed
Under 3 acres	14	24 1 37	0.8
3 to 5 acres	14	55 3 16	1.9
5+ to 10 acres	22	161 1 27	5.6
10+ to 20 acres	17	222 0 14	7.7
20+ to 50 acres	15	472 1 32	16.4
50+ to 100 acres	8	619 0 22	21.5
100+ to 200 acres	4	470 0 19	16.3
Over 200 acres	3	861 0 27	29.8
Total	97	2886 2 34*	100.0

*The actual total in the award is 2887a. 2r. 14p. About an acre has been lost in the above calculation, but the significance of the table is not affected in the slightest. There were four joint owners in small estates whose respective shares cannot be separated. Thus the total number of owners was 101.

An important class of middling peasant proprietors – 22 in all, excluding the vicar – owned 20 to 100 acres each, or rather more than one-third of the parish between them. These, too, consisted largely of true peasant families, native to the village and often of long standing in it.[1] Of the seven who received more than a hundred acres each in the award, four represented peasant families of long residence (Ragg, Johnson, Noone, and Mrs. Sarah Norton, who had been a Freer).

Apart from the creation of a large farm for the Duke of St. Albans in lieu of his great tithes, and of a smaller farm for the vicar in lieu of the small tithes, the enclosure of the parish did not directly create any greater inequality than had existed beforehand. It reflected, with these two exceptions, a state of affairs which had come about while the fields were still open. The small peasant had been losing ground to the larger, and the owner-occupier to the absentee landlord, for some five generations before 1766. The enclosure award merely set the seal

[1] A complete list of the allotments and of the individual costs of enclosure is given in an Appendix, pp. 311-13.

on changes which had been greatly accelerated by the extinction of copyhold tenure in the two manors between 1586 and 1606. Before those momentous dates the smaller peasantry had been protected by the custom of the manor, above all by the custom of inheritable copyholds at a small fixed fine and a small fixed rent. And they were protected not only against their lord but also against their stronger fellows. With the dismemberment of the two manors and the substitution of freeholds for these copyholds of inheritance, the way was left open for the more energetic and acquisitive peasant to buy up the less acquisitive or less fortunate without let or hindrance from any manorial custom. The land-market received an immense stimulus from the dismemberment of the two manors and especially of the larger (Danvers) manor in 1606. The growing volume of Wigston fines and conveyances in the seventeenth and eighteenth centuries bears abundant testimony to this enlarged freedom to buy and sell land within the parish.

The victory of the village over the manor in 1586-1606 was not, therefore, an unmixed blessing for the community, for it let loose forces inherent in peasant society itself which helped to undermine its own foundations with increasing speed during the five generations between 1606 and 1765. Nevertheless, the continued existence of the open fields, and above all of common rights, and of the detailed rules and mutual discussion that governed their management, provided a considerable degree of protection for the smaller farmers in various ways. The open fields, so long as they lasted, prevented the structure of peasant society from being wholly brought to the ground by the burrowing tides of the new individualism. The first great dyke of manorial custom had been demolished, but the second barrier – that of the open-field economy – still remained between the sea and the peasant village.

The open-field system acted as a check on unrestricted acquisitiveness, as exemplified in the by-law which required the larger farmers, under heavy penalty, to let pastures to those who had none at a nominal rent; and it called for communal action in a multitude of ways that helped the smaller men to hold their own. The keystone of the system was the common. Common rights held the whole structure together. With these the smallest proprietor in the village could maintain himself and his family in a tolerably self-sufficient economy that the outside world could not shake. It was when the common rights were extinguished that the whole structure slowly collapsed. Without his rights of common the peasant could no longer live.

The open-field system was vigorously criticised from outside at the time – mainly by those who did not understand its true value and significance as a sixteenth-century squire would have understood it *from the inside* – for its impeding of agricultural and industrial progress through the subjection of the more 'enterprising' farmers to the rules of the majority. But it acted, too, as the last great bulwark of the peasant system when manorial custom (or such of it as was good) had been swept away. And it is in this that the greatest significance of the parliamentary enclosure awards consists, not in any petty injustices they may have perpetrated, or in their financial costs, formidable though these were for the majority of the peasantry. Their significance lies in their sweeping away of common rights, and consequently in plunging the peasant suddenly into a money-economy which he did not understand, loaded with a money-debt at the start. It was not simply the substitution of one system of farming by another, which on balance was perhaps more productive for the country as a whole (though even this is questionable), but the destruction of an entire society with its own economy and traditions, its own way of living and its own culture.

How had the native peasantry fared under the award? It has already been observed that of the seven allotments of a hundred acres or more, four went to proprietors who represented peasant families of long residence in the village, but Sarah Norton (née Freer) was an absentee landlord. Mr. John Ragg received 267 acres (including 17 acres for Wyggeston Hospital land held on a long lease), Mr. John Noone (or his executors) received 125 acres, and William Johnson received 115 acres, of which, however, only 42 acres were his own freehold, the rest being Hospital land held by him on lease. The absentee landlords, who received 824 acres between them (nearly a third of the parish) were the Duke of St. Albans, Mr. Thomas Wightman, Mrs. Sarah Norton, and Mr. John Darker, all of whom have already been discussed.

In the group of eight landowners who received allotments of 50 to 100 acres, one was the parson, two others were Leicester men (one a hosier, the other a butcher), the two Pochins were small gentry who had come into the village in the 1660's with profitable marriages, and the remaining three were representatives of ancient peasant families in Wigston – Mr. John Clarke, Elizabeth Freer, and George Ross. Thus of the fifteen largest allotments, the true peasant families of the village obtained only six.

We may consider the next group of thirty-two proprietors, who each received from ten to fifty acres, as a whole. Here the native peasantry predominated: here we find many of the names familiar to us in the sixteenth and early seventeenth centuries – Freer, Brewin, Smith, Boulter, Jackson, Davenport, White and Clarke. One cannot say, among all the smaller names, exactly how many could be considered as true peasants, rooted in the village; but all but half a dozen or so are readily identifiable as of this type, mostly small owner-occupiers with at least two or three generations' ancestry in the village.

When we move down into the 3 to 10-acre group, more old peasant names come in – Astill, Abbott, Coltman, Dand, Goodrich, Holmes, more Johnsons, Vann, and Ward. The lowest group of all, those who got less than three acres in the award, contains the names of old peasant families who have sunk from a much higher estate – Langton, Pawley, and Simons – all with several centuries of life in Wigston behind them, once prosperous free tenants and now husbanding only a single small field, probably allotted in lieu of certain common rights. There were, indeed, some ten or a dozen ancient peasant families – most of them of medieval origin in the village – whose holdings in 1766 were reduced to a single field like this. The whole enclosure award may be viewed as a pyramid, with a broad base of some fifty proprietors who received less than ten acres, rising to its summit in the Duke of St. Albans, who was nothing but a name in Wigston; and in this pyramid the native peasantry are nearly all near the bottom. As the pyramid rises the familiar names thin out rapidly, and the names are those of absentee hosiers, grocers, M.P.s, peers.

In many instances the old peasant families had sunk in the scale; they had lost most or all of their land before ever enclosure took place. The award for these was only the *coup de grâce*. But there are other instances, which we must not fail to notice, in which the peasant was not so degraded and unsuccessful. He had in fact accumulated a substantial estate, sold out, and moved elsewhere into a profession or a trade in Leicester, and it is only his poor relations who remain in the village to receive their miserable allotment at the enclosure.

The hosiery or framework-knitting trade was expanding yearly in the villages near Leicester, and above all in the town itself, during the early years of the eighteenth century. In the 1680's there had not been above a dozen hosiers in the town. By 1727 the borough contained a larger number of framework-knitters than the town of Nottingham. Some five to seven hundred were said to be engaged in the trade in Leicester; at Nottingham there were about four hundred. The total number of frames in all the midland counties was put at more than 3500. By 1769 the Leicester hosiery trade was said to be worth £60,000 annually; by 1790 there were no fewer than 3000 frames employed in the town, between four and six times as many as sixty years earlier.[1] As the hosiery trade expanded it led to the growth of ancillary trades such as combing, dyeing, frame-smithing, and needle-making, and to a general prosperity from which many other trades benefited, particularly the building trades. The population of the town trebled during the eighteenth century, rising from about 6000 at the beginning of the century to over 17,000 at the end.

As one studies the pages of the *Freemen's Register*, which form a continuous and detailed record of the industrial and commercial life of the town, one is immediately struck by the great contribution made by the surrounding villages to this remarkable expansion in the town. A high proportion of those enrolled each year as freemen, or apprenticed in the borough, are drawn from the neighbouring countryside,[2] and a substantial proportion of the apprentices became masters and employers, above all in the hosiery trade. In this contribution to the town the peasant community of Wigston had a large share. It is in this direction that we must look for the descendants of the successful peasantry rather than in the impoverished cottagers who remained behind in the village to accept whatever fate came their way.

Thus John Coltman, son of a Wigston yeoman, was apprenticed in 1742

[1] Thompson, *Leicester in the Eighteenth Century*, 257. The figure of a dozen Leicester hosiers for the 1680's is derived from an analysis of the *Freemen's Register* for that period.

[2] For example, in 1720, 60 per cent of those apprenticed in the town were drawn from villages outside. In 1750 the proportion was exactly 50 per cent. In 1780 45 per cent of those apprenticed in the town came from outside.

to Isaac Robinson of Leicester, woolcomber, and subsequently built up a large hosiery business from which he was able to retire to a comfortable town house.[1] William Davenport, the son of William Davenport of Wigston, mercer and farmer, was apprenticed about 1710 to Abraham Pougher, whose grandfather, Abstinence Pougher, had established one of the first hosiery businesses in the town in the 1670's; and he, too, blossoms out in the subsequent records as a hosier.[2] A considerable part of the Davenport accumulation seems to have gone, however, to support the dignity of a late seventeenth-century rector George Davenport, rector of Houghton le Spring in County Durham from 1664 to 1677, and a considerable benefactor to that parish and to his native Wigston.[3]

The substantial peasant property of the Smiths seems to have been similarly divided between the church and the hosiery trade. Three members of the family shared 40 acres between them in the award, of whom one was a Leicester hosier and another a parson. The Davenports, the Smiths, and the Vanns, all produced minor gentry and parsons in the later seventeenth century and the eighteenth, and much of their property went in this direction.

Mr. Daniel Vann of Wigston, who died in 1680, left, as we have seen, four stocking frames as his most valuable personal property. The more opulent side of the family seem to have left the village shortly after this, probably for Leicester like so many others, as the name of Vann appears frequently among the hosiers and woolcombers of the town during the eighteenth century. In 1769 we have James Vann of Belgrave, gent. – a fashionable suburb of the town at that time – admitted as a freeman of the town. He was the owner of the major part of the Vann property in Wigston as an abstract of title about this time reveals. In 1775 the Leicestershire pollbook lists Charles Vann, gent., of Nottingham, as a freeholder in Wigston. They, too, had helped to fertilise the new hosiery trade with their capital and their energy.[4]

The Simons were another ancient peasant family in Wigston, going back to the thirteenth century at least. They too were selling out. Amos

---

[1] For the history of the Coltmans in Leicester, see an excellent paper by Florence E. Skillington in *T.L.A.S.*, xviii, 1-40.

[2] *Freemen's Register*, I, 218, 249. Davenport was admitted to the freedom as apprentice to Pougher in 1720. In 1728 he is described as 'hosier'.

[3] Nichols, 387-8.

[4] A Vann was also rector of Peckleton (Leics.) in the 1740's.

Simons sold a close of land in the still open Mucklow Field in 1740, when we find him described as 'of Trowbridge, Wilts., hosier.'[1] And twenty years earlier another member of the family, a son of William Simons, farmer, had been apprenticed to a Leicester woolcomber, and was subsequently admitted to the freedom of the town.

We find some of the Freers and the Brewins similarly being apprenticed to fellmongers and combers in the town; and in 1721 William Hurst, son of a Wigston labourer, was apprenticed to a Leicester comber. He later set up in business in the town as a needle-maker. Both Brewins and Freers seem to have established their own businesses also in later years.

Other Wigston names recur in the registers of freemen and apprentices in Leicester during this period; but enough has been said to leave no doubt that the peasant families of the village, like those of many other villages round the town, made a substantial contribution to the new and growing industries. Several of the larger families, with some solid property behind them, succeeded in founding good hosiery businesses; and of the others, many became framework-knitters in the town or helped to swell such necessary trades as the food and building trades that were growing with the town.

Thus the enclosure award taken by itself would deceive us as to the fate of the old peasantry as a class. The allotment of something under eight acres to William Vann represents only the residue of the Vann property, which by this date had mostly been withdrawn into other spheres, and so, too, with the Simons and a number of others. They had gone to fertilise the growing town just as their ancestors (like the Wykyngestons, the Herricks, the Randalls and others) had gone back in the medieval centuries.

✤ THE COSTS OF ENCLOSURE ✤

The total cost of the Wigston enclosure amounted to £2817 10s. 9d. This represented the cost of obtaining the Act; of surveying, dividing, and allotting the property; of enclosing, sub-dividing and fencing the Duke's allotment and of 'ring-fencing' the vicar's farm; of preparing the award and of meeting the costs of the commissioners, and all other necessary expenses except the ring-fencing and sub-dividing of the

---

[1] L.R.O., 9.D.43 / 186/3.

allotments of the other proprietors, which were to be borne by the individual proprietors. No itemised list of these expenses survives. Since the costs of the Duke and the vicar were borne by the remaining proprietors the total bill was spread over 2411 acres, an average charge of 23s. 4½d. per acre. It was, in fact, apportioned according to the *value* of the respective allotments. The complete list is given in an appendix.

It is difficult to say how heavily these costs pressed upon the smaller proprietors. If we take the typical peasant proprietor for this purpose as one who was allotted twenty or thirty acres, his bill of costs, which had to be paid within ten days of the sealing of the award, was between £25 and £35, something of the order of a year's income for a craftsman or a skilled labourer. One wonders how readily a smallholder in the twentieth century could lay his hands upon, say, £100 to £150 in cash at such short notice. Moreover, this bill did not include the costs of ring-fencing his own fields, which he was obliged to do also in a reasonably short space of time. Moreover, there was the interior fencing of each allotment to be considered. This, too, was a cost which pressed more heavily upon the smaller men, for the smaller the closes the greater the length of hedging and fencing required. A five-acre field to be hedged on two sides required about thirty-eight perches of hedge at a cost of seven to ten shillings per perch,[1] at a total cost of some £14 to £19 for a bank with a ditch on either side, planted with quick – the usual Midland hedge of this period. Thus a peasant proprietor who was allotted twenty acres at the enclosure, divided into four closes of five acres each, was faced with a further bill for between £50 and £75. Even if he had larger fields – two square fields of ten acres each – his interior fencing would cost him nearly as much. At a conservative estimate the cost of interior fencing for the small owner was twice as great as the bill of legal costs he had already been presented with.[2] It is in the light of this formidable and unprecedented financial burden that we shall consider the fate of the peasant proprietor in the next chapter.

---

[1] On this, see Curtler, op. cit., 164, quoting the calculations of Homer, *Essay on Enclosure*, published in 1766, the year of the Wigston award.

[2] This estimate is confirmed by the figures given for a small owner at a Lincolnshire enclosure, whose contribution to the common costs of the enclosure was £4 18s. 2d. as against an estimated cost of £10 8s. 0d. for fencing. (Hosford, 'Some Lincolnshire Enclosure Documents', *Ec.H.R.*, 1949, 73-9.)

X

THE END OF A PEASANT SOCIETY

Farming after the Enclosure

All over Leicestershire the immediate effect of parliamentary enclosure was the conversion of the greater part of what had been open-field arable to permanent pasture, and Wigston was no exception. Even Arthur Young confessed that in the five midland counties of Leicester, Warwick, Northampton, Huntingdon and Buckingham parliamentary enclosure had generally resulted in a decay of tillage and in rural depopulation.[1] This great block of country, filling the entire middle of England, had long been the home of a numerous free peasantry. Scattered all over the four or five thousand square miles of the Midland Plain were hundreds of villages which, since the twelfth or thirteenth centuries at least, had been largely composed of such a peasantry as we have described at Wigston in Leicestershire.[2] To a large extent, therefore, what happened at Wigston is what happened in all those other villages up and down the Midlands, notably the wholesale conversion of arable to pasture, the engrossing of farms by large graziers at a much-enhanced rent, the displacement of the peasant-farmer, and the final collapse in ruins of the peasant society which had prevailed for so long over so wide an area in England.

In one important respect, however, Wigston differed from the majority of villages. Its tillage decayed but its population went on increasing. It was an industrialised village that not only gave some sort of alternative employment to its own dispossessed peasantry but attracted those of the purely farming villages for miles around. Framework-knitting was a domestic industry and it required no capital

---

[1] Cf. Slater, *English Peasantry and the Enclosure of the Common Fields*, 100–7, *passim*. For Leicestershire in particular see *Studies in Leicestershire Agrarian History*, 130–2.

[2] Cf. Dodswell, 'The Free Tenantry of the Hundred Rolls', *Ec.H.R.*, 1944, 163–71.

to hire a frame from a hosier or an undertaker for a shilling a week and to knit the yarn provided by him. And so, ever since the last quarter of the seventeenth century, the village had been attracting the dispossessed and unemployed from outside, and it continued to do so after its own fields and farms were taken out of the peasant economy.

The return of crops made in 1801 to the Home Office is missing for Wigston, or it would have given us a detailed picture of the farming economy of the parish a generation after enclosure.[1] The returns for seven parishes surrounding Wigston all show a small proportion of their area under crops and, by implication, a high proportion under grass, since there was no woodland or waste. The only indication we get of what happened in Wigston itself comes as late as 1832, when we are told that two-thirds of the parish was under pasture and one-third in tillage.[2] This means roughly 2000 acres in grass. In the open-field days about a fifth, or perhaps slightly more, of the land had been in grass, roughly 600 acres. Thus some 1400 acres of arable had been converted to pasture sixty years or so after enclosure, an area equal to nearly half the parish.

There is every reason to believe that what one finds in 1832 was true of the years immediately following enclosure. Within five years of the award an intelligent local farmer, who compiled some notes about the village, wrote that whereas the grain raised on Wigston's three thousand fertile acres had been 'a great help to Leicester market', now (in 1771) there was not enough corn raised to employ the local mill or enough to feed even the inhabitants of the village themselves.[3] And this was the complaint from all over Leicestershire in these days: not enough corn grown after enclosure to feed even the villages.[4]

We begin to find the larger farmers in Wigston described as 'grazier' almost at once. Simeon Bruin is so described in 1770 and George Ross before 1782; and in the 1790's we find John Earp and John Pochin

---

[1] For these returns and those of 1793-4-5, see *V.C.H. Leics.*, ii. 243-4. The Wigston return is missing for all these years.

[2] *Report of the Commission on the Poor Laws* (1834), 44, xxviii. Report of the Asst. Commissioner on Leicestershire.

[3] Nichols, 387, quoting from Mr. George Ayscough's Mss. (now lost).

[4] See, for example, the complaints from Breedon, Slawston, Blaston, and Kegworth in 1801, quoted in *Studies in Leics. Agrarian History*, 131.

similarly described.[1] They were largely engaged in producing meat for the Leicester market, so that even the local supplies of cheese and butter fell off also. No wonder the curate of Breedon said in 1801 that although all the land in north-west Leicestershire was in a higher state of cultivation than formerly' much less *food* was produced than ever before.

The new economy economised chiefly on labour. By 1832 it was reckoned that only forty labourers were sufficient for the proper cultivation of Wigston's three thousand acres. This was probably about a third, perhaps only a quarter, of the labour that had been needed in the old open fields, according to the experience of Kibworth, a large village a few miles away, whose fields had been enclosed about the same time.

Apart from this large-scale conversion of arable to pasture, how was the small landowner, and above all the owner-occupier, affected by the changes that followed enclosure?

If we examine the land-tax assessment for 1781, fifteen years after the award, we find little apparent change: hardly more than one would expect in the normal passage of time. In 1765-6 there had been 99 landowners. Excluding the four small institutional owners (such as the churchwardens and the overseers), the owner-occupiers numbered about 47 – exactly half the total. The larger owners sometimes did not occupy all their land, and the smaller ones often rented more land from the larger, so that one cannot estimate at that date exactly how much of the village land was owner-occupied.

By 1781 the total number of landowners had fallen slightly, but the number of owner-occupiers was undiminished (there were still 48 of them). The owner-occupier farmed 32 per cent of the land in the parish. Out of the 50 small landowners who had been allotted less than ten acres at the enclosure, only six had disappeared fifteen years later, hardly more than a normal rate of change. Even among the larger owners (roughly 40 to 124 acres) there had been four changes among the twenty allottees: John Noone, Sarah Norton, Richard Metcalf, and Elizabeth Horspool had all disappeared.[2] On the face of it, the enclosure had had no effect on the

---

[1] *Register of the Freemen of Leicester*, ii, passim.
[2] Land tax assessments (1773-1832) at the County Record Office, Leicester. Some of these disappearances are due to death (e.g. Sarah Norton in 1778) and the land had passed to heirs of a different name, so that there is no significant change. This may be true to some extent of the small landowners also.

peasant landowner: there was certainly no wholesale selling-out. There were still 33 owner-occupiers paying less than £2 land tax; and amongst those who paid more the native peasantry of the village (or their gentle descendants) were well represented – Boulter, Jackson, Ross, Johnson, Davenport, Clark, and Ragg.

By 1795 – nearly thirty years after enclosure – there were substantial changes. Although the amount of owner-occupied land remained the same, indeed had slightly increased, the number of owner-occupiers had fallen from 48 to 34. Some of the small owners had given up their fields and had let them to larger men; others had sold out altogether. The typical owner-occupier was farming on a bigger scale as a grazier. In addition to his own land he rented that of his fellow-villagers, and also some from large absentee landlords. But the peasant with no capital could not do this. His holding might still have been large enough to support him under the peasant economy, but that had been destroyed by the enclosure; and he could not fit his one, two, or three small closes into the new grazing system. Some let their fields to bigger men, but others, burdened by mortgages, were forced to sell up in the face of the steadily rising price-level, above all of food-prices, which had taken a sharp upward turn in the 1760's and had not ceased to rise since then. The old economy would have protected and sustained them in this situation (as it had done during the price-revolution of the sixteenth century) but they had been precipitated from that natural and largely self-sufficing economy into a full-blown money economy in which they had to buy nearly all the things they needed instead of producing for themselves out of their own natural resources. We shall return to this point a little later.

The existence of hidden mortgages must explain to a large extent the apparent absence of any immediate effect on the position of the peasant landowner after the enclosure of his fields and commons. It is not to be expected that, even when faced with a heavy bill of costs and an even larger bill for his own unwanted fences, the peasant could surrender his inheritance, which lay at the very core of his spiritual as well as his physical life, without a tenacious struggle. The deep roots of the peasant culture, which had grown underground for a thousand years in the Midland Plain, were too powerful to be torn up at once. The peasant borrowed money on the security of his land and fought the new situation in a way that the statistics do not reveal to us.

But he thereby became enmeshed in the very money-economy he had fought instinctively to avoid. He had to meet interest payments at regular intervals, and to get ready money he had to let his fields to a larger man who could use them in the new way. Even if the peasant could have kept his fields in tillage, and even if his common-rights had not been translated into something less valuable and vital, he would still have needed a regular flow of money to meet the obligations that had been thrust upon him. Mortgages enabled him to carry on for twenty or thirty years longer as the apparent owner of his enclosed acres. The shell of the peasant economy still survived; but the heart had been leeched out of it and its spirit was dying pulse by pulse.

The high war-prices of 1793-1815, which enabled so many farmers in England to buy their farms before the end, had little effect on the smaller peasantry. The Wigston land tax assessments show the amount of owner-occupied land rising from 33 per cent in 1795 to 44 per cent in 1811, but this was solely due to the larger men, like Mr. John Ragg, taking on more land. The number of owner-occupiers only rose from 34 to 36 in the same period. Since 1781 the small owner-occupiers (those paying less than £2 land tax) had fallen from 33 to 22. More old peasant names disappear by 1811, and their place is taken by new and bigger men with strange names – Ingram, Blunt, and Seddons.

If, finally, we survey the fifty years between 1781 and 1831, we can see the full measure of the change. The number of landowners fell from about 96 to 64, and the occupying-owners from 49 to 29. The amount of owner-occupied land in 1831 was still 37 per cent – higher than it had been in 1781 and as high perhaps as before enclosure. If we had regard to this figure alone we should have said that the enclosure had had no significant effect upon land-ownership. But the owner-occupier was a bigger man altogether: Mr. John Ragg alone accounted for almost a quarter of the owner-occupied land. The five largest men in this class had 56 per cent of the owner-occupied land. A few small peasant families clung on, like the Coltmans, Bransons, Goodwins, Dands, Hursts and others; but many more, like the Abbotts, Astills, Boulters, Holmeses, and Whites, had lost everything, and others, such as the Ainges, were left with only a cottage. By 1831 the ranks of the peasant landowners, which had hardly been breached fifty years earlier, had been reduced to a mere handful of survivors. The three largest landowners between them owned 35 per cent of the land; seven of them owned more than half the parish between them.

The great agricultural depression after the Napoleonic Wars, and especially since 1824, had. broken a great number of both small landowners and tenant-farmers. Mr. John Buckley, who farmed 400-500 acres at Normanton, near Loughborough, and who knew Leicestershire and Northants well, told the Select Committee on Agriculture in 1833 that the condition of farmers had been worsening since 1824, despite some reductions of rent. Poor rates had not fallen, and the cost of implements and farm-gear from wheel-wrights, carpenters, and blacksmiths had not fallen 'so much as they ought to have done'. A large proportion of tenant-farmers had lost their capital, the land had deteriorated in the past nine years with the neglect of drainage (especially on the stiff Leicestershire clays), yields were down, and labourers were out of work from the beginning of November to the beginning of March. Labourers' wages had fallen from 13s. to 15s. a week in 1824 to 10s. in 1833. Although many small proprietors had suffered less than the tenant-farmers, their estates had fallen considerably in value and many had sold out to manufacturers or great landed proprietors. The numbers of the yeomanry were falling all over the Midlands. Many had borrowed during the war to improve their paternal estates, or to extend them, and these were ruined where they had borrowed up to half the value of their freehold.

We can see all this reflected in Wigston. New men owned and occupied many of the biggest farms by 1831. Among the native landowners Mr. John Ragg had benefited from the misfortunes of his fellows, as the Randalls had done in the depression of the fifteenth century, and had bought them up out of his greater reserves. In 1781 he paid £24 16s. 10d. land tax; in 1831 his son paid £33 12s. 2d., at the same rate in the pound. He had increased his estate by more than one-third, chiefly at the expense of the smaller owners.

The figures of the 1831 census report enable us to fill out this picture and to see the village economy as a whole. The population had risen quickly since 1801, when it had numbered 354 families. Now it numbered 483 families, of whom 93 (rather less than one in five) were chiefly dependent on agriculture. Of these 93, 23 were farmers and 69 were labourers, one family being unaccounted for. Only 13 of the 23 farmers employed any labour; 10 employed none. More than three families in every five in the village were now chiefly engaged in industry or trade.

Twenty years later, the census report of 1851, defective though it is in some respects, shows us how far the engrossing of farms had gone and how far the greater part of the village population had been divorced from the land, other than a cottage garden. The report does not account for the entire acreage of the parish, probably because some farmers in adjoining parishes farmed a good deal of Wigston land (about 500 acres are unaccounted for). These farmers would be returned under their own parishes. But of the 2422 acres which are accounted for, five occupiers out of the total of 27 farmed more than half the total (1246 acres). Indeed, the three Pochins farmed 515 acres between them and the two Langhams (big men from Newton Harcourt, the next parish) had 601 acres. Thus two families of big farmers now farmed about 40 per cent of the parish. Most of the other larger farmers were tenants, newcomers to the village – Elizabeth Eggleston from Nottinghamshire (155 acres), Thomas Watson likewise (105 acres), Samuel Seddon from Cromford in Derbyshire (120 acres) and three more from Northamptonshire. Such Wigston men as still farmed land were mostly among the small farmers except for the Pochins, one of the Langhams, a Burgess, and two Vanns. The peasant system had completely vanished by 1851 and in its place we have the large farm, the absentee landlord, and the capitalist tenant-farmer; and the native peasantry are small occupiers if they are anything at all.

❧ THE END OF THE PEASANT ECONOMY ❧

The peasant economy had been finally extinguished by the enclosure award, though it took a long time to die; and the crucial blow had been the extinction of the common rights of the peasantry. Even where these had been legally established by the claimants, they had been commuted for a small allotment of an acre or two. Many of the smallest allotments in the Wigston enclosure award probably arise in this way. But a small field of one, two, or three acres, divorced from everything else, was useless except in a money economy, and so the peasant abandoned his old economy of mixed farming combined with rights of common pasture (with all the portentous trifles that these rights brought in) and let his field to some bigger man who could make better use of it in the new pattern.

The Wigston award had made no special provision for the maintenance of the old husbandry as was done at Sapcote, a few miles away, in 1778. Here the lord of the manor, who was also rector of the parish, was petitioned by 'sixteen industrious families in humble circumstances' for sufficient land to enable each of them to keep a cow, and he thereupon ordered a pasture close of 32 acres to be laid out for their use. This they held at a reasonable rent which was not increased even by 1810. During that time not one of the cottagers renting these cow-commons ever received parish relief, or ever asked for any. Moreover, not a single plough-team was laid down at the enclosure. Although the parson-squire could have found 'two or three capital farmers' to rent the whole of his estate at much higher rents he continued to let all the consolidated farms at the same rent to the same tenants.[1]

But such squires were rare, and they were battling quixotically against the forces of their time. Only villages which were mostly in single ownership could expect such consideration, and such villages were still exceptional in the Midlands. Elsewhere the tendency to the engrossing of farms, which had grown increasingly strong since the sixteenth century (it was much older than that), received an immense impetus. The peasant, swept out of a traditional thrift economy, which he understood and had always practised, into a money economy whose workings he did not comprehend, starting indeed with a heavy load of money-debt, was bound to go under.

He soon ceased to be a farmer of his own land: he could not fit into the new order of things. Mortgages kept him afloat as an owner for somewhat longer, until the post-war depression after 1814, even perhaps until the worst days after 1824; and then he and his fellows sold out altogether. Few of the peasantry were left by the 1830's.

[1] Nichols (*Sparkenhoe Hundred*), 895-6.

The open-field system had been the solid dyke protecting the peasant against the powerful tide of the money-economy that had been rising in the outside world for centuries, just as manorial custom had protected his ancestors in earlier centuries. The enclosure of the fields and the extinction of the commons made the breach by which this tide was let in. The domestic economy of the whole village was radically altered. No longer could the peasant derive the necessaries of life from the materials, the soil, and the resources of his own countryside and his own strong arms. The self-supporting peasant was transformed into a spender of money, for all the things he needed were now in the shops. Money, which in the sixteenth century had played merely a marginal, though a necessary, part, now became the one thing necessary for the maintenance of life. Peasant thrift was replaced by commercial thrift. Every hour of work now had a money-value; unemployment became a disaster, for there was no piece of land the wage-earner could turn to. His Elizabethan ancestor had needed money intermittently, but *he* needed it nearly every day, certainly every week of the year.

The crumbling of the old system showed itself most obviously in the calamitous rise in the poor-rates. In the early 1750's the expenditure on the poor at Wigston had been moving towards a hundred pounds a year.[1] In the year ending at Easter 1776 it was over £377; by 1783-5 it averaged about £433 a year. Thereafter it rose steadily to a peak of £1776 in 1802. From 1803 to 1812 it fell to an average of just under £800 a year, but from 1813 onwards began to move sharply upwards again, reaching a new high level in 1817 at £2,316.[1] The problem of the poor had become quite unmanageable at Wigston, as in thousands of other parishes in the Midlands and the South. In 1830 £2,505 was raised in levies for the poor; in 1831, £2,070. But in 1832 the total levy shot up to £2,925, just about a pound on every acre in the parish.

The Commission on the working of the Poor Laws was appointed; and in November 1832 an Assistant Commissioner – Mr. Henry Pilkington – arrived at Wigston to hear the local evidence. His report reveals the chaos and misery into which the village economy had by now descended.

The parish contained 2944 acres of good land, capable of producing

[1] See Ch. VIII, p. 230.
[2] *Returns of the Expense and Maintenance of the Poor*, 1803, 1815.

32 bushels of wheat to the acre, 32 to 40 bushels of beans, or 44 bushels of oats. An acre and a half of grass would feed a good beast and carry from five to seven ewes and followers. One-third of the land was in tillage, two-thirds in pasture, and there was no common. Forty labourers were generally considered sufficient for the proper cultivation of the land, an additional number being allowed for harvest. Their average weekly wage was 15s. in the summer and 10s. to 12s. in the winter. At harvest extra men were hired by the farmers for ten weeks at 12s. a week and board. No difference was made between the wages of married and unmarried men.

The magistrates' scale of allowances was 5s. for men and women, 1s. 6d. for children over four years of age and 1s. 3d. for those under that age. It was occasionally necessary to resort to 'the roundsman system'. It was not liked but 'the parish does not otherwise know what to do with the labourers'. The stocking-makers, whose earnings were miserably low – only half those of an agricultural labourer – were almost useless to the farmers.

The cottages belonged to a great variety of persons and were let at rents of between £3 and £5 a year. Some had no gardens: no cottage with a garden could be got under £4. No land was let to the labourers (how different from former days!).

The heavy rates fell disproportionately hard on the farmers. Buildings were assessed at only £465 8s. 4d. and land at £3953 3s. 4d., the latter a valuation made in 1830 and now far too high. In 1832 the rates upon the land raised £2692, upon houses only £233. The rising hosiery manufacturers in the village were being let off very lightly. Since 1820 property values at Wigston, as elsewhere in the county, had fallen by one-half and land was not saleable even at that price. Who wanted land burdened with rates of a pound an acre? The parish was 'eaten up by poor's rates' and the parish authorities 'consider the paupers to be masters', unduly supported by the magistrates who seldom knew them and ordered relief which the select vestry knew to be unnecessary.

There were 208 families 'in regular pay' and the casuals sometimes amounted to 150. What a picture! Nearly one half the families in the village in regular receipt of poor relief and many more receiving intermittent relief! There was no 'house of industry', only a poor-house for the aged, the infirm, and orphaned children. Wigston had not joined any of the workhouse unions of the neighbourhood as the parish authorities did not consider them properly run. They had tried to set up one of their own but had failed 'through the interference of the magistrates, who would not allow us to keep the inmates within the walls, but came to the house of industry, and ordered us to let them out. The paupers do as they like with us, or nearly so. One part in three of our rates is paid to fraud and imposition'. There were fifteen public-houses and beershops in the village, 'all supported by the labourers and paupers, for the farmers cannot afford to go into one.'

Several farmers gave evidence before the assistant commissioner, all on the same theme. It will be enough to quote the words of Mr. William Pochin as an example, if only because he represented, in his name at least, the old order of things that had passed away so completely that it must have seemed only the idle dream of an old man, for only a man in his late seventies or eighties could now remember what the open-field village had once been like.

William Pochin had 'a house and 20 acres of good land of my own. I rent 40 acres more and have many trades in addition, as publican and butcher, but can't get a living by all put together, and am losing my little property fast. The whole of the farms in the parish have changed tenants three times in the space of ten years … A great part of the parish was entirely, at one time, given up and thrown out of cultivation for the purpose of avoiding the poor's rates'.[1]

Farmers could not afford enough labour to keep the land in order. They had to sell hay and straw to meet their 'head landlords' – that is, 'the paupers' rent-days', which generally came round ten to thirteen times a year. The parish would raise money to facilitate emigration but for the fact it was already £1200 in debt. 'We should be very glad to go ourselves if we could turn our effects into money without too great a sacrifice,' said William Pochin. The magistrates were to blame again, because they allowed Wigston men who were little better than paupers to take as many as five or six apprentices to framework-knitting, 'whom they are neither able to feed nor teach a trade.' These men do it to get the small apprenticeship fee, and the neighbouring parishes find the fee

---

[1] A witness before the Select Committee of the Lords on the state of agriculture in 1836 observed of Wigston that it 'presents the monstrous anomaly of land of excellent quality being thrown out of cultivation because unequal to the demands made upon it for poor rates.' (Evidence of Henry William Wilson.)

in order to get rid of their pauper children. So they rid themselves of 'their surplus population' and had a poor rate of only 2s. 6d. in the pound while 'we are paying 20 shillings in the pound.'

The assistant commissioner summed up by saying that 'from what I have learned, I consider that rent will soon cease at Wigston Magna, if it has not already done so in many cases, the farmers seeming to think that the poor's rates are more than sufficient rent'. Rates could not be collected without regular summonses and continual selling up of farmers. 'Property in land at Wigston is gone, and the tenant's capital is gone after it'.[1]

Overdrawn though this picture may be in some of its details, it reveals beyond all dispute the complete disintegration of the village economy, the degradation of at least a half of its total population, and the disappearance of nearly all sense of community. The animosity of the farmers towards 'the paupers' is revealed on every page of the report; and no doubt the underpaid labourers, the unemployed framework-knitters, and their families, felt equally venomous towards their masters, farmers and hosiers alike.

The problem of the uprooted peasantry had become insoluble by the traditional methods of relieving poverty. Moreover it was vastly aggravated by the steady increase in the village population despite a high death-rate. Between 1801 and 1831 another 500 people were added to the crowded streets, mostly housed in small brick cottages newly built or in large seventeenth- and eighteenth-century farmhouses (now abandoned as such) which were divided into two or three parts, each accommodating a family.[2] Infantile mortality rose; puerperal fever carried off more mothers; and consumption – that disease of overcrowded homes – killed young men and women in their 20s and 30s with ever-increasing speed.[3] Wages were low, housing conditions worse than they had been since the early sixteenth century, unemployment had become endemic.

---

[1] Report of the Commission on the Poor Laws, 1834. (Report of the Asst. Commr. on Leicestershire), loc. cit.

[2] One can see surviving examples of this today in all the old streets of the village.

[3] In the non-parochial registers for Wigston at Somerset House the cause of death is frequently given between 1805 and 1816. One death in six was that of an infant, one in three that of a child under five. Equally dangerous was the 20-40 age-group where consumption and puerperal fever raged.

What of those who earned their living in industry? The evidence of two Wigston framework-knitters before 'the Commission appointed to inquire into the Condition of the Framework Knitters' in 1845[1] gives us a complete picture of the industrial side of village life, an even more depressing one than that of the Poor Law enquiry a dozen years before. The village now had about 2300 people, of whom about 500 were employed by the Leicester hosiery manufacturers.[2] A meeting of the framework knitters was held in the village with reference to the newly appointed Commission, and Samuel Hurst and William Wyatt were deputed by it to give evidence at Leicester on behalf of all. Their account of the trade can be supplemented by the details of the census schedule of 1851 for the village.

Samuel Hurst said there were 500 to 550 frames in Wigston altogether, 'including independents and hosiers'. He could not say how many employers there were – 'we have not one of any calculation'. Most of the employers were under-masters, of whom there were several, 'but we have three biggish undertakers'. Most of the small masters kept shops, generally as grocers or drapers. They gave out work to their men on Monday or Tuesday, who then worked it up at home among their families.

The 'largest master in the town' sold bread, grocery, and flour; another kept a grocer's shop, while a third – who can be identified as Edward Holyoak, employing 50 men, 30 women, and 20 boys in 1851 – sold bread. His son – identifiable as John Holyoak, employing 70 hands in 1851 – had a butcher's shop next door and supplied his men with meat. The 'largest master' in 1845 is probably George Loveday, who appears as 'hosiery agent' in the 1846 directory. The Holyoaks, who employed 170 hands between them had possibly taken over his business by 1851. The only other employers of any size in 1851 were Isaac Herbert (25 hands) and John Heard (15 hands).

Although the Truck Act had been in force since October 1831, the Wigston knitters had been entirely ignorant of the illegality of payment in truck until the last few months. Hurst's own employer had paid his wages in ready money only in the past three months. He had formerly

[1] Parly. Papers 1845, 618, xv. The Appendix (Part I) gives the Leicestershire evidence.
[2] Census schedule, 1851 (P.R.O., H.O. 107/2081); *White's Directory of Leicestershire and Rutland*, 1846.

supplied goods during the week and stopped the money on Saturday night, paying the difference between the value of the work done and the goods received, 'if any'. When the provisions of the Truck Act dawned upon the Wigston wage-earners, fourteen years late, they immediately formed an anti-truck association 'and most masters have now stopped it... . The people can have the money themselves. They can lay it out and do a deal better with it.'

The Wigston employers did not work for themselves but were 'undertakers' or middlemen to bigger men in Leicester. Few knitters supplied direct to the warehouse in Leicester; nearly all worked for a middleman. The latter hired frames from the Leicester hosier and let them out to the village framework-knitters at a shilling a week, adding their own charges of fivepence a week for 'taking-in and standing'. The framework-knitters also had to buy their own needles. By the time the fixed charge of 1s. 5d. a week had been met, the knitter could not earn above seven shillings a week. Many young people had given up framework-knitting as the earnings were so low and had taken to sewing and stitching gloves, a new trade in Wigston.

Moreover, there was no rebate on the frame-rent in time of sickness. The rent had to be paid by the knitter because the undertaker had to pay it to the hosier. Samuel Hurst had been ill for five weeks, but the frame-rent went on like the rent of the house. He had been 'a stockinger' for thirty years, and could barely maintain a family. Ten or fifteen years ago he used to get 11 shillings a dozen for his work: now he got 6 shillings. He had a wife and ten children, aged between 2 and 22 years, of whom six lived at home. One, a labourer, brought home 3 shillings a week, and boarded at home. Another 'gets me about 10d. a week', the next 8d. at winding'. The eldest son was in the army. Two children went to the day-school. He paid twopence a week for one, and 'a lady pays for another'. It says something for Samuel Hurst's spirit that he found it necessary to spend twopence a week out of this wretched income on a child's education.

His rent was a shilling a week for 'an oldish cottage but very roomy' – the new cottages were indeed decidedly smaller than the old, for the speculative builder was at large in the village. 'I should not have had it so low, but it belongs to my wife's uncle, and he put us into it … but it is a poor tumble-down place'. All the family slept in one room: he and his wife and two small children in one bed, three children in another, and two more in a crib-bed. As to charity, he got nothing more than a few coals three times during the winter – for the coal stock begun so bountifully by William Lawe on that Sunday evening in May 1595 was now quite inadequate to cope with poverty on the nineteenth-century scale. And as for allotments, nearly fifty had them, 'but not a quarter of those who wanted it'. The starved peasant looked at his ancestors' lands on his Sunday walk, but he looked in vain for even a single furrow of his own.

William Wyatt's evidence before the commissioners was much the same. He worked six days a week, from 6 a.m. until 8 p. m. every day, under a master-man in a shop where there were twelve frames. The master, L—, kept a bread-shop and sold all his bread to his hands, stopping their wages for bread they had had during the week. Wyatt's outgoings were 2s. 8d. frame-rent, 8d. for winding, and 4½d. for needles – a total of 3s. 8½d. 'The earnings I get, when I have them on Saturday night, are so small, I have only a pound of meat on the Sunday, and never have a bit more meat all the week. I can scarcely get a bit of dry bread and not anything at all to it. We all of us lie on one bed … ' but there were a great many worse cases in the village. He generally laid out 3 shillings a week in bread at his master's. Often there was no meat on Sunday, certainly not when he was not in full work; and he had been out of work for twelve weeks at a time. Other times he had been in half-work but still had to meet the full outgoings. Sometimes he was docked another shilling because the hose was slack. His children could not help with the family income. The eldest was only five, and though he tried to wind yarn 'he had not the strength or the knowledge'.

He had tried to get an allotment but had failed. Those who had some ground found it a great benefit although it was not always very good land. Few labourers kept a pig: they could not afford to buy one. Many could not even find tile seed to 'set their ground'. What a vast contrast all this is to the labourer's economy under the open-field system, especially in its heyday in the sixteenth and seventeenth centuries! There were no charitable loan societies in 1845 to lend money to labourers for the purpose of buying a pig or seed: 'they would sooner lend you a rope'.

The average earnings of Leicestershire framework-knitters, over and

above their outgoings, were only 4s. 6d. to 5s. 6d. a week: no wonder their
bitterness was so intense. At Wigston we find among them the Dands,
the Herricks, and descendants of several other old peasant families whose
names have recurred as freeholders and copyholders of inheritance
through several centuries. But where was their inheritance now? Old men
of eighty like William Dand still toiled as framework-knitters; children
of ten like Thomas Smith could be solemnly described in the census
schedule as 'agricultural labourer'. A *labourer* of ten was necessary to the
new system. To this pass the peasant village had come in the end. There
had been more respect and rest for old age, more carefree happiness for
small children, more leisure in the open air for all, in the so-called Dark
Ages than in the early years of Queen Victoria's reign.

❧   THE LAST PHASE, 1870-1900   ❧

The village of 1870 still retained superficially much of its rural
character, despite the great economic and social changes that had
taken place in the preceding three generations. No factories had yet
appeared along the streets; the hundreds of framework-knitters still
worked at home or occasionally in a small workshop with a few others.
Since 1801 the population had increased by about 1000: it was now
2638 (in 1871). There had been two decades of fairly rapid growth
up to 1820 or so, despite a high death-rate; stagnation, or very nearly
so, through the 1820's and '30's, and renewed growth in the 1840's
after the coming of the first railway. The 1850's had seen another
slackening; the 1860's a slow growth again. By 1871 there were 600
inhabited houses, as against only 336 seventy years earlier. Houses
had increased proportionately more than people, but they were in
general smaller than before. Up and down the four village-streets,
which enclosed a rectangle of about forty acres, timber-framed and
brick-built farmhouses of the sixteenth, seventeenth and eighteenth
centuries alternated with short terraces of red-brick cottages, erected
by the score in every decade since 1800. But many of the ample old
farmhouses had been razed to the ground in the '50's and '60's to
make room for a terrace of cottages. Every yard of land along the
streets now had a 'site value'. These red-brick terraces had also crept

northwards along the Leicester road for some distance, and, above all, westwards towards the two new railway stations.

The Midland Railway line, linking Derby and Leicester with the London and Birmingham line at Rugby, had been opened in May 1839, and Wigston was given a station on it, a mile to the west of the village. Then, in 1857, the Leicester and Hitchin Railway, linking Leicester with the Great Northern Railway at Hitchin, opened another station a little nearer the village on the same side. Both stations occupied good meadow-land, once known as Hillow Meadow, in the old Goldhill Field. And only a few years before 1870, yet another railway, linking Leicester with Nuneaton and Birmingham, had been opened. Though it had no station in Wigston itself, it was one of three railways which met very near it, so that Wigston found itself by 1870 an important railway junction on the growing Midland system, with rapid and direct communication with London, Birmingham, and Derby.

Besides the monotonous rows of brick cottages in every street, there were a number of substantial houses in and near the village, occupied generally by families of independent means. The Hall, a small mansion in the Gothick style, had been built by Capt. Baddeley about 1833, standing back from Long Street in its own well-treed grounds. Now, in 1870, it was occupied by Col. Mansfield Turner. The Victorian flavour was well developed, with the Misses Bewick at the Cedars, the Misses White at the Elms, and Thomas Burgess, esquire, at the Grange, descendant of the Leicester hosier of George II's time who had bought an estate in Wigston. And Miss Clara Tealby kept a ladies' day school in Long Street, still the most select of the village streets, with its Hall, its handsome Independent Chapel, and its modest late Georgian almshouses endowed by Mrs. Elizabeth Clarke in 1781.

The more utilitarian life of the lower orders was expressed by a National School, built in 1839 for Church of England children, and by the British School, opened some time in the 1840's by various nonconformist gentlemen each of whom paid for the education of several Dissenting school children. The British School occupied a large, grim chapel-like building, erected 'by four spirited individuals' in 1839 as a Mechanics' Institute on the site of the old Quaker burial-ground. The revolt of the working-class, as they had now become labelled, against the unchecked forces of competitive individualism, of narrow grasping middlemen (small masters were generally worse than large) was already taking form. The wage-earner had been left completely unprotected after the dissolution of the old form of society. With all its shortcomings, it had been a *society* of men and women, a true community in which the philanthropic impulse could, and did, find expression in many ways. That had been dissolved away into nothing; nor had the State as yet displayed much interest in the fate of the new class of industrial wage-earners. To begin with, at any rate, they had to learn to throw up their own defences; and by 1870 they had done so to some effect. Besides the Mechanics' Institute, there was a Working Men's Club with a library attached; several Benefit Societies had grown up in the village; and there was an Industrial Co-operative Society (managed by a woman). But the organisation of the hosiery workers into trade unions had not begun: they were still a domestic industry, and remained so until the end of the nineteenth century.

The chapels, too, expressed some of the revolt of the industrialised workers against an established order which offered them nothing more than a bare living in return for working indoors, all day long and every day. For the Church had done little or nothing to lighten the lot of the poor: indeed the very impropriator of the rectory by the 1870's was a hosiery manufacturer Edward Holyoak, who back in the 1830's was employing 100 men, women and boys as out-workers and paying his workers with bread from his own shop, while his son paid his '70 hands' with butcher's meat from *his* shop. Now Edward Holyoak was very nearly the squire of the village, with an estate of 260 acres or so,[1] worth something over five hundred a year in land alone, impropriator of the rectory, living in a large newbuilt Victorian house on the outskirts of the village. Earls of Leicester, Lenton Priory, the Crown, the Dukes of St. Albans, and now a self-made hosiery manufacturer: the succession of impropriators of Wigston rectory summarised a good bit of its social history.

The church was too closely linked with the masters in the nineteenth century; the wage-earners filled the chapels. Non-conformity had grown

---

[1] *Return of Owners of Land in 1873*, under *Leicestershire*.

strong in Wigston all through the Georgian era. The return made to
Parliament in 1829 revealed 520 Independents, 195 Wesleyan Methodists,
105 Primitive Methodists, and 30 General Baptists – a total of 850
nonconformists[1] out of about 2100 inhabitants. In 1676 they had been
about 4 per cent of the total population; by the 1720's about 16 per cent;
and a hundred years later they were fully 40 per cent. Their strength
had continued to increase in the mid-Victorian decades. The Wesleyans
had put up a new chapel in 1839. Two years later the Independents had
rebuilt and enlarged their attractive old Georgian meeting-place (first
built in 1731), and in 1845 the Primitive Methodists blossomed forth in
a new chapel. Here and there in odd corners behind the main streets,
other little sects flourished obscurely, worshipping the Almighty in their
own way in bare brick tabernacles as ugly as their own cottages. So in
1870 the empty Sunday streets would suddenly resound with the loud
defiant singing of the chapels from one end of the village to the other,
while from the parish church came the more subdued murmur of 'the
Conservative Party at prayer'.

There was still much of the air and feeling of a country village about
the place even in 1870. But the generation that followed in the next 30
years saw a complete transformation into an industrialised, wage-earning
township. The census statistics, decade by decade, show the extent of
the change in one way:

1871	2638 people
1881	4299
1891	7013
1901	8506

Between 1871 and 1901 the population more than trebled, and the number
of inhabited houses rose from 600 to 1840.

The hosiery trade expanded during the '70's. The Wigston men ceased to
be middlemen and agents for the Leicester hosiers, and launched out, some
of them, on their own. And the boot and shoe industry – revolutionised
only 20 years before, but still a domestic industry – took root in the village
also. Then, in 1883, a whole new township began to shoot up on the south-

---

[1] *Return of the number of places of Worship not of the Church of England in each parish, etc.* (1829).

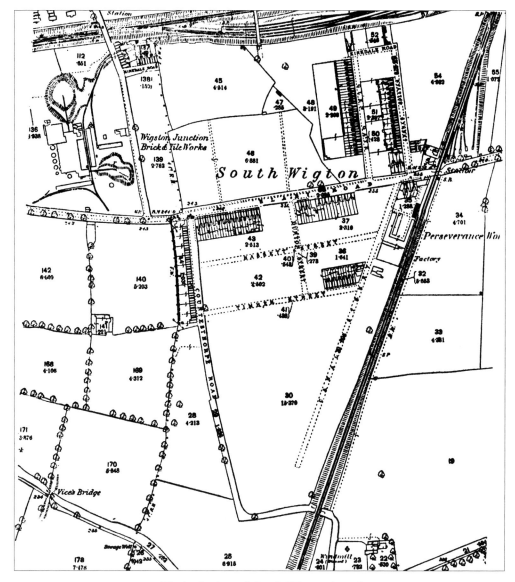

The beginnings of South Wigston (1885)

western edge of the parish beyond the railway stations, where only a few scattered houses had formerly been. This was South Wigston. Within seven years it had six hundred identical brick cottages, a population of 2400, and a Grand Hotel in red and yellow brick.[1]

The meeting of the railways from Birmingham, London, and the North

---

[1] White's *Directory of Leicestershire*, 1890. The earliest houses are dated 1883. Venetia House (now the *Grand Hotel*) came in 1885.

at this point had led to the erection of 'extensive and handsome engine sheds' belonging to the Midland Railway Company, which employed nearly 300 'hands' by 1890; and this in turn led to the almost immediate establishment of three boot and shoe factories, an iron foundry, a large timber-yard, a biscuit factory, and a brick and tile works. One thing led to another: the boot factories brought into being a factory for making elastic web (for those vanished elastic-sided boots of our grandfathers); and the building trade flourished as the township shot up in the fields and helped to create in turn additional employment as it sought new openings elsewhere (See map). Not only were 1200 new houses put up in Wigston itself in these thirty years, but four miles away the town of Leicester was bursting its old bounds and covering hundreds of acres of green fields with brick and slate. The South Wigston Brick and Tile Works helped in this enormous building programme also.

The establishment of the handsome engine-sheds at the Junction had had the same sudden, transforming effect on the entire economy of the township in 1883 as the building of a great abbey church would have had on a small country town in the twelfth or thirteenth century. All the old trades were affected by it, and new trades came in rapidly one after another. Hundreds of new people came in to take up work, and created their own demand for houses and consumption goods of all kinds. The engine-sheds and the railway termini were the Victorian cathedrals; and at South Wigston the new church was naturally built in the same material – cast iron.[1] The whole place was ugly and raw from one end to the other but it pulsed with life and movement. It was one of the minor triumphs of Victorian industrialism, one of its many, unsung odes that are to be found all up and down England.

In 1894 Wigston's new status was formally recognized: it was elevated into an Urban District. But the old ecclesiastical parish was split into two, and nearly 1200 acres on the eastern side, all away from the industrial growth, broke away as the separate civil parish of East Wigston and attached itself to a neighbouring Rural District. This division set the official seal on what had happened to the old village

---

[1] Rebuilt in brick in 1892.

of Wigston: it was now an industrial township and the few remaining farmers wanted nothing to do with it.[1]

In 1901 the total population of the Wigston urban district (excluding the parish of East Wigston) was 8404, of whom 4020 were gainfully employed – 2647 men and boys, and 1373 women and girls. The hosiery industry, as it was now called, employed 969, chiefly women-folk; the boot and shoe industry 726, chiefly men-folk; and the railway was the third largest industry, employing 502 men. Building and construction employed 248; the food, drink, and lodging trades, 194. Farming came sixth, far down the list: 129 earned their living by it – only three per cent of the occupied population. Wigston farming employed only half as many as its building trades, only a quarter as many as those 'on the railway'. The peasant village had been swamped and then submerged completely, and the tide of industrialism rolled on over it unchecked. Fifteen times as many families now lived and got their living off the same area as had done so in the early fourteenth century, at the height of the medieval boom in farming. But a whole culture, a qualitative civilisation, had perished to bring about this quantitative triumph.

[1] It was the opposition of the farmers in the agricultural half of the parish, chiefly their fear of higher rates to pay for urban services they had no use for, that led to this splitting of the old parish.

An Excursus on Peasant Houses and Interiors, 1400-1800

Plan and Evolution, 1400-1642

The village of Wigston Magna lies entirely in the clay country of
the Midlands. No suitable building stone is available for many miles
in any direction. Its peasant houses from a time beyond the memory of
man had been built of mud walls, erected on footings of small round
stones from the Boulder Clay that covers wide tracts of the Midlands.
The frame of the more substantial houses was constructed from local
oak timber, but the smaller houses made use of practically no timber
and relied upon thick mud walls only, such as one sees in some surviving
cottages and barns. One or two of the largest peasant houses in the
village were roofed in the fifteenth century with slates from Swithland,
ten miles the other side of Leicester, but thatch was the roof-covering
for all the rest.

Apart from a solitary lease in the year 1405, which throws a little light
on peasant building at that date, we depend for most of our knowledge
of the peasant houses of Wigston Magna between the fifteenth century
and the early nineteenth upon the probate inventories. The earliest
of these for Wigston is dated 1529, the latest 1802.[1] Between these
two dates about 160 houses are described in sufficient detail (that is,
all the rooms are separately specified) for us to obtain accurate ideas
about the plan and evolution of the peasant house in this village, about
the introduction of new features such as glazed windows, kitchens,
and staircases, and about the growth of household furnishings and
comforts. After the 1730's, however, our knowledge of these houses
is mostly derived from the study of the surviving examples upon the
ground. Of these only two or three examples will be considered here.

---

[1] In effect, inventories which detail each room peter out in the 1730's, but later examples may be
found at long intervals.

283

Our main object is to unearth the plan and contents of houses which have nearly all disappeared from the face of the earth, in Wigston at least, and are no longer available for study.

Though we have sparse documentary evidence about peasant houses in the fifteenth century, and the deserted medieval village sites have not yet yielded up their evidence under this score, there can be little doubt that the great majority of such houses consisted of either one room only, or of two rooms. Almost certainly these were open to the roof in every instance, and where a timber frame was employed it was of the cruck type of construction by this period. Of any earlier type of timber frame we have as yet no evidence from the Midlands. Numerous examples of cruck constructions, however, survive upon the ground. In Leicestershire, rather more than forty examples of cruck-framed buildings have now been discovered, in houses and barns, of which Wigston has one example (much altered in the eighteenth century) in Bullhead Street. On the other hand, the village of Rothley, to the north of Leicester, has no fewer than ten surviving examples of this early type of construction.[1] As to date, the cruck-framed house and barn was well established in the Midlands by the fourteenth century, and was probably being superseded by the post-andpanel type of building from the third quarter of the sixteenth century onwards.

The Wigston lease of 1405 makes it clear that the cruck-framed house with mud walls was the accepted mode of construction for farmhouses at that date. Here the lessee was required 'to make or cause to be made a house upon the said tenement of three pairs of "forkes" within the term of three years' under penalty of twenty shillings.[2] This is a house of two bays of building, having a hall and a private room, the latter being known in Leicestershire as the 'parlour' though invariably used for sleeping. Such two-roomed houses were already not uncommon when the Leicestershire inventories begin, from about 1520 onwards, and must therefore represent a widespread fifteenth-century type.

The one-roomed house is much more difficult to identify in the inventories, for the simple reason that where all household goods are gathered into one room – usually known in Leicestershire as 'the house'

[1] V. R. Webster, 'Cruck-Framed Buildings of Leicestershire', *T.L.A.S.*, xxx (1954), 26-58.
[2] *W.H.R.*, no. 986.

– the makers of the inventory do not need to specify precisely where they lay. On the other hand, some inventories of what are obviously larger houses do not always classify the household goods room by room, and we cannot assume that all houses where the rooms are unspecified consist of one room only. That one-roomed houses existed even in the late sixteenth century and early seventeenth is certain enough from the Wiltshire surveys of 1631–2, which will be considered later, and it is possible to say what proportion of all houses they constituted at that date; but what proportion they constituted at Wigston Magna, or in Leicestershire generally, in the fifteenth and early sixteenth centuries it is difficult to say.

We possess sixteen Wigston inventories for the period 1529–60. Of these nine specify the rooms, and with three exceptions they consist of the standard hall-and-parlour type. Robert Frere's house (1529) also had a 'spence' (probably a buttery), which need not have constituted a separate room but might well have been formed by partitioning off a corner of the hall; and two houses in 1557 had kitchens. Of the houses in which the rooms are not specified, the poverty of the householder and the wording of the record strongly suggest a one-roomed house in two, and perhaps three, instances. The two standard types of peasant house at Wigston in the first half of the sixteenth century are therefore clearly exemplified. There can be little doubt that many of these are survivors from the preceding century and represent the late medieval types.

In the period 1561–1600, for which we have twenty specific inventories, we see very clearly a new, more elaborate, type of house emerging at Wigston. It is not radically different from the older type, and in many instances developed insensibly out of it by additions, and some reconstruction. In perhaps two instances we may well suspect a complete rebuilding, the substitution of a 'modern' house for a late-medieval one.

The principal changes observable in the plan and disposition of the rooms in the forty years after 1560 are:

(1) the greater frequency of kitchens as a third room, added to hall and parlour,
(2) the appearance of upper rooms (invariably called 'chamber'), beginning in the 1560's,
(3) the appearance of glazed windows, first recorded in 1583.

We cannot date innovations such as kitchens or glazed windows or staircases very precisely from the inventories, since they may have been added some years earlier; but when we find them as rare, almost solitary, examples of their kind, we may be fairly sure that they are recent in origin. Thus Richard Pynder's house (1564) is the first at Wigston to record a chamber, an upper room formed by boarding over one of the ground-floor rooms, so giving a loft above. Alice Wheatley's house (1568) had no fewer than five or six ground-floor rooms (hall, parlour, second parlour, kitchen, buttery and spence) and three chambers above. She was the widow of Robert Wheatley, a yeoman-farmer of one yardland, who died about 1562 and whose inventory does not survive. Such a house suggests a complete rebuilding rather than a piecemeal improvement of a smaller and older type, and is more likely to have been built by Robert than by his widow. If so, we may date it as perhaps 1555-60.

At Galby, in east Leicestershire, an upper chamber is first recorded in the inventories of 1559, but does not become common – any more than at Wigston – until the 1570's and 1580's It is possible, indeed likely, that this enlargement of house-space, beginning in the late 1550's, was associated with the change-over from cruck-framed constructions to the post-and-truss frame, which would by its greater use of vertical timbers rather than curved ones heighten the level of the wall-plate and make 'lofting over' a practical proposition.[1]

The addition of a kitchen as a third room involved a modification of the house-plan in many instances. We have to remember in considering the houses of the Midland peasantry that they lay almost without exception – and entirely without exception at Wigston – in villages and not in the open country. Most of them lay on village streets or back-lanes, in nearly all cases on restricted sites. Some presented their front to the street, others presented a gable-end to the street, lying at right-angles to it. Both types of house occupied long, narrow sites, which closely resembled the strip of the open fields in shape. Where a house fronted the street, it tended to occupy the full width of its site except for a narrow path at the side which gave access to the back without going through the house. The addition of a kitchen

[1] For structural details of this change, see Fox and Raglan, *Monmouthshire Houses*, Pt. II, fig. 17 and Pt. III, figs. 34b and 34c.

involved building at right angles to the back of the original house, so converting an original rectangular house into an L-shaped one. The L-shaped farmhouse is one of the commonest plans in the Midlands. It originated almost invariably in this way. Where the original house consisted of two rooms – hall and parlour – the kitchen was naturally built at the back of the hall end of the house, since the parlour was invariably used for sleeping quarters.

Houses which lay at right angles to the village street presented an easier problem when the kitchen came to be added. The parlour end of the house probably lay nearest the street, with the hall beyond it, and presented originally a blank, windowless wall to the street. A kitchen could be added by building on to the house backwards along the croft, and other domestic offices (such as a buttery, a brewhouse, and so forth) could be strung out along the same line as required. This plan meant that the kitchen refuse could be conveniently disposed of in the garden.

There is no evidence in the Wigston inventories, or in the Leicestershire inventories as a whole, for the use of kitchens detached from the main part of the house; nor do the surviving peasant-houses of the fifteenth, sixteenth, and seventeenth centuries show any signs of such separate kitchens. On the other hand, in parts of Southern England such detached kitchens undoubtedly existed in the early seventeenth century, though they were not common. A fine set of surveys of the Wiltshire estates of the first earl of Pembroke and Montgomery, made in 1631-2, gives us details about several hundred houses in some twenty or more villages.[1] Out of 355 houses for which unequivocal information is available, some sixteen had detached kitchens – that is, about one house in every twenty. These separate kitchens are sometimes described as 'out-kitchens' and usually consisted of one room, occasionally of two. Usually the out-kitchen formed an entirely separate little structure, but at Dinton a cowhouse and kitchen were combined to form a separate building, and at Fovant a stable and a kitchen were combined. It is possible that these two examples represent older dwelling-houses of two rooms (medieval in date) which had been replaced by more modern dwellings and relegated

---

[1] *Surveys of the Manors of Philip, first earl of Pembroke and Montgomery, 1631-2*, ed. by Erie Kerridge for the Records Branch of the Wiltshire Archaeological and Natural History Society (Devizes, 1953).

to these humbler uses.[1] In each instance the dwelling-house is described as 'three ground rooms lofted over' which suggests by the completeness of the lofting a new build of late sixteenth- or early seventeenth-century date rather than an older house in process of piecemeal improvement. In some instances, then, a detached kitchen may represent an older dwelling-house, but the problem needs determining by the inspection of surviving examples upon the ground.

Many peasant houses were completely rebuilt during the last generation of the sixteenth century and first forty years or so of the seventeenth, but a great number were medieval and sub-medieval houses which were enlarged and improved over a period of many years. The addition of a kitchen was one such improvement, and the creation of an upper floor by 'chambering over' or 'lofting over' was another. It is possible that the addition of a kitchen ante-dates as a general rule the making of upper chambers, since it did not depend upon any fundamental change in the timber-frame construction.

One finds, in Wigston as in other Leicestershire villages, that the evolution of an upper floor begins with the boarding-over of one of the ground-floor rooms to form a usable space under the roof. In general the parlour is the first room to be boarded or lofted over, since it lay to one end of the house away from the front door. This space was used at first for storage purposes and as sleeping quarters for the children. Some houses remained at this elementary stage for a generation or two, having two or three rooms on the ground-floor but only one boarded over. In a few Wigston houses, however, the hall had also been boarded over by the early years of the seventeenth century. Richard Danne's house (1599) is the first to be recorded as having chambers above both hall and parlour. Simon Brett's house (1600) had chambers above the parlour and kitchen, the hall being still open to the roof. William Johnson's house (1602) had three chambers, but apart from one over the entry their location is not specified. William Langton, miller, had chambers over hall and parlour in 1603. The peasant house with two upper rooms was still uncommon in Wigston before the 1620's. Timber was scarcer in the East Midlands than almost anywhere in England.

---

[1] Ibid. nos. 103, 147. The Wiltshire evidence for detached kitchens confirms what is said in *Monmouthshire Houses*, Pt. III, 115–18.

In better-wooded regions it is probable that complete boarding-over was more common and earlier in date.

The vicarage house is described for us in a terrier of 1606, preserved in the diocesan records at Lincoln. It occupied the same site as the modern vicarage (the terrier makes this perfectly clear) and is described as consisting of three bays 'built all of prickpostes' and covered with thatch. One bay was 'chambered over and boarded', and the whole dwelling was disposed in four rooms, viz. hall, parlour, one chamber, and a nether house. Outside there lay a garden, and an orchard 'hedged and walled about well replenished'.

Prick posts are the smaller posts between the large posts, running from story to story (Innocent, *The Development of English Building Construction*, 113), so that the vicarage was what is loosely called a 'half timbered' house today. We know that the house had not been built in 1518 (when Lenton priory was reprimanded for not having done so), so that the above building probably represents a structure put up about 1520.

The Wiltshire surveys already referred to give us valuable information about the extent to which peasant houses in that county had been 'lofted over' by 1631-2. Out of 355 houses, just over one half (188) had been completely lofted over, though many of these had only one ground-floor room. One house in three (116) was still only partly lofted; and one in every seven (51) was not lofted at all, but consisted only of ground-floor rooms. It is noteworthy that cottages and small farmhouses were still being built in the 1620's with two ground-floor rooms only.[1] Usually farmers occupied houses commensurate with their economic standing, but this was not always so. A conservative farmer of a fifty-four-acre farm at Fovant in Wiltshire occupied a house of only one room lofted over. Both his barn and his hay house were larger than the dwelling house. But a neighbour, farming just under forty acres, had a dwelling house of five ground-floor rooms with one lofted over. One cannot always judge the scale of a man's farming activities by the size of his house in the inventories or, as we shall see, by the number of hearths on which he was assessed in the later years of the seventeenth century.

---

[1] Ibid., no. 109: 'a dwelling house, newly built, of two ground rooms and a garden and orchard.' There are other examples of the same kind.

The Wiltshire surveys show that by the 1630's about half the peasant houses were of a new type, i.e. completely lofted over, and most of them probably represent houses rebuilt or newly built during the preceding generation. The justification for calling them a new type is that they had a complete upper floor, and that this in all probability meant that the cruck-framed house had been superseded by one of the post-and-truss type. We have no similar information for Wigston Magna, but the distribution of the rooms in the inventories suggests that we should have found much the same kind of house-type there. Certainly the new type of house, completely lofted over as far as one can tell, is well in evidence by 1640 at Wigston.

There remains a constructional problem to be touched upon, and that is the appearance of a fixed staircase. The Wiltshire surveys throw no light on this development, and the inventories only do so incidentally when they refer to 'the room under the stairs' or 'the Chamber next the stairs'. It is quite certain that when upper rooms were first constructed the only access to them was by means of a ladder placed against the edge of the boarded floor. Where a house was completely lofted over, an opening was left (perhaps against the back wall, out of the way) through which a ladder, fixed or movable, could be inserted. Only one Wigston inventory specifically mentions this mode of access. Robert Smith's house in 1637 had 'a little ladder to go up by into the chamber'; but the arrangement was so commonplace that there was generally no need to mention it, any more than the inventories vouchsafe information about the sanitary arrangements at any period (except occasionally in town houses).

To digress for a moment on this important subject, Tusser alone throws light upon a dark place. Among the tasks in November he says:

Foul privies are now to be cleansed and fy'd [purged]
Let night be appointed such baggage to hide
Which buried in garden, in trenches a-low
Shall make very many things better to grow …

The peasant economy, as we have remarked before, made use of everything down to the very humblest materials.

The first house in Wigston in which stairs are recorded is that of Robert Brabson, yeoman, in 1642. This was a substantial house of five ground-floor rooms and four chambers above, besides a cellar, and it certainly represents the new type of peasant building, for no cruck-framed house could have offered this accommodation. It is noteworthy that this house had three hearths in 1670, probably in the hall, the kitchen, and the 'new parlour'. More will be said of fireplaces later.

The inventories suggest, not only at Wigston but elsewhere also, that permanent stairs were very rare in farmhouses before 1650, and indeed did not become common until the eighteenth century. The Bedfordshire inventories of 1617-20 contain no mention of stairs in any house, and in the inventories of two Essex parishes we do not find stairs recorded until 1673. At Galby in east Leicestershire they are first recorded in 1669.[1] We cannot attach too much importance to the exact years, since they depend upon the accidental date of a man's death, but it is evident that stairs were rare in rural houses, even of the yeoman class, before 1650.

Another notable improvement in domestic comfort was the glazing of windows. The first house in Wigston to be recorded as having glazed windows was that of John Browne, yeoman, in 1583. The next reference is to another yeoman house, that of Robert Freer in 1594. But the house of William Lawe, gentleman, in 1603 had no glass in its windows, and it seems likely that glazed windows remained rare in the village until the second half of the seventeenth century. We cannot be certain about this as glass windows ceased to be regarded as a piece of movable property when they became commoner, and therefore ceased to be recorded in the inventories. William Langton, miller, had glass in his hall windows in 1603, but in no other rooms, and possibly other householders were similarly sparing with the new amenity.

By the 1630's the peasant houses of Wigston were noticeably larger than they had been in the 1550's before the revolution in housing. Down to 1560, as we have seen, the only types were the one-roomed house and the two-roomed house. In a few rare cases a kitchen had been added as a third room in the middle of the century. Only two kitchens

---

[1] *Jacobean Household Inventories*, ed. by F.G. Emmison for the Bedfordshire Historical Record Society, xx (1938); *Farm and Cottage Inventories of Mid-Essex*, 1635-1749, ed. by F. W. Steer for the Essex County Council (Colchester, 1950). Stairs are first recorded in a yeoman's house at Writtle in mid-Essex in 1673. At Galby in east Leicestershire they are similarly recorded in a yeoman's house (see *Essays in Leicestershire History*, 62).

are recorded at Wigston before 1565, out of sixteen houses of which we have a record.

For the twenty years or so between 1621 and 1642 we have details of no fewer than forty-one houses in Wigston, a very full sample at a time when there were probably about 120 houses in the village. One or two houses may enter twice into this sample but it is still large enough to be fully representative. If we analyse these houses according to the number of rooms in each,[1] we get this result:

No. of rooms	No. of houses
1	2
2	4
3	9
4	6
5	3
6	4
7	7
8	2
9	3
10	1
1 to 10 rooms	41 houses

By the 1620's and 1630's the two original types of peasant house formed a very small proportion of the total – only six out of forty-one. It is likely that the inventories do not reflect the true proportion of one-roomed houses, since the poorer householders generally left no record. But the Wiltshire surveys, which are not open to this objection, reveal only fourteen one-roomed houses out of a total of 355 in 1631-2, or four per cent. The Wigston sample shows about five per cent of one-roomed houses round about the same date. Barley's sample of Lincolnshire farmhouses and cottages in 1635 shows that one-roomed houses constituted nine out of seventy-three for which the rooms are specified, or about one house in every eight. The proportion of Lincolnshire houses with two rooms

---

[1] By 'rooms' I mean rooms devoted primarily to the purposes of living. This includes, for example, kitchens and butteries, but not brewhouses, milkhouses, dairies, shops, and farm buildings generally.

or less was as high as one in three (24 out of 73).[1] In a sample of 136 Wiltshire houses about the same date, the one- and two-roomed houses numbered only nine per cent of the total, and at Wigston they numbered fifteen per cent. Even allowing for the deficiencies of the records, the differences in housing standards between Lincolnshire, Leicestershire, and Wiltshire in the 1630's must reflect real and important differences in economic and cultural standards.

At Wigston rather more than one-third of the peasant houses had one to three rooms. Slightly fewer than a third had four to six rooms, and slightly fewer than a third had more than six rooms by the 1630's. A general revolution in housing had taken place since the 1570's, with the consequence that by 1630 some two-thirds of the village houses were considerably larger than those of one or two generations earlier.

Whatever the size of the peasant house it almost invariably conformed to a fixed plan. The one-roomed house contained a hall only, the two-roomed house a hall and parlour. The three-roomed house (the largest single group), was almost without exception a two-bayed house with a hall, a parlour, and a chamber over the parlour.

The four-roomed houses showed a slight variation. Some consisted of a hall, parlour, kitchen (or buttery) on the ground floor, with one room lofted over to form a chamber; others consisted of a hall and parlour with a chamber above each. It is possible perhaps to distinguish two different dates for the houses, the first type being an older house in process of creating an upper floor, the second perhaps a new building with the two lower rooms chambered over from the beginning.

The five-roomed houses were arrived at by chambering over two of the three lower rooms, and the six-roomed house was often a simple plan of three rooms below (hall, parlour, kitchen) and a chamber over each – again very possibly a newly-built type with a continuous first floor instead of piecemeal boarding. Henry White's house (1638) was of this type, but William Ragge (1623) and John Danne (1637) had four lower rooms and two upper.

John Danne's house had a feature that was now to be found in most of the larger houses, and that was two parlours. These are found in practically all the seven-, eight-, and nine-roomed houses. They usually

[1] M.W. Barley, 'Farmhouses and Cottages, 1550-1725,' *Ec.H.R.*, Second Series, vii, no. 3 (1955).

formed a wing or block at one end of the house, with one parlour at the front ('next the street') and the other behind it ('next the orchard' or 'next the garden'). These rooms were still used as bedrooms, but they indicate a further degree of differentiation among the rooms of the house and an increasing development of privacy for the family.

Besides the appearance of two parlours in the place of one, the greater number of rooms in the 7- to 10-roomed group arose from the multiplication of bedrooms. Two of the three nine-roomed houses (Richard Watts 1641, and Robert Brabson 1642) consisted of hall, two parlours, kitchen, buttery, and four chambers above. The other house had only one parlour, and five chambers above.[1]

The largest house in Wigston of the peasant class was that of Robert Freer the elder, who died in 1625. This contained the usual hall, kitchen and buttery, with no fewer than three parlours, and four chambers above – ten rooms in all. The 'middle parlor' contained nothing but wool, the best parlour was still the principal bedroom, and, apart from one room where the farm-servants slept, the chambers on the first floor were entirely used for the storage of malt, pease, and cheese.

The rectory farm occupied by William Lawe, gent., from the 1580's until his death early in 1603, was the largest house in the village and one in which we might expect to find the earliest innovations, since there was no resident squire. In 1603 this house consisted of the hall, the dining parlour (something unheard-of in any other house), the little parlour, 'the seeld parlour', the men's parlour, larder and buttery, and the kitchen-probably some seven ground-floor rooms. Above were seven chambers, some used as bedrooms, and some for storage. Altogether there were fourteen rooms in the house proper. The domestic offices were exceptionally numerous: brewhouse, dairy house, cheese chamber, bakehouse, and malthouse, the whole furnishing a good picture of a large and well-appointed farmhouse of the Elizabethan period. In 1670 'the parsonage house' was taxed on five hearths. This was of course the rectory farm, and not the humbler vicarage which lay next door and which was still unaltered from its original early sixteenth-century plan.

---

[1] In Lincolnshire in 1635 the largest peasant houses (7 rooms and over) constituted only one in nine of all houses of which the rooms are listed; at Wigston about one in three.

∾ PEASANT INTERIORS, 1500-1642 ∾

The earliest Wigston inventory, that of Robert Frere (1529), shows us the interior of a two-roomed house of the late medieval type to which a 'spence' had been added. This was either a partitioned corner of the hall or an outshot or lean-to at the back of the hall. The furnishings and household goods were meagre in the extreme. Even so, the house contained material objects not possessed by most other houses in the village, such as chairs, a painted cloth as a wall-covering, and some cushions.

The hall contained a table and three forms, four chairs, a cupboard and a screen, four little stools with cushions for each, the painted cloth, two shelves, and some fire-irons. A pen for capons seems to have stood in the hall-a homely medieval touch. In the parlour stood a bedstead and form, a painted cloth hung upon the wall, and on the bed lay an old mattress and a blanket. A coffer completed this bare scene. Some old clothes (jackets, hose, leather doublets, and bonnets), some russet cloth, and some hemp and hemp yarn were also kept in this room. In the spence or buttery were kept the pewter, the brass pots and pans, and the sheets, tablecloths, and so forth. There were also three flitches of bacon, some tubs and vats, and a few carpenter's tools.

Robert Frere's household goods were valued altogether at 24s. 4d. Other inventories made down to 1560 give a range for household goods from 13s. 4d. to £7 9s. 8d. Generally the household goods constituted ten to fifteen per cent of the total inventory by value. Occasionally we have the inventory of a retired farmer, living in his parlour in the ancestral farmstead, and owning only a few pots and pans and some bedding, so far as his household goods are concerned. Such is the case with Thomas Reddeley (1564) who died possessed of two old cows, two coverlets, a pot and a pan, but 'in money' left the considerable sum of £25 6s. 8d.

The most comfortably furnished house in the first half of the century was that of William Astill, yeoman, who died in the autumn of 1554. In the hall were bed hangings and painted cloths, cushions, half a dozen silver spoons; tables, chairs, forms and a cupboard, coffers and spinning-wheels; pewter pots, pans and dishes; and the usual irons in the hearth. In the parlour were two feather beds (an innovation for peasant households) and much good bedding including twenty pairs of sheets (ten of flax, and

ten of hemp and 'harden'). Here the furniture and furnishings totalled
£7 9s. 8d. in value, about one-seventh of the total personal estate. The
hundred sheep on the farm were worth more than all the household
goods together.

Alice Wheatley's house (1568), with its six lower rooms and three
chambers above, was the forerunner of the larger peasant houses that
became common by the middle of the seventeenth century, but its
furnishings were still meagre and showed nothing exceptional for the
period. Their total value was under four pounds and the most valuable
single item was the array of brass pots and pans in the kitchen. It is
possible, however, that this meagre furnishing in a largeish house may
be simply her widow's share of the whole contents, the rest of which
belonged to the eldest son and his wife. But Alice Wheatley, though a
widow, had not retired to her parlour. The inventory shows that she was
a working farmer at the time of her death, with about fifteen acres under
crops, twenty-five sheep, and a few cattle and horses.

By the closing years of the sixteenth century the standard of household
furnishings and comforts of life had very markedly improved among all
classes of the peasant community, in keeping with the general increase
in the size of most village houses. Whereas the household goods of the
average farmer of forty or fifty years earlier had been valued at between
two and four pounds in all, they were now generally appraised at ten to
twenty pounds or more, a five-fold increase in value. A good deal of this
increase is attributable to the general rise of prices in the intervening
period, but the greater variety of household furniture and equipment of
all kinds, the greater numbers of most articles of household use, and the
marked increase in the value of household goods as a proportion of the
total estate, all point to the fact that the real standard of living had risen
among all classes for whom records survive. Whereas household goods
had once averaged ten to fifteen per cent of the total personal estate,
they now amounted to between twenty and forty per cent of the total.
Taking all the evidence into consideration, we may say conservatively
that the material standard of living, measured by the size of houses
and the variety and quantity of their contents, doubled between the
middle of the sixteenth century and the end. It seems certain that the
labouring class shared to some extent, at least, in this increased standard

of living, for such inventories of cottagers as we possess for the late sixteenth century and the early seventeenth show a comparable increase in their household goods also, as compared with the cold poverty of their grandfathers' cottages.

As an example of the great improvement in living conditions, we may compare the house of Robert Freer in 1594 with that of his ancestor already described. The house of 1529 had only two rooms, with a small buttery or spence added. The house of 1594 had seven rooms – the hall, 'lodging parlour' and 'other parlour', kitchen and buttery, a room 'over the entry' and an upper chamber. The furnishings were:

Hall:	two tables, two benches, two forms, one cupboard, three chairs, two stools, shelves, six cushions, the painted cloths, 'the glasse of the 2 wyndowes in the haule with the falinge doere wyndowe', a large collection of pewter, brass, and other ware, the irons about the hearth, some wooden ware, and 'the boerds trasinges & ioyce tree over the haule'. The pen for capons had long been banished from the hall, but '3 reeves of onions' hung there instead, beside the lantern.
Kitchen:	a pair of querns, tubs, oats, and troughs, boards, pails, and other small ware.
Over the entry:	boards and other wood, scythes, draw-rakes with axle-trees, plough-timber, and other implements.
His lodging parlour:	two bedsteads with hangings, feather bed and bedding, a press and a cupboard, 'a watche byll', pitchfork, and staves.
Other parlour:	bedstead and bedding, two coffers, and 'all the butter and cheese in the house'.
Buttery:	two coules (large wooden tubs), barrels, a garner, salting-trough, a woollen wheel, and two loads of coal.
The Chamber:	a bedstead, old iron and an old saddle, some wood, and a 'wyndowe clooth'.

The glass in the hall windows was still a sophisticated rarity for Wigston, and the feather-bed and hangings nearly so. The various rooms are clearly differentiated in their functions, but there were still traces of the relatively primitive living of medieval times in the strings of onions hanging in the principal living room, the pitchfork in the best bedroom, the butter and cheese in the other, and the general mixture of sleeping and storage accommodation elsewhere.

In Robert Freer's house the furniture and furnishings accounted for twenty-one per cent of the total personal estate. In that of Robert Coulson (1596), a much smaller farmer, they account for fully forty per cent. This was a four-roomed house (hall, parlour, spence, and 'far parlour') and contained nothing markedly different from the other. There was simply less of everything, no feather-beds or cushions, and no glass in the windows. The five-roomed house of Richard Danne (1599) was furnished in much the same manner as Robert Coulson's, but here the household goods amounted to twenty-five per cent of the total. In the house of William Langton, miller (1603), the household goods were valued in all at £24 and accounted for thirty-seven per cent of the total personal estate. This was a nine-roomed house, with a hall, three parlours, kitchen, buttery, and spence on the ground floor, and chambers above hall and parlour. The miller's house was furnished in much the same manner and degree as Robert Freer's, with glass in the hall windows and nowhere else, and showed the same confusion of bedsteads and stores of oatmeal, bacon, and cheese.

As an example of a cottage interior, there is the two-roomed house of John Winter, labourer, in 1603. It consisted of a hall and a parlour, and a loft over the entry, and the household goods amounted to thirty-five per cent of the total inventory. There was, indeed, greater comfort in his cottage than there had been in most farmhouses seventy years earlier, as witness the furnishings that are specified. In the hall stood a little framed table, a great chest, a little table, a chair, a cheese press, a cupboard, with forms, benches, stools, hangings, 'and all other small implements'. The parlour contained two bedsteads and bedding, three coffers, and a quantity of linen and hempen sheets, napkins and towels.

In the larger yeoman houses other innovations made their appearance – chamber pots, warming pans, here and there a carpet (as a table covering), and 'joined furniture' instead of roughly carpentered furniture. But even in the 1630's the upper rooms were still used largely for storage. Robert Brabson's house in 1642 (of nine rooms) had considerable quantities of peas and barley in the chamber above the stairs, a great deal of cheese, oatmeal, and butter in the chamber over the hall, wool in 'the Gallery Chamber', and 'divers Implements for husbandry' in the chamber over the kitchen.

✎ Plan and Structural Changes, 1650-1800 ✎

The hearth-tax assessment of 1670 is a useful guide to the variety of house-sizes in the Midland village at a given point of time. The assessments for 1662 and 1664 differ slightly in details, as we might expect, but that for 1670 is the most informative, since it gives a list of those exempted from the tax on the score of poverty. At Wigston Magna, 114 householders were taxed and 47 exempted, a total of 161. In a village (though not necessarily in a town) we may assume that each householder represents a separate house.

Out of the 161 houses, no fewer than 120 had one hearth only: that is, three houses in every four. Twenty-five houses had two hearths, and only 16 had more than two. Of these sixteen larger houses, nine had three hearths, two had four, and five had five hearths. The 4- and 5-hearth houses were occupied by Randle Boulter, Deliverance Freer, Mr. John Horsepool, Thomas Noone, Mr. Francis Smith, Mr. John Pochin, and Mr. Thomas Mawson at the parsonage or rectory farm.

It would be a mistake to equate all the one-hearth houses with cottages, the homes of a rural proletariat. We might assume this from the forty-seven who were exempted from the tax, but even here at least nineteen were widows, some of them of good peasant standing, and some were old men of good stock ending their days in decent quiet. They cannot be described as a proletariat or as paupers. Among the one-hearth houses that were taxed, several were the houses of small or middling farmers, or of craftsmen or tradesmen. James Thornton's house – he was a tailor – had hall, parlour, and kitchen, but only one hearth. John Pallet had only a hall and parlour, and Thomas Vann (labourer) the same. The houses of James West and Walter Simons had a hall, a parlour, and an upper room. William Homes (labourer) had a four-roomed house: hall, parlour, buttery, and chamber. The one-hearth house generally denoted a two-roomed house, but sometimes it was a house of three rooms and occasionally still larger. At Wigston such a dwelling housed three-quarters of the population.

Among the two-hearth houses which can be certainly identified in the inventories that of William Johnson had six rooms, and those of John Vann and Thomas Walker had six and five rooms respectively. Peter Ragg's house had four rooms and Richard Mould's had five. All were described as yeomen in their wills, and other records, and were men well above the average standing. The vicarage at Wigston had hearths and six rooms, and the house of Robert Bruin, butcher, had two hearths and seven rooms. Of the three-hearth houses, only three can be identified. That of William Abbot the elder had seven rooms; that of Francis Smith, gentleman, had eight, William Brabson's house had nine rooms. The seven-roomed house of Thomas Noone, yeoman, had four hearths. Two five-hearth houses, the homes of Thomas Mawson, gent., and John Horsepool gent., had nine and seven rooms respectively.

The number of hearths cannot be related to the number of rooms except in a rough and ready way. If we may generalise, a one-hearth house usually implied two or three rooms; a two-hearth house five or six rooms; three or four hearths imply seven to nine rooms. Above four hearths there is no definite relationship: at this level a man might have more fireplaces installed without necessarily enlarging his house.

Turning now to the inventories, we may take a sample of fifty-five houses in the period 1675-1725 in order to see what changes, if any, had taken place in size and plan since 1621-42. The distribution of houses is as follows:

No. of rooms	No. of houses
1	1
2	15
3	13
4	9
5	3
6	5
7	4
8	1
9	3
10	0
over 10	1
	—————
	55 houses

The most notable change between the earlier period and the later is the increase in the proportion of smaller houses in the village, above all in two-roomed houses. Houses of one to three rooms constituted 53 per cent of the total in 1675-1725, as against 37 per cent in the early part of the seventeenth century. Houses of four to six rooms formed the same proportion in both periods (31 to 32 per cent); but houses of more than six rooms fell from 32 per cent of the total in the earlier period to 16 per cent in the later.

At first sight this is an unexpected change. Remembering the Housing Revolution of the earlier period (1570-1640), with its remarkable increase in the number of rooms in peasant dwellings, one might have assumed that this trend towards larger houses would have continued. But it did not. The trend was apparently reversed, for the number of smaller houses increased sharply by the end of the seventeenth century.[1] It might be assumed that this is the result of the spreading habit of making wills, so that the inventories include a higher proportion of poorer people than before. There is, however, no marked evidence of this at Wigston, judging by the status and occupations given in the inventories, though it probably operated to some extent. The major factor in this change is the accelerating growth of the labouring class at Wigston during the latter half of the seventeenth century and the early eighteenth, a social change which has already been discussed. For this class, recruited both from within the village and from outside it, a great deal of cottage-building became necessary during this period. These cottages were built almost invariably with two ground-floor rooms only – the medieval hall-and-parlour type. In some there was a boarded chamber over one room for storage and the children's beds. From this it is clear that stairs to the upper floor were still a great rarity in the village even in the early eighteenth century.

At the other end of the social scale there was a fall in the number of the larger houses. This is mainly a relative change, which we might expect with the considerable increase in the size of the village, for the well-to-do houses would not increase in number as quickly as those of the poor. But there had been thirteen houses of over six rooms in 1621-42, and there were only nine in 1675-1725 though the sample is appreciably larger. The number of nine- and ten-roomed houses remains the same in

---

[1] Only 11 of the 55 inventories fall after 1700 in date.

each period (four in each), and there seems to be no fall in the numbers of this social class, who are mostly described as 'gentleman' in this later period. What is also noticeable is that the more well-to-do houses in the village grew no larger in the years down to 1725. A house of nine or ten rooms must have represented the optimum size for the big yeomen or the small gentry from about 1600 onwards.

It follows also that in this later period there were no significant changes in house-plans. There remained the basic rectangular type of two ground-rooms or more; the L-plan formed by building at right angles to the hall and parlour block; and the T-plan which seems to derive from the building of two parlours, at the head, so to speak, of the hall block. The only important change one can detect in later years is the building of a regular third or attic floor in the larger farmhouses, with a symmetrical row of windows beneath the eaves, an enlargement which in Wigston and elsewhere in Leicestershire makes its appearance about the middle of the eighteenth century.

Two important changes were made in building materials in the late seventeenth century and the early eighteenth. One was the use of bricks for vernacular building as distinct from country-houses in which brickwork had been known since the fifteenth century; and the other was the greatly increased use of Swithland slates for roofing farmhouses and cottages.

The earliest brickwork in Leicestershire farmhouses and cottages dates from the 1680's. Only a few examples from this decade survive, but from the 1690's and early 1700's there are scores. After a tentative beginning, the use of bricks spread rapidly in the villages in the closing years of the seventeenth century. Often the brick farmhouses and cottages were entirely new buildings, but sometimes peasant buildings of a much earlier period, having a cruck-framed construction, were rebuilt in brick so that the crucks were either partly or wholly concealed.

At Wigston, John Pochin built himself a new farmhouse in brick in the year 1691, in Newgate End near the parish church. This is the oldest surviving brick building in the village, and was probably the second brick house to be erected in Wigston.[1] It stands upon rubble

---

[1] The vicarage house was either rebuilt or substantially enlarged in brick in the 1680's. The living was sequestrated at the time and the sequestrators' accounts have survived (LRO, I.D. 41/31). In 1684, 1000 bricks with carriage cost 18s. A few months later 2000 bricks cost 26s. 8d., plus carriage at 2s. 6d. a load. In 1685 William Coltman was paid 18s. for making iron casements for the house. This building does not, however, survive.

foundations, probably those of an older house, for Newgate End is a medieval street and a farmhouse had probably stood here since the late thirteenth century. The house of 1691 still stands more or less intact, so that its original plan and lay-out may be ascertained without much difficulty. It is a plain rectangular house with a chimneystack at either end. Considerable alterations have been made internally, mainly the insertion of later partitions, windows have been blocked and the front doorway altered, and the pitch of the roof lowered. All these changes were made about the year 1800, possibly a little earlier.

The plan of the original house of 1691 is shown on page 213. The front door opened apparently into a large squarish hall from which the staircase ascended. The original staircase of 1691 remains *in situ*. To the left of the central hall lay the kitchen with a large open fireplace; to the right lay the living-room or parlour, with a cellar underneath. The stairs rose in the centre of the house to a landing off which the three principal bedrooms opened. It is possible that the landing also served as a bedroom for children, though this unsophisticated arrangement may have been abandoned in a house of this type. The two large bedrooms had fireplaces corresponding to those in the kitchen and parlour below. On the second floor, also reached by a stair, were three more bedrooms, probably for servants and children, lit by small windows under the eaves. This floor appears to be an addition to the original house, made about 1800, an addition which involved raising the front and back walls by several courses of brickwork, and the making of a new roof.[1]

This yeoman house of 1691 therefore consisted in its original state of six or possibly seven rooms (counting the entrance hall as a separate room, but not the cellar) and had four hearths. It seems to be the house described in the inventory of John Pochin (son of the builder) in 1731. The inventory is not as detailed as those of earlier decades, but it mentions 'the best parlour' and the kitchen, with the cellar underneath the parlour. On the first floor lay 'the best chamber' (over the parlour)

---

[1] The Rectory Farm, rebuilt in the first quarter of the eighteenth century, has a similar ground- and first-floor plan to John Pochin's house of 1691. But it also had an attic with two large bedrooms, one of which had a plaster floor. It is the earliest of the three-floored houses in the village.

and 'the kitchen chamber' (i.e. the bedroom over the kitchen), and 'the little chamber' over the entrance hall. No other rooms are mentioned, which confirms that the second floor with its three smaller bedrooms was a later addition and not a reconstruction of an earlier attic floor.

The Pochin house was a complete rebuilding in brick, but often the original timber frame was retained when an old house was reconstructed. The ancient mud walls were simply knocked out and replaced by brickwork. But there is reason to believe that in the early period of brickbuilding a timber frame might sometimes be erected anew as for a mudwalled house. A timber-framed brick house dated 1712 survives at Husbands Bosworth, a few miles to the south of Wigston, and inspection suggests that the frame was made to take a 2¼-inch brick filling. Where necessary the timber is cut against the grain in order to fit.[1] How long this wasteful mode of construction persisted is not known; the Husbands Bosworth house is possibly a late example.

Although brick came increasingly into use during the first half of the eighteenth century, much building in the traditional mud continued in those parts where the local clay was especially suitable. Many cheap cottages must have been put up with mud walls, a minimum of timber, and a thatched roof even during the early nineteenth century, especially in the remoter villages where suitable brick-earth was not easily available.

At Wigston brick-earth was found in the village itself, and brick cottages must have been commoner here than in the lonelier villages in the upland country to the south. M.W. Barley considers that 'until after 1775 a brick house in an East Midland village was a rarity', and this was perhaps generally true. But in certain villages, as in those immediately north and south of Leicester, there are considerable numbers of brick houses dating from the 1690's onwards. These are probably the result of the enterprise of local brick-makers in villages that were growing rapidly in population following the spread of framework-knitting.

Similarly, it is difficult to generalise about the spread of Swithland slates as a roofing material. A great number of eighteenth-century farmhouses, early and late, are roofed today with these slates, and the

---

[1] Mr. V.R. Webster, in a letter.

roofs appear to be original and not replacements of thatch. The use of these slates spread steadily, for many purposes besides roofing, during the early eighteenth century, long before the Midland canals of the 1790's carried them cheaply and still more widely. The slates must have been carried by road from the quarries to the north of Leicester, and were certainly reaching south Leicestershire, miles beyond Wigston, by the first decade of the century.[1] By the later decades of the century, many brick-built cottages were being roofed with slates instead of the traditional thatch.

In the second half of the eighteenth century brick-built houses of considerable size and some pretensions made their appearance in Wigston. There was by now a not inconsiderable class of village 'gentry' – the Noones, Horsepools, Pochins, and Davenports, among others – and for the first time they began to build dwelling-houses of an urban kind, which can no longer be considered as peasant or vernacular building. John Pochin's farmhouse of 1691 was still in the rural tradition, despite some traces of sophistication; but the three-storey brick houses are clearly in a different tradition (see plan on page 243).

The three-storied house in Bushloe End was built by Samuel Davenport in 1752, as appears by the inscription on a tie-beam in the stables. It was constructed throughout of brick, with string-courses between each floor, and roofed with Swithland slates. The front door was symmetrically placed in the middle of the facade and opened into a small 'hall' which represented the final stage in the evolution of the hall in small houses: that is, it had become little more than a wide passage from which the stairs ascended to the first floor. It led through the house into a rear courtyard where lay the coach-house and stables. A covered side-passage gave independent access to the kitchen and back quarters of the dwelling-house.

On the ground floor were four rooms, those on either side of the front door being the dining-room and the drawing-room. The kitchen and the parlour lay behind these rooms. The remainder of the plan was simple. On the first floor were four bedrooms, two on either side of a central landing, with a loft over the coach-house which was presumably

[1] Swithland slate headstones in country churchyards give one precise dates for the spread of this slate as a roofing material also. See Herbert, 'Swithland Slate Headstones,' T.L.A.S., xxii, 211-40.

used as a box-room. On the second floor were four small bedrooms for servants and children. The building of this house represented a complete break with the peasant tradition. Its plan shows little or nothing of this tradition: it is virtually a small town-house, copied from Leicester four miles away.

In Newgate End stands another house of the same period and social background. This also was an entirely new building in brick, rising to three stories, the topmost bedrooms having flat ceilings and not the low sloping ceilings to be found on an attic floor, as for example in the Rectory Farm built some fifty years earlier. It was built by the senior branch of the Pochin family in Wigston, almost certainly by the Armston Pochin who was farming four yardlands in 1765. Since the Pochins had acquired a share in the manorial rights (all that was left of the dismembered manor) the new house became known as the Manor House, and is still known by this name.

The house of Armston Pochin was slightly different from that of Samuel Davenport. The front door is again symmetrically placed in the centre of the facade, but it opens into a large hall with only one room on either side – a dining-room and a drawing-room. There is no trace of the original kitchen but it almost certainly lay behind the dining-room and formed an L-shaped house, now disguised by considerable structural changes made about 50-60 years ago. On the first floor were two large bedrooms, and on the second two others. Three of these four bedrooms have their original plaster floors. There were probably bedrooms over the altered kitchen block, so that we do not know the size of the original house. Nevertheless, enough of it stands unaltered to show that, like Samuel Davenport's house, the urban tradition had penetrated into Wigston and the peasant tradition of building was dying fairly rapidly during the second half of the eighteenth century, precisely indeed when the whole peasant economy was being blasted by the enclosure of the open fields and by the climax of the other secular changes which have been traced in earlier chapters.

Even more sophisticated houses were built in the village during the first half of the nineteenth century, such as the stuccoed Gothick of Wigston Hall built by a Captain Baddeley in Long Street about 1833. Wigston had never possessed a squire or a Hall, and it fell to an army captain to provide the semblance at this late date. Such buildings as this, and the mass of nineteenth-century cottage building, deserve to be studied separately. Wigston was industrialised during the nineteenth century and terraces of four-roomed red-brick cottages ('two up and two down') with the attendant small brick-built factory, are now the characteristic grouping. Most of the surviving houses of the peasant community perished in the late nineteenth century with the erection of these cottages and factories. The 'gentry' disappeared from the village, though here and there their houses remain, usually a little battered and gaunt. The Davenport house has become the British Legion Club; Wigston Hall became a small factory during the war of 1939-45. But even in such a village as Wigston, so early industrialised and so near a large city, there remain domestic buildings of every century from the sixteenth onwards which call for detailed study on the spot in order to marry them with the documentary history outlined in this chapter.

✎ PEASANT INTERIORS, 1675-1725 ✎

Much of what has been said about the house-interiors of the early seventeenth century applies without qualification to those of the end of the century and of the early eighteenth. Old house-types persisted in great numbers in the village after the great reconstruction of 1570-1640, and their interiors, too, remained practically unchanged. In the half-dozen largest houses of the village there is a slow sophistication. Looking-glasses, for example, make their first appearance in the house of Francis Smith, gent. in 1677, and he seems to have been the first to keep a maid-servant also. Looking-glasses remained rare: they are not recorded again until 1706, in the house of John Noone, gent. Another piece of sophistication is the dining-room of George Davenport, yeoman, recorded in 1713, the first to be recorded in the village since William Lawe's dining-parlour in 1603. Yet otherwise his inventory contains little or nothing that would not have been found a hundred years earlier in a house of similar standing, beyond a chest of drawers and some cane chairs. Doubtless all the furniture was better made, and there was more of it; but the great bulk of his personal estate lay in his farm goods. His household goods were valued at £52 out of a total personal estate of just under £800 – only 6½ per cent – a far smaller proportion than that in a Tudor household. The earlier trend towards an elaboration of domestic furnishings and comforts had apparently been reversed. Comfort had indeed increased in yeoman farmhouses, but the scale of farming had enlarged still more.

At the other end of the scale are the cottages of William Squire (1678) and William Sutton the elder (1708). The former consisted of hall, parlour, and chamber. In the hall stood a table, a cupboard, two chairs, 'and some small Implements'. In the parlour stood a bedstead, two coffers, and two little boxes. In the chamber, which was probably only a loft over the parlour, stood a chest, two 'wheels', and other implements. A pair of sheets and a pair of blankets constituted all the bedding; and some brass and pewter, a tub and *a peale*, completed the cottage interior. His furniture and other household goods were valued in all at less than forty-five shillings. His two cows were worth twice as much as all his household goods put together. William Sutton's cottage was precisely the same in furnishings, which were valued at forty-six shillings in all.

There are ten inventories for the first decade of the eighteenth century and the houses they describe may be taken as an epitome of those that were standing in the village at that date. Their rooms are described as follows:

William Jacombe (1700) : hall, parlour, kitchen, chamber
(4 rooms)

Richard Meadows (1700) : hall, parlour, new parlour, long parlour, far chamber, chamber over hall, chamber over long parlour
(7 rooms)

William Freer senior (1704) : hall, parlour (2 rooms)

John Lawe (1706) : hall, parlour, buttery, kitchen, chambers over hall and parlour (6 rooms)

John Noone, gent. (1706) : hall, parlour, kitchen, pantry and little pantry, chambers over parlour, kitchen and porch; corn chamber (9 rooms)

Francis Smith (1707) : hall, great parlour, kitchen, buttery, little parlour, best chamber, road chamber, cheese chamber, corn chamber
(9 rooms)

William Sutton the elder (1708) : hall (house), parlour   (2 rooms)

Isaac Freer (1708)   : hall, parlour, kitchen, chamber

                                                                                    (4 rooms)

George Boulter (1708)   : hall (house), parlour, chamber over

                                               hall   (3 rooms)

William Pawley (1709)   : hall (house), parlour   (2 rooms)

The latest detailed Wigston inventory to survive is that of George Davenport clerk, who died in 1736. His ancestors had come to the village as peasant farmers in the 1570's: he seems to have been a retired parson. His house was small: hall and parlour, a back kitchen, a closet or study, and chambers over kitchen, parlour, and hall, seven rooms in all. The hall, as in all other houses of the village, was still a sizeable living-room with a fireplace and furniture, the latter including a clock. The parlour was, however, no longer a bedroom. It contained a table, five chairs, and 'odd things'. The great majority of Wigston people still slept in their parlours, but the transition from a lower to an upper bedroom was beginning in houses like this. Here the three upper chambers were used as bedrooms, and their origin as storage lofts had been forgotten. In the closet were a writing-desk and some books, and probably the plate was kept there also – a silver tankard, half a dozen spoons, snuff box, and gold ring. Outside the house were kept 'one little Galloway' (small horse) on which he made the journey into Leicester, and two fishing nets for quiet meditation among the meadows of the river Sence when reading and writing palled; and at Leicester he found society on winter evenings around the tea-table when he felt inclined, the peasant world of his forebears long ago forgotten.

	Total Personal Estate (nearest £)	Value of household goods (nearest £)	% of household goods by value
1802 William Ward	404	54	13½
1811 Samuel Freer	1670	275*	16
1811 John Smith	424	60	14
1823 John Pochin	549	49	9
1826 Thomas Willson	982	125	13

* Includes 'Brewing vessels, ale, etc.' He was a victualler as well as a farmer.

One last observation is called for concerning the peasant houses of Wigston. In the early and middle decades of the sixteenth century the household goods, as distinct from the farm goods of all kinds, amounted to ten to fifteen per cent of the entire personal estate. In the late sixteenth century and the early seventeenth, they rose to between twenty and forty per cent of the total personal estate, even among the bigger farmers. By the early nineteenth century, the proportion of household goods to the total personal estate was back again to the level of three hundred years earlier.

The rise in the relative value of household goods in the Elizabethan and Jacobean period had been due to a great increase in domestic amenities and comforts. The fall by the early nineteenth century was due to the fact that the scale of farming had greatly increased during the eighteenth century, whereas that of the domestic side had barely moved. Farming had been revolutionised since the early 1600's, but the farmer's household probably enjoyed little more in the way of comforts and amenities in 1820 than their ancestors had in 1620. Certainly there had been no revolution in the house, as there had been from 1570 to 1640. Glass windows had become general, there were carpets on some of the floors, fireplaces in some of the bedrooms; but the greatest improvements had taken place outdoors with the result that the relative proportion of household goods in the farmer's economy had fallen to the level of his Tudor forbears.

APPENDIX

Summary of the Wigston enclosure award of 1766 showing the acreages allotted and the total costs defrayed by each proprietor.

Proprietor	Allotment			Apportioned Cost		
	A.	R.	P.	£	s.	d.
1. Duke of St. Albans	387	1	9	nil		
2. Rev. James Pigott (vicar)	88	3	37	nil		
3. Alban Ainge	11	3	30	12	9	10
4. John Asthill	7	1	12	6	17	0
5. Patient Abbot	9	2	28	14	5	8
6. Ann Ault	0	1	6	0	4	8
7. Joseph Burgess	84	2	23	98	3	11
8. Martha Bruin (of Oadby)	42	1	5	43	13	6
9. Simeon Bruin (of Leicester)	25	2	37	30	15	2
10. John Brailsford	24	2	36	33	15	6
11. George Boulter	25	0	18	31	1	7
12. William Brown	12	0	33	12	19	11
13. Elizabeth Booth	8	0	20	10	12	5
14. Sarah Booth	7	1	32	10	12	5
15. Simeon Bruin (of Wigston)	11	0	14	11	10	4
16. James Bingley	4	3	30	6	12	6
17. Richard Branson	4	3	26	8	2	9
18. William Bates	8	2	25	7	6	8
19. Mary Bruin (of Wigston)	3	2	2	4	18	5
20. Richard Buzard	3	2	31	4	18	8
21. Grace Bruin	2	1	1	1	18	3
22. William Blakesley	0	2	3	0	15	9
23. Thomas Blackwell	3	2	22	4	4	10
24. John Clarke	94	0	37	101	10	2
25. Ann Clarke	20	2	37	27	18	2
26. Elizabeth Clarke	47	3	24	59	2	8
27. Dorothy Coltman	6	0	21	3	16	2
28. John Cooper	8	2	7	14	1	11
29. Jane Crompton	5	3	30	6	14	6
30. Richard Coltman	4	1	19	3	10	6

Proprietor	Allotment			Apportioned Cost		
	A.	R.	P.	£	s.	d.
31. William Coltman	3	1	0	4	13	6
32. Samuel Davenport	49	1	17	61	7	10
33. Richard Dale and Wm. Moor	13	2	38	14	6	11
34. John Darker	108	0	32	114	9	8
35. Cornelius Darker	13	2	30	14	4	1
36. Alice Darker	2	2	6	3	1	8
37. John Dand	3	2	5	4	13	10
38. Elizabeth Freer	50	2	15	71	1	6
39. James Freer	20	0	38	20	15	7
40. William Freer	11	2	27	12	13	2
41. Susannah Freer	12	1	10	15	17	4
42. Jane Freer	2	3	5	3	18	11
43. Thomas Farmer and Richard Turville	8	0	36	11	1	10
44. Thomas Goode	21	1	14	24	15	11
45. David Grant	10	0	28	17	19	0
46. John Goodrich	11	3	28	16	16	4
47. Eleanor Goodrich	5	3	13	9	1	0
48. Thomas Goodwin	25	2	18	30	3	8
49. Elizabeth Horspool	39	1	30	23	19	8
50. Robert Hames	29	2	13	29	13	0
51. Elizabeth Heard	12	2	32	14	5	2
52. Elizabeth Hunt	9	3	31	7	14	6
53. John Hurst	4	0	20	3	9	7
54. Sarah Holmes	5	2	18	6	14	8
55. Thomas Hurst	3	1	38	4	3	2
56. Thomas Jackson	44	1	36	59	0	10
57. William Johnson (farmer)	114	3	10	125	13	1
58. Joseph Johnson	10	1	19	9	5	8
59. William Johnson (cordwainer)	5	0	6	3	14	6
60. Henry Johnson	4	1	28	3	14	6
61. Thomas Johnson	2	0	16	3	9	6
62. John Johnson	2	1	32	3	9	6
63. Susannah Johnson	7	2	18	11	5	4
64. John King and Gilbert Lloyd	14	3	20	18	13	6
65. Alice Law	11	3	33	11	2	8
66. Catherine Langham	6	3	20	7	6	0
67. Mary Langton	2	1	20	3	3	10
68. William Langton	0	1	34	3	6	6
69. Richard Meadows	5	3	3	7	4	6

Proprietor	Allotment			Apportioned Cost		
	A.	R.	P.	£	s.	d.
70. Elizabeth Matthews	2	0	24	10	4	0
71. Richard Metcalf	74	1	18	83	11	8
72. [three trustees]	1	0	29	0	10	2
73. Sarah Norton	122	2	26	143	8	4
74. Thomas North	4	1	12	4	10	11
75. John Noone	1	0	4	6	10	6
76. [executors of John Noone]	124	1	31	125	8	5
77. Narborough Meeting	7	3	15	6	17	6
78. James Oswin	4	1	4	3	10	3
79. John Pochin	65	1	38	87	2	8
80. Armston Pochin	68	3	2	95	18	4
81. John Pawley	1	0	19	1	3	6
82. Edward Pawley	3	1	19	3	7	7
83. John Phipps	6	3	0	4	5	6
84. John Paine and Alice Clarke	18	3	34	27	18	2
85. George Ross	92	0	12	110	8	1
86. John Ragg	267	0	36	342	10	10
87. Benjamin Smith	13	2	7	12	17	0
88. John Smith (hosier)	17	2	19	15	0	6
89. John Smith (clerk)	8	2	10	11	2	7
90. Sarah Simons	1	3	38	3	8	6
91. William Vann	7	3	22	12	4	6
92. Thomas Wightman	206	2	22	190	3	4
93. John Ward	33	2	31	32	13	10
94. Daniel Ward	8	1	14	12	0	5
95. Jonathan White	13	1	14	13	1	4
96. Wigston churchwardens	1	1	0	0	11	6
97. Wigston overseers of poor	6	0	24	3	6	9
98. Wigston Meeting	22	0	38	22	5	7
Total	2887	2	14	2817	10	9

Index

Abandoned area at Wigston, 86
Abbot (Abbott) family, 123, 165, 196, 201, 204, 233, 256, 265, 300
Ab Kettleby, 168

absentee landlords, 197-8, 212, 219, 223, 248, 253
agricultural depression, 266
agricultural development before the Black Death, 57-8
All Saints Church, 15, 90, 95, 180; rebuilt, 80-1; *see also* Rectory
'ancient closes', 95
Anglian cemeteries, 1, 2
Anstey, 68n, 178
Arnesby, 61n, 85, 164
Ashby de la Zouch, 60, 83
Ashby Magna, 159
assessments in Wigston, 143-4, 146; land-tax, 265
Astell (Astill) family, 38, 88, 111, 114, 118, 119, 120, 122, 135, 143, 144, 146, 158, 159, 160, 203, 256, 265, 295
Aston Flamville, 96, 98, 100
attic floor introduced, 302, 303
Ault, Ann, 252
Aylestone, 183

Baddeley, Capt., 306
Bagworth, 203
Baker, Ric., 77
balks, xx, 66-7, 241
Balle family, xxi, 33, 49, 50, 51, 52, 67, 71, 73, 75, 110, 112, 125, 126n
Barkby, 197
Barkby Thorpe, 174n
Barrow-on-Soar, 60
Barwell, 9
Basset, family of Sapcote, 21, 22, 34
Bayl (Bail) family, 33, 34, 50
Beaumanor, bailiff's accounts, 84; mills, 84, 85; estate, 193n
Beaumont, Henry de, i.p.m. 85; John of Cole Orton, 131; Eliz., his widow, 132

Bedingfield, Edmund, of Oxborough, Norf., 103n
Belgrave, 103, 258
Belvoir, 132,193n
Bent family of Cosby, 143, 176
Betrich family, 69, 76
Blaby, 2, 12
Black Death, the, 57, 58, 60, 185, 196
blacksmiths, *see* Smiths
Blackwell Sike, 11, 14, 65, 232
Bloxsom family, 100, 101, 102
bond land and berry land, 105-7
boot and shoe industry, rise of, 279-81
Bosco, de, family, 34
Bosworth, 34
Bosworth, battle of, 96
Bottesford, 60, 85, 90
Boulter family, xxi, 100, 101, 120, 161, 195, 206, 221, 233n, 256, 264, 265, 299,309
Boyter sike, 65
Brabson family, 100, 124, 128, 129, 192n, 222, 226, 229, 236, 290, 294, 298, 300
Brackley, Northants., 33
Bradgate, Thos., of Peatling Parva, 143
Braunston, 174n
'bread money', 206, 207
Breedon, curate of, 263
Brett family, 127, 176, 206, 288
Brewin (Bruin) family, 218, 220, 222, 256, 259, 262, 300
brick houses, three storied, 243, 305
bricks, use of, 302, 304-7
Bridde, Roger, 47
Bringhurst, 1, 12
British School opened, 277
Brock's Hill, Oadby, 2
Brokesby manor in Oadby, 129n, 172
Brooksby family of Oadby, 34
Browne, Robt., his will, 123; John, 183, 291
Buci, Robt. de, 34, 129n, 197
Bugge, Baldwin, 26
Bullhead Street, Wigston, xxi, 12, 13, 44, 45, 46, 90, 96, 125, 284

Burton Lazars, 143
Burton Overy, 3 6, 71, 73, 86, 158
Bushloe End, 305
By-laws, village, xxiii, 97, 238, 254

Campania (Champayne) family, xxi, 21, 24, 25, 26, 50, 96, 112, 126n
capital messuages, 93
'capitalist farming', 217, 219
capitalist peasants, rise of, 141, 146n
Carey, Dame Elizabeth (Nevill, Danvers), tomb of, 108n
Carey, Sir Edmund, of London, and Lady Elizabeth (Danvers) his w., 108
carpenters, 168
Cartwright family, 34, 101, 102, 129, 135, 160, 170, 173
Catesby, Symon, lease-holder of All Saints rectory, 82, 131, 132
Catthorpe, 18
Catton (Ketton) family, 146, 204
Cave, Sir Thos., 248
census of 1831, 266-7
Chamberlain family, 109, 124, 143, 144-5, 159n, 203
Champayne family; see Campania
Chapels, 278-9
Chaplains at Wigston, 73n
'Chaunters lond', 41
Church Nook, Wigston, 92
churches, finest medieval, 61; rebuilding of, 58, 73; of Rutland, 58-9n
churchwardens, 205-6; accounts, 179, 236-7
Clarke (Clark, Clerke) family, 39, 40, 87, 93, 107, 111, 125, 132, 135, 165, 198, 204, 205, 225, 248, 256, 264, 277
Cley family, 201-2, 233
Cleyhill sike, 65
cloth industry of Leicester, decline of, 57
coal money, 206, 207
Cole Orton coal pit, 129, 192
Coltman (Coultman) family, 34, 129, 221, 256, 257, 258n, 265, 303
common pastures, 93, 95
common rights, 254-5, 267
consolidation of 'lands', 151-2
Constables, 205, 208, 210-11; head, 205, 209-10
conversion of arable to pasture, 261-2
convertible husbandry, 162, 233
Cook (Cock, Coke, Coc, Cocus, le Keu) family, 31, 39, 42, 44, 45, 49, 50, 51, 88

copyhold rights, 105, 250; tenure, extinction of, 254
copyholders, 99, 104-6, 109-10
coroner's inquests, 80
Cosby, 8, 143, 176
Cossington, 155n, 162n
Cotesbach, 155n
cottage husbandry, 200-1
cottager or labourer, 171-4, 212, 217, 227, 244-5
Coulson, Robt., 298
Coultman family; see Coltman
Countesthorpe, 12
Cowpasture Farm, Wigston, 14
craftsmen, village, 166-70
Croft, 19, 22, 24, 25, 26, 96, 98
Croft family, 19, 22
crofts adjoining farm-houses, 95
crops, barley, 69, 70, 154-5, 235; hay, 162, 165-6, 235; peas and beans, 69, 70, 154-5, 234-5; rye, etc., 154-6, 234-5; wheat, 69, 70, 154-5, 234-5
crops, medieval, 69, 70; sixteenth century, 234-6
crops and livestock compared, 236
Crow Mill on the Sence, 63, 169, 192
Croxton Kerrial, 9, 110
cruck-framed buildings, 284
customary tenants (see also copyholders) 62, 104-6, 125, 160

Dand (Dann, Danne) family, xx, 99, 101, 102, 115n, 117, 118, 119, 120, 122, 135, 138, 150, 152, 165, 172, 205, 217, 256, 265, 276, 288, 293, 298
Danelaw, the, 7, 8
Danish conquest, 6-7
Danvers, Hy., Lord of Dauntsey, 108, 110
Danvers, Sir John, of Dauntsey, co. Wilts., and Elizabeth his w., 103, 161; dispute with copyholders, 104-6
Danvers, John, of London, 108
Darker family, butchers and graziers, 223, 248, 255
daughters, provision for, 57, 73, 75, 123, 178
Davenport family, 119, 122, 161, 196, 198, 199, 204, 214, 231, 232, 235, 242, 256, 258, 264, 305, 306, 309; manor-house, 192n, 306, 307
debts, 175
Desford, 139

Dicoun, Wm., chaplain, 51, 73*n*
dining-rooms, 307
dismemberment of Wigston manors, 98
Domesday Book, 8, 10, 14, 28, 35, 53
Donington-le-Heath, 85
'double vills', 9
Duchy manor, the, Wigston, 24, 26
Dyve family, 34

East Wigston separated, 281
economic stagnation, 84
Edmondes, John, last rector of Wigston, 130
Edmondthorpe, 60*n*
Edmund, brother of Edward 1, 21, 24
Edward I at Wigston, 79
Enclosure award (1766), 216, 250-9; awards to individuals, 252-3, 311, 313; bill passed, 248 ; commissioners for, 249*n*; costs of, 259-60; labour requirements reduced by, 263; objectors to, 248-50; petition for, 247; summary of acreages, 311-13; temporary, 95, 105, 160-4; pre-Parliamentary, 212
Enderby, 175, 176, 192
engine sheds, importance of, 281
engrossing of farms, 112, 178, 214, 267
ensuring succession to property, 32, 50-2, 73, 122, 124
'eveners', functions of, 241-2
Everingham, Lady Margaret, 40*n*, 96
Evesham, battle of, 24
Evington, 34, 223
expansion of open fields, 63
Eyrig (Eyrek, Erik); *see* Herrick

farm lands in open fields, 150
farming implements, 159-60
farms, increase in size of, 231
Faukes (Faucous) family, 47-9, 65, 71, 72, 110, 112, 125, 126, 142, 222
Faunt family of Foston, 17, 108, 109, 160, 183, 188, 203, 209
Ferrers, Sir Walter Devereux, Lord, 24
field reeves, 205, 217, 241
fifteenth century, paucity of records, 83; evidence of decay, 83, 85; tax quotas cut, 83-8; shrinking villages, 84
fines, appropriation of, by Hospital Masters, 128*n*; for 1570-1603 analysed, 117-21; deficiencies of, 101, 115, 124*n*, 128n; interpretation of, 100, 103, 109
fireplaces, 291

fish, shortage of, 193
fixing of quotas for fifteenth and tenth, 60
Flamville family, 96
Flemyng family, 32, 33
Foston, 17, 18, 54, 169, 183, 203
Fox family, 123-4
Foxton, 127
framework knitters' earnings, 274
framework-knitting industry, 212, 217, 227-8, 257, 261, 273, 276; middlemen, 274
Franklin family of Ecton, Northants., 168
free peasantry, 28, 53
free tenants, high proportion of, 59, 62; families of, dying out, replaced, 110
Freeman's Register, 257
Freer (Frere, Fryer), family, 99, 100, 101, 109, 115*n*, 118, 120, 121, 122, 124, 127, 128, 129, 134-5, 138, 139, 148, 158, 159, 168, 175, 181, 195, 206*n*, 222, 224, 230, 233, 236, 255, 256, 259, 291, 294, 295, 297, 298, 299, 308, 309
free school in St Wistan's, 183, 207
Freman, Wm., of Leicester, 48; Ralph, 99, 101, 118, 119, 121, 122, 129; Joan, widow of Ralph, 119, 122
Friday (Fryday) family, 31, 32, 53, 71, 74, 78, 87
frontier of cultivation, 11, 63
Frowlesworth, 8
Fryday family, *see* Friday
Fryer, *see* Freer
furnishings and household goods, 295-7, 307-8
Futturs lane (Blunts Lane), 148*n*

Galby, 53, 54, 286, 291
Gamel family, 35, 45
Gartree Hundred, 59
Gaunt, John of, 24
gentleman, first Wigston, 87 (*see also* peasant-gentry)
'gentry' in Wigston, 305, 307
glazed windows, 285, 286, 291, 297
Glen, Mercian royal estate, 11
Glen Parva, 2, 197, 207*n*
glove-making, 274
Godwin (Godewyne) family, 44-7, 71, 74, 76, 78, 110
Goldhill (Goldehil) Field, 63, 93, 137, 150, 190
'Gonewarehil', 45, 76

goods, assessment in, 143
graziers, 145, 262
grazing rights in common pasture, disputes on, 238; agreement regarding, 238-9
Great Bowden, 60, 90
Great Easton, 18, 60
Great Glen, 61*n*, 174*n*
Grentemaisnil, Hugh de, 18, 19, 22
Grimston, 172
Groby, 84
Guthlexton Hundred, 59

Hall, Robt., 99, 101, 118, 119, 120, 121, 15 1, 203; Judith (White), 203
Hallaton, 60, 84, 170, 212*n*
Hallcroft, 107, 150
Harcourt family, 33, 34, 74, 87
Hartopp family of Button Lazars, 143
Haudekyn, Ric., chaplain, 73
headlands, 67
hearth tax, 1670, 195, 299
Hecroft, Wigston, xxi, 50
Henry IV, 25
Hereford, Ralph, Earl of, 18
Herrick (Heryck, Eyrig, Eyrek, Erik) family, 31, 35, 42, 43, 49, 78, 87, 111, 126, 128, 157, 165, 173, 175, 193*n*, 204
hidden mortgages, 264
Hinckley, 90, 212, 227
Holyoak, Edward and John, 273, 278
Homes, Wm., labourer, 299
Horsepool (Horspool) family, 195, 199, 263, 299, 300
Horton family of Mowsley, 142
hosiery trade, 279, 282
house, plan of the original brick, 213, 303-4
household goods, rise and fall in value of, 310
house-plans, peasant, 148
houses, improvement in, after 1560, 285, 301
houses, one-hearth, 299; two-hearth and more, 300
houses, urban-type, eighteenth century, 305-6
housing, medieval, 283-4
housing revolution after 1570; kitchens, 285, 286, 287, 291-2; halls, 254, 285, 293, 294; parlours, 284, 293-4; staircase, 286, 290, 291, 301; upper chambers, 288, 293; windows, 186, 283, 285, 291

housing, sixteenth century, 148-9
Howard, Anne, w. of fourteenth Earl of Oxford, 102
Howard, Thos., duke of Norfolk, 102
Hugglescote, 85
Humberstone, 83
Hungerton sike, 65, 161
Huntingdon, earl of, 182
Hurst, Saml., framwork knitter, 273, 274
Husbands Bosworth, 9, 90, 304
Hutte family, 31, 32, 71, 74, 87, 110

Illston-on-the-Hill, 54, 86
impropriators of the rectory, 278
Ingarsby, 86
inns, the *White Hart* in Leicester, 43; the *Angel*, Hallaton, 70
inn-keepers, 170-1
inventories, peasant, 144, 153, 156, 157, 235; probate, 285-310 *passim*; early eighteenth century, 308-9; early nineteenth century, 309
iron, purchase of, 193

Jackson family, 127, 204, 222, 248, 256, 264
Johnson family, 101, 109, 120, 121, 128, 135, 137, 139, 177, 196, 204, 209, 217, 221-2, 223, 253, 255, 288, 300
Judith, Countess, 14, 129*n*, 197

Kent, family of Kirby Muxloe, 41, 112, 145*n*
Ketel, 35
Kibworth Harcourt, 33, 90
Kilby, xx, 8, 143, 144, 145
Kimcote, 'flaxlondes' at, 156
Kirby Bellars, 69
Kirby Muxloe, 41
kitchens, introduction of, 285, 286, 287, 291 -2; detached, 287
Knaptoft, 8, 17, 18, 28
Knighton, 103; brook, 4, 152

labouring class, increase in, 301
Lancaster, dukes of, 24, 25
landless labourers, growth of, 214-15, 242
land-market at Wigston, 115, 121, 195
landowners after enclosure, 263-6
land-ownership, 242-4
Langham family, 267
Langton family, millers, 169-70, 177, 196,

206, 256, 288, 291, 298

Latimer, John, 3rd Lord, 102, 104

Laughton, 103

Lawe family, 38, 109, 113, 120, 133-9 153, 196-7, 198, 206, 232, 275, 291, 294, 307, 308

leaseholders, 125

Leicester Abbey, 69; borough of, 83, 84 87, 90, 103; earls of, 19, 3 6, 6 1; framework knitting in, 212, 227, 257

Leicestershire, Anglian settlement of, 1

Lenton Priory, Notts., Wigston Rectory granted to, 19, 81, 130, 131, 180; appoints absentee rectors, 81; takes over rectorial title, 130, 180; dissolved, 131; neglect of church fabric, 180, 289

Lewyn family, 32, 74

leys, 67, 95, 152, 160, 162-3, 233

Little Date, Wigston, 12

livestock on farms, 157-9, 235-40; cattle, 159, 236-7, 238; horses, 159; pigs, 159; poultry, 159; sheep, 134-40, 157-9, 236-7, 238; enclosure for, 178

Long Clawson, 174

looking-glasses, 307

lost villages, 89, 179

Loughborough, 60, 83, 84, 85, 90

Love (Lufe) family, 48, 49, 81, 112, 126

Loveday, Geo., 'hosiery agent', 273

Lutterworth, 18, 90, 136, 164

Mabile family, 76

Maino the Breton, 18

Major family, 198, 220

Manners, Sir Ric., sheriff, 131; family, 131, 132

Manor House, see Rectory Farm

manorial framework, 95; structure complicated, 96

Market Harborough, 18, 211 60, 83, 84, 90

markets and fairs, none in Wigston, 61

Markfield, 85

Mawson, Thos., 196-7, 210, 299, 300

May Green, the, Wigston, 90

meadow, 4, 64, 67, 68, 95, 101, 152, 164-5, 234

Medbourne, 1, 18, 60

medieval peasant, disposal of property, 51, 73

Melton Mowbray, 8, 60, 69, 83, 84, 90, 172

Mercia, half appropriated by Danes, 7

Meulan (or Mellent) Robt., count of, 19

migration from Wigston, 37, 42-3, 86

migration into Wigston, 87, 88, 211-12

millers, 160

mills, xxi, 13, 14, 169; water, 36, 63, 93, 169

Misterton, 17, 18

Moat Street, Wigston, 12, 90, 96, 148n

'Mokilhow', 63

money-economy, 172, 176-7, 255, 265, 269

Montfort, Simon de, earl of Leicester, 23, 24

Moseho (Bullhead Street), 12, 126

Mould family, xx, 76-7, 88, 127, 176, 300

Mountsorrel, 212n

Mowsley, 79n, 142; End, 92

Mucklow Field, 63, 93, 150, 190

murders, 47, 72n, 77-8

Muston, 168, 173n

Narborough, 61n

National School built, 277

native peasantry, 34

Nevill, Elizabeth, dau. of 4th Lord Latimer (Danvers), 103; John, 4th Lord Latimer, 102-3

new building, brick cottages, 276; substantial houses, 277

Newbold coal-pit, 129

Newgate End, Wigston, 92, 302, 303, 306

Newton Harcourt, 33, 39n, 78, 84, 143, 144, 146, 267

nonconformity, growth of, 278-9

Noone family, 114, 124, 135, 196, 205, 220, 222, 253, 255, 263, 299, 300, 307, 308

Norfolk, Thos. Howard, duke of, 102

normal tenement of villeins and free tenants, 29

Normanton family, 107n

Normanton Turvile, 26, 27, 96, 98, 266

Northampton-Leicester road, 5, 78-9

Norton, Sarah (Freer), 222, 224, 253, 255, 265

Nottingham, 7

Oadby, 2, 8, 11, 13, 14, 34, 128, 129, 222, 223

occupiers of land, 1765, list of, 218

Old English personal names at Wigston, 35

Old Mere, the, Wigston, 4, 95

open arable fields, three, 63

open-field husbandry, xix, xx, 61, 1527, 234, 254; balance of, upset, 240

Overseers of the poor, 205, 206, 229-231

owner-occupiers, decrease of, 265

Oxford, Hugh de Vere, 4th Earl of, 23; John de Vere, thirteenth, 27, 72, 96, 102; Earls of, 36, 61, 95; manor, break-up of the, 102; sale of, 109

Pallet, John, 200

Pallett, Alice, 153

Palmer family, 38, 73, 88, 111, 146, 204, 248

parishioners ordered to make good, 180-1; legacies to church, 181

'parlour' in peasant houses, 284; -s, two, 293-4

pasture (see also ley ground), 67, 68, 101, 233, 239-40

Pawley (Palley) family, xx, 79, 101, 102, 107, 111, 116, 117, 118, 119, 121, 122, 124, 135, 145, 165, 181, 201, 203, 204, 206, 209, 256, 309

peasant charters, xxiii, 76, 167

peasant economy, 190-4, 211, 244-6; changes by time of enclosure, 242; end of, 267-8

peasant families, persistence of, 42, 88, 195-6

peasant-gentry, 53, 73, 196, 198, 214

peasant houses of mud, 283; of one or two rooms, 284, 296; rebuilding of, 288

peasant landowning families, 62, 70, 122; in early sixteenth century, 111-12

peasant's marriage settlements, 123-4

peasant's real property, disposal of, 123

Peatling Magna and Parva, 1, 6, 143

Penne family, 39, 48, 49, 51, 52, 112, 125, 142, 148n

Peter the Chaplain of Wigston, 25, 26

Peterborough Abbey, 18

Pigott, Rev. Jas., vicar, 248, 251

Pikeman family, 33

Pilkington, Hy., report on Poor Laws, 269-72

plecks of hemp and flax, 157

Pochin family, 195, 196, 197, 213, 214, 225, 233, 234, 248, 256, 263, 267, 271, 299, 302, 305, 306, 309

Pollyng family, 31

poor, the, 229, 242

'poore stocke', 206, 207

poor-rates, rise in, 269

population, 1086, 8, 56, 59, 64; 1377, xxiii, 56, 60, 64, 96; 1524, 88, 185; 1563, 90n; 1605, 171; 1801, 267, 276; 1831, 267; 1851, 267; 1871, 276; 1001, 282; trebled between 1871 and 1901, 279

post-and-truss frame houses, 284, 286

Pougher family of Leicester, 258

poverty, growth of, 171, 189; relief of, 229-31

'prick posts,' 289

primogeniture, 75

proprietors, enclosure, 252-3

Pultney family of Misterton, 17

purchasers of farms from Danvers, 113-14

purchasers of Turvile lands, 101-2

Pynder, Ric., his house, 286

Queniborough, 173

Quincy, Saer de, Earl of Winchester, 23

Quorndon, 69; mills, 84, 85

Ragg (Ragge) family, 101, 224, 225, 242, 248, 252, 251, 255, 265, 266, 293, 300

Railways, 277, 280-1

Randall (Randolf, Randulf, Randull) family, 37-42, 43, 51, 68, 71, 73, 74, 87, 93, 112, 125, 142

Rannulf the clerk, 35, 38-9, 44, 112

Ratae Coritanorum, 1

ready money, farmers', 175-6

Rearsby, 203

Rectory appropriated, 82; lease of, 82; Farm, 82n, 294, 299, 303n, 306

'Reddeleiz tofth' in Wigston, 40

Redley (Reddeley) family, smiths, 167, 181, 295

Reede, Wm., first vicar of Wigston, 130

religious changes in sixteenth century, 179

rise in standard of living, 186

roads in enclosure, 251

Robinson, Isaac, of Leicester wool-comber, 258

Rogationtide procession, 79

Roman Leicester, 1; settled by Anglians, 6

rooms, larger number of, after 1570, 292-3

Ross family, xxi, 192n, 222, 225-6, 243, 256, 262, 264

Rotherby, 123

Rothley, houses of cruck-type in, 284

Rudinge, Walter, of Westcotes, 197, 198
rural organisation in the Danelaw, 62-3
Rutland, earl of, 132, 193*n*

Sacheverell, Sir Ric., rectory leased to, 131
St Albans, Duke of, 20, 218*n*, 226, 247, 248, 250-4, 255
St Wistan's Church, 12, 13, 15, 90, 95, 182-3; -yard, 43, 87; shrine, 79; rebuilt, 81; made a free school, 183
St Wolstan's church (St Wistan's), 12-13, 15
Sapcote, 21, 87, 268
Saxby, 3
Saxelby, 172
Scandinavian names at Wigston, 35; settlement, xxi
seignorial authority, none in divided lordship, 63, 97
selion, the, 65-6
Sence, river, xxi, 2, 4, 14, 152
Shakresdale (Shackerdale), 14
Shearsby, 8
Shepshed, 9, 90
Sherman, John, rector, 107
sike, 11, 64-5, 67
Sileby, 90
Simon (Symon, Simons) family, 36, 37*n*, 41, 45, 51, 68, 88, 111, 163, 176, 256, 258-9, 299
Skeffington, 200; family, 25, 26
smaller peasant families in thirteenth- and fourteenth-century records, 37-8
Smith (Smyth, Smythe) family 31, 42, 43-4, 65, 75, 88, 111, 128, 165, 195, 196, 202, 204, 209, 232, 276, 290, 299, 300, 307, 308
smiths, black-, 167-8, 193
Soar, the, 1, 3, 6, 56, 60
social structure of Leicestershire, 59
sokemen, concentrations of, 8; at Domesday, 28
South Wigston, growth of, 281-2
Spa Lane, Wigston, 46
Spencer, John, of Lutterworth, 135, 136; Ric. of Long Clawson, 174
Spowtewell Street (Bullhead Street), 12, 39, 92
Squire, Wm., inventory of, 308
staircases, 286, 290, 291, 301
Stamford, earl of, 239
Stanford family of Leicester, 132 133,

138
stint, old, 121*n*, 174*n*, 233, 238; new, 233, 238
Stoke manor, 26
Stoke Golding, 96, 98
Stoney Stanton, 87
Stoughton, 18, 223
Stowe Nine Churches, Northants., tomb in, by Nic. Stone, 108*n*
strips, xx, 93, 156, 160; size of, 65-6, 68; consolidation of, 231
subsistence farming, 175-9
suits over land, 78
Sulney, Sir John, 26
Sutton, Wm., inventory of, 308, 309
Sutton Cheney, 200
Swan (Swein) family, 35, 37*n*, 71, 72, 78, 87, 110
Swanne family of Coventry, 72, 87
Swannington coal, 85, 192
Swithland, 57; slates, 93, 283, 302, 304; headstones, 305*n*
Symunt family, 50

taxation accounts for 1662-3, 209-10; Commonwealth, 208, 215; freedom from, 177; land-tax, 208-10; medieval, 71, 83-8; monthly assessments, 208; Stuart subsidies, 177*n*; Tudor subsidies, 177*n*
tenant farmers, 223-4
terriers, 150-1, 152, 231-2
Thornton, Jas., tailor, 299
three-field system, 93; size of fields, 93-5
Thurlaston manor, 21, 22, 24, 25, 26, 96, 98; (Newhall), 96
Thurlond, Edmund, parson of Clifton, 131
Thythornhill Field, 63, 93, 150, 190
Tilton, 12
timber, scarcity of, 288
timber-frame houses, 92-3
tithes, 130, 133, 253; on sheep, 134-40
tradesmen, 167
transfers of property, 44-5
Truck Act, breaches of, 273-4
Turbertus (Thurbern), 35, 38
Tur Langton, 207
Turpin family of Knaptoft, 17
Turvile family, 22, 26, 27, 40*n*, 49, 96, 98, 99-102, 110, 118, 119, 120, 121, 124, 143*n*, 170; manor, 95, 98, 102
Tyghe (Tighe), Ant., and Agnes (Pawley),

his w., 116, 117, 118, 119, 120; Wm., and Bridget his w., 118, 119, 121

Ullesthorpe, 36, 71
upper rooms (chambers), introduced, 285, 286, evolution of, 288

Vann (Vanne) family, xx, 101, 122, 196, 258, 259, 267, 299, 300, 313
Vere, Dorothy (Latimer), 102; Elizabeth (Wingfield), 102, 103
vicar, resident and ill-paid, 130, 180; tithe owner, 247, 248; allotment, 251, 255
vicarage, value of, 130, 134, 180; house, 134, 180, 294, 300, 302n; description of, 289
village fields, frontiers of, 11, 63; expansion of, 13-4

wage-labour, 143, 147, 171-4, 263, 270
Waldram (Waldron) family, 34, 119, 129, 198; property, 197
Wallis (Waleys, Wallys) family, 39, 87, 111, 125, 126, 127, 129, 196
Waltham-on-the-Wolds, 10
Walton, family, 38, 47, 78, 116, 117, 124
Walton-on-the-Wolds, 96, 98
Wase, Sampson, of Rotherby, gent., 123; Marg. (Fox), 123-4
Watery Leys (Watry leys), 162n
Watling Street, 8
Watts family, 125, 126, 127, 138, 294
Welham, 18
Welland Valley, the, 1, 6, 18, 56, 60
West, Jas., 299
Westcotes, 197
Wheatley, Alice and Robt., 286, 296
Whetstone, 50
White (Whyte) family, 100, 101, 111, 119, 120, 121, 122, 128, 138, 143, 144, 146, 157, 161, 163, 170, 175, 181, 203-4, 256, 265, 293
Whittington, 85

Whitwick, 74, 85
widows, provision for, 52, 75
Wightman, Thos., woolstapler, of Leicester, 220, 248, 255
Wigston becomes an Urban District, 281
Wigston family, 37, 41, 74, 87, 112, 126; and see Wykygeston
'Wigston Hall', 306-7
Wigston Harcourt, 33
Wigston rectory, glebe, 130
Willoughby Waterless, 8
wills, peasant, xviii, 122-3
Wiltshire peasant houses surveyed, 287-8, 289, 290, 292
Winchester manor in Wigston, 234; honour of, 31, 32, 96, 239
Wingfield, Sir Ant., of Letheringham, Suff., 102, 103; Sir Robt., 103
Winter, John, labourer, 298
Winterborne (Wynturborn) family, 32
Wistan, a Mercian prince, 16
Wistow, 11, 12, 13, 16, 79n, 160n
Woodhouse, 85
working-class organisations, 278
Wreak valley, 69
Wyatt, Wm., framework knitter, 273, 275
Wyggeston Hospital Charters, 9, 13, 34, 36, 38, 42, 48, 63, 72, 110, 125; facts revealed by, 30-1; farms belonging to, 125-6, 221; leasehold lands, 129, 255; tenants required to plant trees, 192
Wyking (Viking) family, 35
Wykyngeston family, xxi, 26; 33, 34, 35, 36, 37, 68, 71, 73, 74, 107n, 112, 126n, 259
Wylde, Nic., 121, 151, 152
Wymeswold, 90, 97, 163, 164
Wymondham, 60n

Yeomen, capitalist peasants, 142
Younger sons, provision for, 52, 73, 75-6, 123, 178